D1599405

Towards a transformation of philosophy

The International Library of Phenomenology and Moral Sciences

Editor: John O'Neill, *York University, Toronto*

The Library will publish original and translated works guided by an analytical interest in the foundations of human culture and the moral sciences. It is intended to foster phenomenological, hermeneutical and ethnomethodological studies in the social sciences, art and literature.

KARL-OTTO APEL

Towards a transformation of philosophy

Translated by Glyn Adey
and David Frisby

Routledge & Kegan Paul
London, Boston and Henley

Transformation der Philosophie
© *Suhrkamp Verlag, Frankfurt am Main, 1972, 1973*

This translation first published in 1980
by Routledge & Kegan Paul Ltd
39 Store Street, London WC1E 7DD,
Broadway House, Newtown Road,
Henley-on-Thames, Oxon RG9 1EN and
9 Park Street, Boston, Mass. 02108, USA
Set in 10 on 12 Times
and printed in Great Britain by
Lowe & Brydone Printers Ltd
Thetford, Norfolk
English translation © Routledge & Kegan Paul Ltd 1980, except for chapter 3
Chapter 3 © Karl-Otto Apel 1972

British Library Cataloguing in Publication Data

Apel, Karl-Otto

Towards a transformation of philosophy. –
(The international library of phenomenology
and moral sciences).
1. Philosophy
I. Title II. Series
193   B3199.A/   79-409 36

ISBN 0 7100 0403 6

CONTENTS

ACKNOWLEDGMENTS

We wish to thank Professor Apel for his helpful comments on the translation and Pru Larsen for typing the manuscript.

Chapter 3 appears in Karl-Otto Apel's own version as published in L. W. Beck (ed.), *Transactions of the Third International Kant Conference*, D. Reidel, Dordrecht, Netherlands, 1972, pp. 90–104, by permission of the original publisher.

Glyn Adey *(Frankfurt)*
David Frisby *(Glasgow)*

PREFACE TO THE ENGLISH EDITION

The essays presented in this volume have been selected from my two-volume German collection that was published in 1973 under the title *Transformation der Philosophie*. The German title was intended to be ambiguous in that it referred both to a hermeneutic reconstruction of the process of *transformation in recent philosophy* and to an outline of the author's programme of a *transformation of (transcendental) philosophy* along the lines of a *transcendental hermeneutics* or *transcendental pragmatics of language*. The present selection which focuses mainly on the second volume of my German collection is more representative for the second meaning of the original title. Consequently , it does not testify so much to my historical-hermeneutic starting-point within a Heideggerian per-spective as to my later attempts to develop a systematic approach through a confrontation with the philosophy of language that is predominant in the English-speaking world. My German edition of selected writings by C. S. Peirce (*Schriften I und II*, Frankfurt, 1967 and 1970) and my book *Der Denkweg von Charles S. Peirce* (Frankfurt, 1975) may be regarded as a parallel attempt in this context. Of course, there was also a permanent exchange with recent currents of thought in Germany e.g. with the Erlangen school, and especially with my friend Jürgen Habermas.

Since 1973, I have elaborated upon the programme of a *trans-cendental pragmatics*, which was outlined in the later essays of the present volume, from several perspectives. One of these is characterized by a controversy – still in progress – with Hans Albert, about the 'Problem of Philosophical Fundamental Grounding in the

Light of a Transcendental Pragmatics of Language' (*Man and World*, 18, 1975, pp. 239–75; cf. Hans Albert, *Transzendentale Träumereien*, Hamburg, 1975). Another perspective is marked by my attempt at a transcendental-pragmatic re-interpretation or transformation of John Searle's speech act theory in my essay 'Sprechakttheorie und transzendentale Sprachpragmatik zur Frage ethischer Normen' (in K.-O. Apel (ed.), *Sprachpragmatik und Philosophie*, Frankfurt, 1976, pp. 10–173, where Habermas's slightly different programme of 'universal pragmatics' *(Universalpragmatik)* is also presented, ibid., pp. 174–272). A third perspective focuses on a further elaboration of the conception of a differentiated (trichotomous) philosophy of science that is outlined in this volume in the essay 'Scientistics, hermeneutics and the critique of ideology'. This is documented by my papers 'The *a priori* of Communication and the Foundation of the Humanities' (*Man and World*, 5, 1972, pp. 3–37), and 'Types of Social Science in the Light of Human Interests of Knowledge' (*Social Research*, 44, 1977, pp. 425–70; reprinted in S. Brown (ed.), *Philosophical Disputes in the Social Sciences*, Hassocks, Sussex, 1979), and finally by my critical discussion of Georg Hendrik von Wright and the critics of post-Wittgensteinian 'New Dualism' in my book *Die Erklären-Verstehen-Kontroverse in transzendentalphilosophischer Sicht* (Frankfurt, forthcoming). Finally, I would like to mention my attempt to integrate the conception of a *transcendental pragmatics of language* into that of a *transcendental semiotics* which is considered as a new (third) paradigm of First Philosophy (after pre-Kantian ontology and the post-Kantian transcendental philosophy of consciousness). I first outlined this project in my papers 'Zur Idee einer transzendentalen Sprachpragmatik', in J. Simon (ed.), *Aspekte und Probleme der Sprachphilosophie*, Freiburg im Breisgau, 1974, pp. 283–326 and 'The Transcendental Conception of Language-Communication and the Idea of First Philosophy', in H. Parret (ed.), *History of Linguistic Thought and Contemporary Linguistics*, Berlin and New York, 1975, pp. 32–61. The first part of an envisaged elaboration will appear in *Philosophic Exchange* under the title 'Transcendental Semiotics and the Paradigm of First Philosophy'.

At this point, I wish to express my thanks to the publishers and to the translators for their efforts in presenting these essays in English. In going over the English text, I have occasionally allowed myself to add new footnotes and to reformulate or supplement the original wording for the sake of clarity.

Frankfurt am Main   Karl-Otto Apel
July 1978

CHAPTER 1

Wittgenstein and the problem of hermeneutic understanding [1]

**The problem and its historical background: 'meaning' and
'understanding' in the tradition of 'hermeneutics' on the one hand,
and the 'logic of language' on the other**

The following study represents an attempt to establish a relationship between the problem that is typical of German philosophy
since Schleiermacher, Droysen and Dilthey, namely that of
'hermeneutic' or 'human scientific' understanding; and the problem
that was central for Wittgenstein and the 'analytic philosophy of
language' which he helped to establish, namely the problem of the
understanding of meaning. The terms themselves, 'understanding'
and 'meaning', which are central to both traditions, suggest that it
must be possible to trace such a relationship. On the other hand,
one must bear in mind that until quite recently the two philosophical
traditions hardly had any contact with one another. This is quite
understandable if one recalls the historical backgrounds against
which the respective problems arose.

Dilthey's problem of hermeneutic or human scientific understanding is concerned with the epistemological generalization of a
methodological problem which had already been formulated in the
individual philological-historical sciences, in jurisprudence, and
especially in Protestant theology. The concrete starting-point of this
methodological tradition was a concern with the adequate understanding of canonical or – in the case of humanist philology –
classical texts. Since Luther's interpretation of the Bible and the
humanist revival of the study of classical authors, the critical
impulse of this hermeneutic tradition has been directed against the
tendency to misunderstand the original meaning of a text, which has

1

arisen as a result of historical distance from the sources. It is this impulse which, in Schleiermacher's philosophical generalization of the hermeneutic problem, has led to the maxim that, strictly speaking, misunderstanding, rather than understanding, arises of its own accord.[2] In Schleiermacher's opinion, therefore, it is no longer sufficient to assert the rules of hermeneutics merely when difficulties occur in the exegesis of a text but rather he requires that all the positive preconditions for understanding be elucidated philosophically from the outset and that they be practically implemented. Dilthey seeks to explicate these positive preconditions for the possibility and validity of understanding as such in terms of a 'critique of historical reason' that is analogous to Kant's *Critique of Pure Reason*.

The provisional title of Dilthey's programme – 'The critique of historical reason' – suggests where nineteenth-century philosophical hermeneutics primarily sought the positive preconditions for understanding. The intention is to make oneself contemporary with the author in question by means of an 'historical understanding' of the age. This approach by the 'historical school' of the human sciences in Germany attempted to transcend the older, humanistic approach which lay in a 'grammatical understanding' of the language of an author, as is demonstrated most clearly in that branch of the historical school that studied the history of language (e.g. Jacob Grimm). Even more characteristic for Schleiermacher (at least for the Schleiermacher who has influenced posterity[3]) and for Dilthey than the supersedence of historical and grammatical understanding by the quasi-psychological personal identification with the author – the 'empathetic understanding' which, starting from the 'life-expression', returns to its source and reconstructs the work from this perspective – is the understanding of language.

It is obvious that this philosophical hermeneutics always presupposes that the major texts in the religious, philosophical and literary traditions possess an irreplaceable, vital meaning which it is essential to reveal afresh to the contemporary world by utilizing all the means and methods of philological criticism. In the nineteenth century, this meaning is, admittedly, stripped of its dogmatic, normative claim to truth; it becomes relativized both historically and in terms of the psychology of experience. But this does not imply that the meaning of the documents themselves is doubted. Basically, Dilthey does not even question the claim to truth of the religious and metaphysical documents. As an 'expression' it is merely traced back to the multi-sidedness of life. From Luther to Dilthey, therefore, the claim to meaning and truth raised by the works in question itself remains a measure of all hermeneutic understanding, and consequently of the philosophical problem of the preconditions for the possibility of hermeneutic understanding.

The motives and presuppositions underlying the problem of the understanding of meaning were completely different in the case of Ludwig Wittgenstein, the trained aircraft engineer, who, in the years prior to the First World War, studied the symbolic techniques and the philosophical implications of mathematic logic under Bertrand Russell.[4] It is not as if Wittgenstein had entered philosophy without any presuppositions concerning the history of thought, but for Wittgenstein, the author of the *Tractatus logico-philosophicus*,[5] such presuppositions seemed unimportant.[6] Nevertheless, they profoundly shaped his thought and this was clearly recognized by the later Wittgenstein. They are essentially the presuppositions of so-called 'logical atomism', the philosophy of the young Russell.[7]

With regard to our problem of the understanding of meaning, these presuppositions may be briefly characterized in the following manner. In the case of Russell and his pupil Wittgenstein, the Leibnizian plan for the logistic construction of a philosophically precise language coincided with the nominalist-empiricist tradition in the critique of language (and of metaphysics), instigated by Ockham.

In order to combine historically this philosophical tradition with the tradition which underlies hermeneutics, one must go back quite a long way in the history of Western thought[8] – namely, beyond the humanism of the Renaissance to the medieval system of the *septem artes liberales*. Here, in fact, (in the so-called *Trivium*), 'logic', together with 'grammar' and 'rhetorics', formed the obligatory introduction for the student to the problem of the understanding of meaning that was naturally of vital importance for a 'satellite culture' like the Christian West, which was so dependent on tradition. But even at that time, there was tension between the advocates of the grammatical-stylistic text interpretation and the advocates of a historically presuppositionless logic of language or of a 'speculative grammar'; and it is not so difficult to trace this opposition between the humanists – as they were later called – and

3

the logicians of language, right up to the present situation in philo-sophy. From this historical standpoint, modern logistic semiotics (since Boole, Peirce, Frege and Russell) emerges as a new flowering of the speculative logic of language, which has incorporated the critical attitude of nominalism towards metaphysics.

The failure to deal with the hermeneutic problem in the 'transcendental semantics' of the early Wittgenstein

On account of the historical presuppositions indicated, one finds in the early Wittgenstein a fundamentally different interpretation of the terms 'meaning' and 'understanding' than in the hermeneutic tradition. Linguistic meaning, with whose understanding the *Tractatus* is concerned, is not the total meaning of an historical, individual text or the conscious-unconscious intention of the author, which -- according to hermeneutic presuppositions -- must be expressed in every single sentence. The early Wittgenstein understands 'meaning' as the information content of linguistic propositions.

The positive preconditions for the possibility of this meaning and of its being understood are reduced for Wittgenstein, in accordance with the synthesis outlined above between logistics and the empiricist tradition, to two postulated, absolute presuppositions: 1 the 'logical form' common to language and world which regulates the syntactic combination of linguistic signs and simultaneously prescribes the categorial form[9] for the facts of the world that are to be described; 2 the 'objects' which, as the 'meaning' of the 'names', that is, of the combinable elements of the proposition, form the formal 'substance' of the world.[10]

A sharp distinction must be made between the preconditions for the possibility of the meaning of propositions and the preconditions for the possibility of the truth of propositions. The latter, too, can be divided into those preconditions of the 'logical form' of language and those of the empirical world that has to be represented through language. For a propositoin to be true, it must either be an 'elementary proposition' itself that represents a world constitutive 'fact', or it must be reducible – as a complex proposition – to true elementary propositions with the aid of the logic of truth-functions.

In contrast with the 'objects' that – as indicated above – constitute the formal meaning substance of the world, the 'elementary facts' that correspond to the true elementary propositions constitute, so to speak, the material truth substance of the world. Wittgenstein expresses this in the famous opening sentences of the *Tractatus*:

1.   The world is all that is the case.
1.1. The world is the totality of facts, not of things.

It is only through the establishment of a fact that any material statement can be made about 'objects' in the world. The objects themselves, although they are presupposed as elements of meaning for the possibility of the statement, cannot determine the material characteristics of the world independently of their configuration in the statement. They are 'colourless' (2.0232).

The point of Wittgenstein's distinction between the preconditions for the meaning and the preconditions for the truth of propositions becomes apparent if one compares the establishment of meaning with the establishment of truth. In order to establish, for instance, whether a complex proposition such as 'All Germans are musical' is true, I must not take only the logic of truth functions into account, i.e. break the complex proposition down into the elementary propositions, 'Müller is musical', 'Schmidt is musical', etc., but also compare the individual elementary propositions with the facts.[11] I must proceed beyond a mere understanding of the logical form. According to Wittgenstein, this is not necessary if one wishes to understand the meaning of propositions, although even the meaning of propositions – as we have seen – depends not only upon their logical form but also upon the extra-linguistic objects which form the meaning of words. In Wittgenstein's view, the distinction between the problem of understanding and the problem of truth rests upon the fact that, in a language constructed in a logically perfect manner, we must presuppose that we have assigned to the words objects as their meanings; but we cannot presuppose *a priori* that the statements in the language are correlated with facts. But we must presuppose *a priori* merely that, by virtue of their logical form, the statements are correlated with possible facts, that is, states of affairs in logical space. According to the *Tractatus*, it is here that the operative point of language as a system of words and sentences lies, namely that with the *a priori* guaranteed presupposition of objective word meanings and, through a combination of the latter in accordance with logical rules, we are able, to a certain extent, to mentally 'construct by way of experiment' a possible situation[12] – and a possible situation means a 'state of affairs' in 'logical space', to which a 'fact' possibly coincides, if our proposition is true.

Wittgenstein summarized this relationship between the preconditions for understanding meaning and the preconditions for the establishment of truth in the following formulation, which is both subtle and far-reaching:

> To understand a proposition means to know what is the case if it is true.
> (One can understand it, therefore, without knowing whether it is true.)
> It is understood by anyone who understands its constituents.
> (4.024) (cf. the subsequent statements up to 4.031)

This statement is subtle and far-reaching since, apart from the distinction between the question of meaning and the question of truth, it also reveals a positive connection between the establishment of meaning and the establishment of truth. If I automatically recognize what is the case if a proposition is true[13] merely because of its logical form, then this implies that an understanding of the logical form of language incorporates knowledge of how I can establish whether the proposition is true. To understand a proposition, therefore, means to be able to state the logico-linguistic method of its possible verification.[14]

But this principle that the neopositivists called the verification principle also leads to a further critical consequence for a theory of the understanding of meaning. If a linguistic proposition does not 'show' what is the case, if it is true, through its logical form, then either it has no meaning or we have not yet understood its meaning which is possibly hidden by the external form of everyday language (cf. 4.002). At this point one can perceive the critical impulse of Wittgenstein's theory of understanding. Like the postulate of a logico-linguistic criterion of meaning, it is expressed in a suggestive formulation in the *Tractatus*:

> Most of the propositions and questions to be found in philosophical works are not false but nonsensical.
> Consequently we cannot give any answer to questions of this kind, but can only establish that they are nonsensical. Most of

the propositions and questions of philosophers arise from our
failure to understand the logic of our language.
(They belong to the same class as questions whether the good
is more or less identical than the beautiful.)
And it is not surprising that the deepest problems are in fact *not*
problems at all. (4.003)

This famous suspicion of nonsensicality with which Wittgenstein
viewed traditional metaphysics apparently provides the absolute
counterpoint to the spirit of a hermeneutic philosophy and its
theory of the understanding of meaning. Schleiermacher's and
Dilthey's hermeneutics concentrated on the immediate existential
shock (*Betroffensein*) brought about by the expression of a living
individual intention which must certainly be revealed, that is, in the
case of a logically deficient form if necessary by means of the
historical and psychological reconstruction of the living motif that
lies behind language. Wittgenstein asserted that this psychological
problem of understanding, together with the traditional 'theory of
knowledge' in general, was philosophically inessential.[15] His critical
impulse is not primarily directed at a deficient disposition on the
part of the interpreter (for instance, insufficient empathetic imagination, insufficient historical knowledge of the situational context), but rather against the meaning claims of the text itself. For
him, the standard for measuring the understanding of meaning is
not a (conscious or unconscious) human intention but simply the
logical form of the language to be understood.

This, at least, is the early Wittgenstein's theory of understanding.
The later Wittgenstein of the *Philosophical Investigations* explicitly
rejected the standard of a 'logical form' of a precision language
which depicts the world, and replaced it with the plurality of rules of
possible language-games, whose function is largely determined by
the 'situational context' and the human 'life-form'.

There can be no doubt that for a closer confrontation with
Wittgenstein from the hermeneutic standpoint it is primarily the
later philosophy that offers a point of departure. But the internal
continuity of Wittgenstein's philosophy which is founded upon the
language analytical approach would be underrated if one tried to
ignore the *Tractatus* completely in a discussion of the later works. It
is the extreme one-sidedness of the theory of understanding in the
Tractatus that provides us with a model that is presupposed not only

7

by the later Wittgenstein but even more by the self-understanding of a philosophical hermeneutics in the form of a contrasting framework. I believe that it is only after one has become completely aware of the opposition between Wittgenstein's *cognitive interest* and that of a hermeneutic theory of the understanding of meaning through studying the *Tractatus*, that one is in a position to realize the contribution made by the *Philosophical Investigations* to the problem of hermeneutic understanding and evaluate it critically.

For this reason, I should like to return to the *Tractatus*, and to a point at which Wittgenstein himself cannot avoid defining his position on the problem of understanding human intended meanings. This is because there exist in language propositions of the form 'A believes that p', 'A thinks p', 'A says p'. The problem which these propositions pose for Wittgenstein lies in the fact that here, apparently, a judgment is contained in another judgment, but not as a condition for the truth of the complex proposition, and this is the only possibility for which provision had been made in the 'logical atomism' of Russell and Wittgenstein. For instance, the proposition 'John believes that God exists' is obviously not a truth function of the proposition 'God exists'; according to the laws of logic, it can still be true even if God did not exist. The point of 'belief-sentences' which is expressed linguistically in an even more acute manner in the form of 'indirect speech', apparently lies in the fact that the truth of what is believed is uncertain and yet the proposition about the belief in which is believed can be true. But propositions of this form are apparently a logical precondition for the possibility of the interpretative 'human sciences'.

The so-called 'belief-sentences' presented Russell and the young Wittgenstein with the following alternative:

1 One could regard a human subject's assertion of a propositional meaning as a relation between two simple objects; then it would be possible to incorporate the belief-sentence into the philosophy of 'logical atomism' as an elementary depiction of facts, that is, one not capable of further analysis. But strictly speaking, this implies a naturalistic view of the dimension of intentionality, which can be suggested, for example, by a behaviouristic interpretation of this relationship. Basically, Russell himself and later the logical positivists opted for this solution.[16]

2 If one could not accept this naturalistic interpretation of the dimension of intentionality then one was apparently obliged to

abandon the conception of a unified scientific language, which reduces all propositions to the depiction of atomistic states of affairs in the external world by means of the logic of truth functions. For our present topic, then, the significance of Russell's and Wittgenstein's difficulties with belief-sentences lies in the fact that here, for the first time, in the analytical philosophy of language the language of the interpretative human sciences which consists of intentional propositions comes into conflict with the language of 'unified science'. Wittgenstein's *Tractatus* is, in fact, the first radical formulation of a unified 'thing-state of affairs-language'; in Wittgenstein's view, it is valid for all meaningful propositions, that is, for all propositions of 'natural science' (4.11).

Remarkable, and extremely characteristic of the theory of understanding in the *Tractatus*, is the interpretation of intentional propositions that Wittgenstein suggested in order to rescue the conception of the unified structure of all meaningful propositions. Wittgenstein says the following on propositions of the form 'A believes that p is the case' or 'A thinks p':

> if these are considered superficially, it looks as if the proposition *p* stood in some kind of relation to an object *A* (5.541).

> It is clear, however, that 'A believes that *p*', '*A* has a thought *p*' and '*A* says *p*' are of the same form '"*p*" says *p*': and this does not involve a correlation of a fact with an object, but rather the correlation of facts by means of the correlation of their objects (5.542).

How is this remarkable reinterpretation of the intentional propositions to be understood?

Wittgenstein's line of thought proceeds in the following manner. The proposition 'A believes that p' is equivalent in meaning to 'A says p', for in A's statement his meaning can be grasped precisely. But this statement on the part of A only exists for us in that the state of affairs about which a statement is made is represented by the state of affairs as signified (*Zeichensachverhalt*), that is, instead of *p* itself, '*p*' (for the state of affairs that the book is lying on the table, we find the signified state of affairs 'the book is lying on the table'). Following his theory of the depiction of the world, Wittgenstein can therefore assert that we are faced with a correlation of facts through a correlation of their objects. In short, he has reduced the psychological understanding of intentional meanings to the semantic understanding of the meaning of propositions.

This procedure is very typical of the approach of the analytical philosophy of language inaugurated by Wittgenstein. The whole problem of 'intentional consciousness' discredited as being 'psychological' is to be replaced by the semantic problem of the world-depicting language. We have already mentioned that in the *Tractatus* the Kantian question concerning the logical form of the consciousness of objects is translated into the question concerning the logical form of the description of objects.

Through this substitution of language analysis for the theory of knowledge, questions about the subject and his intentions, the soul, etc., become, to some extent, superfluous, as does the presupposition of so-called 'intentional acts'. In proposition 5.631 Wittgenstein declares that 'there is no such thing as the subject that thinks or entertains ideas'.

The neopositivists have often understood this statement as a *carte blanche* for a behaviouristic interpretation of the human subject and his intentional acts. But this is precisely what Wittgenstein did not mean. The stress in the statement does not fall upon the subject-complex, but rather upon the verb 'is'. Wittgenstein wishes to point out – and this is obvious from the context – that here the thinking subject is not found like a thing in the describable world (cf. the continuation of 5.631 and 5.5421). Consequently he can assert in the next sentence (5.632): 'The subject does not belong to the world: rather, it is a limit of the world.' And even more pointedly in sentence 5.641:

> Thus there really is a sense in which philosophy can talk about the self in a non-psychological way.
>
> What brings the self into philosophy is the fact that 'the world is my world'. The philosophical self is not the human being, not the human body, or the human soul, with which psychology deals, but rather the metaphysical subject, the limit of the world – not a part of it.

It becomes clear at this juncture that the point behind the reduction of the problem of consciousness to the problem of language does not lie in the denial of consciousness, soul, human subject, etc., but

10

rather in a radical transcendentalization which identifies the metaphysical subject as the limit of the world with the logical subject of language as such:

> *The limits of my language* mean the limits of my world (5.6).

> The world is *my* world: this is manifest in the fact that the limits of *language* . . . mean the limits of *my* world (5.62).

Just how radical Wittgenstein's conception of the transcendentalization of the logical form of language and simultaneously of the intentional subject is, can best be judged by the famous, yet infamous, distinction between what can be said and what merely 'shows itself' to be unstateable. The second transcendental mystical domain in the *Tractatus* includes – alongside the logical form of language which is also the logical form of the world – what Husserl called the 'constitution of the world' by the intentional subject.

In other words, Wittgenstein conceives of the 'transcendental difference' between what can be experienced (that is, according to Wittgenstein, what can be described or stated) and the preconditions for the possibility of experience (according to Wittgenstein, the 'logical form' of language and, at the same time, of the world) in such a manner that he is forced to declare that his own propositions – the propositions of a transcendental semantics – as propositions that attempt to state the transcendental precondition for the possibility of making a statement out of them,[17] are 'nonsensical':

> My propositions serve as elucidations in the following way: anyone who understands me eventually recognizes them as nonsensical, when he has used them – as steps – to climb up beyond them. (He must, so to speak, throw away the ladder after he has climbed up it.)

> He must transcend these propositions, and then he will see the world aright (6.54).

But what, then, are the consequences for the problem of hermeneutic understanding? How can a connection be established between the *transcendental* semantics of the *Tractatus*, the 'critique of pure language' as it has been called,[18] and the problem of *hermeneutics*?

11

The first impression is, surely, that Wittgenstein's outline of the relationship between language and world is of no use whatsoever to hermeneutics. It seems as if the hermeneutic problem of understanding alien world-views has been shown to be ridiculous. For in the pure language of the transcendental subject, postulated by Wittgenstein, in which the world-constitutive states of affairs can be depicted on account of the logical form of language, the concrete human subjects would always already be in agreement with one another about the structure of the world. The problem of understanding would be restricted to the logical interpretation of information about facts. With regard to the interpretation of the world, however, no problem of communication could arise between individuals (and between peoples, cultures, religions), thanks to the existence of *one* language. Even the most private experience of the world would be *eo ipso* intersubjective, since it is structurally mediated through the *one* logical form of language.[19] Wittgenstein confirms this explicitly in the statement (5.64):

> Here it can be seen that solipsism, when its implications are followed out strictly, coincides with pure realism. The self of solipsism shrinks to a point without extension, and there remains the reality co-ordinated with it.

In my opinion, however, this *reductio ad absurdum* of *hermeneutics* by *transcendental semantics* is extremely instructive and provides that contrasting framework which hermeneutics requires for its philosophical self-understanding. In view of Wittgenstein's extreme model, a new light is shed upon an old reservation of hermeneutically orientated philosophy towards the idea of 'transcendental consciousness'.

Dilthey himself felt the need to revitalize or concretize Kant's transcendental subject so that he could realize his plan for a *critique of historical reason* by analogy with the *critique of pure reason*.[20] This impulse recurs in the work of Heidegger who feels compelled to transform Husserl's 'transcendental consciousness' into the facticity of human 'existence' or 'being-in-the-world'. (A further parallel can be found in the monadological conception developed by the neo-Kantians Hönigswald and Cramer.)

The crux of all these attempts apparently lies in the identification of consciousness as that of living or historically existing, communicating people without having to abandon the connection with the transcendental problematic of reflection upon ultimate validity, perhaps in favour of a behaviouristic problematic that replaces intentional consciousness with the sign-mediated behaviour of people in the world.[21]

The *reductio ad absurdum* of the hermeneutic problem in the early Wittgenstein's *Tractatus* lies in the fact that he radically denies the possibility of an approach that is both objective and subjective, empirical and transcendental, since such a possibility is incompatible with the programme of a unified language which only depicts objective facts. The most important consequence of this position for hermeneutics is that Wittgenstein thinks that he can replace the understanding of the pre-notions or preconceptions of individual opinions with a logical analysis of 'the' form of language. If the meaning of a text, for instance, of a metaphysical text, cannot be reconciled with the above-mentioned logico-linguistic criterion of meaning (verification principle), then it is exposed to a 'suspicion of nonsensicality'.

At this point, in my view, the tension and even – at least in the finite situation – the incompatibility of the logico-linguistic[22] and the hermeneutic approach to the problem of the understanding of meaning is revealed with a previously unattained degree of clarity. The same tension was already registered in the Middle Ages (in the Chartres school) and by the humanists of the Quattrocentro (in their polemic against the 'Modistae', the authors of the *Tractatus de modis significandi*).

In the *Tractatus*, Wittgenstein indicates indirectly and involuntarily the dimension in which the hermeneutic problem of understanding – as it were, between the subject and the object of the logical form of language, between what can be described objectively and what can be stated as the transcendental precondition for the possibility of the description of the world – can be located. He asks (5.633):

> Where *in* the world is a metaphysical subject to be found?
>
> You will say that this is exactly like the case of the eye and the visual field. But really you do *not* see the eye.
>
> And nothing *in the visual field* allows you to infer that it is seen by an eye.

At this point, the hermeneutically orientated philosopher feels immediately provoked to contradict Wittgenstein. He is inclined to reply: 'Everything in a concrete text taken from intellectual history suggests that the text was written from a particular perspective, from a particular standpoint, by a concrete historical subject. And the world that is unfolded in such a text is, in fact, like a visual field which is related perspectivally back to the eye of the subject.' This perspectivism of the hermeneutically reconstructible unfolding of the world is realized, for example, in Heidegger's conception of the particular subject's 'being-in-the-world'.

But it must be added here that the world-unfolding perspective of a text need not necessarily coincide with the perspective that the author consciously adopts. The typical work may realize a certain intersubjectivity of expression in contrast with the individual consciousness of the author. In Humboldt's opinion, this is also true of language.[23] This forms the basis of the supraindividual or perhaps its classical or canonical status. This relative intersubjectivity, however, is never identical with the intersubjectivity of the logical form of language that Wittgenstein postulates in the *Tractatus*. Unlike this type of intersubjectivity that Wittgenstein postulates, it is historical and individual. It does not correspond to an intersubjectivity that makes all communicative understanding between people superfluous, but rather it is the representative expression of a *given* path and a historical stage of human communication.

The difference between this basic situation of hermeneutic understanding and the situation presupposed by Wittgenstein in the *Tractatus* can, perhaps, best be illustrated by reference to the transcendental pragmatic idea of the human 'community of interpretation' developed by Royce in the tradition of Peirce.[24]

Whereas in the *Tractatus* Wittgenstein asserts that each individual language user must immediately extract from the logical form of language the interpretative rule that 'shows' him what is the case if a proposition is true, this 'interpretation' – according to Peirce and Royce – develops within the framework of a community of historical human beings that is basically unrestricted. In this 'community of interpretation' which, in Royce's opinion, comprises at least three members, one person makes another understand what a third (who, in principle, has spoken earlier) means with regard to reality. Moreover, in order to interpret the material content of what was said, he can use the verification principle (in the form of Peirce's 'pragmatic maxim'). But in order to realize this principle of interpretation under the conditions of historical language, which even in the case of members of a 'language community' is not simply identical in the sense of formal logic, 'interpretation' *qua* 'translation' is required from the language of one person into that of another by a third person.

By referring to William James's famous image, one can say that if the linguistic communication of opinions is compared with cashless transactions based on credit then with any attempt to realize the 'cash value' (that is, an attempt at verification) the problem of exchange cannot be ignored so long as we do not have a unified currency.

The resulting *two-dimensionality of the problem of interpretation* can be related to an old semantic problem, namely that of the distinction between *extensional* and *intensional* meaning. In the *Tractatus*, Wittgenstein advocates a thesis of *extensionality* concerning the reduction of the meaning of complex propositions (in accordance with the logic of truth conditions) to the meaning of elementary propositions. The problem of intensional meaning is removed by the reduction of belief-sentences to semantic propositions. Underlying this reduction, as we have seen, was the identification of the human subject's meaning with the logically possible meaning of language as such. If this identification is retracted, in the light of the variety of languages and the historical mutability of each individual language, then one finds that Royce's conception of the triadic structure of interpretation in a human community (the translation from language to language, even within a so-called 'language community') represents the basically infinite development of the intensional meaning of propositions (and, within the latter, the development of the presupposed intensional word meanings). This development of meaning in the continuum of human conversation is obviously the topic of understanding and interpretation in the sense of 'hermeneutics' or the hermeneutic 'human sciences'.

The problem of hermeneutic understanding and the 'language-game' theory of the later Wittgenstein

After this 'confrontation' with the theory of understanding in the

Tractatus, let us turn to Wittgenstein's later work, that of his *Philosophical Investigations*.[25] We shall attempt to examine the work of the later Wittgenstein by raising the same questions that we have asked of the *Tractatus* in a heuristic confrontation with the hermeneutic tradition.

Even a cursory glance reveals that the question of the meaning of 'meaning' and 'understanding' stands, in fact, at the centre of the later Wittgenstein's philosophy: moreover, it is precisely the confrontation with the traditional conceptions of the understanding of 'opinions' or 'intentions', which Wittgenstein had dealt with in the *Tractatus* in a few apodictic yet obscure sentences, that takes up most space in the later works.

Basic difficulties in the assessment of the later Wittgenstein's 'doctrine'

It is certainly not immediately possible to infer from these Socratic discussions of examples and mental experiments anything which might represent the doctrine of the later Wittgenstein. The difficulties encountered by such an attempt do not even arise primarily because Wittgenstein's book, as he himself says, is 'only an album' that comprises 'sketches of landscapes'. Much of the mainly indirect information about his arguments, which are as subtle as they are fragmentary, is suggestive enough to create a conception of Wittgenstein's new 'theory' for the reader. The real difficulty, however, is that, according to Wittgenstein, such a thing cannot exist. If there is continuity between the early and the later Wittgenstein's philosophy, then it lies in the consistent development of the suspicion of nonsensicality towards a philosophy that seeks – like the sciences – to establish propositions or theories about the world:

> Philosophy is not a body of doctrine but an activity.
>
> A philosophical work consists essentially of elucidations.
>
> Philosophy does not result in 'philosophical propositions', but rather in the clarification of propositions . . . (4.112).
>
> The correct method in philosophy would be . . . whenever someone else wanted to say something metaphysical, to demonstrate to him that he had failed to give a meaning to certain signs in his propositions . . . (6.53).

These fundamental statements in the *Tractatus* (and in the analytical philosophy which developed from it) can be applied without any reservations to the later writings; in fact they form the basis for the methodological standpoint here, namely, for the 'therapeutical' philosophy which 'treats' a philosophical question 'like an illness' (§ 255). It is their aim to demonstrate to anyone who becomes entangled in a question unanswerable in terms of science or everyday activity (i.e. a metaphysical question) that he has not grasped the function of language correctly, that he has succumbed to the temptation of a verbal 'image', of a metaphorical 'appearance' (§ 112).

The temptation can even lie in the grammatical form of the question. This is the case, for instance, in the famous Cartesian question '*What* is thinking?', which suggests as an answer the postulation of a special 'entity', perhaps of a '*res* (or *substantia*) *cogitans*', or at least the assumption that there are 'mental acts' or a 'centre of acts'.

On this problem, Wittgenstein says the following: 'Where our language suggests a body and there is none: there, we should like to say, is a *spirit*' (§ 36). As a result there arises the 'philosophical problem about mental processes and states' or, on the other hand, behaviourism:

> The first step is the one that altogether escapes notice.
> [Confused by the analogy with the description of the physical.]
> We talk of processes and states and leave their nature
> undecided. Sometime perhaps we shall know more about
> them – we think. But that is just what commits us to a particular
> way of looking at the matter. For we have a definite concept of
> what it means to learn to know a process better. (The decisive
> movement in the conjuring trick has been made, and it was the
> very one that we thought quite innocent.) – And now the
> analogy which was to make us understand our thoughts falls to
> pieces. So we have to deny the yet uncomprehended process in
> the yet unexplored medium. And now it looks as if we had
> denied mental processes. And naturally we don't want to deny
> them (§ 308).

In Wittgenstein's view (cf. § 89), a similar, apparently innocent transition from everyday language to a nonsensical metaphysical question is made, for example, in Augustine's *Quid est ergo tempus?* (*Confessiones* XI, 14). And according to Wittgenstein, Augustine unintentionally reveals where the transition to nonsense, to the 'idling' of language (§ 132), is to be sought when he continues: *Si nemo ex me quaerat scio; si quarenti explicare velim nescio.*

Wittgenstein believes that the correct interpretation of Augustine's remark lies in the fact that we know what time is as long as we use the word 'time' in practical situational contexts within which we have learned its function (for instance, in the question 'Do you have time [*Zeit*] today?', or in the scientific context of the question 'How can we measure the simultaneity [*Gleichzeitigkeit*] of two events?'). In this linguistic usage that has become stabilized through practice, the essence of time 'shows itself', but we alienate this essence from its usage by the hypostatization of the 'ontological question': 'What is time?', whose apparent meaning rests upon the external, grammatical analogy with a language-game like the following: 'What is that lying there?' – (Answer) 'A stone'. According to Wittgenstein, this is also valid for other ontological questions of essence.

> When philosophers use a word – 'knowledge', 'being', 'object', 'I', 'proposition', 'name' – and try to grasp the *essence* of the thing, one must always ask oneself: is the word ever actually used in this way in the language-game which is its original home? – What *we* do is to bring words back from their metaphysical to their everyday use (§ 116).

The examples quoted so far for the emergence of nonsensical (metaphysical) questions and the corresponding formation of theories can tentatively be interpreted in such a manner that ultimately it is merely a matter of recognizing the restriction of a given ontological approach to the existence (*Sein*) of physical things and of excluding the analogous treatment of mental phenomena.[26]

But Wittgenstein's rejection of philosophical theory-formation is far more radical. This becomes most evident in his discussion of the traditional theory of the concept, that is, the question which has been raised since Socrates, concerning the 'what' content, the definable *quidditas* or *essentia* of any word-meaning. In a discussion of the questions concerning the essence of the 'game' and the 'number', Wittgenstein attempts to demonstrate that it is impossible to verify any conjecture concerning a uniformly determinable mental content, an idea or an essence. This still applies even if no hypostatization of this essence in accordance with the preformed image (*Vor-Bild*) or model of an existing thing is intended. In Wittgenstein's view, such a conjecture is also completely unnecessary for the understanding of the function of words. It is quite sufficient that a 'family resemblance' exists between the numerous 'ways of using' a word which are determined by the situational context:

> 67. I can think of no better expression to characterize these similarities than 'family resemblances'; for the various resemblances between members of a family: build, features, colour of eyes, gait, temperament, etc. etc. overlap and criss-cross in the same way. And I shall say: 'games' form a family.
>
> And for instance the kinds of number form a family in the same way. Why do we call something a 'number'? Well, perhaps because it has a – direct – relationship with several things that have hitherto been called number; and this can be said to give it an indirect relationship to other things we call the same name. And we extend our concept of number as in spinning a thread we twist fibre on fibre. And the strength of the thread does not reside in the fact that some one fibre runs through its whole length, but in the overlapping of many fibres.

Perhaps Wittgenstein himself succumbs to the suggestiveness of an image at this point. At least one might pose such a question, especially if one bears in mind that Wittgenstein himself is somehow able to establish something like a generally valid, theoretical statement about the essence of the meaning of a word – namely, that it shows itself in its specific 'usage' in the linguistic and situational context.[27] It should be noted at this point that we are not accusing Wittgenstein of having recognized what is common to the ways of using a *specific* word in the disjunction of the respective common elements (between A and B, B and C, C and D, etc.). Wittgenstein himself raises this objection and invalidates it by means of an ironic comparison: 'something runs through the whole thread – namely the continuous overlapping of those fibres'. But the supposed recognition of this disjunctive similarity in the ways of using a specific word is not at stake in what Wittgenstein claims to have recognized as the common element (the general essence) of the term 'meaning of a word' (in a different context, the function of

19

language), namely, that it only shows itself in the use of words.[28]

Here lies a real difficulty in interpreting the later Wittgenstein since he denies (and by virtue of his own presuppositions he must deny) that he himself in the new concept of the 'language-game', for example, claims to have recognized theoretically something about the uniform essence of language. For instance, that it is entangled in the ways of interacting, in the 'life-form' as a social 'habit' or 'institution' and therefore its structure is interwoven with the *a priori* free structure of possible experience in the situational world. Wittgenstein explicitly raises this question in § 65 of the *Philosophical Investigations* and, with the unrelenting consistency that he had demonstrated in the *Tractatus*, he now thinks that he must deny to his own statements the status of a theory. His 'examples' are not intended to reveal what is common to 'language-games' as such: 'Here giving examples is not an indirect means of explaining . . .' (§ 71). The examples are intended to provoke in the reader merely an *ad hoc* application, that is, they are to help him on occasion to allow his philosophizing to come to rest since his questions dissolve themselves:

> For the clarity that we are aiming at is indeed *complete* clarity. But this simply means that the philosophical problems should *completely* disappear.
>
> The real discovery is the one that makes me capable of stopping doing philosophy when I want to. The one that gives philosophy peace, so that it is no longer tormented by questions which bring *itself* in question. Instead, we now demonstrate a method, by examples; and the series of examples can be broken off. Problems are solved (difficulties eliminated), not a *single* problem (§ 133).

Moreover, since he is dissatisfied with the previous formulation which after all still spoke in terms of a *single* method whose significance Wittgenstein must have discovered, he proceeds to give an even more precise formulation to his thesis:

> There is not *a* philosophical method, though there are indeed methods, like different therapies (§ 133).

But, one is forced to ask, how are these *ad hoc* approaches of the critique of language supposed to fulfil their therapeutic function?

How can they convince the unhappy victim of metaphysical rumination of the nonsensical nature of the questions he raises if they cannot have recourse to a theoretical insight into the essence of language's function, of 'meaning', 'sense' and 'understanding', an insight which must be superior to the traditional presuppositions? This insight itself may only be capable of being formulated with the 'vagueness'[29] which fits the concrete conversational situation, and it may, therefore, be open in principle to new, unpredictable situations of application; but in my view this does not invalidate its claim as an ontological insight, in the sense of the invalidation suggested by Wittgenstein by the image of the mere family resemblance of intended meanings.

At this point we must break off the discussion of the paradox which remains unresolved both in the *Philosophical Investigations* and in the *Tractatus*, namely, the paradox of how Wittgenstein saw himself as a philosopher. Nevertheless, the implicit question of whether it is possible to reveal the nonsensicality of metaphysical questions without adopting, in a disguised form, a metaphysical – or, for that matter, philosophical – standpoint oneself, appears to be the decisive question that Wittgenstein passed on to contemporary philosophy.

The new basic conception of *Philosophical Investigations* compared to the *Tractatus*

In the following we shall return to the more specific question concerning the relationship of Wittgenstein to the problem of hermeneutic understanding. We shall conclude the necessary digression on the fundamental difficulties which confront the interpreter of Wittgenstein with the decision to understand Wittgenstein's examples and 'ladder' sentences in such a manner that they incorporate a theory of 'language', 'meaning' and 'understanding' which is relevant to our topic. We shall now compare the basic structure of this theory with that of the *Tractatus*.

As I have indicated (cf. pp. 39–40, n. 14), it seems to me that the essential change lies in the fact that the presupposition of a *single* precision language is abandoned. This language would be one which, by means of its 'logical form' that it shares with the describable world, lays down the framework within which every analysis of language and reality is carried out. This metaphysical or transcendental semantic presupposition is now replaced by the new working hypothesis of an unlimited number of different, but more or less related, 'language-games' which develop and disintegrate historically. As becomes gradually evident in Wittgenstein's examples, these language-games can be characterized in their heuristic conception as units of linguistic usage, life-form and world (situational) interpretation that are constituted by a behavioural rule.

This abbreviated conceptual definition might serve to accentuate the common aspects of the later Wittgenstein's novel basic approach and the philosophy of the *Tractatus*. All the functions which are attributed to the 'logical form' of language or the linguistically representable world in the *Tractatus* are transferred in the *Philosophical Investigations* to the 'rule' of the respective language-game. The rule constitutes the so-called 'depth grammar' (§ 664) of language which contains the criteria of sense and nonsense and, at the same time, prescribes the *a priori* ontological structure of the situational world that belongs to the respective language-game. Apparently the differentiation and relativization of these functions of the logic of language which are called 'transcendental' in the *Tractatus*, is brought about by the inclusion of human activity (the social 'life-forms', 'habits' or 'institutions') in the basic conception of the language-game. A significant consequence of this *pragmatization*[30] is that – together with the absolute ideal of exactitude – the monopolistic position of the (natural) scientific understanding of the world is abandoned in favour of the various standards of the interpretation of the world which are instrinsic to the respective language-games.

According to the later Wittgenstein the expression 'the sun rises' would not be false within the framework of a modern astronomical theory but rather it would be meaningless; in the context of a farmers' or tourists' language-game, on the other hand, it would be meaningful (and verifiable). Consequently, a question such as the one concerning the parts of an armchair which Wittgenstein himself uses to carry his earlier adherence to logico-metaphysical atomism *ad absurdum* (cf. § 47), acquires its standards, for example, in the language-game of removal men who want to take the armchair to pieces in an expert manner. (Generally, atomic physicists will not ask about the parts of an armchair.) The decisive criterion for the appropriateness (e.g. sufficient precision) of linguistic usage is 'our real need' as the 'axis of reference' of the language-game (§ 108).

The fact that the practical 'life-form' is taken into account in the basic conception of the language not only results in a pragmatization of the criteria of meaning for descriptive or informative linguistic usage. It also means that the traditional orientation of the philosophy of language towards the descriptive function of language is placed in question. The meaning of questions and commands, for instance, cannot be reduced to the establishment of facts; nor even in the sense that – like Frege and Wittgenstein himself in the *Tractatus*[31] – one distinguishes between the assertion of a 'fact' and the 'showing' of a 'state of affairs', and tries to recognize the latter even in imperative statements and questions as a meaning-content that remains neutral to their modality. For it is precisely the mood of a sentence (declarative, imperative, interrogative and also indicative, subjunctive, optative, conditional, etc.) that expresses the entanglement of linguistic usage with the situational reference of the life-form in the language-game.[32] Moreover, the 'deep grammar' of sentence modes should by no means be restricted to the typical forms distinguished by traditional grammar. This is even refuted by the fact that only in the context of a large unit of language and life activity (that is, in the context of the 'language-game') does a sentence acquire its meaning (cf. § 23).[33] The language-game model places the basic orientation of the ontology of language, which stretches from Aristotle to the *Tractatus*,[34] even more radically in question in its critique of the biased nature of the theory of meaning in favour of the so-called 'denotational' or 'naming' function of words (cf. §§ 1–15). Wittgenstein is prepared to accept this mode of speech as being at most the abbreviation for the description of the manner in which words are used in the language-game so long as this is not associated with the notion that words are actually used like names:

> Nominalists make the mistake of interpreting all words as *names*, and so of not really describing their use, but only, so to speak, giving a paper draft on such a description   (§ 383).

The reference to human activity or a 'life-form' in the language-game model, however, has a further consequence which seems to threaten to undermine the thematic realm of the philosophy of language as a whole. In the catalogue of conceivable language-games that Wittgenstein draws up in § 23 of the *Philosophical Investigations*, it is noticeable that the language-game of commanding also includes acting in accordance with commands. In addition, the following are mentioned: 'constructing an object from a description [a drawing]', 'forming and testing a hypothesis', 'presenting the results of an experiment in tables and diagrams', 'play-acting', 'singing catches' and 'solving a problem in practical arithmetic'.

It is evident at this point that it is not only so-called 'linguistic usage' in the traditional sense that belongs to the 'language-game' but also *all* thought and action which is 'interlaced' in some way with linguistic usage. The context of the *Philosophical Investigations* makes it clear that this includes all human behaviour which involves an 'understanding' of 'meaning' and is (therefore) itself 'intelligible'. With this statement it seems to me that a starting-point is provided for our substantive confrontation of hermeneutics with Wittgenstein's later writings. The model of the language-game implies both the immediate world (situational) understanding which is an aspect of 'meaning something' and, in the narrower sense, the 'hermeneutic' understanding of the intentions that reside in the immediate understanding of the world and are expressed in the actions and deeds of human beings.

In order to grasp the significance of this implication one has, however, to bear in mind Wittgenstein's critique of metaphysics and primarily, in this connection, the rejection of the notion of specific mental-spiritual activities or events alongside the visible events or activities with which we are familiar. This rejection is especially directed against the identification of 'meaning' or 'understanding' with spiritual experiences of mental acts, and the identification of the intended or understood meaning with specific mental contents. Throughout the entire text of the *Philosophical Investigations* one encounters Wittgenstein's repeated attempt to expose psychologistic metaphysics with the aid of language criticism. The following is a characteristic example. If someone who has to solve a difficult mathematical problem suddenly says 'now I understand', then with the word 'understand' he does not wish to 'denote' a specific 'spiritual condition', an experience, nor does he wish to 'describe' a fact with the sentence in which the word occurs. Rather, he wishes to say 'now I know how to proceed' (cf. §§ 154, 179, 180, 321 ff.). Wittgenstein himself interprets this case as follows: 'One might rather call them [i.e. the words] a "signal"; and we judge whether it was rightly employed by what he goes on to do' (§ 180). According to Wittgenstein, one can only answer the question concerning the 'meaning' of 'meaning', 'sense', 'meaning something' and 'understanding' in such a manner that one simultaneously answers the question of the criteria[35] for the meaning, or rather for the understanding of meaning in a given case. But this means that the question cannot be answered by reference to a secret event in the spirit, but rather, at best, by references to the 'conditions' of given behaviour (cf. §§ 154, 155, 269). The following example is also typical:

> Wittgenstein asks: 'How does it come about that this arrow
> —→ *points*? Doesn't it seem to carry in it something besides
> itself?' According to Wittgenstein, the traditional answer
> comes: 'No, not the dead line on paper; only the psychical
> thing, the meaning, can do that'. [i.e. constitute the referential
> functions of the sign.] Wittgenstein himself, however, replies:
> 'That is both true and false. The arrow points only in the
> application that a living being makes of it.
> 'This pointing is *not* a hocus-pocus which can be performed
> only by the soul'   (§ 454; cf § 435).

The following example provides the crucial test of the critique of language for the non-identifiability of 'meaning' with an 'experience':

> 'Tell me, what was going on in you when you uttered the words
> . . .?–The answer to this is not: "I was meaning . . ."'
> (§ 675).

Nor, in Wittgenstein's view, is it a mental act of intentionality (for instance, in Brentano's or Husserl's sense) distinguished from psychic events that constitutes the sense or meaning of sentences or words. In this context, Wittgenstein recommends the following mental experiment:

> If I say 'Mr. Scot is not a Scot', I mean the first 'Scot' as a proper
> name, the second one as a common name . . . Try to mean the
> first 'Scot' as a common name and the second one as a proper
> name – How is it done? When *I* do it, I blink with the effort as I
> try to parade the right meaning before my mind in saying the

words. – But do I parade the meanings of the words before my mind when I make the ordinary use of them?   (p. 176).

At this point, Wittgenstein draws attention to the fact that the meaning function of words is fixed by their standard usage in such a manner that the intentional act of meaning something is not only superfluous but also hardly has a chance of asserting its intention *against* such a usage:

> When I say the sentence with this exchange of meanings I feel that its sense disintegrates. – Well, *I* feel it, but the person I am saying it to does not. So what harm is done?   (ibid.)

According to Wittgenstein, therefore, it is not the fact that in speaking we 'parade the meanings before our minds' which is decisive for the meaning of verbal utterances but rather that the utterances occur in a language-game in which meaning, on the one hand, and understanding on the other, are fixed by means of a public rule, an institutional 'habit'.

In short, Wittgenstein refuses to search for a specific theoretical 'explanation' of the phenomena of meaning and understanding. In his view, everything is made evident when the language-game is described in which the phenomena in question reveal themselves:

> 654 Our mistake is to look for an explanation where we ought to look at what happens as a 'proto-phenomenon'. That is, where we ought to have said: *this language-game is played*.
>
> 655 The question is not one of explaining a language-game by means of our experiences, but of noting a language-game.[36]

But what is the significance of this approach for our problem of hermeneutic understanding? Can the traditional problem of the interpretation of texts and the reconstruction of the (conscious or unconscious) intentions of their authors be formulated with the aid of the language-game 'theory'?

Since we have denied such a possibility as far as the logic of language in the *Tractatus* was concerned, it will be useful to illustrate the new situation in this confrontation by returning to the situation created by the *Tractatus*. Even the young Wittgenstein had maintained that one cannot describe what 'meaning', 'intended meaning' and 'understanding' are in the same way as one can a natural process; they reveal themselves to be the preconditions for the possibility of the description of a natural process in and against the function of language. This basic analytical approach is also preserved by the later Wittgenstein, the difference being, however, that the function of language is no longer governed by a 'transcendental logic' of world depiction, but rather it disintegrates into the unlimited diversity of actual 'language-games' which are the components of 'life-forms' or 'habits' and, as such, reveal *a priori* a particular situational world through their meaning.

In this differentiation and relativization of the limiting conditions and criteria of 'meaning' and the 'understanding of meaning' to 'life-form' and 'situational context' it seems as if the concrete mediation – which has always been required by philosophical hermeneutics – between subject and object, between transcendental philosophy and the historically empirical has in fact been taken into account. It would appear that the 'language-games' as model units of linguistic usage, life-form and world interpretation represented the living incarnation of the function of the intellectual realm, which can more readily provide the basis for a *Critique of Historical Reason* in Dilthey's sense than can the conception of the transcendental 'subject as such'.

As we have seen, the language-game approach certainly entails a rejection of the psychologistic terminology and mode of thinking which dominates the usual conception of 'hermeneutics' as conceived by Schleiermacher and Dilthey. If neither 'experiences' nor 'mental intentions' form the real object and substance of understanding, then the theory of hermeneutic understanding cannot be founded either on empathetic reliving (*Nacherleben*) or on the mental reconstruction of someone else's creative acts which are expressed in the medium of the printed text (or in the medium of the work of art, or actions, or institutions). What – in the conception of the later Wittgenstein – could replace these basic notions of traditional hermeneutics?

It seems to me that we are confronted with a strange alternative at this point through the conception of the language-game. Initially one might think that hermeneutic understanding *qua* empathetic reliving is replaced by the objective 'description' of the language-game, in whose context the meaning that is to be grasped, the intention, 'shows itself'. This methodological principle indeed often appears to closely follow both Wittgenstein's recommendations and also the method which he himself demonstrated. But, second, one might maintain that in order to understand the meaning which reveals itself in a language-game one must presuppose not a detached description of the language-game as a whole, but rather participation in the language-game, since – according to Wittgenstein's own maxim derived from his critique of language – an understanding of meaning commonly exists within the framework of a functioning language-game.

Hermeneutic understanding and the 'description' of language-games

Let us tentatively follow for a moment the first suggestion which is based upon Wittgenstein's own method. It also represents a widespread tendency in the modern cultural sciences, ethnology, cultural anthropology, linguistics, and sociology which replaces the immediate empathetic interpretation of documents and other living expressions of a foreign culture with the objective description (and categorical analysis) of the total life-context, and in particular with the objective description of 'institutions', in order to gain objective criteria through such a conscious estrangement which can be used to combat the prejudices and over-hasty conclusions of the empathetic imagination.[37]

This methodological tendency is, however, ambiguous. It either already presupposes the understanding which it wishes to replace and actually seeks to reinforce such understanding – by means of an objective estrangement – or it must subscribe to a radical behaviourism that does indeed seek to replace understanding by the description of an objectively given process.

Many points in Wittgenstein's *Philosophical Investigations* (and this is even more true of Ryle's related studies) create the initial impression that Wittgenstein would actually like to replace the reconstruction of intentions with 'looking at' and 'describing' objective behaviour. In this case, all those arguments will apply to him that have always disqualified radical 'physicalistic' behaviourism as the basis of the so-called 'human sciences'.[38] One example is the argument that one cannot proceed from even an extremely precise description of behaviour – for instance, a description of the statistically relevant features of behaviour – to a decision as to whether it constitutes language, that is, in Wittgenstein's words, whether the behaviour follows a rule of its own accord.[39] Above all, it would be impossible to appreciate how Wittgenstein, on the basis of a mere description of objective data, achieves a critique of meaning (e.g. an exposure of language idling in the case of metaphysical 'language-games'). Moreover, should we assume that Wittgenstein understands the differentiation and relativization of the transcendental 'logic of language' in language-games in such a manner that now what 'only shows itself' as the precondition for the possibility of all objective description will itself become accessible to this same objective description?

Repeatedly, however, Wittgenstein explicitly repudiated behaviourism.[40] Like every '-ism', in his eyes it would have been merely a philosophical disease. Undoubtedly, one is more faithful to Wittgenstein's reference to 'looking at' and 'describing' language-games (as well as to the indisputable fruitfulness of so-called 'behavioural research' in the cultural sciences) if one simply presupposes the understanding of intended meanings, whose function is to be revealed through description, in the function of the description itself. The description of a language-game in which opinions are both expressed and understood – either in words or in the form of subsequent behaviour – is indeed nothing more than a relative estrangement of one's own meaning and understanding. Basically, all the attempts to distance oneself from and to objectify behavioural criteria and institutional contexts in the modern cultural sciences cannot gloss over the fact that the starting-point of the description (the question raised, the cognitive interest) is dependent upon a self-understanding,[41] no matter how pre-reflective this might be, and also that the cognitive gain from the quasi-objective description lies in the deepening of this self-understanding. What is revealed in every aspect of this objectivistic, quasi-behaviouristic tendency in modern science and analytical philosophy is ultimately only that circuitousness of human self-understanding which was recognized by Hegel: its 'mediation' through 'exteriorization' (*Entäusserung*).[42] Dilthey especially is very conscious of this structure when he counters Nietzsche's introspective psychologism with the thesis that man knows himself only on account of his history.[43]

If, however, one does not understand Wittgenstein's method of describing language-games in a behaviouristic manner, but rather as the estrangement of human self-understanding,[44] then a problem arises which Wittgenstein neither raises nor answers in the

Philosophical Investigations. This question concerns the structure of language-games that are related to others by their mode of description, for example, the language-game of language criticism whose existence Wittgenstein himself bears witness to in the *Philosophical Investigations.* If the description of language-games as units of linguistic usage, life-form and world interpretation is intended to take over the function of the hermeneutic understanding of intended meanings, then precisely the type of language-game that is related to other language-games must become a key problem for a hermeneutics based on Wittgenstein's work. Such language-games ought to be constructed and, in particular, the question should be raised as to whether, and if necessary, how such hermeneutic language-games differ from the normal descriptive language-games that are concerned with the description of non-human nature. This question is primarily of interest because the historical human sciences are concerned with situational contexts which are not interwoven with one's own language-game in the present (as is, for example, the situational context of describing a landscape) but rather they belong to the language-game in the past that must still be reconstructed.

In Wittgenstein's sense, for instance, narrating a story either from personal experience or one that has been handed down, translating within the framework of a conversation, or construing the meaning of an old text (exegesis, interpretation) are all hermeneutic language-games. If one bears in mind the comment that language-games are 'part of a life-form' and are interwoven with 'activities', then one must include in the historical hermeneutic language-game all the detailed technical studies that a historian carries out in order to trace the sources and make critical use of them, and also everything gained from history's auxiliary sciences, even the activities of an archaeological expedition, and the results of an excavation. On the other hand, one must also include the activities in which hermeneutic understanding is applied: the sermon, the lecture, schoolteaching, jurisprudence, the performance of a play or a concert, or an exhibition of paintings or sculpture. Furthermore, one must include the institutionally rule-governed behaviour of the audience in which the assimilation of the spoken, performed or exhibited understanding takes place and only in so doing does it complete the application of hermeneutic understanding.[45]

So far we have been trying to imagine those language-games in Wittgenstein's sense that are hermeneutically related to other language-games, but by doing so we have surely become aware of the fact that our examples are far removed from the model of the *description* of one language-game by means of another. This model seems to be more readily realized in the philosophical language-game that we ourselves,[46] in an attempt to proceed in a manner analogous to Wittgenstein's, have just been playing and are still playing. The hermeneutic language-games that have been presented, however, seem to form new language-game units with those language-games which they are interpreting, units which only become visible at the level of our philosophical structural analysis.[47] It is in fact important to establish whether the structure of the language-game (the type of sense or nonsense possible in it) is being described philosophically, or whether the concrete meaning-content of a language-game is being interpreted in a hermeneutic language-game. In the latter case, the unity of a quasi-discourse must be created between the two language-games, even if they have taken place in periods that are far removed from each other and in very different situational contexts.[48] Accordingly, the specific function of the hermeneutic language-game would be to mediate the human interpretation of the world and the associated outline of existence in the continuum of discourse or, to put it in largely Wittgensteinian terms, a mediation between one 'life-form' and another.

Hermeneutic understanding and participation in language-games

In my opinion, it is necessary at this point to take up the above-mentioned Wittgensteinian alternative to the conception of hermeneutics as the *description* of language-games. This alternative argues that the understanding of meaning always presupposes *participation* in the language-game, through whose context the meaning structure of a situation is revealed *a priori*. Can the characteristic features of hermeneutic language-games be made more readily intelligible perhaps by the new starting-point than by our first approach which, starting from the external description of language-games, was at best able through an aporetic discussion to suggest indirectly the true nature of hermeneutic language-games?

I would maintain that we must first realize that we are now concerned with the quasi-transcendental philosophical perspective of the language-game 'theory', since we have already dealt with the quasi-behaviouristic aspect. Or, to put it more pointedly, whereas it originally seemed as if – according to Wittgenstein's doctrine – the understanding of meaning was to be replaced by the external description of behaviour, this doctrine now seems to assert that only within the framework of a language-game does human behaviour become accessible, i.e. as meaningful and intelligible behaviour.[49]

It is only at this point that many of the later Wittgenstein's most valuable achievements can be recognized. One of these is, for instance, the truly revolutionary insight for all philosophical thinking that a 'private language' is, in principle, impossible, or rather – formulated differently – one cannot follow a rule all by oneself, guided perhaps by introspectively accessible standards.[50] Anyone who wished to introduce a language for empirical data accessible only to himself (e.g. pains) that was intelligible only to himself (one not consistently connected with standard usage and consequently untranslatable) would not possess any criteria for the correct use of language. He would be unable to distinguish between the arbitrary and the norm, since every operative norm which provides criteria for such distinctions is dependent, among other things, upon the fact that other people can check whether the norm is being followed. Another person, however, would be unable to recognize from his outward behaviour whether he were following a rule or not, unless they had already agreed upon this rule, or the other person could reach an agreement with a third person who could check the behaviour of the first by recourse to a public rule (for instance, 'habit' or 'institution'). Without reference to such a public controlling instance the other person might regard even fortuitous (natural, spontaneous) movements as rule-governed behaviour, since no behaviour is conceivable that human beings could not 'explain' externally using a rule that had been invented *ad hoc*. In the case in question, the other person might perhaps think he 'understood' what he merely 'explains' in accordance with an externally imposed rule.[51] The other possibility would be that an instance of human behaviour, although rule-governed and therefore intelligible, is 'explained' externally by other people as being a natural spontaneous phenomenon of movement since they do not participate in the associated language-game. In short, understanding and intelligible behaviour only exist if one presupposes the existence of a language-game, i.e. a public 'habit' or a social 'institution'.[52]

It is only now when, instead of quasi-behaviourism, a transcendental philosophy of the preconditions for the possibility and validity of meaning and understanding – a philosophy embodied in the concept of the language-game – opposes the modern philosophy of the human subject,[53] that the confrontation between Wittgenstein and traditional hermeneutics seems to reach its climax. The precondition of mutual participation in a language-game obviously replaces the *methodological solipsism* of attaining understanding through *empathy for* (*Einfühlung in*) another person. It is evident that the self-understanding which the methodological solipsist seeks to offer as his investment, so to speak, towards the empathetic understanding of other people (if not even as the presupposition for a proof by analogy of their existence as thinking beings) is itself mediated through the public rule of a language-game and the 'life-form' that is interwoven with the latter.

It is interesting to note the pertinent change in Dilthey's standpoint. In his *Einleitung in die Geisteswissenschaften* (1883), he still holds the view that 'an isolated individual treading the earth, supposing (he) live(d) long enough to develop . . . would evolve these functions (sc. philosophy, religion and art) out of himself in complete isolation'.[54] Later, however, in the fragments of *Der Aufbau der geschichtlichen Welt in der Geisteswissenschaften* he writes: 'Every word, every sentence, every gesture or polite formula, every work of art and every historical deed is intelligible because the people who express themselves through them and those who understand them have something in common; the individual always experiences, thinks and acts in a common sphere and only there does he understand.'[55]

Among the examples that Dilthey uses in order to illustrate how understanding is conditioned by the 'common sphere' are some which are very close to the language-games presented by Wittgenstein, or rather the 'life-forms' that are interlaced with them. The following passage can serve as an example:[56]

> Every square planted with trees, every room in which seats are arranged, is intelligible to us from our infancy because human planning, arranging and valuing – common to us all – have assigned its place to every square and every object in the room.

The child grows up within the order and customs of the family which it shares with the other members and its mother's orders are accepted in this context. Before it learns to talk it is already wholly immersed in that common medium. It learns to understand the gestures and facial expressions, movements and exclamations, words and sentences, only because it encounters them always in the same form and in the same relation to what they mean and express.

Consequently one understands elements of actions, e.g. 'the picking up of an object, the dropping of a hammer, the cutting of wood with a saw',[57] since the specific connection in which they occur is familiar: 'The relation of the action to the mind which it . . . expresses is regular and so we can make assumptions about it.'[58]

To this extent, it is possible to establish common ground between the hermeneutic function of Wittgenstein's language-game model and Dilthey's 'common sphere' which, like Hegel, he also calls the 'sphere of objective mind'. But the comparison between the later Wittgenstein and the later Dilthey actually becomes interesting for our purposes in that Dilthey draws upon the above-mentioned examples not, in fact, for 'hermeneutic understanding' but rather for pre-scientific, 'elementary' or 'pragmatic' understanding. He writes:[59]

Understanding arises, first of all, from the interests of practical life where people are dependent on communicating with each other. They must make themselves mutually understood. The one must know what the other wants. Thus, first of all, the elementary forms of understanding arise.

These are indeed forms of understanding envisaged by pragmatic, behaviouristic conceptions of sociology and social psychology (especially of G.H. Mead), and it is these, above all, which are also elucidated through the language-game 'theory' of the later Wittgenstein.

The limitations of the language-game model in the light of the *'Hermeneutic circle'* of understanding

In Dilthey's opinion, the problem of artistic, or even scientific, hermeneutic understanding only arises when – still within the framework of elementary understanding – 'uncertainties', 'difficulties' and 'contradictions' occur,[60] e.g. when foreign customs, institutions and life-forms are encountered, or when one's own traditions start to become unintelligible. In fact, from the last example the two great currents developed which gave modern hermeneutics its character as the art of understanding; these are the philological criticism developed by humanism and the Protestant exegesis of the Bible. How is one to analyse this characteristic point of departure of the hermeneutic desire and necessity to understand in the light of the language-game model?

Let us recall at this point what led us to consider participation in a functioning language-game as the precondition for the possibility and validity of understanding. This heuristic aspect of a possible interpretation of Wittgenstein emerged when the attempt to regard the external description of a language-game as a model (as a limiting case of the estrangement) of hermeneutic understanding led to the conclusion that the description of a language-game can only result in a substantive understanding of the meaning which 'shows itself' in the latter if it creates a new language-game unit, the unity of discourse, with the language-game described. It now seems that we are reaching a result which indicates the contrary. The model of participation in the existing rule-governed unity of a language-game can only serve as a model for the situation of hermeneutic understanding if we consider the weakening and ultimately the disintegration of this unit (into the historically objectified language-game and the historically objectifying language-game of the interpreter).

The confrontation between these apparently contradictory results indicates, however, that the philosophical problem of hermeneutic understanding lies precisely between the two models that are at least suggested by Wittgenstein's conception of the language-game. We are not concerned here with 'understanding' of the type that, in Wittgenstein's view, is even correlated *a priori* with a given expression of intention through the rule of an existing language-game (a 'habit') so that the expression and the understanding connected with it mutually explicate each other within the framework of the language-game and reveal their 'essence' to the description.[61] Nor are we concerned with an 'objective description of behaviour' of the type in which the underlying rule could be applied externally, so that it could not be considered, in principle, as the 'motive' of both one's own behaviour as well as the other person's. Rather, we are concerned with a procedure which is compelled to confront itself, to a certain extent, in an objective manner with the quasi-transcendental rule of the language-game – a rule which distinguishes between sense and nonsense in human behaviour and reveals *a priori* a structure of possible objects in a situational world. Nevertheless, it must do this in order to 'understand' a possible motivation of one's own and another person's behaviour in the light of this quasi-objective rule.

Let us take an example. From Wittgenstein's perspective the meaning of Godfrey of Bouillon's intentions is determined by the rules of the language-game or life-form of the medieval crusade. These rules in a sense constitute the quasi-transcendental framework of the 'life-form' and 'world' of Godfrey. But the modern historian, who no longer participates in this life-form, must first reconstruct them from the given records of Godfrey's words and deeds (and also those of other crusaders). Whatever the *precondition* for the possibility of intelligible meaning, it must be capable of becoming *objective* for him in a sense-phenomenon that is itself *conditioned*, but in such a manner that it is nevertheless *understood* as the *precondition* for the possibility of similar discoverable meanings, even concerning one's own existential possibilities. We can formulate it differently. It must be possible to derive from what is objective an outline of meaning for the world that is capable of correcting the hitherto accepted outline of meaning, in the light of which the objective initially acquired its meaning – a meaning which presumably appeared strange.

Dilthey's real concern was to analyse this structure. He called the phenomenon in which the rule of the life-form – which is no longer self-evident – becomes concrete for the interpreter the 'expression' of life (and later, following Hegel, the 'objectivation of mind'). Moreover, he called the structure, according to which the rule that has become objective in the 'expression' can correct the rule in the light of which it became objective, the 'hermeneutic circle'. Should we claim that Dilthey discovered the structure of the hermeneutic language-game?

In his later writings, Wittgenstein dissolved the 'logic form' of language, which is at the same time the logic form of the describable world, into the rules underlying the unlimited variety of possible language-games. In this new conception of the model he also made the subject-object correlation of traditional transcendental philosophy (including the accompanying 'reference theory' of language) concrete as the functional unity of linguistic usage, life-form and situational world. Did he thereby also account for the historicity of language, life-form and situational world?

It is true that Wittgenstein compared language to an organically growing town,[62] that he included the functions of language in the 'natural history' of mankind,[63] that he regarded language-games as things which are not governed by a mathematically precise rule in the form of a calculus, and that he reckoned with the emergence and decline of language-games and their associated life-forms.[64] But it is precisely through his recognition of this latter point that Wittgenstein shows that the rational explanatory power of his language-game model only extends as far as the fixed correlation of life-form, linguistic usage and structure of the world of situational experience by means of an existing rule. In particular Wittgenstein's critique of metaphysics has an important consequence here. It relativizes possible meaning to possible functioning language-games, and consequently he resolves the problem of *a priori* true statements through the concept of so-called 'grammatical sentences' which actually communicate nothing but instead simply illustrate the rule of the specific language-game in so-called 'patterns' or 'paradigms' of the real world (e.g. 'Every body has an extension', or 'The command commands that it be obeyed').[65]

But in my opinion, the limitation of this conceptual model is expressed in these functions of the language-game 'theory' that were also central for Wittgenstein himself. The dualistic scheme of the transcendental difference between the logical form and the possible content of the world, which dominates the *Tractatus*, is not really overcome in the concept of 'language-games', but rather it is merely differentiated. It is for this reason that Wittgenstein, with his conceptual model, cannot actually apprehend what is *historical* in understanding, the mediation between the disintegrating and the emerging language-games (the normal phenomenon of the mediation of tradition) and, on the other hand, mediation over the ages,' the revitalization of the past and its assimilation into the present life-form. From the standpoint of his model, Wittgenstein can, at most, concede its existence. Dilthey, however, achieves the maximum rationality in his philosophy precisely at the point where the historical mediation between language-games and also the mediation between the form (the *a priori* rule) and the content (the objectified meaning) of human life-forms, is at issue. He achieves it in the notion of the 'hermeneutic circle'. But this notion is perhaps only a type of code for the unsolved problem of a critical revival of the rationality of Hegelian dialectics.[66]

Notes

1 This is an extended version of a lecture given on 28 October 1965 at the meeting of the Old Marburgers in Höchst/Odenwald.
2 F.D.E. Schleiermacher, *Hermeneutik*, sections 15 and 16 (*Werke*, I/7, 1838, pp. 29 f.); cf. H.-G. Gadamer, *Truth and Method*, London, 1975.
3 Cf. the reconstructed history of the development of Schleiermacher's hermeneutics in H. Kimmerle, *Die Hermeneutik Schleiermachers im Zusammenhang seines spekulativen Denkens*, Heidelberg dissertation, 1957.
4 Cf. G.H. von Wright, 'Ludwig Wittgenstein, a Biographical Sketch', *Philosophical Review*, 64, October 1955, pp. 527–44.
5 The *Tractatus* first appeared in 1921 in the last volume of Ostwald's *Annalen der Naturphilosophie*, then in 1922 as a German-English edition in London. In the quotations below, we follow Wittgenstein's decimal notation of the sentences.
6 Cf. the preface to the *Tractatus*.
7 Here, however, I wish to ignore a certain Kantianism – presumably mediated through Schopenhauer and Heinrich Hertz – which characteristically distinguishes even the young Wittgenstein from Russell, and left such clear traces even in his later works that the interpreters of Wittgenstein and his successors (Stenius, Maslow, Winch, Cavell, etc.) have constantly been compelled to follow transcendental philosophical paths.
8 Cf. on the following K.-O. Apel, *Die Idee der Sprache in der Tradition des Humanismus von Dante bis Vico*.
9 In Wittgenstein's reference to the 'logical form' of both language and world, the Kantian problem of a 'transcendental logic' of the experiential world recurs. It is, of course, primarily no longer a question of the logical-psychological preconditions for the possibility of the conceivability of objects or events in space and time, but rather it is a question of the logico-linguistic preconditions for the unambiguous representation of *possible* facts. In Wittgenstein's view, these pre-conditions already imply a decision concerning the *a priori* form of objects and events in space and time, without it being necessary or permissible to assume *a priori* true objective knowledge (*a priori* synthetic judgments). It is merely the fact that 'objects' are 'conceivable' only in a 'state of affairs' (*Sachverhalt*), that is, mediated through 'propositions', which elevates the 'logical space' of the linguistic constitution of meaning to the *a priori* of possible spatio-temporal experiences (cf. *Tractatus*, 2.011–2.0141). But this establishes merely the

possibility, not the necessity, of certain *categories* as the preconditions for the possibility of describable spatio-temporal experiences, since the connection between language and sensuousness in experience cannot be dealt with in a transcendental philosophical manner. Such a connection is thought to be the domain of psychology. Wittgenstein's transition from Leibniz's logic of possible worlds to the transcendental logic of possible experience is not effected by recourse to a 'consciousness as such', but rather by recourse to 'language as such': 'It used to be said that God could create anything except what would be contrary to the laws of logic. The reason being that we could not *say* what an "illogical" world would look like.' (3.031). For Wittgenstein, *a priori* synthetic judgments, e.g. on the so-called 'causal law' or on the 'structure of colour', are replaced by '*a priori* insights about the forms in which the propositions of science can be cast' (6.34; cf. 6.32–6.33; further 6.35–6.361, 6.362, 6.3751). Cf. as an alternative to this purely semantic transformation of transcendental philosophy, the semiotic-pragmatic transformation in the work of C.S. Peirce (see 'From Kant to Peirce' in this volume). In my view, however, the language game conception of the later Wittgenstein also suggests a transcendental pragmatic transformation of Kant's philosophy. Cf. 'The communication community' in this volume.

10 Cf. *Tractatus*, 2.021–2.0232. The 'objects' are both dependent and independent of the 'logical form' of the world. In the first place, they are dependent in so far as they can only be conceived in a 'state of affairs', and second, not every object is conceivable in all states of affairs (e.g. a sound or a feeling cannot be found in a geometric space, nor can it either possess a colour); rather, each object implies – and this constitutes its 'internal' (= categorial) structure – certain possible states of affairs as its 'logical space' (cf. 2.011–2.0141). In addition, however, the objects form the 'substance of the world' independently of the logical form of states of affairs, which is presupposed so that a 'new meaning' can be communicated through a combination of the 'names' in a proposition that denote objects (cf. 3.23.026–4.031).

11 Cf. ibid., 2.223. For the sake of illustration, our example disregards the fact that for Wittgenstein neither the facts nor the 'objects' of everyday language can be considered to be elementary states of affairs. Cf. on this problem E. Stenius, *Wittgenstein's Tractatus: Critical Exposition of its Lines of Thought*, Oxford, 1960. Further, see W. Stegmüller, *Main Currents in Contemporary German, British and American Philosophy*, ch. 9.

12 *Tractatus*, 4.031; cf. 4.021 ff.

13 Cf. ibid., 4.022: 'A proposition *shows* its sense. A proposition *shows* how things stand *if* it is true. And it says that they do so stand.'

14 To this extent, it is quite possible that Wittgenstein was the first to use this formulation propagated by Moritz Schlick as the 'verification principle'. This is suggested by G. E. Moore's article, 'Wittgenstein's Lectures in 1930–33', *Mind*, 63, no. 249, 1954, pp. 1–15, and also by a remark of the later Wittgenstein (cf. J. Hartnack, *Wittgenstein und die*

moderne Philosophie, 1962, n. 54). This assumption has since been corroborated (cf. L. Wittgenstein, *Schriften III, Ludwig Wittgenstein und der Wiener Kreis*, Frankfurt, 1967, pp. 243 ff.).

Wittgenstein's criterion for the distinction between sense and non-sense certainly cannot be simply equated with the neopositivist principle of verification, but nevertheless the necessity of both an historical and a substantive derivation of the latter from the philosophy of the *Tractatus* must be emphasized. It was the *Tractatus* which encouraged the Viennese neopositivists to decide in advance by means of a 'logical analysis of language' (Schlick, Carnap) whether a proposition is either logically or mathematically 'provable' (Wittgenstein speaks here of a 'meaningless tautology') or 'verifiable' (i.e. in Wittgenstein's terms, reducible by means of the logic of truth functions to a proposition compatible with reality) or finally, completely 'meaningless' (in Wittgenstein's terms 'nonsensical'). Wittgenstein, of course, did not provide an 'empirical criterion' for the elementary propositions that are compatible with reality, but rather he *postulates* the existence of such propositions and the 'states of affairs' correlated with them merely as the basis for the intelligibility of meaningful propositions (cf. in particular 4.2211). The neopositivists' search for 'protocol sentences' as the 'basic statements' of all scientific theories, on the other hand, amounts to the attempt to verify Wittgenstein's propositions about the very 'transcendental' structure of language and the world. Even this relationship postulated by Wittgenstein between elementary propositions and the facts which they depict was to be corroborated empirically, but this means – according to the *Tractatus* – that what 'shows itself' in or against the function of language as the transcendental precondition for the possibility of this function had to be described as an inner-worldly relationship between objects – just as if one could observe the relationship between language and world from a third point outside this relationship (cf. 4.12). This confusion of what 'shows itself' with what can be 'stated' in 'meaningful' propositions (i.e. according to the definition provided by the logic of language: verifiable propositions) in Wittgenstein's opinion forms the $\pi\rho\tilde{\omega}\tau\text{o}\nu$ $\psi\epsilon\mu\delta\text{o}\varsigma$ of traditional metaphysics, the basis of the latter's misunderstanding of the logic of language, upon which its nonsensicality rests (cf. 4.003).

I think that one has to concede that the paradox of neopositivist attempts to satisfy the 'verification principle' by the formulation of an 'empirical criterion of meaning' (cf. Stegmüller, op. cit., chs 7 and 8), confirms the profundity of Wittgenstein's conception of the criterion of meaning. At the end of this development stands the decline of neopositivism itself into 'constructive semantics' and the 'empirical pragmatics' of language usage, but this means that Wittgenstein's language-related approach to the problem of the criterion of meaning was the only one possible. Of course, we are no longer dealing with the single, ideal, logical-ontological language of the *Tractatus*, but rather with purely conventional systems of rules or with those that, as 'language-games' in the sense of the later Wittgenstein, can be extracted from everyday language usage which has been proven through practice. With reference to the 'deep grammar' of these language-games, the later Wittgenstein still understands the verification principle in the form in which he had suggested it as a logico-linguistic principle in the *Tractatus*. Cf. Wittgenstein, *Philosophical Investigations*, I, § 353: 'Asking whether and how a proposition can be verified is only a particular way of asking "How d'you mean?" The answer is a contribution to the grammar of the proposition.' In other words: there are as many possibilities of verification as there are language-games (cf. on this point, n.35 below).

15 Cf. *Tractatus*, 4.1121.

16 On the difficulties of this approach, cf. Hans Skjervheim, *Objectivism and the Study of Language*, Oslo, 1959.

17 The semantic side of Russell's theory of types is condensed by Wittgenstein into this point, that is, into the recognition of the absolute transcendental difference. According to this theory, no proposition 'can make a statement about itself, because a propositional sign cannot be contained in itself . . .' (3.332).

18 Cf. Stenius, op. cit.

19 This means that it is not only *potentially* intelligible to others, since – in default of a 'private language' – it can only become intelligible to the person who experiences it through the public language. This position, which is suggested by the later Wittgenstein, is not only compatible with hermeneutics but, in my opinion, belongs to its *transcendental hermeneutic* foundations. In the early Wittgenstein's transcendental semantics, however, communication is *guaranteed* to some extent by the *a priori* structure of the understanding of the world that is the same for all human subjects.

20 Cf. the preface to the *Einleitung in die Geisteswissenschaften* (*Gesammelte Schriften*, vol. 1, Leipzig, 1923, 2nd ed., p. xviii) where he writes: 'In the veins of the knowing subject constructed by Locke, Hume, and Kant there runs no real blood, but the diluted juice of reason in the sense of mere thought activity.'

21 Charles Morris, *Signs, Language and Behavior*, New York, 1955, is representative of this approach.

22 We refer here to the absolutization of the *syntactic-semantic* structure of an unambiguous and consistent *language-system*, accompanied by an abstraction from the *pragmatic* context of *language usage*, which, moreover, must be presupposed in *hermeneutics* as the *historically* concretized context.

23 Cf. W. V. Humboldt, 'Über das vergleichende Sprachstudium' (*Gesammelte Schriften*, vol. 4, 1905, pp. 1–34, pp. 27 ff.): 'In that they [sc. the individual national languages] confront what is knowable as subjective, they confront human beings as objective. For each is a reminder of man's general nature and even if they cannot also be at all times a complete expression of the subjectivity of mankind, languages nevertheless continually approximate to this goal.'

24 Cf. especially J. Royce, *The Problem of Christianity*, New York, 1913, vol. 2, pp. 146 ff.

25 *Philosophical Investigations* was first published in Oxford in 1953 (two years after Wittgenstein's death) in a dual-language edition by G.E.M. Anscombe and R. Rhees. As far as possible we shall quote from the paragraphs of the first part that Wittgenstein himself (in 1945) prepared for publication; otherwise, we shall refer to the page numbers of the original dual-language edition.

The following comments in the 1945 preface merit special attention since they characterize Wittgenstein's later work:

> After several unsuccessful attempts to weld my results into . . . a whole, I realized that I should never succeed. The best that I could write would never be more than philosophical remarks . . . The philosophical remarks in this book are, as it were, a number of sketches of landscapes which were made in the course of . . . long and involved journeyings . . . Thus this book is really only an album (*Philosophical Investigations*, 2nd ed., 1958, p.vii).

26 Using this interpretation, numerous parallels would be set up between Wittgenstein (and Ryle, who developed Wittgenstein's references to the metaphysics of mind in his book *The Concept of Mind*, London, 1949, in a critique of the 'Cartesian myth') and Heidegger, 'critique of the traditional "ontology of the existent"', which also implies a critique of Descartes.

27 Cf. also the following general theses: '*Essence* is expressed by grammar' (S 371); 'Grammar tells us what kind of object anything is' (§ 373).

28 Can one *formulate* the 'hypothesis' about the mere family resemblance between the meanings of a word without – at the level of reflection and generality of the formulation – drawing upon an insight into its essence, an insight which is certainly not explained through the hypothesis? This seems to me to be the problem.

29 Cf. §§ 69 ff. as a rejection of the ideal of exactitude. They are apparently intended to elucidate the previously suggested impossibility of the philosophical determination of essence, but it seems to me that they advocate *de facto* a thesis which is not incompatible with the claim raised by the philosophical determination of essence.

30 A clear parallel to Wittgenstein's development is to be found in the introduction and development of the 'pragmatic dimension' in Morris's semiotics. This also took place in the 1930s (cf. C. Morris, *Foundations of the Theory of Signs*, Chicago, 1938; cf. also my essay 'Sprache und Wahrheit', in vol. 1, *Transformation der Philosophie*, Frankfurt, 1973, pp. 138–66, and 'Charles W. Morris und das Programm einer pragmatisch integrierten Semiotik', in C.W. Morris, *Zeichen, Sprache und Verhalten*, Düsseldorf, 1973, pp. 9–66.)

31 Cf. Wittgenstein, *Philosophical Investigations*, § 22. Also Stegmüller, op. cit., (see n. 11), p. 574 f.

32 As Searle has demonstrated – developing Austin's position in a systematic theory of 'speech acts' – this fact can, of course, be reconciled with the logically abstract assumption that there are meaning contents which are neutral with reference to modality. Such a theory of 'speech acts'

reveals the 'performative-propositional' dual-structure of the 'deep grammar' of the sentences that explicate such a grammar and thereby clearly separates the pragmatic features which are the result of human life-forms of interaction from those meaning contents which may be explicated through their truth conditions (cf. J.R. Searle, *Speech Acts*).

33 This aspect, which was rediscovered by Wittgenstein, has probably been lost in traditional 'grammar' as a result of its abstractive detachment from rhetorics.

34 Cf. in this context E.K. Specht, 'Die Sprachphilosophischen und ontologischen Grundlagen im Spätwerk L. Wittgensteins', *Kantstudien, Ergänzungsheft*, 84, 1963.

35 Herein lies the pragmatized generalization of the logico-linguistic verification principle; cf. n. 14 above.

36 Wittgenstein's affinity to Husserl's kind of phenomenology but also his distance from it are evident at this point.

37 Arnold Gehlen, in particular, has expressed the methodological point of this tendency in a strong polemic against 'understanding' in Dilthey's sense. Cf. A. Gehlen, *Der Mensch*, 4th ed., 1950, pp. 413 ff. as well as his *Urmensch und Spätkultur*, 1956, p. 9 *passim*, and also my essay 'Arnold Gehlen's "Philosophie der Institutionen"', esp. section III, in *Transformation der Philosophie*, vol. 1, pp. 204 ff.

38 Cf. for instance, Skjervheim, op. cit. (see n. 16).

39 Cf. also pp. xxx f. below.

40 Cf. *Philosophical Investigations*, §§ 197, 307, 318.

41 Taking Heidegger as his starting-point, Gadamer, in particular, has demonstrated that self-understanding as 'understanding-oneself-in-the-situation' is not identical with self-reflection. Cf. Gadamer, *Truth and Method*.

42 Through its implicit critique of language (and metaphysics), Wittgenstein's language-game analysis demonstrated that outside natural science all objective description and structural analysis derives from self-understanding and returns to the latter, enriched by estrangement. Through its implicit 'cultural criticism', Gehlen's *Philosophie der Institutionen* demonstrates the same point; and even Konrad Lorenz's research, which bears the name 'behavioural physiology', reveals through its outstanding elucidation of human situational understanding (for instance, through contrast with that behaviour of animals which is 'analogous' to human moral behaviour) that – unlike physics, for example – it has a hermeneutic root. Furthermore, such research reveals that even in this context recourse is made to human self-understanding, which returns to itself after a long detour, with the corresponding effect of estrangement.

43 Cf. W. Dilthey, *Gesammelte Schriften*, vol. 5, Stuttgart, 1968, p. 180; vol. 7, Stuttgart, 1968, p. 250.

44 Wittgenstein himself seems to make such an interpretation legitimate through his preference for exotic examples, or for those constructed in a mental experiment which are intended – as contrast to our normal behaviour – to open our eyes to the 'depth grammar' of our language-

games. He adheres to this method of estrangement particularly in *Remarks on the Foundations of Mathematics*, Oxford, 1967.

45 At this point, one could establish connections both with Royce's triadic analysis of interpretation (cf. pp. 14–15 above) and also with Gadamer's 'philosophical hermeneutics' which attempts to integrate the traditional problem of the 'application' of understanding into the concept of understanding *qua* mediation of tradition.

46 The writer and his audience (readers).

47 Here a characteristic segment of what Litt has shown to be the 'self-upgrading of language' emerges; namely, the upgrading of the possible levels of generality of language's intended meanings. To some extent, this is a dialectical model in opposition to Russell's involved (semantic) 'theory of types'. Cf. T. Litt, *Mensch und Welt*, Munich, 1948, ch. 13.

48 From the standpoint of a radical historical hermeneutic philosophy, one might object that even the philosophical structural analysis of language-games must have established with the latter the unity of discourse. This is, of course, correct in the sense that the philosopher cannot discuss the structure of human language-games like a behaviourist from another planet, and undoubtedly the historian (especially the historian of language) will always be able to detect in philosophical writings their historical connections with human discourse. On the other hand, an undeniable reflective emancipation from the historical context of discourse lies in the fact that – at a higher level of generality of intended meaning – the philosopher is able to state explicitly the necessity of the historical context of discourse for hermeneutic understanding. He demonstrates this in a formal manner by his discussion of the difference between first-level language-games and second-level (i.e. hermeneutic) language-games in as far as he thereby reveals the third-level structure of the philosophical language-game which, as the present essay suggests, can also explicate its own structure by a fourth level of self-reflection through which the entire reflective 'self-upgrading of language' that began with hermeneutic understanding is brought to a conclusion.

49 As far as I am aware, Winch, in his book *The Idea of a Social Science*, was the first to explore this aspect of a possible interpretation of Wittgenstein consistently. In the following, we draw upon this interpretation for valuable suggestions.

50 Cf. *Logical Investigations*, §§ 199, 243, 257 and elsewhere.

51 In this case, 'understanding' would indeed be – as neopositivism conceives it – nothing more than 'empathy' that leads to a hypothesis of 'explanation'. Cf. on this interpretation, T. Abel, 'The Operation called "Verstehen"', in *Readings in the Philosophy of Science*, New York, 1953.

52 It is remarkable that this insight converges in turn with Gehlen's anthropology which is strongly influenced by pragmatic approaches, such as G.H. Mead's. (Cf. Mead's book *Mind, Self and Society*, Chicago, 1934.)

53 In Wittgenstein's conception of the language-game, the methodological solipsism of modern philosophy from Descartes' *Meditationes* to

Husserl's *Cartesian Meditations* does indeed encounter an opposing standpoint similar to Heidegger's, as it is expressed in §§ 26 and 31 ff. (on 'being-with' and 'understanding') of *Being and Time* in particular.

But with both Heidegger and the later Wittgenstein the question arises as to whether a philosophy of 'ego cogito', which has freed itself from the illusion that primarily it must prove the existence of others (and of a real external world), does not, as a philosophy of responsible *reflection* upon the *eis ipsibus* intersubjective and linguistic-social bases of thought, retain the function of a philosophical ultimate grounding and of the ability to take up reflection at any time, regardless of the situation.

54 *Gesammelte Schriften*, vol. 1, pp. 422 ff.; trans. in H.A. Hodges, *Wilhelm Dilthey: an Introduction*, London, 1944, reprinted, 1969, pp. 139 f.

55 *Gesammelte Schriften*, vol. 7, pp. 146 f.; trans. in W. Dilthey, *Pattern and Meanings in History* (ed. H.P. Rickman), London, 1961/New York, 1962, p. 123.

56 Ibid., pp. 208 f.; trans. in Rickman, op. cit., pp. 120 f.

57 Ibid., p. 207; trans. in Rickman, op. cit., p. 119.

58 Ibid., p. 206; trans. in Rickman, op. cit., p. 117.

59 Ibid., p. 207; trans. in Rickman, op. cit., p. 119.

60 Ibid., pp. 210 f.

61 According to Wittgenstein, one can recognize what a command is (as an intention) by how it is normally obeyed (i.e. understood). Wittgenstein comments: 'orders are sometimes not obeyed. But what would it be like if no order were *ever* obeyed? The concept "order" would have lost itself purpose' (§ 345).

62 *Philosophical Investigations*, S 18.

63 Ibid., § 25.

64 In a spirited manner, Stegmüller has attempted to enlarge Wittgenstein's statements in the direction of an integration of historicity into the concept of a language-game. Compared with a game of chess, for instance, 'the moves in the language-game' are not *historically invariant*. The 'rules governing the use of a word' must therefore be formulated in such a manner that – amongst other things – 'the previous dialogue is taken into account' (Stegmüller, op. cit., p. 448).

65 Cf. *Philosophical Investigations*, §§ 251, 252, 458. Also Specht, op. cit., pp. 127 ff.

66 Cf. on this problem K.-O. Apel, *Analytic Philosophy of Language and the 'Geisteswissenschaften'*, Dordrecht, 1967.

CHAPTER 2

Scientistics, hermeneutics and the critique of ideology: outline of a theory of science from a cognitive-anthropological standpoint

Introduction: the cognitive-anthropological problem

The following study is to be understood as a programmatic sketch. If one compares its title with the subtitle then it is apparent that the concept of 'science' in the 'theory of science' must certainly be much broader than the concept of 'scientia' which is contained in 'scientistics' since the projected 'theory of science' is meant to incorporate 'hermeneutics' and the 'critique of ideology' as well as 'scientistics'. In fact, the attempt will be made in the following sketch to demonstrate the possibility of a conception of science that is relevant to the philosophy and methodology of science, and that, none the less, is not restricted to the 'logic of science'.

The basis for the postulated enlargement of the concept of science should be provided by an enlargement of traditional 'epistemology' in terms of a 'cognitive anthropology'. By 'cognitive anthropology' I mean an approach that enlarges the Kantian question of the 'preconditions for the possibility of knowledge' in the sense that not only are the preconditions for an objectively valid, unified world conception for a 'consciousness as such' specified, but so too are all the preconditions that make possible a scientific problem as a meaningful one.

In my opinion, the meaning of the problems of physics, for example, cannot be made intelligible solely by recourse to 'unifying' (synthetic) functions of consciousness ('categories'). This meaning also presupposes a 'unified interpretation' on the basis of a linguistic 'agreement' by the investigators of nature as well as the possibility of a realization of the question by an instrumental intervention in nature. This instrumental intervention in nature, which is pre-supposed *a priori* in every experiment, to some extent specifies that living engagement in the world through the sense organs which is already presupposed in pre-scientific experience: human beings' 'comparison' of themselves 'with' nature becomes the 'measure-ment' of experimental science. For example, the pre-scientific concept of 'heat' expresses the 'comparison' of an organism with its environment in contrast with the instrumentally precise 'measured intervention' of the thermometer and the scientific language-game whose 'paradigm' lies in the thermometer.[1] Modern natural scientists have not only approached nature – as Kant already asserted – with an *a priori* outline of law-like processes in thought (or in the spatio-temporally schematized imagination), but they have related this outline in the form of an instrumental apparatus (i.e. as it were, as artificial nature) to nature proper. Largely by means of this technical intervention which, to a certain extent, translates human questions into the language of nature, was it possible for natural scientists – as Kant put it – to 'oblige nature to answer their questions'.[2] The fact that the concern here is with a precondition for the possibility of physical knowledge that is necessarily added to the categorial synthesis as a function of reason and constitutes an integrative element of the physicalist language-game, is made particularly evident, in my opinion, by the semantic revolution in the definition of physics' basic concepts carried out by Einstein. As a result, for example, the meaning of 'simultaneity' must certainly be so defined that the technical and material pre-conditions for the measurement of 'simultaneity' are taken into account in the definition. Natural constants such as the speed of light therefore belong to the 'paradigms' of the language-game of relativity theory; one speaks of 'material' or 'physical preconditions for the possibility of experience'.[3]

On the one hand, the preconditions for the possibility and validity of knowledge just outlined cannot solely be traced back to logical mental functions nor, on the other, can they be classed with the object of knowledge that is to be apprehended since they are always presupposed by all knowledge of objects. The Cartesian subject-object relationship, however, does not suffice for the establishment of a cognitive anthropology. A pure consciousness of objects, taken by itself, cannot secure any meaning from the world. In order to arrive at a constitution of meaning, consciousness – which is basically 'eccentric'[4] – must become engaged concentrically; that is, embodied in the Here and Now. Any constitution of meaning refers back, for example, to a particular perspective which expresses a standpoint. Once again, this means a living engagement on the part of the knowing consciousness.

Yet, remarkably, not only is the respective *individual* constitution of possible meaning mediated through a living engagement of the knowing consciousness but so too is the *intersubjective validity* of any constitution of meaning. That is, only through linguistic signs do my intended meanings become mediated with the possible meaning intentions of other human beings in such a manner that I can really 'mean' something. Hence, I only have valid intended meanings because a language exists in which not only my intended meanings are fixed. This agreement with others concerning possible intended meanings, which always to a certain extent operates in linguistic 'meanings', is a precondition for the possibility of agreement on experiential data in the Kantian 'synthesis of apperception'. However, over and above this, it opens up a dimension of experience of a distinctive kind.

From a cognitive-anthropological viewpoint, linguistic signs no more belong to the objects of knowledge than do the sense organs or the technical instruments that mediate their intervention in external nature. For the signs, too, as preconditions for the possibility of any intended meaning, are already presupposed in order for objects of knowledge to be constituted. None the less, language as a medium of signs cannot be reduced to the logical conscious preconditions for knowledge that are represented by Kant's 'transcendental consciousness'. Rather, like material-technical intervention that is included amongst the presuppositions for experimental natural-scientific knowledge, language refers back to a distinctive subjective *a priori* that was not considered in traditional Cartesian epistemology. I wish to call it 'the bodily *a priori*' *(Leibapriori)* of knowledge.[5]

It seems to me that the life *a priori* of knowledge stands in a complementary relationship to the *a priori* of consciousness. In other words, both preconditions for the possibility of knowledge

48

mutually and necessarily supplement one another in the whole of knowledge, whilst in the actual production of knowledge either the life *a priori* or the *a priori* of consciousness takes up the leading position: 'knowledge through reflection' and 'knowledge through engagement' stand as polar opposites. For instance, I cannot simultaneously gain a significant aspect of the world and reflect upon the standpoint that I must necessarily take up in so doing. All experience – and this applies even to the theoretically guided, experimental experience in the natural sciences – is primarily knowledge through engagement in life; all theory-formation is primarily knowledge through reflection.[6]

I would maintain that in so far as a cognitive anthropology must treat the living engagement of human beings as a necessary precondition for all knowledge it can and must also elevate a further precondition for knowledge to the rank of an *a priori*: the type of living engagement of our knowledge is related to a specific *cognitive interest*.[7] The experimental engagement of modern physics, for example, is related *a priori* to a technical cognitive interest.

This does not mean that psychologically verifiable motives of technical utilization are amongst the preconditions for the possibility and validity of natural-scientific theory-formation. Such motives are certainly in no way typical of the subjective notions of the major theoretical researchers in the natural sciences. Yet in my opinion, the question of such motives misses the question of the *a priori* valid connection between technology and natural science and thereby the question of the necessary interest that first makes possible this type of knowledge. This interest seems to me to lie simply and solely in the prior dependency that the problems of modern physics have upon the possibility of operative verification that has in principle already been presupposed. This dependency of the problem of modern physics expresses its life *a priori* that lies in the presupposition of instrumental intervention by means of which human questions and problems can be put to nature. The modern natural scientist must be guided by a technical interest in the sense of this *a priori* dependency of the problems upon instrumental verification. In this supra-individual, quasi-objective connection, his cognitive interest differs from that of the natural philosophy of the Greeks or the Renaissance and, in turn, that of Goethe or the romantics. And in this methodologically relevant interest, the whole of the exact natural sciences differ, above all, from the divergent practical interest and world engagement that lies at the basis of the so-called 'human sciences'.[8]

In this way I arrive at the actual theme of my essay. By presupposing the already outlined cognitive-anthropological categories, I wish to take up anew and, if possible, to bring closer towards a solution the old disputed question of the relationship between the natural and human sciences which has now been made more complicated by the development of the 'behavioural' sciences.[9] The solution that is intended here is expressed in the trichotomy of concepts in the title: 'scientistics', 'hermeneutics' and 'the critique of ideology'. It must be demonstrated that by means of this methodological trichotomy the diverse methodological approaches of present-day empirical sciences can be defined and related to one another. Therefore my argument will fall into two parts. The first and more comprehensive part will be concerned with the assertion of a complementarity between 'scientistics' and 'hermeneutics' (or expressed differently, between explanatory natural sciences and interpretative human sciences). This complementarity thesis is directly against the idea of a unified science. The second part is concerned with a dialectical mediation of 'explanation' and 'understanding' in the critique of ideology.

The complementary relationship between scientistics and hermeneutics: a critique of the idea of a unified science

Nowadays, whoever upholds a theory of science on the basis of *a priori* differentiated cognitive interests must confront the contrary presuppositions of the positivistic or neopositivistic thesis of a 'unified science'.[10] These presuppositions will first of all be analysed from a cognitive-anthropological standpoint.

A comparison of the now dominant neopositivist theory of science with Kant's epistemology reveals that the question of the preconditions for the possibility of knowledge has not been enlarged – as in my projected cognitive anthropology – but rather, on the contrary, it has been reduced as much as possible. Whereas Kant maintained that a 'transcendental logic' was necessary for the philosophical clarification of the preconditions for the possibility of experience – a logic whose specific problem was the constitution of experience by means of a 'categorial synthesis' – neopositivism maintains that it can get by with formal logic in its mathematically precise and enlarged form and that, with its assistance, it can trace all knowledge back to 'the' empirical data. The problem of a synthetic constitution of empirical data – at least in the relevant form of a neopositivistically conceived 'logic of knowledge' – is to play no role at all.[11]

The significance of this particular reduction of the question of the presuppositions of knowledge becomes evident when one considers that our cognitive anthropology already makes the constitution of empirical data dependent not only upon a synthetic achievement of human reason as such (as with Kant) but also upon an engaged understanding of the world, i.e. upon a *cognitive interest that constitutes meaning.*

In contrast, neopositivism wishes to eliminate the question of cognitive interests as well as that of evaluation – at least from the basic problematic of the logic of science. It wishes to see in such questions secondary problems associated with a cognitive psychology or a sociology of knowledge, i.e. questions which themselves can again be dealt with by interest-free sciences as purely factual problems. In this way, all sciences are to be certified as themselves interest-free, as purely theoretical treatments of facts, as cognitive operations, which fundamentally obey the same methodology, namely, that of a unified 'logic of science'.

On the basis of such presuppositions, neopositivism is inclined to suspect an ideological mixture of theoretical insights and inadmissible practical goals in the conception of so-called 'transcendental' preconditions of knowledge in so far as these can be made responsible for the diverse constitution of even empirical data in different sciences. As far as theoretical insights are concerned, they belong in empirical psychology or sociology. Where practical goals are at issue, they are subject to a critique of ideology which itself – as a constituent part of unified science – should be free from practical interests.

The presuppositions for the idea of a 'unified' science referred to earlier may be illustrated by the manner in which neopositivism judges the distinction between so-called 'causal explanatory' natural science and 'interpretative' human sciences (*Geisteswissenschaften*) that has been drawn by Dilthey and others.[12]

In so far as epistemological status is claimed for this distinction, it is declared to be ideology-laden metaphysics in the following

manner. The title *Geisteswissenschaften* and the so-called
methodological distinction between an internal 'understanding' and
a merely external 'explanation' express the fact that certain object
domains (of human life) are to be removed from the unbiased
clutches of explanatory science and made the preserve of a
secularized theology of the mind (in the tradition of Hegel or
Schleiermacher).

However this may be, it none the less remains true according to
neopositivism that there is a psychological aspect of the distinction
between 'explanation' and 'understanding'. Man is capable of internalizing certain causal relations between events in the external
world (i.e. those which one recognizes as stimulus and response in
organisms' behaviour) and, to a certain extent, of experiencing
them internally. For instance, the reaction of running away in the
face of an enemy attack by the person who is afraid; or the
aggressive reaction of the angry person in the same situation; or
the search for warmth by the person who is cold, the search for
nourishment by the hungry – and many other similar instances. Man
recognizes such complex behavioural reactions to a certain extent
internally and is therefore accustomed to interpolate them automatically in mentally associating events with events in the outside
world.

In what follows I shall provide an example from Theodor Abel[13]
who, in his essay 'The Operation called "Verstehen"', has analysed
understanding in the light of a neopositivist theory of science. If, for
example, I see that in the event of a sudden drop in temperature my
neighbour stands up from his writing desk, chops wood and lights
his fire, then I automatically interpolate that he was cold and
therefore sought to bring about a situation in which he was warm. In
Abel's opinion, we term such 'interpolation' 'understanding'.
According to Abel, however, this does not provide us with a specific
scientific method that could be logically distinguished from causal
explanation. For the logical significance of intuitive understanding
lies in the fact that, through the 'internalization' of observed
behaviour we are led to conceive of a 'behavioural maxim' which
corresponds precisely to a 'causal hypothesis' for a possible causal
explanation of behaviour. If the causal hypothesis produced in this
manner can be objectively verified then we are actually provided
with an 'explanation'. In this way, the distinction between 'understanding' and 'explanation' consists in the fact that 'understanding'

is only equivalent to a component of the *logical* operation of explanation: the establishment of a causal hypothesis. However, according to the neopositivist 'logic of science', this heuristic component does not affect the scientific nature of the operation of explanation since, taken by itself, it cannot be corroborated logically but, at most, psychologically. Logically, only the *possible* correctness of a hypothesis corresponds to the psychic sense of evidence which understanding guides towards the discovery of behavioural maxims. Only the deduction of verifiable observational statements from the causal hypothesis, i.e. to some extent prognosis testing, secures the scientific nature of an 'explanation'. In full agreement with Hempel's and Oppenheim's theory of explanation,[14] Abel concludes that although the 'understanding' of the so-called *Geisteswissenschaften* remains significant as a heuristic prelude to science, it is irrelevant for the 'logic of science'.

From the standpoint of cognitive anthropology, what could one say to the reduction of understanding and hence of the so-called *Geisteswissenschaften* to a pre-scientific heuristic in the service of explanatory science?

First of all, one could point to the difficulties in the neopositivist conception that the supporters of a unified 'logic of science' themselves have raised in recent decades. Amongst such difficulties are, for example, that the manner in which a historian establishes a causal hypothesis with the aid of understanding cannot at all be interpreted and confirmed as a subsumption of events or circumstances under general laws.

William Dray[15] was led to this conclusion in 1957 when he tested Popper's thesis that the 'individualizing' historical sciences are not to be distinguished from the 'generalizing' natural sciences in terms of the logic of explanation. Rather, they are only to be distinguished psychologically on the grounds that they are not primarily interested in the construction of general law-like hypotheses but in the specific limiting or initial conditions which, by presupposing certain trivial laws, can be used as the causes of particular events.[16] In contrast, Dray asserts that for basic reasons historical explanations do not fulfil the conditions of a subsumption under general laws. In arguing this, he gives the following example. A historian could perhaps explain the unpopularity of Louis XIV in the period before his death in terms of the fact that the king had pursued a policy that was detrimental to French national interests. In order for this to be a causal explanation in the sense of the 'logic of science' the logician would have to be able to explicitly formulate the general law which the historian implicitly presupposes in the form of a statement like: 'A ruler who pursues a policy that runs contrary to the interests of his subjects will be unpopular.'

But the historian will reject this imputation as incorrect, and will also reject any attempt at the specification of causal hypotheses as insufficient, with the exception, however, of the following formulation: 'Any ruler who carries out the policies of Louis XIV in the same manner and under exactly the same circumstance, loses his popularity.'

However, viewed logically, this statement – which does not trace back the individual *explanandum* to a general *explanans* but appeals to the particular in the *explanans* itself – is certainly not a general law-like hypothesis. Rather, it is merely the formal assertion of the necessity of an individual event without any explanatory value.

This shows, therefore, that the historian's explanation at least cannot be viewed as a *deductive-nomological* explanation. However, nor can it be interpreted as an *inductive-nomological* explanation that only derives the statistical probability of a kind of event from laws. For such an explanation in the 'empirical social sciences' remains in principle outside the historian's claim to explain the 'necessity' of a specific event. On what basis, then, does the specific *historical explanation* gain its plausibility? Dray provides the following viewpoint for this plausibility: a historical explanation does produce a relationship between an event and the necessary conditions for the occurrence of this event. Yet these conditions are:

1   not sufficient conditions for the prognosis of the event;
2   as necessary conditions, they are valid only in the context of a given total situation.

What lies hidden behind these restrictions?

Ad. 1:

The fact that the conditions discovered by the historian are not sufficient for a prognosis rests ultimately on the fact that all the events which the historian 'explains' are mediated in their *constitution* by the intentions of acting human subjects. Hence, the preconditions for these events are not 'causes' but 'rational grounds' for action. However, as rational grounds for action they must also be 'understood' by the historian outside the actors' situation.

Furthermore, they cannot be treated in the logic of explanation of events in the exact same way as are causal conditions in the framework of a prognosis on the basis of laws. For law-like hypotheses can be falsified by negative instances, whereas behavioural maxims, which enter into conditions as rational grounds, cannot be falsified by facts.

Yet here we have again reached the point at which Abel could counter with the argument that in so far as intelligible behavioural maxims cannot be falsified by facts they possess no explanatory value. Rather they express a mere possibility of behaviour.
Ad. 2:
But here Dray's other standpoint helps us further. Historical explanations reveal the necessary conditions for events (actions) but only within the context of a given total situation. In fact, this contains an allusion to the positive task of 'understanding' as a decisive condition for the possibility of a so-called 'historical explanation'. This is revealed most clearly by a contrast with Abel's theory of understanding.

In his analysis of understanding, Abel completely overlooked the problem of the hermeneutic connection between the human behaviour that is to be understood and the pre-understanding of data about the world to which behaviour intentionally refers. The data seems to him to be given in roughly the same manner as occurrences in the cognitive situation of the natural sciences. Thus, understanding exists only in the interpolation of an internally experienced context in the objectively explicable law-like context of facts. In so doing, this analysis expresses a pre-linguistic-analytical theory of understanding,[17] a theory which did not take into account the later Wittgenstein's insight, namely, that empirical data itself is constituted in the context of a language-game. In such an account, understanding is only treated as a psychologically relevant auxiliary function in the connection of data but not as a precondition for the possibility of data itself. In contrast, a linguistic, hermeneutic analysis commences from the fact that intelligible human behavioural reactions, as linguistically-related intentional forms, themselves possess the quality of understanding. As a result, such an analysis would affirm that the data of the world, in whose context the behaviour that is to be understood emerges, must itself be understood from the intentional understanding of the behaviour that is to be understood. The world is then no longer the 'existence

55

of things inasmuch as [in the sense of the natural sciences] they form a law-like connection' (Kant) but the 'total situation' of a specific 'being-in-the-world' (Heidegger) in which we can participate through the understanding of language.

Here we return to Dray's reply to the question of the preconditions for the possibility of a historical factual explanation that cannot be traced back to general laws. According to Dray, the necessity for this lies in the consideration of a given total situation out of which the antecedent conditions for explanation of facts must first be understood as the possible grounds for intentional actions. How does such understanding actually take place in the historical sciences? How does it achieve that pragmatic sufficient certainty which Dray allows to enter into factual explanation as a situationally conditioned necessity?

The older hermeneutic tradition (Schleiermacher, Droysen, Dilthey) spoke in terms of the fact that the historian must place himself in the total situation of the actions that are to be understood. This statement possesses the truth of a metaphor. However, to return to Dray's example, how does the historian place himself in the situation within which the French people judged Louis XIV's politics shortly before his death? How is the state of affairs of a past situation of human action constituted at all for the historian?

By presupposing the world understanding of an objective unified science, we came to the remarkable conclusion that the historian must select those events, out of all those that actually took place in the period before Louis XIV's death, which come into question as conditions for the actions of Louis XIV's contemporaries. In fact, the historian would not proceed in this manner since neither he himself knows nor could he experience from anyone the 'total previous events' prior to Louis XIV's death. They exist only in the metaphysics of positivism. That is, the natural sciences, on the basis of their semantic pre-understanding of the world, can only have recourse to specific classes of events at the time of Louis XIV, e.g. to earthquakes, solar eclipses and the like. In many instances these can be assigned to historically handed-down events of a constellation of human action. The natural and historical sciences are capable of working together, for instance, in the dating of so-called prehistoric finds.

None the less, the primary orientation of the historian *vis-à-vis* past events is drawn, in Wittgenstein's terms, from a 'language-game' different from that of the natural scientist. It is a language-game that is already being played prior to the actual scientific language-game of the historian: it is that of cultural tradition or, better, that of a specific cultural tradition that is itself capable of being made a historical theme. The historian's language-game lies in a critical corroboration and enlargement of the primary tradition. At the same time, however, it is the case that the historian is, in principle, dependent upon the plausibility of linguistic tradition; for example, narrative and oral or written 'histories'. In order to consider each individually (by means of a so-called critique of sources), the historian must, of course, in principle, presuppose them as mediums of communication (along with various human forms of 'being-in-the-world'). Out of the situational perspective of traditional 'histories', that he himself again understands out of the situational perspective of 'the' history, to which he himself also belongs,[18] the historian in fact obtains the 'data' that are relevant to the antecedent conditions for a 'historical explanation' of events. And in fact their plausible connection with the respective event to be understood lies in a new narrative of a history in which possibly many events, mediated by the situational relation of participating human subjects, are placed in connection with one another.[19]

In so doing, this process of hermeneutically mediated remembrance of events and their relations is, in principle, just as little terminable as is the process of verification of natural scientific causal hypotheses. Yet like the latter in the research situation, it none the less achieves a pragmatically sufficient validity.

This seems to me to be the context within which the result of Dray's analysis of his example of historical explanation is best understood. Dray writes:[20]

> The force of the explanation of Louis XIV's unpopularity in terms of his policies being detrimental to French interests is very likely to be found in the detailed aspirations, beliefs, and problems of Louis's subjects. Given these men and their situation, Louis and his policies, their dislike of the king was an appropriate response.

Dray's distinction between a logic of 'historical explanation' that rests upon the explication of action situations and a logic of natural scientific explanation that is deduced from causal hypotheses none the less does not yet reveal the distinction and enlarged relationship of the natural and human sciences, of scientific and hermeneutic methods, in the correct light. In fact, political history is not the correct place to make completely intelligible the cognitive-anthropological meaning of hermeneutic understanding. For despite the hermeneutic presuppositions that we have suggested, political history is always concerned with an objective science that explains facts and events within a temporal framework. The 'understanding' of meaning still functions here as an instrument for the explanation of the fact that certain events have occurred as a result of other events, even if this objective context, in contrast to the causal nexus in natural science, may also be mediated by the understanding of rational grounds, emotional dispositons, socially binding behavioural expectations, institutionalized values and individual goals. This explains why the positivists always equate the concept of the motive of an action with the cause of an occurrence.[21] In so doing, however, before it can be objectified as the cause, the motive must be understood in a completely different setting according to its meaning. In its *a priori* bond with the objectification of an event in time, the questions of political history none the less still possess a certain unmistakable analogy with natural scientific causal analysis.

In contrast, in my opinion, genuine hermeneutic inquiry stands in a complementary relationship to natural scientific objectification and explanation of events. Both types of inquiry are mutually exclusive and yet none the less thereby supplement one another. One can clarify this structural relationship most fully if one takes up the question of the linguistic preconditions for the possibility and validity of natural science itself and thinks it out to its logical conclusion within the context of a cognitive anthropology. A natural scientist, as *solus ipse*, cannot seek to explain something for himself alone.[22] And in order merely to know 'what' he should explain, he must have come to some agreement with others about it. As Peirce recognized, the natural scientist's community of experiment always expresses a semiotic community of interpretation.[23] Yet this agreement at the level of intersubjectivity, precisely because it is the precondition for the possibility of objective science, can never be replaced by a mode of procedure of objective science. Here we confront the absolute limits of any programme for objective-explanatory science. Linguistic agreement concerning what one means and what one wants is *complementary* to objective science in the sense defined above.

We now still have to show that intersubjective agreement, which cannot be replaced by any method of objective science, can nevertheless become a theme of scientific inquiry. In other words, it must be shown that not only 'descriptive' and 'explanatory' sciences that presuppose the subject-object relationship but also 'interpretative sciences' that presuppose the intersubjective relationship are possible and even necessary. Their mode of inquiry must possess a relationship to pre-scientific human communication similar to that of the causal explanatory natural sciences to the so-called 'knowledge of work' (Scheler) as a preliminary stage. This is in fact the case. It seems to me that man has basically two equally important but not identical *complementary* cognitive interests:

1   an interest that is determined by the necessity for a technical praxis as the basis of insights into natural laws;
2   an interest that is determined by the necessity for social, morally relevant praxis.

The latter is directed towards agreement – one that is already presupposed by technical praxis – upon the possibility and norms of a meaningful human 'being-in-the-world'. This interest in the understanding of meaning is not only directed towards communication amongst contemporaries but also towards the communication of the living with past generations in the manner of a mediation of tradition.[24] It is indeed primarily through this mediation of tradition that human beings achieve that accumulation of technical knowledge and that deepening and enrichment of their understanding of possible meaningful motivation which gives them their superiority over the animal kingdom.

In fact, the mediation of tradition – above all when it occurs in crises – is the only cognitive-anthropological location out of which the hermeneutic sciences can emerge and out of which they, as a reality of European and Asiatic high culture, did emerge. Its centre is formed by 'philologies' in the widest sense of this word, that is, including literary studies. Of course, these sciences may not be understood – as often occurs in objectivistic theories of science – as mere auxiliary sciences of history, as if the interpretation of historical texts meant only supplying information about past occurrences. The 'classical' or canonical traditional texts (religious, philosophical, poetic and legal literary documents) are not

59

primarily 'sources' for the historian which the philologist has merely to edit. Rather, 'philologies' are the genuine hermeneutic human sciences since they are not at all primarily concerned with spatial and temporal processes but with the 'interpretation' of 'meaning' that only (indeed) has its vehicle, its *conditio sine qua non* in the sphere of spatio-temporal events.[25]

The 'life-*a priori*' of knowledge is revealed in the fundamental problematic of the hermeneutic human sciences not as the presupposition of the instrumental incursion into nature but as the dependence of the intersubjective manifestation of meaning on the meaningful perceivable 'expression'. It is revealed in linguistics, for example, as the articulation of possible meaning in linguistic sounds that can be dealt with phonologically. This living expression of dialogically communicable meaning can certainly in limiting cases – as in calculus language – become a rigid 'sign-instrument'. In that moment in which language becomes a sign-instrument, the understanding of meaning indeed no longer depends upon the individual interpretation of the living expression but rather only upon participation in the conventional fixing of the (syntactic and semantic) rules of a sign system. Yet even here the sign-instrument still serves as a vehicle of the 'understanding of meaning'. It is the established result – in accordance with its form – of pre-understanding in the 'community of interpretation' which must also belong to the construction of calculus languages.

So much for the first main thesis of a theory of science which does not – as is usually the case – commence from the subject-object relationship as the sole presupposition and problematic of human knowledge. Ultimately, the proposed assertion of a *complementarity* of scientistic and hermeneutic sciences starts out from the fact that the existence of a communication community is the presupposition for all knowledge in the subject-object dimension and that the function of this communication community itself – as the intersubjective meta-dimension for the objective description and explanation of data in the world – can and must become a theme of scientific knowledge.

Josiah Royce, the American Hegelian, expressed this insight – connected with the founder of pragmatism, Peirce – in the following form: the human being must not only 'perceive' sense-data and 'conceive' ideas in the confrontation with nature; he must also, at the same time and in the regular exchange with the other members of a historical 'community', 'interpret' ideas. For example, when it is a matter of verifying opinions then it is insufficient to secure the 'cash value' of ideas by means of experimental operations that lead to sense-data perceptions. Rather, the 'face value' of the ideas to be verified must already have been secured through 'interpretation'. Hence, in a basic triadic relationship A makes clear to B what C means. This is true even of so-called solitary thought in which I (A) must make clear to myself (B) what my idea, opinion or intention (C) already at hand means. This triadic process of mediation of interpretation secures the historical continuity of knowledge in that A represents the present which the future (B) mediates the meaning or opinion of the past (C).[26]

The actual problem of the philosophical foundation of hermeneutics, i.e. the study of the scientific interpretation of (intended or, at least, expressed) meaning may be formulated, in my opinion, in the following question: Is there a *methodological abstraction* through which a scientific investigation of intended or expressed meaning is possible at the level of intersubjective agreement between human subjects?

The philosophical founders of hermeneutics in the nineteenth century (Schleiermacher and Dilthey) answered this question in the affirmative and in fact replied in the following manner: By means of abstraction from the question of the truth or normative claim of the expression of meaning to be understood (e.g. the text that has been handed down), a progressive, universally valid objectivation of meaning is possible. Herein should lie the parallel between interpretative human sciences and the objective and progressive natural sciences. In place of the normatively binding understanding of the pre-scientific mediation of tradition there emerges – as a result of the intention of the theory of science – the normatively unbinding but scientifically universally valid understanding of the hermeneutic 'sciences of the spirit' (*Geisteswissenschaften*).

If one takes the practical (existential) consequences of this conception seriously then this leads to the problem of nihilistic 'historicism' that Dilthey himself had clearly seen and that later Robert Musil the writer – taking up a notion from Nietzsche – formulated as the problem of 'The Man without Qualities'.[27] In fact, the person who scientifically objectivated all binding truths and norms and had collected in the contemporaneity of an 'imaginary museum' anything but understandable meaning would be similar to

61

a person who was unable to acquire any qualities, a 'person of possibilities', as Musil also termed him, who was unable to actualize his life. Such a person would have lost all connection with tradition and would have been reduced by the historical-hermeneutic sciences to precisely this state in which history was virtually absent. These sciences themselves and their neutralizing objectivation of binding norms and truths would replace real tradition and hence history itself.[28]

Recently, Gadamer in particular, commencing from Heidegger's hermeneutics of existence and, like Heidegger himself, from Dilthey's *Lebensphilosophie* approach (i.e. not from his objectivistic and historicist approach), has placed in question the presuppositions for the historicist foundations of the human sciences.[29] Gadamer questions the meaning and possibility of a systematic, progressive objectivation of meaning in the hermeneutic sciences that leads to the emasculation of historical tradition. He sees in this conception an unreflected temptation to follow the natural scientific (scientistic) methodological ideal that is still present in Dilthey's work. And he goes so far as to make the dismantling of all methodological abstractions the precondition for the philosophical analysis of meaning in the hermeneutic sciences. According to Gadamer, hermeneutic understanding cannot, as Schleiermacher first demanded, leave out of account a decision as to questions of norms or truth. It must, whether it likes it or not, include its 'application' to practical questions of life and also to historical existential engagement as a precondition for its possibility and validity. As the model for a philosophical analysis of the integral function of understanding, Gadamer recommends the understanding of written law applied by the judge or the understanding of a drama as applied by the director who stages it. Here, understanding does not destroy the binding nature of tradition but mediates it with the present. According to Gadamer, the same is *also* the task of the historical-hermeneutic sciences. With regard to their hermeneutic basic features, Gadamer equates the model of the good interpreter with which the human scientist can be identified with the model of the director or judge.

In my opinion, it is not easy to decide between the historicist and existential-hermeneutic foundation of the meaning of the human sciences in the sense of an alternative.

It seems to me that the strength of Gadamer's 'philosophical hermeneutics' lies in the critique of the objectivistic methodological ideal of historicism, but that he goes too far when he disputes the meaning of the methodological-hermeneutic abstraction from the question of truth and equates the model of the judge or director with that of the interpreter. In my opinion, Gadamer correctly points out that the historicity of the interpreter is one of the pre-conditions for the possibility of understanding in the human sciences; and that it is not a Cartesian or Kantian subject or con-sciousness as such that progressively makes the world available as an objective complex but rather that in the end the contemporary being-in-the-world must understand itself in its possibilities in terms of the tradition that is to be appropriated. Hence, the conception of an emasculation of historical tradition by the 'imaginary museum' of meaning objectified in the human sciences is an illusion. Its dubiousness lies in the fact that the human scientist hides or re-presses the unavoidable determination of his understanding by its inherent historical engagement and thus, instead of thereby assist-ing the intended dedogmatization of the understanding of meaning, actually assists its ideologization.

Despite this, it seems to me that the scientific understanding of meaning, in the sense of philological hermeneutics, presupposes – just like each individual scientific method – a *methodological abstraction*. This methodological abstraction is already suggested in the pre-scientific realm by the interpreter's situation. The in-terpreter's own specific function within the mediation of meaning in the context of practical situations in life is already completely different from that of the director or even the judge. Similarly, the legal historian's systematic activity of interpretation is completely different from that of the judge, even though he too does not undoubtedly serve the objective neutralization of the meaning of law in an 'imaginary museum' but rather, as Gadamer rightly suggests, is integrated in the process of the practically applicable mediation of tradition. Of course one must concede that affiliation to a historical situation of life-practice on the part of the scientific interpreter of texts or the language interpreter is presupposed as the precondition for the possibility of his understanding. In that this is the case, not merely reflexive distancing but also pre-reflexive engagement is a part of hermeneutic understanding. Yet the scien-tific interpreter's pre-reflexive engagement is fundamentally different from that of the director or even the judge.

63

The responsibility of the director and even more of the judge lies in the first instance in the application of understanding to the situation in which he is placed. With reference to the practical mastery of this task he must undertake, in creative interpretation, responsibility for the truth or normative commitment of the meaning to be understood to a much greater extent, for instance, than a legal historian who is interpreting the canonical texts of Roman law. The legal historian's responsibility is primarily to the meaning of the text that in his original intention is merely one that is still difficult to understand. Herein already lies the abstraction from the question of normative commitment and its delegation to practical lawyers who, within the division of labour in the mediation of tradition, have taken on the function of the 'application' of understanding. The legal historian will certainly not be allowed to think that he could make himself contemporary with the public for the texts of the *corpus iuris* through the study of language and history as Schleiermacher – as a precondition for the ultimate identification with the author – demanded. Nor will he be allowed to renounce Schleiermacher's hermeneutic ideal in favour of a conscious actualization of understanding.[30] Gadamer rightly demands from the interpreter of a text that he thinks out the history of the text's reception, which basically co-determines the historical situation of the interpreter and hence the preconditions for the possibility of understanding. Yet for the scientific interpreter, this 'reflecting on the distance of time' does not take place in the interest of the 'application' of understanding but rather in the interest of Schleiermacher's methodological ideal of making oneself contemporary with what is to be understood.

It seems to me that at this point a new light is thrown upon the question that has been in dispute since Nietzsche's 'untimely' observations 'On the Uses and Disadvantages of History for Life'. This is the question of whether historical understanding can lead to the emasculation of history (as an effective mediation of tradition). Along with Gadamer, we have already ruled out this possibility in the sense that the human scientist should not deceive himself into thinking he can take up a neutral standpoint outside history. Thus, the power of history as the mediation of tradition still also exists in the age of historicism. On the other hand, however, the element of truth in talk of the emasculation of tradition through historical understanding is certainly not to be overlooked. Here, however, the concern is not with an emasculation of history as the mediation of tradition as such but with the actual 'traditions' of the pre-industrial or pre-scientific age,[31] with the powerful historical process of emasculation of specific 'traditions'. In this epochal crisis that has been noticeably much more decisive for non-European cultures in the twentieth century than for European culture in the nineteenth century lies the substantive problem of (nihilistic) historicism. Moreover, this problem is of such a concrete nature that it cannot be shown to be an illusory problem by the formally correct demonstration by existential analysis that hermeneutic understanding cannot extricate itself from the context of the historical mediation of tradition.

In fact, the mediation of tradition, without which man would indeed never be able to exist, must take on another form in our post-historicist age than in the period before the emergence of the historical, hermeneutic human sciences. The immediacy of the dogmatic and normative (institutionally secured and socially binding) 'application' of the understanding of tradition as it occurred up to the Enlightenment in Europe and up to the present in most non-European cultures, cannot be reproduced. The mediation of tradition must become a complicated scientifically mediated process in as far as the – even though only provisional – objectivation and distantiation of the meaning to be understood is possible by means of the hermeneutic abstraction from normative validity. And, in my opinion, it is also an illusion to believe that the hermeneutic human sciences can carry out on their own the complicated function of the mediation of tradition that they have themselves made necessary. It is not enough for them simply to give up that positivistic self-understanding and to consciously integrate themselves into the functional context of intercultural agreement and, in particular, the mediation of tradition. In my opinion, the hermeneutic human sciences become just as ideologically corrupted through the (existentialist or even Marxist) demand for a binding application of their understanding as they do through the positivistic non-reflection, i.e. repression, of historical engagement as a precondition for the possibility of their understanding of meaning. If there were at all to be a rational integration of the results of the hermeneutic sciences, if this is not to be relinquished to art or existential self-understanding, then this task could only be undertaken by philosophy and, in particular, by the philosophy of history.

In solving this problem, however, the philosophy of history cannot solely draw upon the historical-hermeneutic human sciences. It must include a further large group of sciences and a methodological approach that can be reduced neither to the questions raised by scientism nor those raised by hermeneutics.

In arguing this, I come to the second major thesis of my outline for a theory of science. Unfortunately I can indicate the necessary reflections here only in simple outline and in the form of very speculative assertions.

The philosophical solution to the problem of historicism by the dialectical mediation of objective-scientistic and hermeneutic methods in the critique of ideology

It seems to me necessary for a reasonable philosophical assessment of the so-called problem of historicism to choose as our point of orientation not so much ours in the West as that of non-European cultures. These cultures which had to and still must take over the European technical-industrial form of life and its scientific foundations are forced to distance themselves and estrange themselves from their traditions much more radically than we are. They can in no way desire to compensate for the emergent break with the past solely by hermeneutic reflection. For them there exists from the outset the necessity to achieve a quasi-objective, historical-philosophical system of reference alongside hermeneutic reflection upon their own and foreign traditions. This system of reference must make possible the integration of their own position in the world-historical and human-planetary context that, without their doing, is shaped by European and American civilization. They will simultaneously draw upon the unavoidable estrangement from their own tradition as well as upon the fact that intellectual interpretations of the world, e.g. religious and moral orders of values, are to be conceived in the closest connection with social forms of life (institutions). What they seek above all is a philosophical and scientific orientation that mediates the hermeneutic understanding of their own and foreign traditions of meaning by sociological analyses of those economic and social orders to which they belong. It is this that makes intelligible the fascinating power of Marxism for intellectuals in developing countries.

Yet how is the philosophical study of the problem of historicism illuminated in the situation of non-European cultures?

The answer to this question can, first of all, be sketched out in a speculative language which I wish at least to ascribe a heuristic value to. Spirit as such does not simply appear in time as Hegel suggested in his system of historical idealism but on the basis of a mediation with the history of nature that is advanced in human social behaviour. This may be stated differently. When Gadamer makes the 'productivity of time' responsible for the fact that the guiding idea of classical hermeneutics – making oneself contemporary with and ultimately identifying oneself with the author of the text that is to be understood – must remain an illusion,[32] then in this 'productivity' which is irritating to the understanding, it seems to me that the vague suggestion of the unintended and the still not intendable in all human expressions of life is to blame; namely, the fact that the non-intelligible history of nature – still even now – continues in intelligible intellectual history.

Were human beings' motives for action or at least the conceptions of meaning in their literary works transparent to them, then in principle making-oneself-contemporary in understanding, the mutual identification of individual monads (Schleiermacher's debt to Leibniz), the 'elevated discourse of minds' of all revered authors, the transcendence of time (Petrarch, Bembo) would all be possible. In other words, if human beings were completely lucid about their intentions, then only two complementary cognitive interests would be justified: the scientific interest in technically relevant knowledge of nature and the hermeneutic interest in intersubjective agreement about possible interpretable motivations in life. Yet up to now, human beings have neither 'made' their political and social history nor are their so-called intellectual convictions, as they are laid down in linguistic documents, the pure expression of their intellectual 'intentions'. All results of their intentions are, at the same time, the results of actual forms of life that they have not yet been able to take up in their self-understanding. It seems to me that at this dark suggestion in the natural history of human beings which is carried forth in human intellectual history the strivings towards hermeneutic identification founder, especially with the authors of spatially and temporally distant cultures. Precisely for this reason, all understanding, in so far and as long as it is at all successful, must understand an author better than he understands himself in that – in

67

Hegel's sense – it reflexively goes beyond the author's understanding of the world and himself and does not merely empathetically reconstruct (as with Schleiermacher and Dilthey) his inner experiences. None the less, these are limits to reflexively transcending understanding that are not only due to the finite nature and defective self-transparency of the interpreter. It also encounters contradictions in the expressions of life that are to be understood – either within texts that have been handed down, or between them and the accompanying actions of the authors – that cannot be resolved at all by hermeneutic methods which make implicit meaning explicit. These are contradictions which are determined by the intermeshing of sense and nonsense, intended actions and naturally determined reactions and which constitute a barrier to 'understanding'. A philosophy of history that seeks to be understood merely as an integration of the hermeneutic *Geisteswissenschaften* must founder here upon the factual that lacks meaning and upon the contingent that is plainly irrational.

Yet it is precisely these factually contingent factors of human history – and hence of the history of ideas – that are not yet able to be raised to intersubjective agreement, precisely because they are not, as motives, subjectively transparent but are merely factually effective and can only be analysed by means of a quasi-objective explanatory science.

In any conversation between people it is apparent that one party no longer attempts to take the other seriously hermeneutically with regard to his intentions but rather distances himself from the other objectively as a quasi-natural entity, where he no longer attempts to create the unity of language in communication but rather seeks to evaluate what the other person says as the symptom of an objective situation which he seeks to explain from outside in a language in which his partner does not participate. Typical of this partial breakdown of hermeneutic communication in favour of objective methods of acquiring knowledge is the doctor's relationship to his patients, and in particular, the psychotherapist's relationship to the neurotic patient. In my opinion, this model of partially suspended communication may indeed be made just as fruitful as the positive basic model of conversation for the foundation of the theory of social science. In particular, the philosopher of history who seeks to solve the problem of historicism must, in my opinion, not only unify the hermeneutic function of the translator with its practical application – as Gadamer desires – in order to mediate tradition with the present. At the same time he must also adopt the objective distantiating cognitive role of a doctor or, more specifically, a psychotherapist in relation to the behaviour and meaning claims of what has been handed down and of contemporaries. In fact, this is what he does when he not merely draws upon the results of the hermeneutic methods of the so-called *Geisteswissenschaften* but also upon the objective structural analyses of the empirical social sciences in order to explain, for instance, the constellations of interests in political and also intellectual history that cannot be proven by literary methods.

Here we are once more led back to the problem of 'historical explanation' and its remarkable intermediate position between hermeneutics and scientistics. We have already emphasized earlier that political history, despite the whole dependency of intended meanings upon hermeneutic understanding, nevertheless explains events in a certain analogy to natural science; it explains events that are actually occurring in the objectifiable temporal order. In our earlier example of a 'historical explanation' we have none the less emphasized that the objective context of events as a result of historical reconstruction is mediated through an understanding of the intentions of participating human beings. It will thus proceed in this manner whenever the historian takes human beings as the subjects of their actions and intentions completely seriously; when, for example, he seeks to answer the question of the causes of war merely by means of the statements left behind by responsible politicians concerning their motives. Yet one can conceive of the opposite instance, too, as when understanding of the reasons is methodologically mediated by an analysis of objective, operating factors of which the responsible actors are not at all conscious as meaningful motives. Something approaching this has been achieved, for example, for the explanation of the causes of the First World War by Hallgarten in terms of the economic world situation of imperialism.[33] In this study, the official motives of politicians are, to some extent, ignored and in their place as causal factors are the verifiable needs of big industry for market outlets.

Of course, a more precise methodological analysis would show that the empirical data which assists the sociologically orientated historian in the quasi-objective establishment of the state of interests is far from being equated with securing data in the natural sciences. Company reports, balance sheets, price lists, bills, etc., are ultimately also 'texts' in which human intentions are expressed. Correspondingly, one can very easily confirm in the case of so-called social-psychological behavioural research that their statistical data constantly goes back to hermeneutic operations for gaining data such as interviews.[34] Yet the significance of the quasi-scientistic cognitive achievements of sociological and psychological behavioural research will never be reached by referring to their ever present hermeneutic presuppositions. In my opinion, it lies in the alienation of the traditional self-understanding of individual human beings and human communities by theoretical structures that interpret human life-expressions in a language in which the originator of the life-expressions cannot immediately participate (and which also cannot be translated into their language by philological operations). Compared with hermeneutic understanding which, in principle, strives for the maintenance and even deepening of communication, psychological and social-psychological behavioural analyses can quite easily function like causal explanations – on the basis of laws – which are applied to the object from outside. This is shown, above all, in the fact that – in exactly the same manner as prognostically relevant natural scientific knowledge – they make possible technical domination over their object, as in the case of the manipulation of the employer by the manager versed in organizational psychology, the consumer by the advertising expert, and the voter by the politician schooled in psephology.

At this point, however, the scientific self-understanding of the behavioural sciences actually becomes a morally relevant factor in history. If, like neopositivism, one wishes to value the quasi-objective cognitive achievements of the behavioural sciences as the beginnings of a universal natural science of man, then one must necessarily see their goal as securing and enlarging the domination of man over man. Of course, this also presupposes that human behaviour can never be fully mastered by prognoses. Otherwise, the social engineer himself could no longer 'commence' with his knowledge of social domination. None the less, the naïve legitimation of fragmentary attainable knowledge of social domination by the philosophical self-understanding of the scientist can have disastrous practical consequences.

Fortunately, there exists – in contrast to the natural sciences where this is, in principle, impossible – the 'reaction' of human objects to the results of behavioural explanation which must figure as a fundamental failure in the scientistic self-understanding of the social psychological sciences. Furthermore, this 'reaction', which behavioural 'explanation' counterposes with a new kind of procedure, at the same time provides an indication as to how the quasi-objective cognitive achievements of the behavioural sciences can be meaningfully incorporated into a (cognitive-anthropological) theory of science.

The sole explanation for the fact that human beings can react to the causal analytical explanation of their behaviour with a new kind of behaviour lies in the insight that human beings can, by self-reflection, translate the language of psychological and sociological 'explanations' into the language of a deepened self-understanding that transforms their motivational structure and thereby robs the 'explanation' of its foundation. This leads us back to the model of psychotherapy referred to earlier. In this remarkable cognitive model, there exist, in fact, both elements, namely:

1 the objective and distanced behavioural 'explanation' which presupposes the partial breakdown of communication; and
2 the subsequent 'transcendence' of the 'explanation' in a deepened self-understanding which is dialectically mediated. With the aid of psychoanalytic theory the doctor recognizes:

1 the quasi-natural, explicable and sometimes even predictable consequences of repressed meaningful motives. In so doing, he makes the patient into an object.
2 At the same time, however, he seeks to transcend the merely explicable causal constraint in that he understands the meaning of the repressed motives and provokes the patient through communication to apply this interpretation of meaning to a revision of his autobiographical self-understanding.

As already indicated above, however, the model of psychotherapy can be transferred, to some extent, to the relationship of the philosophy of history to the self-understanding of human society. Indeed, there might even exist a real connection between the quasi-natural causal processes of a specific mode of societal practice and the neurotic symptoms of individuals in this society. The inability to trace back certain social modes of behaviour 1) to

71

causally active needs and to reconcile them 2) as intelligible needs with society's tradition of meaning might also encourage individuals to repress motives immanent to these needs.

It seems to me that these reflections prompt the methodological demand for a dialectical mediation of social scientific 'explanation' and historical-hermeneutic 'understanding' of traditions of meaning on the basis of the regulative principle of a transcendence of the elements of our historical existence that lack reason. Here, the social-scientific 'explanations' would have to be so established (and published!) that they did not give power over the ignorant to those who know, but represented a challenge to all to transform causally explicable modes of behaviour into intelligible actions by a process of taking stock. The *terminus technicus* of this dialectical mediation of 'understanding' and 'explanation' is called 'the critique of ideology'. As the 'psychoanalysis' of human social history and as the 'psychotherapy' of actual crises in human actions it seems to me to represent the sole meaningful logical foundation and moral justification for the objective and explanatory sciences of man.[35]

Its guiding cognitive interest corresponds to the life-*a priori* of a psychosomatic self-diagnosis and self-therapy of mankind. The regulative principle of this cognitive engagement would not be the liberation of the spirit from the body, or the cognitive 'transcendence' of matter in the absolute idea but rather the pure expression of the spiritual in the corporeal, the 'humanization of nature' and the 'naturalization of man'.

Notes

1 A central suggestion of Wittgenstein's later work is that determinate natural phenomena, but in particular artificial standards, instruments or even work procedures including their material preconditions are co-constitutive of the 'deep structure' of a language-game as 'models' or 'paradigms' and hence also co-determine the *a priori* valid, so-called 'essential structure' of our understanding of the world. Recently, it has been made fruitful for the understanding of the history of science by Thomas S. Kuhn (*The Structure of Scientific Revolutions*, Chicago, 1962). Indeed, in so doing, Kuhn terms precisely what Wittgenstein understood by a 'language-game' – namely, the quasi-institutional unity of linguistic usage, behaviour (work procedures, instrumental technology) and world understanding (theory-formation) that is interwoven in the practice of life – a 'paradigm'. In this concept, which in Kuhn as

similarly in Wittgenstein indicates a practical cognitive *a priori* established through practice, I wish to discover an illustration of the cognitive-anthropological concretization of epistemology that I have postulated. However, there is a proviso: it seems to me that Kuhn and Wittgenstein underestimate the logical connection between the diverse 'paradigms' or 'language-games' which, in the progress of natural science, the cognitive *a priori* of eccentric, non-engaged reflection brings to bear in the form of ever more comprehensive theory-formations. Cf. below on the complementarity of reflection and engagement.

2 Cf. I. Kant, *Critique of Pure Reason*, trans. N. Kemp Smith, London, 1933, BXIIf. Kant himself here implicitly refers to the instrumental *a priori* that we have postulated and, in my opinion, he again took up the problem – that he had overlooked in his 'critical reason' – of a bodily -*a priori* (*Leibapriori*) as the transcendental precondition for physical experience in his 'Opus postumum'. Cf. K. Hübner, 'Leib und Erfahrung in Kants Opus Postumum', *Zeitschrift für Philosophische Forschung*, 7, 1953, pp. 204 f. Also, H. C. Hoppe, *Kants Theorie der Physik: eine Untersuchung über das Opus postumum von Kant*, Frankfurt, 1969.

3 Cf. P. Mittelstaedt, *Philosophische Probleme der modernen Physik*, Mannheim, 1953, pp. 15 f. The *methodical a priori* character of 'material preconditions for the possibility of experience' is illustrated even more strikingly by P. Lorenzen's conception of a 'protophysics' of measurement. Cf. G. Böhme (ed.), *Protophysik*, Frankfurt, 1976.

4 Cf. H. Plessner on the 'eccentric positionality' of human beings in *Die Stufen des Organischen und der Mensch*, Berlin/Leipzig, 1928.

5 Cf. K.-O. Apel, 'Das Leibapriori der Erkenntnis (eine Betrachung im Anschluss an Leibnizens Monadenlehre)', *Archiv für Philosophie*, 12, 1963, pp. 152–72.

6 Erich Rothacker in his *Die dogmatische Denkform in den Geisteswissenschaften und das Problem des Historismus*, Mainz/Wiesbaden, 1954, has dealt with the distinctiveness and necessity of engaged knowledge.
O. Becker, in his book, *Grösse und Grenze der mathematischen Denkweise*, Freiburg/Munich, 1959, has clarified the significance of eccentric reflection for the formation of increasingly comprehensive relativity or transformation theories by the law derived from the history of science of 'pythagorean necessity' (the abandonment of intuitionally significant knowledge in favour of mathematically abstract universal validity).

7 Cf. Jürgen Habermas, *Knowledge and Human Interests*; see also K.-O. Apel, *Analytic Philosophy of Language and the 'Geisteswissenschaften'*, Dordrecht, 1967. Further, K.-O. Apel, 'Types of Social Science in the Light of Human Cognitive Interests', in Social Research, 44, 1977, reprinted in *Philosophical Disputes in the Social Sciences* (ed. S. Brown), Hassocks, Sussex, 1979.

8 The thesis of a *technical cognitive interest* in no way implies that the claim to *truth* by natural scientific knowledge may be *reduced in an instrumentalist manner*. It should be stressed along with Peirce and in

opposition to this pragmatism (taken from Max Scheler) in the style of
Nietzsche, James and Dewey, that only the possible *meaning* of
experimental knowledge is *a priori* revealed and limited by the context
of verification of technical practice. In terms of its *meaning, human*
knowledge cannot be simply a pure knowledge of objects in relation to a
'consciousness as such' but only knowledge of a personally engaged and
practically interested nature. In this fact lies, in my opinion, the
cognitive-anthropological radicalization and transformation of Kant's
critique of knowledge. Indeed we cannot meaningfully conceive of
another form of knowledge that is *meaningful for us* and hence perhaps
true. On the transformation of the 'critique of knowledge' that is based
on the 'critique of meaning', see my *Der Denkweg von C. S. Peirce*,
Frankfurt, 1975.

9 Cf. also K.-O. Apel, *Die 'Erklären-Verstehen' Kontroverse in trans-
zendentalpragmatischen Sicht*, Frankfurt, 1979.

10 Cf. the studies in the journal *Erkenntnis* (1930–38) which was continued
in the USA as the *Journal of Unified Science* (1939) and the *International
Encyclopaedia of Unified Science* (1938 ff.).

11 In its place, the analytical philosophy of language approach of modern
neopositivism since the early Wittgenstein has once more treated the
problem of a transcendental constitution of the meaning of so-called
'data' as that of necessary linguistic conventions. Cf. Apel, *Analytic
Philosophy of Language and the 'Geisteswissenschaften'*. In the
development of the Popperian 'Logic of Scientific Discovery', the
Kantian supposition of a synthetic constitution of empirical data is,
rather, replaced by the assumption that the data is always interpreted
in the light of (the creative spontaneity of) theories. But as far as these
theories are concerned, no question seems to be allowed as to their
constitution in the light of *internal, meaning–constitutive cognitive
interests* which, for example, are very different in the case of the
explanation of understanding and the *understanding of explanations*.

12 My characterization of the positivistic critique of ideology is based in
part upon E. Topitsch, *Sozialphilosophie zwischen Ideologie und
Wissenschaft*, Neuwied, 1961.

13 In H. Feigl and M. Brodbeck (eds), *Readings in the Philosophy of
Science*, New York, 1953, pp. 677–88.

14 Cf. Feigl and Brodbeck, op. cit., pp. 319 ff.

15 W. Dray, *Laws and Explanation in History*, Oxford, 1957.

16 Cf. K. R. Popper, *The Open Society and its Enemies*, vol. 2, 5th ed.,
London, 1966.

17 In the nineteenth century, the philosophy of science's reflection upon
the distinction between the 'natural sciences' and the *Geisteswissenschaften* was originally psychologically orientated – like J. S. Mill's
positivism to which it reacted. That is, it was suggested that the
Geisteswissenschaften 'understand' life as the expression of something
internal whereas the natural sciences 'describe' the uninterpretable
'background of life' (Dilthey) and 'explain' it according to laws derived
inductively. Today, where the positivist programme of a 'unified

science' emerges in a language-analytical formulation (in order not to
appear to be a metaphysical reductive theory!), philosophical
'hermeneutics' also has every reason to accept this new basis for
argument. It can then, for its part, and without any recourse to the
terminology of a metaphysics of the spirit (or of life), refute the positivist
thesis of an objective, analytical unified science on the basis of its own
language-analytical presuppositions (cf. Apel, *Analytic Philosophy of
Language and the 'Geisteswissenschaften'*). The distinction between
'objectivations of the spirit' (Hegel and Dilthey) that are to be
understood from within, on the one hand, and 'natural processes' that
are to be explained from outside, on the other, may then be replaced –
or, if one wishes, made concrete – by the distinction between those
objects with which the investigator can enter into linguistic communication and those with which no communication is possible. The
investigator must deal with the latter – even as data – on the basis of the
linguistic anticipation of externally applied theories; the former
confronts him, as it were, with the data of their situated world derived
from a linguistic understanding of the world to which he himself
contributes as a partner in communication. Behavioural explanations
applied to 'dumb' objects can only be verified by observations, whereas
hermeneutic 'hypotheses' of understanding are primarily verified by the
replies of the communication partner. Even 'texts' can 'reply'! It is
interesting in this context that Chomsky, the founder of so-called
'generative' or 'transformational' grammar, has shown that even
linguistic usage, which certainly appears easily objectifiable as
anonymous and unconscious group behaviour, cannot be described
without interpretative communication with the 'competent speaker'.
Indeed, on the basis of external observations – such as available
statistical criteria of distribution as adopted by the behaviouristically
orientated Bloomfield school – it cannot be decided either whether
someone in fact 'speaks' or according to which rules he does so. Cf. the
works of Chomsky in J. A. Fodor and J. J. Katz (eds), *The Structure of
Language*. The reply to Wittgenstein's question as to how one can
decide whether someone is following a rule reaches similar conclusions.
Cf. P. Winch, *The Idea of a Social Science*, London, 1958. On Chomsky,
and Winch, cf. also J. Habermas, 'Zur Logik der Sozialwissenschaften',
Philosophische Rundschau, Sonderheft, Tübingen, 1967, and chs 5 and 6
in this volume.

18 According to Heidegger and Wittgenstein, 'history as such' becomes a
meaningless ontological hypostatization. There is only 'our own'
history!

19 A. C. Danto, in his *Analytical Philosophy of History*, Cambridge, 1965,
distinguishes in this sense historical explanation as 'narrative
explanation' from deductive explanation in natural science. Earlier,
Wilhelm Schapp (*Geschichten Verstrickt: zum Sein von Mensch und
Ding*, Hamburg, 1953) had already developed a similar approach. This
phenomenological-hermeneutic approach was already compared with
the 'analytical philosophy' in the Wittgensteinian tradition in

H. Lübbe's 'Sprachspiele und Geschichten', *Kantstudien*, 52, 1960–1.
20 Dray, op. cit., p. 134. Cf. also G. H. von Wright's account for the peculiar 'necessity' of the 'ex post factum' understanding of human actions in *Explanation and Understanding*, London and New York, 1971, p. 117 and p. 205, n. 26.
21 Cf. W. Stegmüller, *Main Currents in Contemporary German, British and American Philosophy*, pp. 479 f. On this see Apel, *Analytic Philosophy of Language and the 'Geisteswissenschaften'*, pp. 19 f.
22 Cf. Wittgenstein's mental experiments on the problem of a 'private language'; *Philosophical Investigations*, 1.SS, 197 ff., 199, 243, 256.
23 Cf. my *Der Denkweg von C. S. Peirce*.
24 Cf. H.-G. Gadamer's interpretation of the hermeneutic human sciences on the basis of the functional context of the mediation of tradition in *Truth and Method*, London, 1975. On this cf. K.-O. Apel in *Hegelstudien*, vol. 2, 1963, pp. 314–22.
25 Cf. E. Rothacker, 'Sinn und Geschehnis', in *Sinn und Sein*, Tübingen, 1960, pp. 1–9.
26 Cf. J. Royce, *The Problem of Christianity*, New York, 1913, vol. 2, pp. 146 ff. On this see K. T. Humbach, *Das Verhältnis von Einzelperson und Gemeinschaft nach Josiah Royce*, Heidelberg, 1962, pp. 110 ff.
27 Cf. on this point, E. Heintel, 'Der Mann ohne Eigenschaften und die Tradition', *Wissenschaft und Weltbild*, 1960, pp. 179–94.
28 Cf. J. Ritter, 'Die Aufgabe der Geisteswissenschaften in der modernen Gesellschaft', in *Jahresschrift 1961 der Gesellschaft zur Förderrung der Westfälischen Wilhelms-Universität zu Münster*, Hamburg, 1963, pp. 278 ff.
29 Cf. Gadamer, op cit.
30 In my opinion, Betti correctly attacks the implicit call for actualization that also seems to be directed at the human 'scientist' in existential hermeneutics. Cf. E. Betti, *Die Hermeneutik als allgemeine Methodik der Geisteswissenschaften*, Tübingen, 1962.
31 It seems to me that the difference between Gadamer's position, on the one hand, and that of J. Ritter and H. Schelsky on the other seems in fact to rest in part upon the ambiguity of the concept of 'tradition'.
32 Cf. Gadamer, op. cit. pp. 262 ff.
33 G. W. F. Hallgarten, *Imperialismus vor 1914*, 2 vols, 1951.
34 This is demonstrated especially in H. Skjervheim, *Objectivism and the Study of Man*, Oslo, 1959. On the difficulties faced by the translation of communicative experience into the measuring data of the social sciences, cf. Habermas, 'Zur Logik der Sozialwissenschaften', pp. 95 ff.
35 On the development and critical discussion of the theory of science model outlined here cf. Habermas, *Knowledge and Human Interests*; A. Lorenzer, *Sprachzerstörung und Rekonstruktion*, Frankfurt, 1971; G. Radnitzky, *Contemporary Schools of Metascience*, Göteborg, 1968/ Boston, 1973; K.-O. Apel *et al.*, *Hermeneutik und Ideologiekritik*, Frankfurt, 1971; K.-O. Apel, 'Communication and the Foundation of the Humanities', *Acta Sociologica*, 1972, pp. 7–26 (rpd. in *Man and World*, 5, 1972, pp. 3–37); and also Apel, 'Types of Social Science'.

CHAPTER 3

From Kant to Peirce: the semiotical transformation of transcendental logic

The transcendental dimension of modern 'logic of science'

In comparing Kant's *Critique of Pure Reason* as a logic of science with the modern 'logic of science' one might find the profoundest point of difference between them in the fact that one is an analysis of 'consciousness', the other an analysis of 'language'.

Kant's concern is to make the *objective validity* of science under-standable. For this purpose he indeed puts transcendental logic in the place of the psychology of knowledge as it was developed by Locke and Hume; but his method of inquiry is still related to the 'synthetic unity of *consciousness*' as its 'highest point'. And in accordance with this preconception he makes his synthetic *a priori rules*, which he puts in the place of Hume's psychological laws of association, rules of the function of psychic faculties such as intuition, imagination, understanding, reason.

It is quite different with the modern 'logic of science': There is not only no talk about psychic faculties, even the very problem of consciousness as a subject of scientific knowledge (in contradistinc-tion to the objects of science) is nearly eliminated from the dis-cussion. What has been put in the place of these requisites of Kant's transcendental logic is not, as many like to believe, *formal logic* in its renewed form as mathematical logic, but – for a closer consider-ation – the logical syntax and the logical semantics of scientific *languages*.

These languages as semantical frameworks provide the new subject for *a priori* rules which prescribe the possible form of description and explanation for 'things in as far as they form a context ruled by laws'. And the Kantian problem of the *objective validity* of scientific knowledge for every consciousness was to be resolved in the modern logic of science by logical syntax and logical semantics, which would guarantee the logical consistency and the verifiability (confirmability) of scientific hypotheses or theories.

The historical point of this syntactic-semantic reconstruction of epistemology becomes apparent if one puts the question of what has become of the Kantian consciousness in the modern logic of science, i.e.: of the transcendental subject of scientific knowledge. The official answer could be: This supposition is no longer needed. In as far as the question refers to man as a subject of science the subject may be reduced to an object of science, that is, of human science as behavioural science; in as far, on the other hand, as the question refers to a logical condition of the possibility and validity of science the transcendental function of the Kantian subject may be substituted by the logic of scientific language: the logic of language and the empirical confirmation of propositions or systems of propositions together take the place of Kant's transcendental logic of objective experience.

However, this official view of the modern logic of science, in my opinion, has fallen short of the real problems with which it is confronted. It implies an ideological moment which conceals the failure of the original programme of the modern logic of science, the programme of logical empiricism. For the substitution of the transcendental function of the subject of knowledge by 'the' logic of scientific language could be seriously propagated just as long as one could hope to guarantee the *intersubjectivity* of the possible validity of empirical science by the syntax and semantics of *one* so-called *language of things or facts*. This was just the point by which the young Wittgenstein in his *Tractatus* felt entitled to call the 'logic of language' 'transcendental', apparently with an allusion to Kant (*Tractatus* 6.13), and to identify the *subject* of scientific knowledge as a thing which does *not exist* in the world, with the function of language as a limit of the world (ibid. 5.62; 5.631; 5.632; 5.64).

In the meantime, however, it became clear that neither the logical consistency nor, far less, the empirical testability of science can be warranted by the logical syntax and semantics of *one language of things or facts*. It proved necessary in two places to introduce the so-called *pragmatical dimension*, i.e. the dimension of the *interpretation of signs*, as a condition of the possibility and validity of scientific propositions.

1 One of the two aporetic situations was the famous problem of verification, where it was necessary to connect the reconstructed language of science with the observable facts. It became apparent here as a consequence of the very form of language-analysis that the modern logic of science cannot confront the theories or hypotheses of science with bare facts but only with so-called *basic statements*. But in order to provide validity for the basic statements themselves one requires an intersubjective agreement of the scientists as the pragmatic interpreters of scientific propositions, that is, as subjects of science in as far as they cannot in principle be reduced to objects of empirical science.

Moreover, the language of this intersubjective agreement cannot, in terms of logical semantics, be identical with the logically reconstructed language of science; it must rather coincide practically with the not yet formalized language needed for communication between empirical scientists and the designers of semantical frameworks about the pragmatic interpretation of a language of science.

2 By this last observation we have also already indicated the second, still more fundamental, point, where the substitution of the transcendental function of the epistemological subject by the syntactic or semantical rules of a scientific language was doomed to failure. A formalized language of science just cannot make use of the *one* postulated logical form of language or of the world, which, according to the early Wittgenstein, is *transcendental*. A formalized language of science has to be introduced and legitimized as a conventional framework by scientists, who can and must provide the framework with a pragmatical interpretation in a *meta-language*.

By this it has been shown, in my opinion, that the pragmatic dimension of the sign-function, which was introduced into the modern logic of science by Charles Morris, cannot, as logical empiricists would like, be reduced to a topic of empirical psychology. The pragmatic dimension may rather be considered as the semiotical analogue to the transcendental synthesis of apperception postulated by Kant. Just as Kant, as an analyst of consciousness, had to postulate as a presupposition of epistemology, that by cognition something like the *synthetic unity of consciousness* has to be reached – in just the same way modern logicians of science, starting from a semiotic basis of analysis, could, or rather should, postulate, that it must be possible, for something like the *unity of intersubjective interpretation of the world* to be reached by the way of interpretation of signs.

(Advocates of modern, analytical philosophy might perhaps object that the difference between the modern logic of science and that of Kant consists in the very fact that one is not entitled to postulate a transcendental unity of interpretation of the world but has to be satisfied with a 'critical conventionalism' concerning the interpretation of scientific propositions by experts. I think that in this objection K. R. Popper, the later Wittgenstein, and the later Carnap would agree. One could, however, give the following answer to the objection from a quasi-Kantian point of view: *critical* conventionalism, in contradistinction to *dogmatical* (metaphysical) conventionalism, may not have the intention to reduce knowledge to *mere* convention; it may rather intend to make a difference, by the way of a *fallibilistic* reservation, between *ad-hoc*-conventions of experts and the absolutely intersubjective consensus concerning the validity of scientific propositions. That means, however, that critical conventionalism, understood rightly, does not exclude but presupposes the postulate (the regulative idea) of an absolutely intersubjective *unity of interpretation.*)

Perhaps these critical remarks about the situation of the modern, analytical 'logic of science' are able to convince you that this discipline via *pragmatics* and especially by the problem of *intersubjective interpretation* implied in pragmatics is directed back to a Kantian type of 'transcendental philosophy'. If this should be the case you will not have overlooked that the way suggested by my remarks does not lead back to the historical Kant, nor even to nineteenth-century type neo-Kantianism but rather to a language-analytical or semiotical transformation of transcendental philosophy.

Peirce's semiotical transformation of Kant's transcendental logic

It is a remarkable fact that the very programme sketched out just now has in fact been developed in detail by an American contemporary of German neo-Kantianism. It was Charles S. Peirce, the Kant of American Philosophy, as one may perhaps call him, who initiated the three-dimensional semiotic, which nowadays has been introduced into the modern 'logic of science' by Charles Morris, as the triadic foundation of his 'logic of inquiry'; and this logic of inquiry was intended from the beginning – that is: since the deduction of the 'New List of Categories' in 1867 – as a critical reconstruction (in the sense of setting up an equivalent) of Kant's *Critique of Pure Reason.*

I cannot – within the limits of this essay – develop *in extenso* my interpretation of Peirce's Philosophy.[1] But I will try to make clear my chief thesis, that Peirce's philosophical approach may be understood as a semiotical transformation of Kant's transcendental logic, in a discussion with some renowned investigators of the relationship between Kant and Peirce.[2]

Jürgen von Kempski is to be credited for having for the first time analysed in a serious way the close relationship between Peirce and Kant in his book *C. S. Peirce und der Pragmatismus* (1952). He has shown that Peirce in 1892 succeeded in deducing his three universal categories (firstness, secondness, thirdness) from a classification of the propositional functions[3] into *singular, dual* and *plural* ones, and in this way has set up an analogy to Kant's metaphysical deduction of the categories from the table of judgments. Von Kempski holds, however, that this metaphysical deduction so to speak is hanging in the air, because there is no corresponding transcendental deduction of the categories from the 'highest point', that is: from the transcendental synthesis of apperception (von Kempski, op. cit., pp. 57 ff.). Kant's highest point, so holds von Kempski, is for Peirce 'occult transcendentalism', and therefore he could not understand, much less resolve, the chief problem of Kant's: the problem of explaining the *necessity* of our ideas being determined by categories. Hence Peirce could not manage the transition from his 'logical forms' to the categories of experience, and finally had to give up the Kantian approach and to put in its place a phenomenological discovery of the categories and a pre-Kantian metaphysics for an inductive verification of the categories (ibid., pp. 58 ff.). By this Peirce fell into line, as an original outsider, with neo-Kantianism, or rather with its dissolution at the turn of the nineteenth century by the phenomenological turn.

It cannot be denied that von Kempski's analysis wins much plausibility not only by the suggested historical parallels but also by the development of Peirce's philosophy in its later period (especially by its establishing *phenomenology* or *phaneroscopy* as

81

prima philosophia) and the preceding conception of a metaphysical cosmology on the basis of 'objective idealism'.

Nevertheless, one may get quite another picture if one starts from Peirce's early writings of the sixties and seventies and analyses from this perspective Peirce's hierarchical classification of sciences of 1902–3. Even at this time phenomenology as *prima philosophia* has by no means taken the place of a logical deduction of the categories but only has to illustrate their virtual application after their formal deduction in the mathematical logic of relations (not belonging to philosophy!) and previous to their quasi-transcendental deduction in the normative, semiotical 'logic of inquiry'.

(It may be admitted in this context that Peirce did not succeed in setting up a consistent systematic representation of his philosophy, and that the fragments of his designed architecture leave a lot of free play to the interpreters.)

But let us turn to the transformation of Kant by the early Peirce. Von Kempski (p. 59) has realized that Peirce – in his opinion only in his later works – has found a kind of substitute for the 'highest point' of Kant: namely the category *thirdness*, which he conceives in 1903 as a 'synonym of representation' (Peirce, 5.105) and thus takes as the basis of his logic (of inquiry). Von Kempski is aware of the fact that *thirdness* as a *mediation* by signs or *representation* of something to an *interpretant* is in Peirce's language something like an analogue of Kant's objective unity of ideas in a self-consciousness. But he holds that *thirdness* in Peirce's philosophy remains a conception of an abstract logical structure and in so far cannot take over the function of the 'highest point' in a transcendental deduction. Peirce did not realize – according to von Kempski – that 'the necessity of the possibility of objective knowledge is identical with the (thinking) I', and he is said to have rejected Kant's doctrine that 'the supreme legislation of nature' lies in our understanding (von Kempski, op. cit., pp. 60 f., 63, 65 f.).

It must however be stated that Peirce himself in plain contradiction to these theses has claimed for himself the 'Copernican step': so in 1871 he writes in his review of Berkeley, after having introduced his own theory of reality: 'Indeed what Kant called his *Copernican step* was precisely the passage from the nominalistic to the realistic view of reality. It was the essence of his philosophy *to regard the real object as determined by the mind*. That was nothing else than to consider every conception and intuition which enters necessarily into the experience of an object, and which is not transitory and accidental, as having objective validity . . .' (Peirce, 8.15).

And in full accordance with this claim of the 'Copernican step' Peirce in 1868 and in 1878 appeals to Kant's supreme principle of synthetic judgments, in order to answer with its help the question how synthetic judgments are possible. He says in this context: 'Whatever is universally true of my experience . . . is involved in the condition of experience' (ibid. 2.691; cf. 5.332 M).

How can these transcendental arguments be reconciled with Peirce's rejection of 'occult transcendentalism', quoted by von Kempski?

The answer is that Peirce's rejection of 'transcendentalism' does not refer to the idea of the 'highest point' of a 'transcendental deduction' but to those features of Kant's procedure which in Peirce's opinion are psychologistic and circular.[4]

The investigations of M. Murphey in particular have shown that Peirce, in his long study and transformation of Kant, which resulted in the 'New List of Categories' of 1868, had the transcendental deduction of the categories just as much before his eyes as the metaphysical deduction.

As to von Kempski's criticism of Peirce's having neglected the transcendental synthesis of apperception, one may find equivalent counter-evidence in Peirce's reproaching Kant because his method 'does not display that direct reference to the *unity of consistency* which alone gives validity to the categories'.[5]

The phrase 'unity of consistency', used by Peirce in his criticism, shows the direction in which Peirce himself is searching for the 'highest point' of his 'transcendental deduction': His concern, it is true, is not with the objective unity of ideas[6] in a *self-consciousness* but rather with the semantical consistency of an intersubjectively valid *representation* of the objects by signs, which consistency, according to Peirce, can only be decided about in the dimension of sign-*interpretation* (afterwards called *pragmatic* by C. Morris). The young Peirce characterizes the unity of consistency he was searching for as follows in 1866: 'We find that every judgement is subject to a condition of consistency: its elements must be capable of being brought to a unity. This consistent unity since it belongs to all our judgements may be said to belong to us. Or rather since it belongs to the judgements of all mankind, we may be said to belong to it.'[7]

This early utterance shows that the 'unity of consistency' Peirce was looking for lies beyond the personal unity of self-consciousness, which is Kant's 'highest point'. Peirce confirms this in 1868 in his semiotical *Theory of Mind*, where he says:

> Consciousness is a vague term . . . consciousness is sometimes used to signify the *I think*, or unity in thought; but the unity is nothing but consistency, or the recognition of it. Consistency belongs to every sign, so far as it is a sign . . . there is no element whatever of man's consciousness which has not something corresponding to it in the word . . . the word or sign which man uses *is* the man himself . . . the organism is only an instrument of thought. But the identity of a man consists in the *consistency* of what he does and thinks . . .

From here Peirce comes immediately to the decisive conclusion which leads to the 'highest point' in the sense of a *semiotical unity of consistent interpretation*: He says: 'the existence of thought now depends on what is to be hereafter; so that it has only a potential existence, dependent on the future thought of the *community*' (5.313–16).

But how should it be possible to deduce from the 'highest point' which is suggested here the *categories* or even the *principles* of possible *experience*? Do not Peirce's formulations bear the appearance of being prepossessed by a pre-Kantian rationalism which confuses the formal logic of language with the transcendental logic of the constitution of possible objects of experience?

This objection may be not without warrant if directed against the modern analytical 'logic of science', for example, against modern deductive theory of explanation set up in the framework of a formalized language; but it does not hold for Peirce. He by no means considers the formal logic of conceptual – or propositional – symbols as a sufficient substitute for Kant's transcendental logic, but on the contrary he initiates for this purpose, with the help of Kant's Copernican turn, his new 'synthetic logic of inquiry'; and he postulates in his quasi-transcendental semiotic, besides conceptual *symbols*, two other types of signs which are thought to make the transition possible from the stimulation of sensation and the qualities of feeling to conceptions and judgments respectively. But the real basis of this transformation of transcendental logic is provided by the fact that Peirce in 1867 performed a 'transcendental deduction' of the *three types of signs* parallel with the *three kinds of inferences* as illustrations of the *three universal categories* which are implied, as he shows, in the *sign-relation* (*semiosis*) as provisionally 'the highest point' of his 'transcendental logic' (cf. Murphey, ch. 3).

The *sign-relation* or *representation* can be made explicit, according to Peirce, by the following scheme of definition: A sign is something that stands for something in some respect or quality to an interpretant (5.283; 2.228). This schema implies, according to Peirce, three categories:

1 Simple *quality* without relations, which makes up the respect or point of view, under which something is expressed *as* something in its *suchness* (category *the first*, later called *firstness*). To this category corresponds the sign-type of 'icons' which has to be implied – as Peirce later makes clear (8.41; 3.363; 5.119) – in every predicate of a perceptual judgment in order to integrate felt qualities of the real world into the synthesis of a hypothesis which makes up the argument of a perceptual judgment.

2 The *dyadic relation* of the sign to its denoted object or rather objects (category *the second*, later called *secondness*). To this category corresponds the sign-type of 'indices' which has to be found – as Peirce later makes clear (5.287, 296, 352; 8.41 ff.) – in every perceptual judgment (for instance as a function of the *pronouns* and *adverbs*) in order to warrant the space-time-identification of the objects which are to be determined by predicates.

3 The *triadic relation* of the sign-function as a 'mediation' or 'representation' of something as something to an interpretant (category *the third*, later called *thirdness*). To this category corresponds the sign-type of conventional 'symbols', which is the subject or medium of the central function of synthesis *qua* the representation of something as something by concepts. But this *representation* by *symbols* would be 'void' without the integration of the function of *indices* and of *icons*, just as with Kant conceptions without intuitions are 'void'. On the other hand the function of *indices* and *icons* is blind if not integrated into the function of representation to an interpretant, just as with Kant intuition without conceptions is 'blind'. Indeed: only *interpretation* fills the *index*-function with meaning, say of the pulse or of a signpost as well as the *icon*-function of a model or a diagram or even of a picture. (The last point should be seriously regarded by the syntactic-semantic philosophy of formalized languages.)

But in order to show how this semiotical deduction of three

fundamental categories and of three types of signs may help to explain the possibility and validity of experience, it is necessary to co-ordinate with Peirce the three fundamental kinds of inference to the three kinds of categories and the three types of signs: that is to parallel *thirdness* and conceptional *symbols* with *deduction* as a rationally necessary agent, *secondness* and *indices* with *induction* as the confirmation of the general by facts in space and time, and finally *firstness* with *abduction* as the synthetic cognition of new qualities of suchness.

(This characteristic complementation of the analytic logic of deduction by a synthetic logic of induction and abduction or hypothesis was also in the sixties of the nineteenth century brought about by a criticism of Kant's treatise *Die falsche Spitzfindigkeit der vier syllogistischen Figuren*. At this time indeed Peirce was already convinced by Duns Scotus that the study of the syllogism had to precede the study of the forms of judgment since only in this way are the logically significant differences of the judgment to be found (cf. Murphey, pp. 56 ff.).

The discovery of *abduction* or *hypothesis*,[8] which is an inference from a given result of a possible deduction and a presupposed general premise to the contingent (minor) premise of a syllogism, proved to be especially important for Peirce's pragmatistic logic of inquiry: for *hypothesis* is according to Peirce the single kind of inference by which our knowledge is expanded in the sense of Kant's synthetic judgments of experience, which therefore, according to Peirce, may be interpreted as unconscious abductive inferences. But now, since every abduction or hypothesis presupposes a general premise and therefore has to be tested by induction, abduction and induction together provide the answer to the question implicitly asked by Kant, according to Peirce – to the question: how synthetic judgments are *possible* and *valid* (5.348 and 2.690).

Abduction or *hypothesis* explains *possibility* of experience in so far as it brings about the synthesis as a reduction of the manifold of sense-impressions and qualities of feeling to the unity of consistency in perceptual judgments (and also in explanations by law). Here in the first place the *icon*-function of predicates has to be mediated with the intensional meaning of the predicates as symbols; as, for instance, in the statement: 'This (which looks so and so) is likely to be a case of plague.'

86

Induction, on the other hand, explains the empirical justification of the general presuppositions of all experience, be they implicit in perceptual judgments or explicit in law-like statements. Here in the first place the *index*-function of language as the identification of objects here and now has to be mediated with the *extensional* meaning of the predicates as symbols of classes; as, for instance, in the statement: '*This* (or *here*) *is* a case of plague.'

But now, according to Peirce, it is possible to examine in a procedure antecedent to the actual verification or falsification of a proposition whether or not a proposition is a genuine *hypothesis* implying a general element which *can* be confirmed by *induction*. For this purpose one has to *deduce* possible experimental consequences from the general (law-like) meaning of the predicate by an experiment of thought with the form of an operationally conditioned prognosis. This very procedure which realizes the interdependence of analytical and synthetical phases within the logic of inquiry is explained by Peirce in his *Pragmatic maxim* as a method of 'How to make our ideas clear' (5.388–409).

Peirce now applies this method last but not least to the conception of 'reality' as it is used in propositions like 'The object of my experience is *real*, it is not a mere *illusion*'; and by an explication of the meaning of reality in the light of possible experience as analysed in his 'synthetic logic' he reaches the final and characteristic conception of the 'highest point' of a possible *unity of consistency* of our knowledge. For the sake of conciseness I quote a summing up of this 'highest point', which precedes by years the explicit foundation of pragmatism:

> The real . . . is that (more exactly: the object of the opinion[9]) which, sooner or later, information and reasoning would finally result in, and which is therefore independent of the vagaries of me and you. Thus, the very origin of the conception of reality shows that this conception essentially involves the notion of a *Community*, without definite limits, and capable of a definite increase of knowledge (5, 311, from 1868!).

In other words, the 'highest point' of Peirce's transformation of Kant's transcendental logic is the 'ultimate opinion' of the 'indefinite community of investigators'. At this point one may find a convergence of the semiotical postulate of the transindividual *unity of interpretation* and of the postulate of the logic of inquiry concerning the *validation* of experience *in the long run*. The quasi-transcendental subject of this unity is the *indefinite community of experimentation* which is identical with the *indefinite community of interpretation*.

From this last presupposition of a quasi-transcendental logic Peirce cannot, it is true, deduce the 'principles' of science as synthetic judgments *a priori* in line with Kant's intentions. But from his highest point of view he can make plausible that those absolute *principles a priori* are not needed and that the maintenance of those principles amounts to preserving a remnant of metaphysical dogmatism. This he can show just by appealing to Kant's supreme principle of synthetical judgments in connection with his own logic of synthetic inferences, for from his postulate of the ultimate opinion he can deduce as transcendentally necessary not any propositions but the universal validity of synthetic inferences *in the long run*; that is, of the *method* of induction and abduction.

This he did in 1869 and 1878 (5.341–52 and 2.690–3). In a way he has put Kant's *regulative principles* of experience in the place of Kant's *constitutive principles* of experience, on the assumption that the regulative principles in the long run turn out to be constitutive. Thus by shifting the necessary and universal validity of scientific propositions to the end of the (indefinite) process of inquiry it is possible for Peirce to escape Hume's scepticism without insisting with Kant on the necessity and universality of propositions which for the moment are accepted by experts. These propositions can, nay must, on Peirce's transcendental presuppositions, be conceived as fallible, that is corrigible, by hypotheses which come nearer to the ultimate opinion. (There is no doubt that most of the modern logicians of science prefer this fallibilistic and melioristic but not sceptic conception to the Kantian doctrine, which clings to the Platonic idea of science as *episteme*. Very similar to Peirce's conception is in this respect for instance the position of K. R. Popper.)

If one considers this position as a plausible and consistent transformation of Kant's transcendental logic of experience, then one will hardly be satisfied by the criticism which Murphey brings forward against Peirce's understanding of Kant in his great monograph on *The Development of Peirce's Philosophy* (pp. 25 ff.). Murphey's criticism is chiefly directed against the fact that the young Peirce in his Kant-studies does not accept Kant's 'critical' distinction between noumena and phenomena and in consequence cannot justify synthetical judgments *a priori* as principles of the possible experience of phenomena but takes his refuge with faith as a foundation of the principles. However, if one looks at this situation in the light of Peirce's final achievement of the transformation of transcendental logic, the approach of the young Peirce seems to be consequent and legitimate:

1 From his semiotical conception of cognition Peirce could not accept Kant's distinction between knowable objects of experience and things in themselves which are supposed to be thinkable as existing (and even as affecting the senses!) but basically unknowable. Our claim for cognition, according to Peirce, reaches as far as the truth-claim of meaningful hypotheses, for, on the other hand, for Peirce, as we have seen, there is no cognition which would not, by its very essence, be a hypothesis, that is, an abductive inference. Peirce's arguments against the very meaning of the conception of unknowable things in themselves – which I unfortunately cannot bring to the fore in this place – rank foremost among the strongest objections which have been directed against Kant since the days of Jacobi.[10] Still more convincing, in my opinion, is Peirce's positive transformation of the famous Kantian distinction, which takes into account Kant's legitimate motives without getting entangled in the nonsensicalities. Instead of laying down the difference between unknowable and knowable objects Peirce distinguishes between the real as the knowable in the long run and whatever may be the result of an actual cognition basically underlying to the reservation of fallibility (5.257, 310). The problem of unknowable things-in-themselves by this turn is transformed into the problem of infinite approximation, which, indeed, is a paradoxcal problem too.

2 But now the distinction between unknowable things-in-themselves, which affect the senses, and phenomena which are predetermined as to their formal structure by the mind (that is, Kant's transcendental idealism) is the precondition for the Copernican turn. How can Peirce appeal to the latter and nevertheless reject the former? The answer is: Peirce does not, as we have seen, refer the Copernican turn to the mind as the *faculty of the principles* but to the mind as the *faculty of synthetic inferences*. He therefore is entitled, in my opinion, to cling to Kant's central doctrine, that a transcendental foundation of the objectivity of science is necessary and possible, and nevertheless postulate that all scientific propositions as hypotheses may be corrected by experi-

ence, that is: by confrontation with the real here and now as brute fact and by perception of its pre-conceptional qualities.[11]

3   Finally, regarding the foundation of the principles of science in practical faith, which was criticized by M. Murphey, one has to state that this position of the young Peirce is consistent wth his final pragmaticistic transformation of Kantianism. Also the later Peirce could not accept the Kantian distinction between theoretical and practical reason which he apparently rejected back in 1861.[12] For, together with the distinction between noumena and phenomena Peirce has also to nullify the Kantian distinction between regulative ideas and moral postulates: the indefinite process of inquiry as a real enterprise of human practice, the progress and outcome of which is in fact uncertain, is itself the object of logic and of a moral engagement.

At this point Peirce's semiotical transformation of the 'highest point' of the transcendental logic reaches its *highest point* in what later has been called Peirce's 'Logical Socialism':[13] A man who wishes to proceed logically in the sense of Peirce's synthetic logic of inquiry has to surrender all the private interests of his finite life, also the private interest in *his* personal salvation (which is existential in Kierkegaard's sense) to the interest of the *indefinite community* since only the community has a chance to reach the ultimate truth: 'He who would not sacrifice his own soul to save the whole world, is illogical in all his inferences, collectively. So the social principle is rooted intrinsically in logic' (5.354 ff., 2.654 f.).

Unlike the pragmatism of James, who in his essay *The Will to Believe* of 1897 defends the subjective interest of the single man in a belief for his life just because he cannot wait for the ultimate opinion, the young Peirce considers his point of 'logical socialism' also as a practical postulate of ethics. For he expects – or hopes – that the social progress of science will bring about simultaneously a rationalization of human conduct,[14] whose 'habits' may be conceived as being analogous to natural laws and therefore may establish in the long run the 'concrete reasonableness' of the universe.

This last thought of Peirce's is also a consequent transformation of Kantianism; for Kant's categorical imperative in its most speculative version reads: 'Handle so, als ob die maxime deiner Handlung durch deinen Willen zum allgemeinen Naturgesetz werden sollte.'

Notes

1 Cf. K.-O. Apel, 'Der philosophische Hintergrund der Entstehung des Pragmatismus bei C. S. Peirce', in C. S. Peirce, *Schriften I*, Frankfurt, 1967; and K.-O. Apel, 'Peirce's Denkweg vom Pragmatismus zum Pragmatizismus', in C. S. Peirce, *Schriften II*, Frankfurt, 1970. Both introductions were reprinted under the title *Der Denkweg von Charles S. Peirce*, Frankfurt, 1975.

2 Quotations of Peirce are, as usual, from *Collected Papers*, vols. 1–6 (ed. C. Hartshorne and P. Weiss), Cambridge, Mass., 1931–35; 2nd ed., 1960, vols. 7–8 (ed. A. W. Burks), 1958; 2nd ed., 1960, as for example: CP, 5.263 = Collected Papers, vol. 5, paragraph 263.

3 Peirce had discovered the later so-called *propositional functions* under the title *Rhemata*, cf. CP, 3,420. Cf. J. v. Kempski, *C. S. Peirce und der Pragmatismus*, Stuttgart, 1952, pp. 5 ff.

4 Thus the young Peirce writes in 1861: 'Psychological transcendentalism says that the results of metaphysics are worthless, unless the study of consciousness produces a warrant for the authority of consciousness. But the authority of consciousness must be valid within the consciousness or else no science, not even psychological transcendentalism is valid; for every science supposes that and depends upon it for validity.' (Quotation from M. G. Murphey, *The Development of Peirce's Philosophy*, Cambridge, Mass., 1961, p. 26.)

5 Quoted from Murphey, op. cit., p. 65.

6 A decisive nuance of Peirce's interpretation of Kant is concealed by the fact that Kant's term *Vorstellung* is usually translated into English by 'representation'. With Peirce, however, such a translation already implies a semiotical transformation of this very conception.

7 Quoted from Murphey, op. cit., p. 89. Cf. Peirce, 5.289 n.: 'Just as we say that a body is in motion, and not that motion is in a body, we ought to say that we are in thought and not that thoughts are in us.'

8 Peirce understood this discovery as an interpretation of Aristotle. Cf. his *Memoranda Concerning the Aristotelian Syllogism*, November 1866 (CP, 2.792–807).

9 Cf. the formulation in 5.407 (1878!).

10 See for instance the following argumentation of 1905 (5.525): 'Kant (whom I *more* than admire) is nothing but a somewhat confused pragmatist . . . but in half a dozen ways the *Ding an sich* has been proved to be nonsensical; and here is another way. It has been shown (3.417) that in the formal analysis of a proposition, after all that words can convey has been thrown into the predicate, there remains a subject that is indescribable and that can only be pointed at or otherwise indicated, unless a way, of finding what is referred to, be prescribed. The *Ding an sich*, however, can neither be indirected nor found. Consequently, no proposition can refer to it, and nothing true or false can be predicated of it. Therefore, all references to it must be thrown out as meaningless surplusage, but when that is done, we see clearly that Kant regards

Space, Time, and his Categories just as everybody else does, and never doubts or has doubted their objectivity. His limitation of them to possible experience is pragmatism in the general sense; and a pragmaticist, as fully as Kant, recognizes the mental ingredient in these concepts.' Cf.5.452.

11 Cf. above pp. 84 ff. about the cognitive function of the 'indices' and 'icons'.

12 Peirce writes in 1861: 'Faith is not peculiar to or more needed in one province of thought than another. For every premise we require faith and no where else is there any room for it. This is overlooked by Kant and others who drew a distinction between *knowledge* and *faith*.' (Quotation from Murphey, op. cit., pp. 26 f.)

13 Cf. to this topic the dissertation of G. Wartenberg, *Logischer Sozialismus*, Frankfurt, 1971.

14 For a criticism of Peirce's 'scientism', see ibid.; also ch. 4 in this volume.

CHAPTER 4

Scientism or transcendental hermeneutics? on the question of the subject of the interpretation of signs in the semiotics of pragmatism

The problem: what is the appropriate interpretation of the pragmatic dimension of the sign function?

Following Charles W. Morris's foundation of semiotics,[1] it has become usual in the philosophical analysis of language and, accordingly, in the philosophy of science to distinguish between three aspects of semiotics and their associated disciplines: syntax or rather *syntactics, semantics* and *pragmatics.*

1 *Syntactics* deals with the relationships between signs. Since the logical structure of formalized languages can be reflected in them, syntactics marks the starting-point of modern, mathematical logic in language analysis and the philosophy of science (cf. R. Carnap, *Logical Syntax of Language*).

2 *Semantics* deals with the relationship of signs to extra-linguistic objects or states of affairs, which are represented by signs.[2] Consequently, it marks – amongst other things – the starting-point of a modern, empiricist logic of science which replaces the traditional ontological problem of truth (as represented by Aristotle's correspondence theory of truth) by the question – to be dealt with in a metaphysically neutral way – of how states of affairs are represented semantically by propositions or systems of propositions (cf. Tarski's semantic explication of the concept of truth).

3   Finally, *pragmatics* deals with the relationship between signs and their users, human beings. In the modern analysis of language and philosophy of science, it marks the starting-point of the Peirce-inspired semiotics of American pragmatism, which is primarily interested in the function of language, knowledge and science in the context of human life-practice.

It is no secret that in the course of the development of analytical philosophy, the focal point of interest as far as a philosophy of science is concerned shifted from syntactics to semantics and then to pragmatics. One can give numerous reasons or motives for this development. Here are the most important:

1   Within the analytical logic of science, i.e. within *logical empiricism*, the problem of the *empirical criterion of meaning* (originally termed the 'verification principle') could not be resolved by the construction of the 'logical syntax' or 'logical semantics' of the language of science. Given these abstract presuppositions, the problem proved to be that of the confirmation or falsification of theories by empirical scientists, which means that it was a problem of the pragmatic application and interpretation of theories or language systems.[3] Only in this pragmatic dimension of language analysis (that Morris offered at the right moment to logical empiricism at a critical phase in its development)[4] was it possible for the neopositivist question concerning the verification principle to converge with the pragmatic maxim of Peirce's clarification of meaning and with Bridgman's operationalist principle of definition and criterion of meaning. It should be added that in the field of mathematics even *constructivism*'s and *operationalism*'s critique of Platonism at the level of meaning converges to some extent with the empiricist critique of meaning in the pragmatic dimension of semiotic analysis. It was at the level of the foundations of mathematics and partially for the same reasons as in logical empiricism that the inadequacies of the original syntactic-semantic conception of science were revealed, e.g. the crisis of logicism and Hilbert's *Metamathematics* arising from Gödel's and Church's theorems. The *single* world calculus of a single formalized scientific language, the dream of neo-Leibnizianism, proved to be a Utopia and therefore the esoteric basic notion of a purely syntactic-semantic conception of science became fundamentally untenable. Russell and the young Wittgenstein had believed in 'the logic of language', which was both syntactically and semantically decisive. Logical empiricism,

however, was now compelled to abandon such faith in favour of a conventionalism of 'frameworks' which had to be tested pragmatically. At this point, it becomes evident that in abandoning its secret Platonic–Leibnizian metaphysics, logical empiricism also lost the theoretical basis for its critique of metaphysics.[5]

2 Within language-analytical philosophy in the narrower sense, i.e. in the case of Wittgenstein and his British pupils, the question of an adequate interpretation of language and meaning led away from the syntactic-semantic model of 'logical atomism' towards the radically pragmatic model of 'language-games', i.e. of the use of language in the context of rule-governed 'life-forms'.[6]

3 Within the analytical philosophy of science in the wider sense, e.g. in the Popperian school and in the Swedish school of H. Törnebohm, interest increasingly moved away from metamathematically inspired 'justificationism' towards the problem of the *growth of science* in the pragmatic context of a social milieu.[7] An extreme example of the accentuation of the pragmatic dimension in the philosophy of science is Kuhn's *The Structure of Scientific Revolutions*[8] which was inspired by the later Wittgenstein and American pragmatism.

4 But the above-mentioned problem of the social milieu of science points towards the affinity of the 'pragmatic turn' in analytical philosophy with other highly topical approaches in the philosophy of science, e.g. Bertalanffy's general systems theory, cybernetics, decision and game theory, Kotarbinsky's praxeology and the theories of action and behaviour in the modern social sciences.

5 Finally, one must mention in this context the affinity between the pragmatic turn and the *philosophy of science of the New Left*. It is obvious that a neo-Marxist conception of science which raises questions concerning the social preconditions (e.g. cognitive interests) and the practical functions of the sciences for society, can only enter into a dialogue with the analytical philosophy of science through pragmatics.[9]

A philosophical observer – or rather, an observer versed in the history of philosophy – who is confronted by this development cannot overlook a profound ambiguity in the 'pragmatic turn'. This is indicated, at least, by the manner in which *neopositivism*, partly in agreement with Morris, interpreted his semiotics (and *operationalism*). Initially *pragmatics*, unlike *syntactics* and *semantics*, was to be excluded from the philosophical logic of science and handed over to an empirical science (e.g. a behaviouristic psychology).[10] But one could counter such an attempt and argue with Peirce and consequently Morris against Morris that if *mediation* through signs (*semiosis*) is to be regarded as the triadic basic structure of a modern approach to the theory of knowledge and science, then it is obvious that the pragmatic relationship between the sign and its interpreter must be accorded at least the same significance and epistemological status as the syntactic relationship between signs, and the semantic relationship between signs and states of affairs. In fact, it emerges from Morris's justification of semiotics that *syntactics* and even *semantics* only become intelligible as far as their truth claims (in terms of the analysis of language or the theory of science) are concerned as abstractive considerations of partial functions of *semiosis* in general. It is pragmatics which analyses the whole function in whose context the results of the syntactic-semantic analyses of systems of language or science become meaningful. It is, therefore, only the *pragmatics of signs* that is able to make the modern *analytical logic of science* complete.

But if this is the case, the following question arises which throws some light upon the *ambiguity* of the 'pragmatic turn'. Can the pragmatic sign dimension, and this also implies the problem of human beings as the subjects of science, possibly be reduced to a topic of empirical science? Or should not this problem, as much as that of both logical syntactics and semantics – and precisely as a complement to these abstractions – be treated as a problem of the preconditions for the possibility and validity of the sciences and their languages?

At this point, one might object that in neopositivism (e.g. Carnap[11] and Richard Martin[12]) the attempt has already been made to develop *pragmatics* as an *axiomatic-constructive, formalizable discipline* that would be correlated with an empirical-descriptive pragmatics in the same manner as constructive semantics is correlated with empirical-descriptive (linguistic) semantics and constructive syntactics is correlated with descriptive (linguistic) syntax.

However, this conception of a constructive pragmatics which would be correlated with an empirical, descriptive pragmatics cannot answer the question that I wish to raise. For in the realm of the pragmatics of signs, it becomes clear that even in the case of syntactics and semantics the correlation between an axiomatic-constructive discipline and an empirical-descriptive discipline presupposes a condition which cannot, for its part, be made intelligible in the form of a correlation between axiomatic construction and empirical description. For description presupposes that the human subjects of language construction and description are able to communicate with one another[13] about the possible correlation between constructed and empirically described language. This communication is neither empirical description nor formalizing construction, but rather it is what makes both of them possible. In the case of constructive semantics, therefore, it leads back to everyday language as the actual ultimate meta-language of language construction and language interpretation.[14] Yet precisely this communication between the human subjects of science as sign-users should obviously be the subject matter of a self-reflective pragmatics of signs as an ultimate 'meta-science', so to speak.

The neopositivist philosopher of science would counter with the argument that an ultimate self-reflective meta-science of pragmatics is not possible and that communication between sign-users can only be the subject matter of an empirical social science. In what follows, I shall refer to this position as *scientism*. The crucial point of scientism lies in its belief that whereas philosophical self-reflection of the subjective preconditions of science is impossible, it must be possible to reduce the human subject of science to an object of science. For scientism, a pragmatically orientated philosophy of science is a social science of science as behaviour.[15] Thus *pragmatics* itself once again becomes the subject matter of a scientific language viewed as a *semantic* system. Moreover, since the *subject* of this scientific language can only be understood as an *object* and so on *ad infinitum*, scientism implies the reductive elimination of the subject of science.

Morris, who – as a *behaviourist* and in common with the neo-positivists – firmly asserts that the users of language and their sign-mediated modes of behaviour represent a natural object of investigation of the empirical science, just like the objects denoted in the semantic dimension of meaning, nevertheless emphasizes – as a practitioner of *semiotics* – that the *'interpretant'*, as the *rule which permits one to say of a sign vehicle that it denotes certain types of objects or situations* is not itself an object belonging to this set. The description of the pragmatic dimension cannot be applied to its own dimension at the time of its usage. Morris concludes from this that the final 'interpretant' (to be provided in a community of interpreters) is inaccessible to analysis.[16] Yet how does Morris himself know anything about the final 'interpretant', that which, as the precondition for the possibility of *designation*, cannot, in principle, be identified with a *designatum*?

The *problem of the final 'interpretant'* in Morris's writings is reminiscent of the *problem of the final meta-language* in constructive semantics. In both cases, logical empiricism's philosophy of science, which only recognizes the alternatives of construction or description but not the concept of a reflective-interpretative cognition, prohibits one from accounting for knowledge that one has, in fact, always drawn upon. If one inquires for a moment about the historical origins of this standpoint, one is referred to the semantic aspect of Russell's *theory of types*. As in the case of Gilbert Ryle,[17] it is obviously the acceptance of the semantic theory of types, which has become almost natural for twentieth-century analytical philosophy, that makes it impossible for Morris himself to reflect upon his recourse to reflective, interpretive knowledge of the subjective preconditions for the possibility of sign-mediated knowledge. In fact, unreflective recourse to such knowledge is demonstrated by the semantic theory of types itself, which claims to formulate a philosophical insight concerning *every* use of symbols in general, and consequently contradicts itself.[18]

Although the form of his attempt was paradoxical, the young Wittgenstein was the only person to reflect upon the question of the linguistic preconditions for the possibility and validity of the theory of types and consequently of the logical analysis of language itself. For Wittgenstein, the semantic theory of types implies that nothing can be said about the 'logical form' of language, since this would presuppose a self-reflective language.[19] Yet since, on the other hand, the 'logical form' of language is also the logical form of the (describable) world and therefore the real subject matter of (analytical) philosophy, the semantic theory of types, in its paradoxical representation in Wittgenstein's *Tractatus logico-philosophicus*, implies the dissolution of philosophy by philosophy itself.[20]

In Wittgenstein's writings it is quite obvious that the elimination of the question concerning the preconditions for the possibility and validity of the function of language and therefore of the analysis of language is identical to the elimination of the question concerning the subject of science. Furthermore, it is obvious that such an elimination also leads to a paradox:

5.631:   There is no such thing as the subject that thinks . . .

5.632:   The subject does not belong to the world: rather, it is a limit of the world.[21]

The first of these two statements provides the starting-point for the neopositivist (or, in a broader sense, analytical) *programme of a reduction of the subjectivistic-mentalistic-intentionalistic language of philosophy and the human sciences to an extensionalistic-behaviouristic 'thing language'*.[22] The second statement, however, describes a paradoxical limiting case of that position which will be described below as an *alternative to the scientistic reduction of the subject of science* to an object of science. In the *Tractatus*, Wittgenstein not only implicitly suggested[23] that this position was the presupposition for his transformation of the critique of knowledge into the critique of language, but also he makes explicit reference to it when he says of the logic of language, and therefore of the describable world, that:

6.13:   . . . Logic is transcendental.

In what follows, however, the *transcendental philosophical alternative to scientism* will not be developed from the young Wittgenstein, but rather as an *answer to the question concerning the subject of the pragmatic dimension of the sign function* or of science. The problem of the subject in pragmatic semiotics differs from the limiting problematic of the subject of pure language in the *Tractatus* since, in the former case, the subject of interpretation cannot contract to 'a point without extension', such that there only remains 'the reality co-ordinated with it'.[24] Rather, the subjects of the pragmatic dimension of the sign function must be taken into account in a very striking, anthropologically and socio-historically comprehensible sense as the precondition of the possibility for the perspectivistic interpretation of reality 'as something'. Contrary to the stipulations of the *Tractatus*, communication between these subjects does not simply amount to an exchange of information about what is the case[25] but primarily it attempts to secure a pre-understanding as to how one can interpret the world, i.e. how one can assess the world, and evaluate it as something with regard to human needs, interests and goals. In view of this striking, 'empirically' comprehensible problem of the subject in the pragmatics of signs, the problem of a transcendental philosophical alternative to scientism indeed becomes more complicated. Is it not plausible to reduce the subject of science to an object of science, if – as indicated above – it is historically and sociologically comprehensible as the subject of the pragmatic dimension of the sign function?

In reply to this question, Kant's *model of transcendental philosophy* permits only one alternative that is compatible with Wittgenstein's answer. The subject of science as something that can be experienced must either be subsumed under the categories of natural scientific objectivation – especially the category of causality – or it cannot be discussed at all in terms of what can be experienced. In other words, even for Kant the subject of science as such constitutes the 'limit of the world'. In the history of philosophy, a third reply to the question of the human, historical and social subject of science has been formulated only by the tradition of *objective idealism*. This philosophical tradition which was prefigured by Leibniz and Herder was most clearly expressed in Hegel's *conception of 'objective mind'*. Dilthey and others rediscovered it and considered it to be, to some extent, the *implicit philosophy of the hermeneutic, interpretative human sciences*. In short, the representatives of this tradition believe that the subject of cognition not only experiences what is other than himself – as a world that is describable and explicable externally – but also experiences himself in reflexive contemplation and in the other (at least in the other person, in his words and actions). By virtue of its speculative, dialectical concept of the identity of subject and object, *objective idealism* combines experience in the sense of *hermeneutic understanding* with *transcendental reflection*, and sets both in opposition to scientific empiricism in the sense of scientism.

From what we have said above about the characteristic features of the pragmatic dimension of the sign function, the dimension of the 'interpretant' and the 'interpreter', it is evident that a transcendental, philosophical interpretation of this dimension must not only have recourse to Kant but also, in some form, to the objective idealist tradition of the hermeneutic human sciences. I shall therefore refer to the alternative to scientistic pragmatics, that is, the behaviouristic reduction of the subject of science as *transcendental hermeneutics*. The central question of the present study runs as follows: *Are there any starting-points in pragmatic semiotics for a non-scientistic, transcendental hermeneutic reply to the question concerning the subject of the sign function?*

To elucidate this question we shall have recourse to the founder of semiotic pragmatism, Charles S. Peirce (1839–1914), who still considered himself to be a Kantian[26] and who, especially in his later cosmology of evolution, sought to revitalize Schelling's and Hegel's objective idealism.[27]

Peirce's semiotic transformation of transcendental philosophy: the real but unbounded community of experiment and interpretation and interpretation as the transcendental subject of the sign function and of science

The discovery of the pragmatic dimension of the sign function and consequently of sign-mediated knowledge can be traced back to Peirce's semiotics, his doctrine of categories and relational logic.[28] Its crucial point lies in the recognition that *cognition, as a sign-mediated function, is a triadic relationship that cannot be reduced to a dyadic relationship*, as is possible in the case of all *observable* reactions in the object world. What is essential to cognition is not the actual reaction of an object in the world towards another (the category of 'secondness'), but rather the interpretation of something *as* something which must be mediated through signs (the category of 'thirdness'). All the basic elements of the triadic relationship must be present, otherwise the cognitive function would be deprived of its basis. Amongst other things, this means that cognition can be reduced neither to the relation-free givenness of mere sense data (classical positivism, especially that of Ernst Mach), nor to a dyadic subject-object relationship (which merely elucidates the resistance experienced when the self clashes with a non-self), nor to dyadic relationship between theories and facts in the sense of semantics (logical positivism), although – according to Peirce – all this must be included. Nor can cognition be understood as the bare mediation through concepts as in *Kant's transcendental synthesis of apperception.*

This shortcoming of Kant's critique of reason, which had already been sensed by the fathers of German philosophy of language, Hamann, Herder and Wilhelm von Humboldt, could in fact be rectified in the development of neo-Kantianism by Ernst Cassirer who, in his *Philosophy of Symbolic Forms*, to some extent incorporated the sign function into the transcendental synthesis of apperception. Neo-Kantianism emerged at the same time as American pragmatism, but its *semiotic transformation of transcendental philosophy* differs from Peirce's conception in that – despite its semiotic embodiment of the mediating function of cognition – it leaves the Kantian presupposition of a transcendental cognitive idealism unaltered as far as this mediated subject-object relationship is concerned. In this respect, Peirce's semiotic transformation of Kantianism is far more radical. He draws three consequences for the foundations of philosophy from the triple sign relationship:

1 There can be no knowledge of something as something without a *real sign mediation on the basis of material sign vehicles.* In Peirce's opinion this includes not only the conventional conceptual 'symbols' of language, but also the unconventional, or not merely conventional, 'indices' and 'icons'. On the one hand, these guarantee the situational reference of speech or its capacity for aesthetic expression and depiction of structures. On the other, they enable human beings to integrate, to some extent, causal connections and relationships of similarity in nature and technology – instruments and models – into the sign function of language, and therefore into the function of cognition. Peirce maintains that, as a result, the conventional language of conceptual 'symbols' can be fixed in the 'here' and 'now' of the situation on the basis of the identifiable objects and perceptible qualities of the world. On the other hand, we can understand extra-linguistic nature as a set of sign references for us and, in addition – by way of a privative analogy to the symbol-mediated semiotic process – as an objective semiotic process.[29] This concretization of the mediating function of cognition by that of the sign function contains the *semiotic* transformation of epistemology in the narrower sense.

2 The sign can have no representational function for a consciousness without the presupposed *existence* of a *real world* which, in principle, must be thought of as being representable, and that means *knowable*, in various respects. In Peirce's view, the negation of the existence of the real as a member of the triadic relationship as practised by epistemological idealism, or the negation of its fundamental cognizability as in Kant's hypothesis concerning the thing-in-itself, destroys an essential presupposition of the semiotically

conceived cognitive function. In order to be meaningful, the concepts of error, appearance, illusion, mere contention, etc., all presuppose the existence of something real that is knowable. Kant's distinction between what is real and knowable as mere appearance on the one hand and the thing-in-itself on the other, which is in principle not knowable but only conceivable, overlooks the fact that cognition, when understood semiotically, stretches as far as the establishment of meaningful hypotheses whose truth is open to confirmation. To this extent, the assertion that an unknowable thing-in-itself exists is intended to be accepted as knowledge. According to Peirce, however, such an assumption is a self-contradictory hypothesis, since it defines what is actually the object of cognition as unknowable. In Peirce's view, only the distinction between what is *knowable* in the long run and what is actually *known* can be meaningful.[30] This distinction corresponds to *fallibilism* and *critical conventionalism* which concedes to human knowledge merely provisional validity.

This standpoint of *'sense-critical realism' (sinnkritischer Realismus)*[31] reveals the consequence of the semiotic transformation of the *critique of knowledge*. Like Wittgenstein and the neopositivists, it replaces Kant's concept of questions that are unanswerable in principle since they are excessive with the meaningless questions without, however, declaring that all metaphysics is meaningless.

3 There can be no representation of something as something by a sign without *interpretation by a real interpreter*.

Peirce's more detailed definition of this third member of the sign relationship, which is also his *answer to the question of the subject of science*, demonstrates most clearly to what extent semiotic pragmatism, on the one hand, as an epistemology based on a triadic relationship, can be grouped together with transcendental philosophy, and on the other hand, to what extent it remodels the latter so that the naturalistic-behaviouristic, reductionist tendency of popular pragmatism becomes intelligible.

Primarily, the semiotic transformation of the concept of knowledge requires a real subject of sign usage that must replace pure consciousness. On the other hand, this replacement of object-consciousness by sign interpretation necessitates the transcendence of all finite subjectivity through the cognitive process *qua* interpretative process. In 1868 Peirce wrote:[32]

There is no exception . . . to the law that every thought-sign is

> translated or interpreted in a subsequent one, unless it be that
> all thought comes to an abrupt and final end in death.

Ultimately, even the *sense-critical* definition of what is *real* as what
is *knowable* requires the transcendence of every finite cognitive
subject. In Peirce's view, the real as such and as a whole must be
considered unknowable in terms of a finite consciousness and the
latter's capacities for conceiving of the world. In fact, Peirce
postulates that the real which can only be meaningfully conceived of
as what is to be known and what is knowable, can at no point in time
actually be known in a definite sense. This would imply that the
category of *thirdness*, which relates what is general in the concept or
law to the infinite process of interpretation, is reduced to the category of *secondness*, which is valid for finite facts. As early as 1868,
Peirce found the answer to the question raised here concerning the
subject of the semiotically conceived cognitive process. Peirce
formulated the idea of a 'community without definite limits, and
capable of a definite increase of knowledge'.[33]

Since Peirce, unlike Kant, no longer believes that he can deduce
the objectivity and necessity of individual scientific empirical judgments transcendentally, although he still believes this to be possible
in the long run, as far as the objectivity of scientific inference is
concerned,[34] he has to replace Kant's ultimate presupposition and
'highest point', namely, the *transcendental synthesis of apperception,
by the postulate of an 'ultimate opinion'* upon which, after a sufficiently lengthy research process, the unlimited community of scholars
would agree.

Peirce had reached this stage of the semiotic transformation of
transcendental philosophy prior to the establishment of *pragmatism*,
which first emerged in the review of Berkeley (1871),[35] and then in
the unpublished Logic of 1872-3.[36] Despite the realistic concretization
of the problem of knowledge which develops even at this point,[37]
the logical structure of his thought shows that the question concerning
the subject of science should not be reduced in a naturalistic manner.
Whilst it is true that a real community is postulated as the subject,
and cognition is not exclusively understood as a function of consciousness but rather primarily as a real, historical process of
interpretation, both the sense-critical definition of reality and truth
as well as the justification of the necessary validity of synthetic
procedures of inference in the research process, are not made with

recourse to the actual, empirically describable function of cognition in the actual community. Rather, they are made with reference to the convergence of processes of inference and interpretation in the unlimited community – a convergence that must be postulated as normative. The *consensus* postulated with the aid of a critique of meaning guarantees *the objectivity of knowledge*, and replaces Kant's transcendental 'consciousness as such'. In fact, it functions as a regulative principle which, as an ideal of the community, must first be realized in and by the real community. Moreover, the uncertainty concerning the actual attainment of the goal must be replaced by an ethical principle of engagement and hope:[38] this is Peirce's principle of 'logical socialism'.[39] In this principle, the problem of a dialectical mediation between theoretical and practical reason is expressed for the first time in Peirce's writings, but the envisaged mediation is suggested in such a manner that there can be no doubt about its transcendental-philosophical normative character.

This seems to alter with the establishment of *pragmatism*, especially in the famous essays 'The Fixation of Belief' and 'How to Make Our Ideas Clear' (1877–8) which were subsequently popularized by William James. Here the process of inference and interpretation of sign-mediated cognition is embedded in the life-process of feedback-monitored behaviour. The aim of this process no longer seems to be the establishment of a consensus concerning truth in the unlimited community of investigators but merely that 'settlement of opinion' which restores the security of behaviour that has been disturbed by doubt, through establishing a new habit of action, which is tested practically (experimentally). This also seems to be the direction suggested by the pragmatic concretization of a realism that is critical of meaning. This is expressed, for instance, in the following statement:[40]

> the whole function of thought is to produce habits of action . . .
> To develop its meaning, we have, therefore, simply to
> determine what habits it produces, for what a thing means is
> simply what habits it involves.

There can be no doubt that popular pragmatism developed out of such formulations, as ultimately did Morris's semiotic behaviourism as well, in which the meaning of signs is reduced to the describable behavioural dispositions that are actually mediated by the signs themselves. Consequently, the subject of pragmatic sign interpretation is reduced to an object of the empirical social sciences.

In a sense that must still be elucidated, it is indeed possible to infer the (linguistic) meaning of symbols in terms of the use of language from the average behaviour of those communicating. In so doing, one makes, however, several tacit presuppositions which cannot be grounded through descriptions on the basis of observations. Such a presupposition might, for example, be that the reactions of the receivers of a message are generally based upon a proper understanding of the meaning of the message, and in addition are answered in terms of a typical 'perlocutionary effect' which is produced by speech acts. Neither the correct understanding, in the sense of an 'illocutionary effect', nor the typical reaction – which is separated from understanding – in the sense of the 'perlocutionary effect' – is a natural fact, as Austin's and Searle's analysis of speech acts has demonstrated.[41] Furthermore, one presupposes that one is in a position to understand the rule that underlies the use of language and can test this understanding through communication with competent speakers. This is presupposed since it is impossible to ascertain whether one is dealing with linguistic behaviour at all on the basis of observations and their statistical evaluation. In other words, one cannot determine whether the rule which one applies externally to the observed data in such a case in order to 'explain' them linguistically, is the rule that is *followed* by the communicating objects *themselves*, such that by following this rule they could produce an unlimited number of sentences that actually (i.e. in the course of their normal behaviour) never occur.[42]

The reflexive discussion of the above-mentioned tacit presuppositions of the successful quasi-behaviouristic analysis of meaning reveals that, even as an analysis of general linguistic usage, such an analysis is unable to reduce the meaning of symbols to observable modes of behaviour. Even the detached quasi-objective analysis of linguistic usage can only be regarded, in terms of the philosophy of science, as the limiting situation of estrangement within the framework of intersubjective communication. The 'pragmatic maxim' of the elucidation of meaning that Peirce incorporated within his logic of research is not, however, concerned with linguistic generalizations about language usage, but rather with a normative clarification of the meaning of symbols in a communicative situation. An instance within Peirce's lifetime is the fundamental crisis in physics which made a clarification of the concepts of space and time necessary. Obviously, meaning cannot be elucidated here by recourse to actual language usage or average behaviour because it is precisely the normal use of language – even, for instance, that of scientists – which could rest upon misunderstandings that must be removed.

Indeed, nothing was further from Peirce's intention when he introduced the 'pragmatic maxim' of the elucidation of meaning than to replace the understanding of the meaning of ideas by the observation or description of their actual consequences. Even the above-mentioned deceptive formulations reveal quite a different intention if one examines them more closely. Peirce writes, 'To develop its meaning [i.e. the meaning of a thought], we have therefore to *determine* [and not 'observe' or 'describe' – my emphasis] what habits it produces.' By the rash use of one word 'produce' Peirce does not mean what habits it 'entails as actual consequences', but rather – as the word 'involves' indicates, which replaces it in the next sentence – he means what habits it *would* entail for a correct interpretation according to a rule.[43] In the succeeding comments it is also made clear that the habits which Peirce equates with the meaning of an idea cannot be understood in the terminology of Hume or behaviourism as causally determined observational facts, but rather as rules which – in the sense of 'thirdness' – can mediate between our self-controlled, subjective action and possible observational facts: 'Now, the identity of a *habit* depends on how it *might* lead us to act, not merely under such circumstances as are likely to arise, but under such as *might possibly* occur, no matter how improbable they may be.'[44]

Even from these passages, which were written against the background of the 'normative logic' of research which was referred to as such from 1903 onwards, it becomes evident that in his semiotic pragmatism Peirce was not concerned with the reduction of meaning to the objective facts of empirical social science, but rather he was concerned with the *meta-scientific rules of the explication of meaning with reference to possible experimental experiences*. The understanding of meaning is not replaced here by the observation of experimental data, but rather it is related to possible experimental experience in a *mental* experiment.[45]

But at this point a difficulty seems to arise. If one follows Peirce and seeks to *define* the habits with which one could explicate the meaning of an idea with reference to possible experience, then one must have already understood, to some extent, the meaning of the ideas that are to be explicated. There seems to be a logical circle here, a circle familiar to us from P. W. Bridgman's semantic operationalism. As a result of methodological reflection upon Einstein's definition of basic physical terms such as 'simultaneity', 'length', etc., Bridgman formulated demands similar to those already established by Peirce on the basis of his semiotic pragmatism. Bridgman was confronted with the following problem: namely, that the meaning of concepts – a meaning that is to be defined by a 'set of operations' – must already have been presupposed in order to establish the class of roughly similar operations (the concepts of time and space, for instance, are understood, from the outset, phenomenologically, in that *various* classes of measuring operations are envisaged).[46]

But in my view this problem itself can be resolved if one considers not a *reductive* sense of the 'pragmatic maxim', but rather a *hermeneutic* one. Only those who, like Bridgman and the behaviourists, wish to 'reduce' meaning to either prescribable or describable modes of behaviour must adhere to a deductive logic, which is forced to see a *circulus vitiosus* if in order to determine conceptual meanings through modes of behaviour one presupposes that their meaning has already been understood. When meaning is clarified, however, with the aid of mental experiments that accord with the 'pragmatic maxim', it is by no means a matter of such a reduction but rather of the explication of a vaguely preunderstood meaning. This takes place when the imagination is allowed to anticipate possibilities in praxis and experience to which the meaning of the sign refers. Unlike the logically formalizable type of theory-formation, this method does not deduce states of affairs from states of affairs. Rather, it works towards agreement about the meaning of concepts which must be presupposed by every formalizable type of theory-formation. As a meta-theoretical principle, the 'pragmatic maxim' merely makes explicit in some respect that referential structure of concept-symbols which involves all understanding in the *circulus fructuosus* of hermeneutics.

Naturally, the hermeneutics of the 'pragmatic maxim' only represents the meta-theoretical (or meta-scientific) limiting case of a hermeneutics of the elucidation of meaning in general. It represents the illustration of conceptual meaning with reference to possible *experimental* experience. We shall return to this point. In his later works, Peirce illustrated the limiting case of a meta-scientific hermeneutics, which was contained in the 'pragmatic maxim', by if-then propositions in the form of 'contrary-to-fact-conditionals', and, in so doing, also distinguished his method of elucidating meaning by means of reference to the future ('mellonization')[47] from every empiricist reductionist theory.[48] The *counter-factual* structure of 'mellonization' provides Peirce with the opportunity for realizing the perspective of the normative logic of research even in his semiotics. Unlike Morris, he explicitly distinguishes in his essays on 'pragmaticism' (1905 ff.) between three types of *interpretants* of symbols: 'emotional', 'energetic' and 'logical inter-pretants'.[49] Only the first two classes correspond to the empirically (i.e. psychologically) determinable effects of the symbols upon the interpreter. In contrast, the 'logical interpretant' of a proposition, for instance, is:[50]

> that form of translation in which the proposition becomes applicable to human conduct, not in these or those special circumstances, nor when one entertains this or that special design but that form which is most directly applicable to self-control under every situation, and to every purpose. This is why he [sc. the pragmaticist] locates the meaning in future time; for future conduct is the only conduct that is subject to self-control.

In accordance with the above postulated rule for the possible attribution of meaning, however, the 'ultimate logical interpretant', which must break off, in practical terms, the infinite interpretative process in favour of a 'real living conclusion', is also for Peirce a 'habit' but one that is normatively prescribed:[51]

> The deliberately formed, self-analyzing habit – self-analyzing because formed by aid of analysis of the exercises that nourished it – is the living definition, the veritable and final logical interpretant.

A more detailed interpretation of Peirce's semiotic pragmatism reveals, therefore, that he also subscribes to the normative logic – which he had already established in 1868 – of the mediation of theory and practice with regard to the transcendental-philosophical goal of a consensus of truth in the unlimited community of scholars. Moreover, this teleological research process that is postulated by transcendental philosophy is regarded by Peirce the *pragmaticist* as the path towards a practical completion of the rationalization of the universe by means of self-controlled 'habit' formation. The subject of this habit formation, however, can no more be reduced to an object of the empirical social sciences than can the 'habits' *qua* 'logical interpretants' to which Peirce refers. Nor is it a pure consciousness as such as in Kant's (and even Husserl's) classical transcendental philosophy but rather a *real community of experiment and interpretation*, in which an *ideal, unlimited community* is simultaneously presupposed as a *telos*. This community can be *experienced* in a sense, as can its signs and actions, but not as an object of experience that could be described extrinsically and explained as an observational datum. Rather, it is experienced as the *intersubjective medium of communication* about the conceptual preconditions for the possibility and validity of descriptions and explanations of observational data.

The transcendental hermeneutic interpretation of Peirce's semiotics and the problem of the non-instrumental practice-relatedness of sign interpretation: the interpreting community as an interacting community

In developing Peirce's semiotics, Royce illustrated the *relationship between the meta-scientific problem of intersubjective communication and the scientific problem of cognition* by an economic image. In order to redeem the 'cash value' of an idea or hypothesis by experimental verification, one must first fix its 'nominal value' in the community of scholars through *interpretation*. In other words, man's *perceptive* cognitive exchange with nature presupposes an *interpretative* cognitive exchange between human beings – a kind of exchange of idea-values through translation.[52] In my opinion, Royce who, unlike Peirce, was not primarily interested in a meta-scientific theory of the elucidation of scientific concepts, but rather in social-philosophical theory of intersubjective communication in general, seems to have highlighted in this image a transcendental-hermeneutic presupposition of cognition which had hitherto hardly been reflected upon. I believe that he throws light upon the point at which the natural and human sciences are both connected and differentiated. This is a point which cannot be apprehended in a pre-semiotic theory of knowledge.

The *pre-semiotic theory of knowledge*, which must include Kant and classical positivism as well as Schleiermacher's and Dilthey's theory of human scientific understanding, can only reflect upon the problem of knowledge in the dimension of the *subject-object* relationship. Since such a theory is based on the unity and evidence of object consciousness and self-consciousness, whose methodological conception is solipsistic, it is unable to apprehend the fact that – as sign-mediated knowledge – the *subject-object* relationship of apperceptive cognition is always mediated through the *subject-subject* relationship of interpretative cognition. In other words, in the time-honoured tradition of nominalist epistemology that only recognizes in the sign an instrument for communicating what is already known, *language is neglected as the mediating instance of the cognition* of something *as* something. But neglecting language always implies *neglecting the intersubjective mediation of tradition*, which is connected with each interpretative application of language in perceptive-apperceptive cognitive acts. One notices perhaps that the interpretation of something *as* something includes the element of 'convention' alongside sensual and rational elements. But one does not register the cognitive character of this element as the interpretation of the meaning of linguistically handed-down word meanings or concepts, which must precede any subsumption of sense-data under these concepts. In reflecting upon the 'conventional' element of cognition, one only registers the accomplished decision of an isolated human subject in the interpretation of the data, but not the *achievement of intersubjective agreement* which is operative in every interpretative application of language. In short, one fails to notice that intersubjective communication *qua* mediation of tradition in a 'community of interpretation' is the transcendental-hermeneutic precondition for the possibility and validity of all objectively orientated knowledge (including pre-scientific knowledge). In my opinion, Royce deserves credit for being the first to draw attention to this relationship. In so doing, he was able to draw equally on Peirce's semiotic pragmatics and Hegel's insight into the dependence of self-knowledge upon the recognition by others. The two motifs intermingle in his 'philosophy of social loyalty'.

With his analysis of the relationship between 'perception', 'conception' and 'interpretation', Royce not merely indicated the direction

111

of a hermeneutic transformation of transcendental philosophy. As we have suggested, he also went on to pave the way for a decisive insight into the relationship between the natural and human sciences. To what extent was he successful?

Ultimately, pre-semiotic epistemology – one that is bound to the subject-object-relationship and is methodologically solipsistic – can only comprehend hermeneutic 'understanding', if it reflects upon such subject matter at all, as a method which is in competition with the scientific 'explanation' of observational data. It might regard such understanding as intuitive 'empathy' towards objective experiential data of a given class that can be internalized in the sense of empathetic reconstruction (*Nacherleben*). The limits of this framework are not basically exceeded by Schleiermacher's or Dilthey's hermeneutics. In fact, Dilthey specifically understood the objectivation of the spirit to be reconstructed in its 'expression' as a parallel to the observable objectivity of things in the domain of the objective natural sciences.[53] Given this starting position, it is not difficult for modern scientism to look upon the insistence upon understanding as a cognitive method as the irrational attempt to compensate for the difficulties involved in 'covering law explanation'. Modern scientism then opposes this illegitimate claim of the so-called 'human sciences' with the 'cup of coffee theory' of understanding, according to which empathetic understanding can merely fulfil the function of a psychologically and heuristically relevant facilitation of the discovery of law-like hypotheses in the service of explanation.[54]

In contrast to this theory, the transcendental hermeneutic interpretation of hermeneutics, as outlined by Royce, is able to demonstrate that 'understanding' cannot be understood as a rival enterprise to 'explanation' but rather as a cognitive phenomenon that is complementary to the scientific knowledge of objective facts. Both are included, in fact, in the sign-mediated knowledge of something *as* something: mediation between subject and object in the form of an interpretation of the world *and* mediation between human subjects in the form of the interpretation of language. Both modes of sign-mediated knowledge are *complementary* even in their origin, in the sense that they supplement each other and are also mutually exclusive.[55] This is what is revealed in the divergence between objectively orientated knowledge *qua* 'observation' and 'explanation', and intersubjective 'communication' within the 'community of interpretation', of natural scientists, which is implicitly conceptualized by Peirce and explicitly by Royce. Natural scientists cannot replace intersubjective communication by mutual observation and explanation of behaviour since even the implicit communication that is carried out in the form of the interpretation of language (in connection with the interpretation of the world) cannot be replaced by objective observation and the explanation of linguistic data.

Even someone – like the poet – who pays *great attention* to language as a medium in his description of the world is nevertheless far removed from *objectifying* language and *observing* it. Rather, he listens to language as he would to someone who has something to say.[56] Moreover, even someone like the cultural historian who interprets language as an expression or objectivation of the mind does not previously reduce it to an object of observation and explanation with which he would then establish an *empathetic* relationship in the service of explanation. His contemplative quasi-objectivation rests upon a methodological *estrangement* of the mediation of tradition that lies in the communicative situation. The sociologist and the linguist go further along the path of methodological estrangement without, however, being able to totally transcend the communicative situation in favour of observation and explanation.[57]

In my opinion, these reflections which were developed from Royce indicate that only a *semiotically* transformed transcendental philosophy is capable of comprehending adequately the origin of the hermeneutic question which is contained in the interest in communication that is *complementary* to the scientific cognitive interest. By positing the communication community as the subject of cognition – itself a sign-mediated function – such a transcendental philosophy overcomes the methodological solipsism of traditional epistemology according to which other human subjects and their communicative actions can only be conceptualized as objects of an isolated cognitive subject which can, at best, understand them through empathy.

However, in its pragmatic form, which is used by Royce in his economic image, Peircean semiotics – for all its merits – is limited in its scope, a limitation which – in a sense different from that previously assumed – must also be attributed to *scientism*. At this point, we must return to the fact that the 'pragmatic maxim' only describes the *meta-scientific limiting case* of a transcendantal hermeneutics *qua* method of elucidating meaning.

As a component of a normative logic of research, the 'pragmatic maxim' – as we have just demonstrated – is certainly not a formal-izable method of reduction in the sense of explanatory science. Nevertheless, as a *pragmatic* maxim it is related from the outset to experimental experience in the sense of science. Only in so far as the meaning of symbols can be illustrated by possible experiences – which can be gained within the framework of purposive-rational, feedback-monitored behaviour by interchangeable human subjects in experiments that are fundamentally repeatable – are the symbols in question (e.g. statements) identified as meaningful.[58] Conse-quently, communication can only refer to such questions as could be answered in the long run by an intersubjective, and thus objective, law-like knowledge. But since this knowledge – as the exploitation of the cash value of experimental results through the establishment of the nominal value of symbols in the interpreting community of scholars – must in turn be mediated through communication, Peirce seems to recognize no distinction between the process of experimental research in the natural sciences and the process of communication in the human community of interpretation. It would appear that the extent to which the meaning of all potentially meaningful symbols can be interpretatively elucidated is determined by the extent to which the community of researchers achieves an experimentally tested, objective knowledge of laws – and a corresponding techno-logical 'know-how'.

Royce abandons this scientistic framework of the problem of communication in so far as he is no longer primarily concerned with knowledge of – experimentally testable – states of affairs, but rather with man's self-knowledge. In his view, this self-understanding is mediated through mutual understanding in the 'community of interpretation'. Accordingly, Royce is the first person within the pragmatic movement to progress from the discussion of the inter-pretation of signs to the discussion of the hermeneutic problem of understanding intended meanings. Peirce, as a result of his con-centration on the experimentally-mediated *consensus omnium* concerning states of affairs, seeks to integrate man himself as a sign into the supra-individual inferential process of sign interpretation.[59] Royce, on the other hand, substitutes man as the subject of intended meaning for the sign in the semiotically analysed process of inter-pretation. In so doing, Royce applies the relational-logical analysis of the semiotic process, which convinced Peirce that interpretation was the paradigm for the category of 'thirdness', to the process of intellectual history and historical-philological knowledge. Royce believes that the *triadic structure of sign interpretation* reappears here in the *triadic structure of the mediation of tradition*, or rather in the triadic structure of the minimal 'community of interpretation' of three human subjects which transmits tradition. Of these three human subjects, one (A) must assume the function of the mediating interpreter who makes intelligible to a second (B) – or, if necessary, 'translates' – what a third (C) means – or has expressed. (It must be added here that the same structure characterizes the individual subject's thought: as a 'discourse of the soul with itself' (Plato) in which someone (A) communicates with himself (B) about himself (C), it has to integrate itself, to some extent, into the community of interpretation which is the agent of the mediation of tradition – a necessity which, despite the *a priori* triadic structure of the mind in a process of language acquisition and socialization that can either succeed or fail, must constantly be realized afresh.) Since this triadic structure implies an irreversible order of progression, in which the subjects cannot change place, Royce recognizes the ontological structure of historical time as lying in the logical structure of interpretation: 'Wherever the world's processes are recorded . . . the present potentially interprets the past to the future, and contrives to do so *ad infinitum* . . . we can simply define the time order, and its three regions – past, present, future – as an order of possible interpretation.'[60]

On the other hand, this structure of interpretation is also the key to the world of social relationships:[61]

> Metaphysically considered, the world of interpretation is the world in which, if indeed we are able to interpret at all, we learn to acknowledge the being and the inner life of our fellow-men; and to understand the constitution of temporal experience, with its endlessly accumulating sequence of significant deeds. In this world of interpretation . . . selves and communities may exist, past and future can be defined, and the realm of the spirit may find a place.

In Royce's philosophy of interpretation which, to some extent, translates Peircean semiotics from the pragmatic transformation of Kant into a neo-idealist transformation of Hegel, the supreme point of affinity between American philosophy and the German tradition of philosophical hermeneutics is reached.[62] After a psychologizing digression through Schleiermacher's and Dilthey's theory of identical empathetic reconstruction, the latter tradition also returns to Hegel's line with Gadamer's conception of the *mediation* of tradition.[63] It seems necessary at this point to confront the semiotic philosophy of interpretation with Gadamer's question concerning the relationship between hermeneutic 'truth' and the 'objectivity' of scientific 'method'. In Gadamer's view it is not sensible to measure the possible 'truth' of human scientific interpretation by the standards of 'scientific objectivity', which must be realized in progressive approximation. The ultimate reason for this lies in the fact that – unlike the subject of scientific description or explanation – the human subject of hermeneutic understanding does not have his paradigm in Kant's 'consciousness as such', but rather in Heidegger's 'existence' (*Dasein*) which is itself historical. This existence can derive meaning from the products of tradition only in so far as it outlines the horizon of meaning of its own ability-to-be (*Seinkönnen*) and having-to-be (*Zuseinhaben*). For Gadamer, therefore, the truth of interpretation is not one of progressive, methodical approximation to the ideal of objectivity, but rather one of the revelation of meaning which results from the 'fusion of the horizons' of past and present in the historical situation. This truth of the mediation of tradition which is appropriate to the *hic et nunc* in the sense of 'consciousness of historical reception' stems of course from an interpretation which overcomes the self-understanding of the past through reflection. But this truth must also correspond to a finite situational understanding and self-understanding and can, therefore, never definitely overcome the past. To this extent, the present can never understand the past 'better than it understood itself', but rather it can only understand the past differently.[64]

If one compares Gadamer's *existential-hermeneutic* position with *semiotic pragmatism's theory of interpretation*, then the *meta-scientific scientism* of Peirce's theory of interpretation is once again confirmed. Peirce no longer presupposes – not even for the natural sciences – a 'consciousness as such' as the transcendental subject of objective truth. Like Popper at a later stage,[65] Peirce grounds even the possible objectivity of natural science on the historical process of communication in the community of scholars. But he still assumes that this process of communication, if it were not disturbed, would in the long run produce the *consensus omnium* which corresponds in semiotic terms to the 'transcendental consciousness as such' and guarantees objectivity. Moreover, in view of the fact that – given the 'pragmatic maxim' – all communication about meaning is related to possible experimental experience, Peirce believes that even all understanding of meaning *qua* sign interpretation would attain its inherently possible intersubjective truth with the consensus of scholars with regard to their subject matter. Royce abandons this *scientistic restriction of the problem of communication* in favour of the hermeneutic mediation of tradition in the widest sense. But, like Hegel, Royce conceives of the mediation of tradition within the community of interpretation as the teleological process of man's self-knowledge. Nor is man's progress towards self-knowledge simply connected with its possible perfection by means of a regulative principle, as Peirce asserts, but rather it is guaranteed by a manifestly infinite, absolute system of the self-representation of the mind.[66] The result was that, on the one hand, Royce the Hegelian[67] was the first to demonstrate how the problem of pragmatic semiotics, which he had taken up, converges with human scientific hermeneutics, and that, on the other hand, Royce – as an absolute idealist – seems to be further removed from Gadamer's situational hermeneutics than does pragmatism.[68]

In view of this complicated situation, we shall temporarily ignore the relationship between Gadamer's post-existential hermeneutics and the reflectional certainty of absolute idealism. We shall attempt to determine more precisely *what prevents hermeneutics from subjecting itself to the regulative principle of Peirce's elucidation of meaning* – a principle which seems to secure the progress of interpretation in the form of meta-scientific objectivity.

It should be possible to find an answer to this question along the lines of an extended pragmatistic semiotics by considering an element of practical relevance which, in everyday conversation and in the interpretation of cultural traditions, makes possible an understanding of meaning that is not related to an experimental experience that can be reproduced at will by interchangeable human subjects. The simplest example seems to be a dialogue between two people in which they do not communicate with one another about states of affairs, but rather they mutually express their volitional intentions.[69] Here, one person anticipates the expected reaction of the other in the outline of what he says and thereby endows it with meaning. The other person will understand what he says in terms of what is to be achieved within their reciprocal relationship. Here, both parties initially elucidate the meaning of their respective utterances in the light of the expected praxis, that is, their 'interaction',[70] and also with reference to related possible experiences. This interaction cannot be repeated since it irreversibly alters the situation. The verbal utterances themselves are not the constantly citable vehicles of a universally valid interpretable meaning, but rather they too are components of the irreversible praxis of interaction.[71]

But it could be objected that this elucidation of meaning in the light of irreversible interaction can itself only be rationally validated in so far as it is mediated through a reference to possible purposive rational action that is valid for all people at all times. Each party in communication that is based on interaction has cause – to a certain extent – to elucidate for himself the possible rational meaning – and, in contrast, the possibly irrational intentions[72] – of his own linguistic acts and the expected behavioural reaction of the other person with the aid of a game theory of possible strategies for asserting one's will. This would reduce the problem of the interpretation of meaning – even in the case of the confrontation of wills that is related to irreversible practice – to mental experiments in the sense of Peirce's 'pragmatic maxim'.

However, this scientistic line of argument – in the broadest sense – overlooks the real point of a *dialogue based on interaction*. It rests upon the tacit, methodologically solipsistic presupposition that practical communication between human subjects can, or rather must, always presuppose the self-understanding and the corresponding will towards self-assertion on the part of the individual parties as instances which establish goals. Moreover, it presupposes that this communication can be understood as an attempt at mutual instrumental manipulation concerning the goal established through the will towards self-assertion. But, this very old, deeply rooted presupposition on the part of the traditional philosophy of the human subject is contradicted even by the empirically substantiated fact that a child only gains an understanding of itself and a corresponding orientation of its volitional intentions towards possible goals through language acquisition and socialization, which develops from contact with its mother. It is not, therefore, from the outset an ego-subject of possible objectivations and instrumental techniques (which might possibly also include the use of language), but rather it first attains this ego-subjectivity and the possible goals of instrumental techniques through identification with a role which falls to it in the community of interaction and linguistic communication.

In this *identification with a role* on the basis of linguistic communication and interaction there lies a *genesis of habits*[73] which cannot be reduced to the establishment of 'habits' in the sense of the 'pragmatic maxim' (even if this genesis alone can give rise to the behavioural dispositions which the later Peirce hoped would rationalize the universe in the form of an 'evolutionary love' that was directed towards the 'ultimate good').[74] Identification with a social role certainly stabilizes action based on reciprocity but not in the sense of the *if-then-rules of purposive rational behaviour* (perhaps by manipulating the other person), but rather in the sense of *internalized norms of social interaction* that are always presupposed in all purposive rational behaviour. Moreover, every word of the language learned in the course of socialization is not only and primarily an instrument for the individual participant in communication with whose aid he can attain the goal of what he says. It is always the embodiment of the institutionalized norms of social interaction and, in addition, the result of an age-old agreement about the normatively binding meaning of things and situations. To this extent, language as a whole has always been the 'institution of institutions' for a communication community, as the humanists, in their capacity as custodians of the secret philosophy of rhetoric, well knew.[75]

But as the historically constituted life-form of a given society, language is not only the normatively binding 'institution of institutions'. As a self-reflexive[76] medium of unlimited communication (especially of translation from one language into another) it is also the 'meta-institution' of all dogmatically established institutions. As a *meta*-institution, it represents the instance of criticism for all unreflected social norms and, at the same time, as the meta-*institution* of all institutions, it always represents a normatively binding instance which does not abandon the individual persons to their merely subjective reasoning,[77] but rather it compels them to participate in intersubjective communication on social norms as long as they maintain communication. But this almost binding force of critical communication as the institution of unlimited community formation *only* exists when the meaning of the linguistic signs that are used is related to possible praxis and possible experience. To this extent, the position of an expanded pragmatic semiotics is corroborated.

119

But the praxis referred to here and its relationship to experience is not that of experiments which can be repeated by anyone at any time. Rather, it is that of unique and uncertain interaction, i.e. the change (or substantiation) of the social situation. There is reason to believe that a language whose symbols cannot be explicated as meaningful, not merely with regard to a potential technical praxis of inter-changeable experimenters, but also with regard to the potential experiencing of historical interaction, completely loses its function. (This alone would be sufficient illustration for the fate of an idling language-game similar to the fate which Wittgenstein envisaged for metaphysics!)

On the basis of these reflections it ought to be possible to deter-mine more precisely the relationship between pragmatic semiotics *qua* theory of interpretation and hermeneutics in Gadamer's sense, and also to answer the question, which we initially raised concerning the subject of sign interpretation, in terms of a transcendental hermeneutics.

It is now obvious why a hermeneutics with a human-scientific orientation that conceives of the interpretation of symbols in the widest sense as a function of the historical mediation of tradition cannot commit itself to the 'pragmatic maxim' of the elucidation of meaning. From the hermeneutic perspective, this method of eluci-dating meaning (and similarly a correctly interpreted 'operationalism') represents the *meta-scientific limiting case of understanding of meaning*. It represents the attempt by means of an idealizing abstraction to relate all meaning to operations and correlated experiences which every isolated human subject can have at any time, independently of his historical interaction with others, and which – to this extent – are *a priori* intersubjective and this means they are also objective. One can detect here the basic desire of every progressive empirical analytical science to make the hermeneutic aids of intersubjective communication superfluous for the future by means of a definitive mode of agreement about meaning and thereby to establish once and for all the preconditions for the possibility and validity of logically and empirically testable theories. In parenthesis one might add that the ideal of this definitive meta-scientific agreement would be the abrupt replacement of historically constituted everyday language – including the experimentally proven language of science that developed from the latter – by a universal calculus language, which would be both guaranteed to be non-contradictory and experimentally and pragmatically capable of application. This was the original dream of logical empiricism.

Yet even this scientistic limiting case of the hermeneutic understanding of meaning is subject, as such, to the basic law of the historical mediation of tradition, according to which all elucidation of meaning presupposes a *pre-understanding* in the form of everyday language, to which all detailed explication is related through its conditions of adequacy. This basic hermeneutic law governs the already-mentioned 'circle' of the pragmatic-operationalist elucidation of formalized scientific languages, in the form of the reciprocal presupposition of a precision language – as a partial explication of everyday language – and the historical everyday language, with whose aid the constructed language must be interpreted as a more precise form of the scientific language and also related to experimental experience. Each successful pragmatic or operationalist elucidation of meaning remains, to some extent, a historical transition from the historical mediation of tradition of the interpreting community which belongs to the interaction to the historically indifferent clarity of the concepts that are related to experimental experience.[78]

But the adequate pre-understanding of tradition, which is constantly required, postulates that it is only meaningful to seek such a transition in the case of those concepts or expressions which are themselves open to an operational interpretation. Consequently, the attempt is made to clarify 'space' and 'time', for example, as basic concepts of natural science with reference to possible measuring operations, and the attempt is made to relate even the interpretation of earlier concepts in the history of science to the ideal of operational clarification and also to measure the intended meanings of their originators against this ideal. The same procedure would even be reasonable for dispositional terms relevant in social science such as 'intelligence', 'aggressivity', 'social prestige', even if agreement concerning the standards of operationalization in this case – unlike that of natural scientists – presumably implies a normative socio-historical engagement. Terms such as 'the standard of living', 'the stage of development of productive forces' or 'rule of law' in themselves certainly imply normative standards of empirical assessment, which are both dependent upon irreversible historical interaction and communication and, in turn, influence the latter. Concepts such as 'freedom', 'justice', 'happiness', 'the dignity of human beings' can, however, be demonstrated to be meaningful only through such a reference to moral praxis to which a historical community of interpretation is traditionally committed or to which it actually commits itself in emancipatory engagement.

It is evident that the subject of uncurtailed sign interpretation which one has to presuppose for the hermeneutic human sciences is indeed itself historical, as Heidegger and Gadamer have assumed. By extending Peirce's semiotics, one can claim that we are dealing with the *interpreting community of an unlimited community of interaction*. This community can trace itself back (i.e. reduce itself) to the community of scientific experimenters only in such cases where it is not a question of developing the world as history through morally engaged practice, but rather of simply converting law-like knowledge of the world as a cosmos into technical skill by means of experimental tests. This habitualized skill itself undoubtedly represents a kind of rationalization of the universe, to put it in Peirce's terminology. But the question as to if this instrumental rationalization represents the 'evolutionary love' of the 'ultimate good' must surely depend upon whether the historical human community of interaction can make it serve a human self-liberation towards a realization of the unlimited critical community of interpretation. The scientistic alternative to this perspective could consist in a self-stabilization of man, which is analogous to instinctual behaviour and is achieved at the level of cybernetic manipulation.[79] Ultimately this would not be controlled by any human communication community.

At this point, it seems that our reply to the question concerning the relationship between the hermeneutics that Gadamer has developed within the German tradition and pragmatic semiotics must be expanded upon. Initially, we had to defend the legitimacy of the existentially inspired hermeneutics against a scientistic curtailment of the problem of the historical mediation of tradition by means of the distinction between technical and scientific practice and experience, on the one hand, and the morally relevant practice and experience of interaction on the other. Now, from the perspective of Peirce's semiotics – which we have extended in the form of the historical community of interaction – the post-Hegelian tradition of German hermeneutics, including existential hermeneutics, must once again be critically placed in question. The following questions are addressed to Gadamer in particular, since he has summarized this tradition.

Is it sufficient to analyse the elucidation of meaning *qua* mediation of tradition as a situationally bounded manifestation of the 'fusion of horizons' which, as a 'game' that has been entrusted to the 'productivity of the age', will always produce different results of practical 'application'?

Is it sufficient to derive, as a quasi-methodological postulate,[80] from an analysis of the 'historicity' of understanding nothing more than the demand for the 'consciousness of historical reception'?

To put it more precisely: the interpreter, who becomes aware of his own function in the interpretative process in the sense of 'consciousness of historical reception', knows that he cannot avoid the 'application' of his understanding to historical praxis. Is he not forced, therefore, to relate his activity to possible communication in a community of action, i.e. to historical praxis?

Does he not require in this situation a methodologically relevant principle so that his interpretative activity is related to unlimited potential progress; and this ultimately means the ideal limiting value of an absolute truth of interpretation?

In my opinion, these characteristic questions of a normative logic of research in the spirit of Peirce's semiotics recur even if the idea of the progress of interpretation is not restricted in the narrow sense of scientistic pragmatism to the elucidation of meaning with regard to potential experimental experience and technological 'know-how'. If, instead of the scientistically restricted interpreting community of experimenters, the historical community of interaction is regarded as the subject of sign interpretation, then it appears that even here – regardless of the fact that the interpretation is now entwined in an irreversible manner with an activity which changes certain conditions – a regulative principle of potential unlimited progress can be discovered. In my view, the regulative principle in question is to be found in the *idea of the realization of that unlimited community of interpretation which is presupposed by everyone who takes part in critical discussion* (that is, by everyone who thinks!) *as an ideal controlling instance.* If one considers that the real communication community that is presupposed by the person critically discussing in the finite situation never corresponds to the ideal of the unlimited community of interpretation, but rather, is subject to the restrictions of consciousness and interest that are manifested by the human species in its various nations, classes, language-games and life-forms, then from this *contrast between the ideal and the reality of interpreting community* there arises the regulative principles of *practical* progress, with which the progress of interpretation could, and ought, to be entwined. The undeniable reference of interpretation to a human subject who is himself historical, and who also irreversibly changes conditions with his interpretation, need not therefore surrender normative hermeneutics to a relativistic historicism. Rather, it can itself be conceptualized as a dimension of possible progress at the level of intersubjective communication. If we were not entitled to conceive of a *practical* progress towards realizing that ideal communication community which we must anticipate counter-factually in all attempts at communicative understanding, then we must, in fact, conclude along with Gadamer that there can be no genuine progress in hermeneutic understanding either, but only 'understanding differently'.

As a methodologically relevant principle of hermeneutics, the ideal of unlimited communication which is relevant in practical terms for the interacting community would also remove a misunderstanding, namely, that contemplation of the historically accomplished application of interpretation must *eo ipso* play off a subjectively actualizing understanding against a historical, objective understanding of tradition.[81] For the creation of an unlimited communication community also includes the intentions ('text meaning' *and* 'author's meaning') of the spatially and temporarily separated communicating partners. Moreover, it is certainly an obligation on the part of a consciously applied interpretative method to make the actual application difficult, perhaps for the present, in the interests of an unlimited communication. (Here undoubtedly lies the specific task of the historical, philological human sciences which links them with the practical function of the foreign language interpreter, but distinguishes them in a hermeneutically relevant manner from that of the judge, the preacher, or the artistic 'interpreter' – e.g. director or conductor.)

On the other hand, the postulate of unlimited communication certainly compels us – in Gadamer's sense – to ultimately extricate the 'hermeneutic abstraction' from truth or from the ethically binding force of tradition, although this abstraction is useful in the narrower sense of methodological concentration. But this must not lead to an unrestricted rehabilitation of the authority of classical texts as is suggested by Gadamer, who seems to demand that the *interpreter* should seek the reasons or causes of failures in understanding (i.e. ultimately the causes or failures of possible agreement) only on his own side. If the 'anticipation of perfection' (Gadamer) with respect to the interpretandum, which admittedly must form the heuristic starting-point of every textual interpretation,is conceived of as an anticipation of the *truth* in the sense of a potential *consensus omnium*, then the fact that this anticipation leads to disappointment must also make it legitimate to reveal the reasons for the failure of communication by means of a critical understanding of the socio-historical conditioned nature of the *interpretandum* or of its author(s). In my view, the goal of unlimited communication – and this means that of the abolition of all obstacles to communication – also includes the legitimation to temporarily suspend *hermeneutic communications* with the *interpretandum* in order to turn instead to *causal* or *functional* 'explanations' of the empirical-analytical social science.[82] As an extension of hermeneutic methods, in the form of a *critique of ideology* and within the framework of the transcendental hermeneutic theory of universal communication, these methods are legitimate as long as the explanation does not become an end in itself but rather is *considered to be* capable of conversion into a reflexively heightened self-understanding of the communicating parties.[83] In the case of historical text-interpretation, the hermeneutic verification of this conjecture on the part of a critique of ideology cannot, of course, be provided by the authors of the texts that had been handed down. This is the task, as it were, of those who read these texts: to learn to understand themselves better than they did before through the exposure of compulsive motivations as obstacles to self-understanding in the authors of the interpretanda.[84]

It seems to me that this *regulative principle of an unlimited community of interpretation* which realizes itself in the long run both theoretically and practically does justice to Hegel's concept of understanding in an even more decisive manner than does Gadamer.[85] Hegel's concept of understanding consists in the reflexively transcending self-penetration of the mind as opposed to Schleiermacher's and Dilthey's postulate of the identical, empathetic reconstruction of other people's intellectual production. This holds true even if the goal of the whole process of reflexively transcending interpretation is transposed into an infinite future and its realization is entrusted not to a self-sufficient philosophy but rather to a philosophically-guided mediation between hermeneutic activity and the practice of interaction. If, however, it is possible or even inevitable to establish the regulative principle of an absolute truth of understanding in an unlimited community of interpretation and interaction, then it cannot be denied that it is possible, to some extent, even now for the critical self-consciousness – which does not regard itself in a methodologically solipsistic manner, but rather as a member and representative of the unlimited community of interpretation – to confront itself as empirical and finite consciousness with the unlimited community. Even if the dialogue of the unlimited community of interpretation cannot be replaced by the monologue of a single intellect,[86] philosophical reflection – with the aid of everyday language which is its own meta-language[87] – can, nevertheless, reach a level at which it can comprehend the goal in formal anticipation and represent it at any time. In my view, it is only by securing this reflective achievement that philosophy can recognize the claim of its own statements to general validity and meaningfully realize such a claim.

With this thesis we return, in conclusion, to Royce's reply to the question of the subject of sign interpretation. Royce was unable, I think, to mediate sufficiently between his absolute idealism of the unlimited interpreting community that knows itself to be in a state of infinite self-consciousness and the pragmatistic key notion of the explication of meaning through potential real praxis and its correlated experience.[88] The idea of an expectation of possible experience that is not based on repeatable, experimental operations but rather on interaction, which we have associated with Royce's idea of the historical 'community of interpretation', was first introduced into pragmatism by Royce's and William James's pupil, George Herbert Mead.[89] Mead, however, no longer based his approach on Royce's transcendental hermeneutic problems. He turned instead to Darwin's theory of evolution and John Dewey's 'naturalistic' pragmatism. His pupils (e.g. his editor Charles W. Morris) regarded him as a social behaviourist, despite the fact that he tended to make behaviour intelligible through the situation of intersubjective communication rather than by reducing the situation of intersubjectivity to objectively describable behaviour.[90] Mead's interactionism and social pragmatism became the secret philosophy of American social psychology. Royce's transcendental hermeneutics, on the other hand, fell into oblivion along with the philosophy of idealism. As a result, American philosophy produced no synthesis of the two approaches, which – as we have attempted to indicate here – could have complemented

Peirce's answer to the question of the subject of sign interpretation, and provided a definitive answer.

Notes

1 Cf. Charles W. Morris, 'Foundations of the Theory of Signs', in *Encyclopaedia of Unified Science*, I, no. 2, Chicago, 1938.
2 Following semantic pragmatism, the possibility of an *intensional* semantics, which would be independent of pragmatics, is not discussed here. In semiotic pragmatism the so-called *intensional* meaning of signs is dealt with in the pragmatic dimension under the term 'interpretant'. Peirce, who coined this term, says the following concerning the relationship between intensional meaning and interpretant: 'When we speak of the depth, or signification, of a sign we are resorting to hypostatic abstraction, that process whereby we regard a thought as a thing, make an interpretant sign the object of a sign.' (*Collected Papers*, vol. 5, Cambridge, Mass., 1934, § 4488.)
3 Cf. R. Carnap, *Introduction to Semantics*, Cambridge, Mass., 1942, § 38.
4 Cf. E. Tugendhat in *Philosophische Rundschau*, vol. 8, 1960, pp. 131–9, and K.-O. Apel, *Transformation der Philosophie*, Frankfurt, 1973, vol. 1, pp. 308 ff.
5 Cf. K.-O. Apel, 'Heideggers philosophische Radikalisierung der Hermeneutik und die Frage nach dem "Sinnkriterium" der Sprache', in *Transformation der Philosophie*, vol. 1, pp. 308 ff.
6 Cf. J. O. Urmson, *Philosophical Analysis*, Oxford, 1956; and K.-O. Apel, 'Wittgenstein und Heidegger: Die Frage nach dem Sinn von Sein und der Sinnlosigkeitsverdacht gegen alle Metaphysik', in *Transformation der Philosophie*, vol. 1, pp. 225 ff.
7 Cf. G. Radnitzky, *Contemporary Schools of Metascience*, Göteborg, 1968, Chicago, 1973.
8 Chicago, 1962.
9 This is confirmed for the domain of orthodox Marxism-Leninism by the writings of Georg Klaus (*Semiotik und Erkenntnistheorie*, Berlin, 1963; *Die Macht des Wortes: ein erkenntnistheoretisch-pragmatischer Traktat*, Berlin, 1964) and Adam Schaff (*Introduction to Semantics*, New York, 1962). For a largely neo-Marxist interpretation and development of pragmatics, cf. Utz Maas and Dieter Wunderlich, *Pragmatik und sprachliches Handeln*, Frankfurt, 1972. Further Jürgen Habermas, 'Vorbereitende Bemerkungen zu einer Theorie der kommunikativen Kompetenz', in J. Habermas and N. Luhmann, *Theorie der Gesellschaft oder Sozialtechnologie*, pp. 101–41.
10 Cf. Carnap, *Introduction to Semantics*, § 5, cf. § 39.
11 Cf. R. Carnap, 'On Some Concepts of Pragmatics', *Philosophical Studies*, 6, 1955, pp. 85–91.
12 Cf. R. Martin, *Towards a Systematic Pragmatics*, Amsterdam, 1959.
13 Strictly speaking, they should also be able to communicate with the

human subjects who use the language that is to be described. Cf. pp. 185 ff. and 200 ff. below.

14 Cf. Gerhard Frey, 'Das Residuum der naturlichen Sprache', *Methodos*, 3, 1951, and also the introduction to K.-O. Apel, *Die Idee der Sprache in der Tradition des Humanismus von Dante bis Vico*. Cf. also my criticism of the Carnapian standpoint of Helmuth Schnelle (*Sprachphilosophie und Linguistik*, Reinbeck, 1973) in my contribution to K.-O. Apel (ed.), *Sprachpragmatik und Philosophie*, esp. pp. 44–53.

15 On the difficulties of this position see A. Naess, 'Science as Behaviour: Prospects and Limitations of a Behavioural Metascience', in B. B. Wolman (ed.), *Scientific Psychology*, New York, 1965.

16 Cf. Morris, 'Foundations of the Theory of Signs', p. 34.

17 By subjecting his statements about the reflexive hierarchy of possible 'performances' to the semantic theory of types, Ryle denies them their claim to be valid with regard to 'performances' in general: 'The operation which is the commenting is not, and cannot be, the step on which that commentary is being made . . . A higher order action cannot be the action upon which it is performed' (*The Concept of Mind*, London, 1949, p. 195). Ryle fails to notice that in these very statements he has recourse to a judgment upon his own statements, even those that are 'commentaries'. But this judgment cannot, of course, be classified under the psychological *regressus ad infinitum*; rather, as a *philosophical* judgment it takes place at a *transcendental* level of generality. Ryle and Morris, by their treatment of the pragmatic self-reflection of speech or semiosis respectively, testify to the paradigm-function of the Russell/ Tarski axiom of the impossibility of self-referential speech in a language of scientific philosophy which should be free of semantic antinomies. I have recently tried to make plausible the thesis that this fundamental presupposition of twentieth-century analytical philosophy represents a confusion of *philosophical rationality* with *logico-mathematical rationality*. Cf. my essay, 'Types of Rationality Today' in Th. Gerach (ed.), *Proceedings of the International Conference 'Rationality Today'*, Ottawa, 1977, 1978.

18 Cf. also M. Black, 'Russell's Philosophy of Language', in P. Schilpp (ed.), *The Philosophy of Bertrand Russell*, Evanston, Ill., 1944, pp. 227–55.

19 Cf. *Tractatus logico-philosophicus*, §§ 3.332, 4.12, 6.13. For a more detailed interpretation, cf. my article 'Wittgenstein und Heidegger', in *Transformation der Philosophie*, esp. pp. 232 ff.

20 Cf. the last sentence of the *Tractatus*, §§ 6.53 ff.

21 Cf. also § 5.641.

22 On the insoluble contradictions contained in this programme, cf. H. Skjervheim, *Objectivism and the Study of Man*, Oslo, 1959. In addition, cf. K.-O. Apel, *Analytic Philosophy of Language and the 'Geisteswissenschaften'*.

23 For a development of these allusions in a Kantian sense, cf. E. Stenius, *Wittgenstein's Tractatus*, Oxford, 1960; and also my above-mentioned writings.

24 Cf. *Tractatus*, § 5.64
25 Cf. ibid., § 4.024.
26 Cf. the preceding essay in this volume.
27 Cf. on what follows my *Der Denkweg von Charles S. Peirce*, Frankfurt, 1975. As is usual the quotations refer to the volumes and paragraphs of C. Hartshorne and P. Weiss (eds), (vols 1–6), A. Burks (ed.), (vols 7–8), *Collected Papers*, Cambridge, Mass., 1933–61. For my criticism of Morris's behaviouristic transformation of Peirce's semiotical approach, cf. also my introduction ('C. W. Morris und das Programm einer pragmatisch integrierten Semiotik') to C. W. Morris, *Zeichen, Sprache und Verhalten*, Düsseldorf, 1973, pp. 9–66. (This is the German translation of *Signs, Language, and Behavior*, New York, 1946.)
28 For a detailed analysis of the connection between relational logic, the doctrine of categories and semiotics in Peirce's writings, cf. Apel, *Der Denkweg von Charles S. Peirce*. For critical consequences of a semiotical approach in First Philosophy, cf. my essay, 'Zur Idee einer transzendentalen Sprachpragmatik', in J. Simon (ed.), *Aspekte und Probleme der Sprachphilosophie*, Freiburg/Munich, 1974, pp. 283–326, and my 'Transcendental Semiotics and the Paradigms of First Philosophy', in *Philosophic Exchange*, 2, no. 4, 1977.
29 Cf. pp. 80 f. above. At this point the *objective idealism* of the later Peirce comes into play, cf. e.g. 5.119.
30 Cf. *Collected Papers*, vol. 5, para. 257: 'ignorance and error can only be conceived as correlative to a real knowledge and truth . . . Over against any cognition, there is an unknown but knowable reality; but over against all possible cognition, there is only the self-contradictory. In short, *cognizability* (in its widest sense) and *being* are not merely metaphysically the same, but are synonymous terms.' Cf. also 5.265 and 5.310 f.
31 Cf. Apel, *Der Denkweg von Charles S. Peirce*, pp. 51 ff. on Peirce's 'sense-critical realism'. [Translators' note: The term 'Sinnkritischer Realismus' was coined by Apel and has no real equivalent in English philosophical vocabulary. It has been translated throughout as 'sense-critical realism'.]
32 *Collected Papers*, 5.284.
33 *Collected Papers*, 5.311; cf. also 8.13: 'the catholic consent which constitutes the truth is by no means to be limited to men in this earthly life or to the human race, but extends to the whole communion of minds to which we belong, including some probably whose senses are very different from ours, so that in that consent no predication of a sensible quality can enter, except as an admission that so certain sorts of senses are affected.'
34 Cf. the article 'Grounds of Validity of the Laws of Logic' (1869; esp. 5.342–352) and the article 'The Probability of Induction' (1878; esp. 2.690–693).
35 Cf. 8.33.
36 Cf. 8.358 ff.
37 Peirce however still considers himself here to be an 'idealist' or a

'phenomenalist' of the Kantian type. Cf. 5.310 (1868), 8.15 (1871).
38 Cf. ibid., 5.354 ff.
39 Cf. G. Wartenberg, *Logischer Sozialismus*, Frankfurt, 1971. In this
   book, the parallel between Peirce's substitution of the absolute subject
   of philosophy – mediated through American transcendentalism
   (especially through Henry James senior, who was inspired by Fourier)
   – and the young Hegelian substitution of the 'infinite community'
   (David Friedrich Strauss, Feuerbach) or 'society' (Marx), is
   emphasized.
40 Peirce, *Collected Papers*, 5.400.
41 Cf. J. L. Austin, *How to do Things with Words*; J. R. Searle, *Speech
   Acts*.
42 In my opinion, this is the point at which Peter Winch's implicit critique
   of behaviourism in *The Idea of a Social Science*, ch. 1, coincides with
   Chomsky's critique in 'A Review of B. F. Skinner's "Verbal
   Behavior"', in J. A. Fodor and J. J. Katz (eds), *The Structure of
   Language,* pp. 547 ff.
43 In 1909 Peirce wrote the following to William James:
   The final Interpretant does not consist in the way in which any
   mind does act but in the way in which every mind would act . . . . 'If
   so and so were to happen to any mind this sign would determine
   that mind to such and such *conduct.*' By 'conduct' I mean *action*
   under an intention of self-control. No event that occurs to any
   mind, no action of any mind can constitute the truth of that
   conditional proposition (8.315; cf. 5.482 and 5.491).
44 *Collected Papers*, 5.400. My emphasis.
45 Cf. in this context, the decisive formulation of the 'pragmatic maxim' in
   How to Make Our Ideas Clear (Oxford, 1962): 'Consider what effects,
   that *might conceivably* have practical bearings, we *conceive* the object
   of our *conception* to have. Then, our *conception* of these effects is the
   whole of our *conception* of the object' (5.402). In a footnote added in
   1906, Peirce himself refers to the derivations from 'conceive' – which
   we have emphasized here – in order to allay the suspicion that in 1878
   he had sought to 'reduce' the 'intellectual purport' of symbols to
   something that did not possess the universal character of concepts (e.g.
   sense-data or actual actions).
46 Cf. A. C. Benjamin, *Operationalism*, Springfield, Ill., 1955, pp. 69 ff.
47 Cf. *Collected Papers*, 8.284.
48 Within the present framework, we cannot discuss how and to what
   extent the *counter-factual* structure of 'mellonization' enables Peirce to
   relate, on the one hand, the meaning of all scientific concepts to a
   transcendental framework of *possible* experience – following Berkeley
   and Kant – and, on the other, to replace empirical or transcendental
   idealism, which seems to be linked to the method of 'mellonization',
   since Berkeley or Kant, with sense-critical realism. (Cf. my
   introduction to Peirce, *Der Denkweg von Charles S. Peirce*, esp. pp.
   255 ff. and p. 309, n. 90.)
49 Cf. esp. *Collected Papers*, 5.476.

50 Ibid., 5.427.
51 Ibid., 5.491.
52 Cf. Josiah Royce, *The Problem of Christianity,* New York, 1913, vol. 2, pp. 146 ff. On Royce, cf. K. T. Humbach, *Das Verhältnis von Einzelperson und Gemeinschaft nach Josiah Royce,* Heidelberg, 1962, pp. 110 ff. and J. E. Smith, *Royce's Social Infinite,* New York, 1950.
53 Cf. W. Dilthey, *Gesammelte Schriften,* vol. 5, Stuttgart, 1958, pp. 317, 319, 328; cf. vol. 7, pp. 309, 217.
54 The 'cup of coffee theory' of understanding was, to my knowledge, first formulated by Otto Neurath (*Empirische Soziologie,* Vienna 1931, p. 56) and later developed by Hempel and Oppenheim (in *Philosophy of Science,* 15, 1948) and Abel ('The Operation called "Verstehen"', in Feigl and Brodbeck (eds), *Readings in the Philosophy of Science,* New York, 1953, pp. 677–88). For an attempt at undermining this whole approach, cf. my 'Communication and the Foundation of the Humanities', in *Acta Sociologica,* 15, 1972, pp. 7–26 (expanded version in *Man and World,* 5, 1972, pp. 3–37). Cf. also my 'Types of Social Science in the Light of Human Interests of Knowledge', in *Social Research,* 44, no. 3, 1977, pp. 425–70, and ch. 2 in this volume.
55 When Heidegger in *Being and Time* (S 31) considers the methodologically divergent 'types of knowledge' – 'understanding' and 'explanation' – to be 'existential derivatives', of the primary understanding that helps to constitute the 'disclosedness' of existence, and that receives its light from the 'for-the-sake-of-which' of 'potentiality-for-being' and 'having-to-be', then it seems to me, that despite the emphasis upon 'being-with', it remains trapped in an existential-ontological type of methodological solipsism. In my opinion, in the fundamentally grounded unity of understanding as the disclosedness of *my* being-in-the-world, the tension between the public interpretedness of the world mediated by language and my experience of the world – especially experience of the opposition of the external world that is discovered through the experimental approach of each individual child – is not sufficiently taken into account.
56 One might compare this with the later Heidegger's strange statements about a 'speaking of language' (cf. *Unterwegs zur Sprache,* Pfüllingen, 1959, pp. 254 ff.). The platonic Socrates calls the rhapsodes as interpreters of the poets 'ἑρμηνέων ἑρμηνῆς' (Ion 535a) and the poets themselves 'ἑρμηνῆς . . . τῶν θεῶν' (Ion 534e). Hölderlin writes, 'Man has experienced a great deal,/Named many of the celestial beings,/Since we are a discourse/And *can hear from one another*' (my italics). In my opinion, this last version comes closest to the truth.
57 Cf. n. 42 above on Winch's and Chomsky's critique of behaviourism.
58 In his discussion of Peirce in *Knowledge and Human Interests,* Habermas has pointedly revealed this scientific restriction of the referential horizon of the 'pragmatic maxim' as the 'transcendental framework of instrumentalism'. However, Peirce is also familiar with the explication of meaning of a historical statement through reference to a possible unique verification in the future. In his first published

definition of pragmatism in Baldwin's *Dictionary of Philosophy and Psychology*, 1902, he seeks a 'still higher grade of clearness of thought', than the 'pragmatic maxim' can offer him. This would lie in the consideration 'that the only ultimate good to which the practical facts to which it [sc. the pragmatic maxim] directs attention can subserve is to further the development of concrete reasonableness' (5.3). On the conflict between instrumentalism and ethics or the metaphysics of teleological evolution in Peirce's later writings, cf. my introduction to Peirce, *Der Denkweg von Charles S. Peirce*, pp. 155 ff.

59 This was expressed in very crass terms in an early essay:
> For, as the fact that every thought is a sign, taken in conjunction with the fact that life is a train of thought, proves that man is a sign; so, that every thought is an *external* sign, proves that man is an external sign . . . Now the organism is only an instrument of thought. But the identity of a man consists in the consistency of what he does and thinks . . . The individual man, since his separate existence is manifested only by ignorance and error, so far as he is anything apart from his fellows, and from what he and they are to be, is only a negation (5.314–17).

60 Royce, *The Problem of Christianity,* vol. 2, pp. 146 f.
61 Ibid., pp. 160 f.
62 Humbach, *Das Verhältnis von Einzelperson und Gemeinschaft nach Josiah Royce,* p. 111, is unable to see any connection between Royce and his German contemporary Dilthey.
63 On the relationship between Gadamer and Hegel, see also my review of *Truth and Method* in *Hegelstudien,* vol. 2, 1963, pp. 314–22. In addition, see my 'Reflexion und materielle Praxis', in *Transformation der Philosophie,* vol. 2, pp. 9–27.
64 H.-G. Gadamer, *Truth and Method,* London, 1975, p. 263.
65 This statement has been invalidated (overtaken) in a sense, since Popper has grounded the possible objectivity of knowledge on the quasi-Platonic realm of a 'Third world'. Cf. his *Objective Knowledge: an Evolutionary Approach,* Oxford, 1972, chs 3 and 4.
66 On one occasion, Royce illustrates the theoretical possibility of such a system by a map which also depicts itself – which depicts itself, etc., *ad infinitum*. He compares self-consciousness with such a map. (Cf. 'The One, the Many and the Infinite', appendix to *World and the Individual,* New York, 1900, London, 1901.)
67 This characterization is only valid for Royce with strong reservations. Nevertheless, it adequately illustrates the shift of emphasis towards the problem of (intellectual) history and society which distinguishes Royce from Peirce.
68 This impression is strengthened by the development of American pragmatism after Peirce, which does not take up Peirce's esoteric (quasi-transcendental philosophical) 'pragmaticism', but rather the situational common sense-pragmatism which he indicated in 'The Fixation of Belief'. In several respects, this finitistic pragmatism of the psychologist William James and the social educationalist John Dewey

represents the American counterpart to European existential
hermeneutics.
69 It must be added that, strictly speaking, no actual dialogue can be
conceived of that does not include a confrontation of wills and the
related strategy of employing language rhetorically.
70 'Interaction' is not used here, as it frequently is, in the sense of a
reciprocal interaction between two objects, but rather in the sense of
action based on reciprocity that is possible only between human
subjects – a type of action which anticipates the reaction of the other
person. Cf. J. Habermas, 'Labour and Interaction', in *Theory and
Practice,* trans. J. Viertel, Boston/London, 1974, pp. 142–69.
71 The relationships outlined here and below can be analysed in a much
more concrete manner with the aid of the theory of speech acts
developed by Austin and Searle. Cf. also Maas and Wunderlich,
Pragmatik und sprachliches Handeln.
72 Cf. Max Weber's intended hermeneutics of purposive rational action.
73 Cf. G. Funke, *Transzendental-phänomenologische Untersuchung über
'universalen Idealismus', 'Intentionalanalyse' und 'Habitusgenese',*
Padua, 1957.
74 Cf. n. 58 above.
75 Cf. my study, *Die Idee der Sprache in der Tradition des Humanismus
von Dante bis Vico.*
76 This is true of everyday speech as opposed to formalized language.
77 Cf. my critical review of Gehlen's 'Philosophie der Institutionen', in
Philosophische Rundschau, vol. 10, 1962, pp. 1–21; reprinted in
Transformation der Philosophie, vol. 1, pp. 197 ff.
78 This transition on the part of a meta-scientifically orientated
communication of meaning corresponds to another transition that has
a correspondingly inverted structure. This transition is from the
operationalized, scientific-technological specialized language to the
everyday language of informed 'public opinion', and it alone is capable
of incorporating the results of science and technology into the political
and moral framework of a democratic formation of the will.
Presumably, the specifically modern task of the hermeneutic sciences
of communication, rather than that of the pragmatic-operationalist
elucidation of meaning, would be regarded as the constant realization
of this transition. Cf. K.-O. Apel. 'Wissenschaft als Emanzipation?', in
Zeitschrift für allgemeine Wissenschaftstheorie, no. 2, 1970; reprinted in
Transformation der Philosophie, vol. 2, pp. 128–54.
79 To some extent, this would be the technocratic apotheosis of Peirce's
pragmatism along the lines of Gehlen's anthropology and social
philosophy.
80 Gadamer emphasizes, of course, especially in his controversy with
Betti (cf. E. Betti, *Die Hermeneutik als allgemeine Methodik der
Geisteswissenschaften,* Tübingen, 1962, n. 118), that he is not
suggesting a 'method', but rather describing 'what exists'. But one
cannot fail to recognize the implied *demand* that one should also
remember the historical connection between interpreter and

interpretandum as a connection which is necessary for the interpretation since it determines the 'pre-understanding' and, to this extent, one should develop a 'consciousness of historical reception' towards the interpretandum. Moreover, this demand can only be understood as normatively relevant. If one wished to deny this the 'ontological' embedding of the interpretation in a 'theory of the game' (Gadamer, *Truth and Method,* pp. 97 ff.) one would draw dangerously near to an objectivistic description of the behaviourist type (such as is suggested by Wittgenstein's language-game theory). The historical interpretative process of the mediation of tradition which, unlike explicable natural processes, is not mere subject to laws, but rather must still be developed by ourselves in a responsible manner (and is 'intelligible' only on account of this fact) can only be understood ontologically if the philosophical concept also expresses a methodologically relevant, normative engagement. The later Peirce understood this very clearly when, in the fourth phase of his intellectual development (1902 ff.), he established a *normative logic* of research, that takes up the Kantianism of his first phase as a corrective to the naturalistic tendency of his earlier pragmatism (second phase) and even his cosmology of evolution (third phase). In my view, even the 'meta-ethics' of the Oxford school (similar to the unhistorical language-game theory of the later Wittgenstein upon which it is based) overlooks the fact that, strictly speaking, one cannot describe in a value-neutral manner an intelligible event which has its concrete place in the history that we must develop. Games theory and functionalist ontology rest upon an abstraction that a hermeneutics of historical integration must 'transcend'.

81 It will not be discussed here to what extent this accusation is valid for existential hermeneutics (Heidegger, Bultmann, Gadamer?) – and thereby establishes a parallel with popular pragmatism. Cf. Betti, *Die Hermeneutik als allgemeine Methodik der Geisteswissenschaften.*

82 Cf. 'Scientistics, Hermeneutics and the Critique of Ideology', ch. 2 above; also Habermas, *Knowledge and Human Interests,* part 3.

83 I believe in this sense that Winch is correct in his postulate (see n. 42 above) which stands in opposition to naturalistic sociology even if his demand that alien or past cultures be understood only in the sense of their actually correlated language-games does justice neither to the hermeneutic prerequisite of the 'fusion of horizons' (Gadamer) nor to that of a critique of ideology with an emancipatory intention (cf. my critique in *Analytical Philosophy of Language and the 'Geisteswissenschaften',* and ch. 5 in this volume).

84 As an illustration of this admittedly delicate method of depth-hermeneutics one could cite, for example, E. H. Erikson, *Young Man Luther: a Study in Psychoanalysis and History*, New York, 1958.

85 Cf. Gadamer, *Truth and Method,* p. 161.

86 Cf. Gadamer's critique of Hegel, ibid., p. 351.

87 Cf. my paper 'Sprache und Reflexion', *Akten des XIV Internationalen Kongresses für Philosophie, Vienna, 1968,* vol. 3, Vienna, 1969, and

my revised version in *Transformation der Philosophie*, vol. 2, pp. 311–29.

88 In his last years, Royce (1855–1916) was greatly interested in Peirce's posthumous writings that had been acquired by Harvard in 1914. Even at that time he attempted to organize an edition of Peirce's writings. Cf. W. F. Kernan, 'The Peirce Manuscripts and Josiah Royce', in *Transactions of the C. S. Peirce Society*, vol. 1, 1965, pp. 90 ff.

89 Cf. G. H. Mead, *Mind, Self and Society*, Chicago, 1934.

90 Cf. J. Habermas, *Zur Logik der Sozialwissenschaften*, Frankfurt, 1973, pp. 152 f.

CHAPTER 5

The communication community as the transcendental presupposition for the social sciences

Programmatic theses

To be more precise, the title of this study should read: 'The transcendental language-game of the unlimited communication community as the precondition for the possibility of the social sciences'. By means of this title I wish, from the outset, to indicate two *theses*:

1 In contrast to the now dominant 'logic of science' I am of the opinion that any philosophical theory of science must answer the Kantian question of the transcendental presuppositions for the possibility and validity of science.

2 Unlike those who adhere to an orthodox Kantianism, I am, however, of the opinion that the reply to the question raised by Kant does not lead back today to Kant's philosophy of a transcendental 'consciousness as such'. Rather, I believe that the reply to the question as to the transcendental subject of science must be mediated by the real achievement of twentieth-century philosophy, namely, by the insight into the transcendental importance of language and, thereby, of the language community.

I do not believe that the question of the transcendental preconditions for the possibility and validity of science is identical with the question of possible *deduction* of theorems within the framework of an axiomatic system that itself remains to be grounded. Nor do I believe that this question must therefore lead back to a *logical circle*, a *regressus ad infinitum*, or even to a *dogmatic* establishment of ultimate principles.[1]

Furthermore, I do not believe that the transcendental question must be limited, as in Kant's work, to the 'justification' of classical theory-formation in physics or Euclidean geometry,[2] even though, given such a restriction, it still remains relevant if it is taken together with the cognitive-anthropological relativization of the notion of the *a priori*.[3] But, in view of the already accomplished transformation of the epistemological problem into the problem of an analytical philosophy of language, it seems to me that a *Cartesian* radicalization of the transcendental problem of reflection is required. This cannot, however – as is the case even with Husserl – trace the question of the *validity of meaning* back to the Cartesian question of someone's *evidence for consciousness*.

The fact that the *evidence for consciousness* in Descartes', Kant's and even Husserl's sense is insufficient to ground the *validity* of knowledge is demonstrated, for example, by the problem of *a priori* validity in Euclidean geometry in Kant's sense or in the so-called 'colour statements' in Husserl's sense. On the one hand, it is very plausible to argue that the axioms of Euclidean geometry and the 'colour statements' ('what is green is not red' or 'what is coloured is also extensive') are *a priori synthetic statements* because we can certainly *think* of their particular content as being different without contradiction but cannot intuitively *conceive* of its being different. This phenomenological and cognitive anthropological assertion is based upon personal intuitive evidence in the light of individual phenomena. But precisely for this reason it does not suffice to ground the *a priori intersubjective validity* of Euclidean geometry and colour statements. For this, it is necessary, in addition, that personal intuitive evidence – linked through pragmatic-semantic rules to a 'language-game' in the later Wittgenstein's sense – is elevated to a 'paradigm' of the language-game. Only then is the *personal evidence for consciousness* transposed by means of linguistic agreement into an *a priori validity of statements for us* and only then can it be *valid*, in terms of the *consensus* theory of truth,[4] as *a priori* binding knowledge. By means of the – implicit or explicit – elevation of personal evidence for consciousness to a paradigm of the language-game, the *argumentative sense* of the intuitive certainty of each consciousness for the community of communication and interpretation is, to some extent, secured. And it is the securing of meaning in the *communicative synthesis of interpretation* – and not simply the 'synthesis of apperception' – that provides the basis for the 'highest point' (Kant) of a semiotically transformed transcendental philosophy.[5]

In my opinion, a modern transcendental philosophy is primarily concerned with reflection upon the meaning – and thus also upon the implications of the meaning – of argument as such. This is manifestly what is *ultimate and irreducible* for all who argue – no matter what their position. For by arguing – and this means even in the light of any doubt however radical, which, as doubt, should have a meaning – they have established for themselves and implicitly recognized both the transcendental presuppositions of epistemology and the theory of science in terms of the transcendental language-game of an unlimited communication community. Taking Kant as a starting-point, one might say that in the 'synthesis of apperception', in which the self posits both its object and itself as thinking entities, the self must, at the same time, identify itself with the transcendental communication community which alone can confirm the *validity of meaning* of its own knowledge of self and the world. Without this *transcendental-semiotical* presupposition of *cognition* – not reflected upon by Kant and Fichte – the latter cannot become the subject of *argument*. It would then at best retain the status of an experiential certainty that is blind to meaning like that merely private experience of pain which, according to Wittgenstein, 'cancels out' when it is a matter of understanding my or your pain.[6] Consequently, where *fundamental grounding by means of transcendental reflection* is concerned, the person who philosophizes need not *choose* membership of a critical communication community either dogmatically or on the basis of an 'irrational decision' (Popper). For as a party to an argument, he has already implicitly recognized the presupposition of an unlimited and critical communication community. He can only explicate this presupposition more or less adequately and intentionally reinforce the norms contained within it, or he can fail to perform this *transcendental reflection*, or intentionally renounce the norms of the transcendental language-game as obscurantist. The latter would indeed be an 'irrational' choice which, if completely carried out, must also destroy the possibility of solitary self-understanding and hence of self-identification. One cannot decide to affirm or negate the norms of the transcendental language-game from a position outside the language-game.[7] The negation of this constitutes the basic error of *methodological solipsism*.[8] As an ego that already presupposes the communication community, one can at best decide about self-affirmation or self-negation. This forms the freedom of choice of the finite person that cannot be further justified, a freedom which must, however, always be drawn upon if our concern is not the reflective foundation but rather the *practical realization* of the norms of the critical communication community that is always presupposed. We shall return to this point later.

This postulated mediation of transcendental philosophy by the problem of language of communication is recognized in the expanded title of this paper by reference to two *fundamental philosophical statements* which, in my opinion, perform a key function in the *transformation of Kantianism*. The first is the later Wittgenstein's concept of the language-game, the second is the 'indefinite community of investigators' that is postulated as the subject of possible consensus as to truth by Peirce (in the course of his semiotical transformation of Kant's 'transcendental logic').[9] This latter conception has been extrapolated or generalized by Royce as the 'Community of Interpretation' and by George H. Mead as the 'Community of Universal Discourse'.[10]

Indeed, in my opinion both the Wittgensteinian concept of the 'language-game' and Peirce's concept of the 'community' can be interpreted in such a manner that, on the one hand, the functional point of Kant's transcendental idealism is retained (i.e. an equivalent can be established for the 'highest point' of Kant's transcendental deduction and for the 'highest maxim of synthetic judgments' according to which the preconditions for the possibility of experience are at the same time the preconditions for the possibility of the objects of experience); whilst on the other, a mediation of Kant's transcendental idealism with a realism, and even historical materialism of society that has indeed always been presupposed (as the subject-object of science) is implied.[11] The possibility and even necessity for such an interpretation is conditioned by the fact that a sense-critical transcendental philosophy does not, as does Kant's, commence from the metaphysical presupposition of a distinction between the thing-in-itself and the empirical world of appearances, nor from the presupposition of a transcendental subject as the limit of the empirical world. Rather, it commences from the fact that the ideal norms that must be presupposed in order for any argument to have meaning (i.e. the postulates concerning the formation of consensus in knowledge of the real world and in agreement as to a continuation of the real world through historical praxis), are in principle destined to be realized in a concrete society.[12] Thus, this transcendental presupposition of science is neither idealistic in the sense of traditional philosophies of consciousness nor materialistic in the sense of an ontological official 'dialectical materialism' or a scientistic, positivistic objectivism that conceals its ontological implications. Rather, it will be concerned with a genuine *dialectical conception that lies on this side of idealism and materialism*. It will be concerned with a dialectical conception in so far as it 'mediates' from the very start the opposition between transcendental idealism and a 'historical materialism' that is related to society.

In my opinion, the dialectical mediation lies, on the one hand, in the fact that the inalienable normative and ideal presupposition of the transcendental language-game of an unlimited communication community is postulated in any argument, indeed in any human word (in fact, more precisely, with any action that is to be intelligible); on the other, in the fact that in the historically given society the ideal communication community is always still to be realized. From out of the antagonism between the normative-ideal and material-factual elements in our transcendental presupposition of a communication community there arises a dialectical feature of the philosophical theory of science that emerges at that moment in which the communication community, which forms the transcendental subject of science, also becomes the object of science: at the level of the social sciences in the broadest sense. For now it becomes relevant that, on the one hand, the subject of a possible truth consensus of science is not an extra-worldly 'consciousness as such', but rather the historical-real society; on the other, however, the historical-real society can then only be adequately understood if it is treated as the potential subject of science – including social science – and if its historical reality is always both empirically and normatively critically reconstructed in the light of the ideal of the unlimited communication community that is to be realized in society.

At this point, the conflict that exists from the outset between the transcendental-philosophical foundational starting-point that I have outlined and the now predominant analytical 'logic of science' must also be brought into the open. The roots of this latter approach seem to me to be determined by the presupposition – hardly reflected upon by the logic of science – that the tidy *separation of the subject and object of science* is not only to be justifiably upheld in the realm of natural science but also in the social sciences too. The self-evidentness of this presupposition is today agreed upon not only by *neopositivists* and *critical rationalists* (in Popper's sense) alike, but also by *vulgar Marxists,* in the sense of orthodox dialectical materialism, who are to be distinguished from the *critical neo-Marxists* in that they abandon the dialectical problematic of society as that of the subject and object in favour of a logically clear, scientistic objectivism. In fact, it seems to me that the rubicon in contemporary discussion of the foundation of the theory of science is typified by the question as to whether, by virtue of the fact that in the social sciences man is both the subject and object of science, these sciences are, in principle, different from the natural sciences. In what follows, I wish to consciously cross this rubicon.

At this point, I wish to draw out the implications of this step with a certain degree of completeness. In part, this is because, in what follows, I wish to concentrate upon one of these implications: upon the distinction and dialectical mediation between 'understanding' and 'explanation'. However, in my opinion, recognition of society as the subject-object of science also implies a series of further consequences which, from the analytical logic of science's perspective, appear much more 'doubtful' than the traditional distinction between explanation and *understanding*.

1   First of all, there already exists a fundamental distinction in the *identification* of the objects of science at the level of so-called *description*. This distinction is based on the question as to whether the so-called 'data' can be made 'available' through repeatable experiments as instances of possible explanations by means of laws – or can at least be subsumed under class concepts – or whether they should be treated as spatio-temporally individualized elements of the totality of an irreversible historical process that is itself mediated through these elements. We can derive *two completely different concepts of experience* from this. Only the former opens up the transcendental horizon for such entities as contingent 'laws' or inductive corroboration in the sense of the 'logic of science'. In contrast, the latter opens up the transcendental horizon for an experience – to some extent in the sense of Hegel's concept of experience[13] – which includes not only inductive corroboration or

141

falsification but, above all, the qualitative *revision* of its *conceptual* presuppositions through self-reflection.

It seems to me that Popper, with his concept of the formation of risky hypotheses that consciously creates by means of methodology possible falsification and the construction of possible alternative hypotheses, stops half-way on the road to a dialectical concept of experience.[14] He systematically and energetically distances himself from the inductivistic-positivistic concept of an experience that always retains its semantic-categorial presuppositions behind its back. Of course, he is able – as a result of the methodological reduction of Kant's epistemological problem – to reflect the transcendental problem of the empirical horizons only in the form of the restricted framework of a pluralism of theories within the implicitly absolutized natural scientific experience. This scientistic restriction of reflection prevents him from recognizing historical self-experience of society as the fundamental alternative to the basically repeatable experience of nature – an alternative that is relevant for the theory of science. For instance, it prevents him from seriously recognizing that the implicitly recognized *reflexive self-experience of science* as an innovative process of hypothesis formation and correction is also the paradigm for the experience of objects in the historical and critical social sciences. If Popper recognized this consequence, he would indeed have to abandon the separation of subject and object, and thereby the deeply-rooted presupposition of modern scientism, and would hence have to concern himself with a dialectical problematic of history in Hegel's sense.[15]

2   Even 'more doubtful' than this implication of our step over the rubicon of the modern logic of science for the theory of experience is the associated *transcendence of the concept of value-free science* that Max Weber also made obligatory for the social sciences. The recognition of what Weber termed 'purposive-rational understanding' as a 'good reason essay' which, as such, cannot be reduced to a causal motivational explanation already necessitates a critical evaluation of human behaviour, even if the latter remains confined to the normative *standard of instrumental rationality* and seeks to understand the goals in question without evaluating them.[16] The same is true of a systems theory of society that understands its object *functionally*. But the difference here is that, at least implicitly, a positive evaluation not only of the functional efficiency

but also of system formation and adaptation, in the sense of the self-preservation and self-improvement of the quasi-organic life of society, is also included.[17] However, such an absolutization of the value of system formation by the functionalist systems theory of society must, from the outset, stand in opposition to the transcendental-normative presupposition of all sciences that I have emphasized; namely, that the realization of truth depends *a priori* upon the realization of the *unlimited* communication community within the historically given society. That is, it takes place within the society which must be organized in *limited* functional systems in order to secure its physical self-preservation. From this conflict between the implicit evaluation on the part of a functionalistic systems theory of society and the normative preconditions of its own truth-claim we can infer that a *critical social science,* which conceives of its *object* simultaneously as the possible subject of science, cannot thereby abandon the goals of human actions that are still to be evaluated.

This does not imply that – as is commonly asserted by the theorists of value-free social sciences[18] – normative standards can be derived from the empirical, or more precisely, that imperative prescriptions can be derived from the description of facts, and to this extent that the 'logical divide' between is and ought is ignored.[19] Rather, it implies that experiences in the sense of the historical self-experience of society – as opposed to the empirical-analytically describable experiences of nature and of methodically reified human 'behaviour' in the sense of a social quasi-nature – cannot be gained or be the subject of a discussion without a certain normatively relevant engagement in the sense of possible or required advancement of history through subjective-intersubjective praxis. The fact that human action, in contrast to observable behaviour, cannot be recognized as action as such without evaluation, is already demonstrated, as has been suggested, by the instance of purposive-rational understanding. Here, indeed, the goals under consideration do not need to be evaluated, as supporters of value-free social science since Max Weber are accustomed to emphasizing. On the other hand, the action must be evaluated along with how it is understood in so far as a 'good ground' in terms of the ideal of purposive rationality must be *found*. This demonstrates that 'empirical-analytical' experience of human actions is not possible in the strict sense. Human actions are not to be described precisely *as that which they are* without one having first understood the (immanent) norms of their successful outcome and recognized them as standards of evaluation. Furthermore, the abandonment of the evaluation of purposes does not imply that as such they could be found without the heuristic presupposition of an evaluation of purposes. In short, value-free factual judgments cannot stand at the start of historical experience, and they do not need to be taken as the starting-point of historical value judgments. Rather, the latter are derived from the horizon of meaning that historical experience, as the reconstructable self-experience of a potential communication community, first makes possible. If empirical-analytical science in Popper's sense must recognize the presuppositions of *theoretical* horizons, for its so-called 'observation statements', then the historical self-experience of society must, in addition, recognize *value-horizons* for its 'derivation of data'. In my opinion, the function of these horizons may not, as in the case of empirical-analytical experience or description, be reduced to a purely psychologically relevant function of heuristics that has nothing more to do with the logic of empirical judgments that it makes possible. This is already shown in the fact that historical experience cannot seriously be separated from its narrative representation in the colloquial, or more precisely, educated language which always suggests valuation: after reading the introduction or some random checks one usually knows where the author of a historical work stands.

Even more important than reference to the necessity of evaluation in the experiential horizon of history is the insight that the normative presupposition of values in the sense with which we are concerned here in no way needs to be *subjective* in the sense of a decisionism without intersubjectively binding obligations – a meaning of subjective that has become common ever since Max Weber. The abstract logical distinction between intersubjectively binding factual judgments and subjective value judgments has always been transcended by the validity-claim of any argument that has to be redeemed in favour of an intersubjectively binding *minimal ethics*.[20] This minimal ethics that is implicitly recognized by any partner to an argument and which implies, amongst other things, an engagement in the sense of the historical realization of the unlimited communication community, is even presupposed by value-free empirical-analytical science as the precondition for the possibility of reaching a consensus and thereby of finding the truth. Consequently, at the very least, this minimal ethics of 'logical socialism' – first discussed by Peirce[21] – can and must be made the standard for its value judgments by a critical social science that has to reconstruct the historical self-experience of the human species.[22] The contradiction that must be overcome between the real and the ideal communication community and which is already recognized in the transcendental presupposition of science, thereby immediately supplies the starting-point for an evaluative critique of ideology.

3   The necessity for evaluation in the critical social sciences outlined above indicates the final and most radical consequence that is implicit in the theory of science's recognition of society as the subject and object of science: namely, the *distinction between theory and practice*. The apparently similar distinction that was established by Kant with reference to the foundation of natural science in the form of the distinction between theoretical and practical reason cannot be maintained as the foundation for the critical social sciences.

Even the purely theoretical character of the causal explanatory natural sciences can only be asserted in a way that is free of ideology if, at the same time, one reflects upon the fact that value-free theory-formation in natural science is *a priori* framed in such a way that it is, in fact, the precondition for the possibility of the technological utilization of its results.[23] This *a priori* interlocking of interests itself and especially that of a methodologically pure theory with a practice in the sense of technical utilization is valid *a fortiori* with reference to the social-technological function of the so-called empirical-analytical social sciences. That this is the case, is manifested in the mostly quite naively formulated demand that the perfection of scientific progress in modern industrial society must lie in the extension of man's natural scientific control over nature through the social-scientific *control* of man *over man*. But this demand is not merely and obviously of practical relevance, but as a practical, relevant demand it is deeply ambiguous. If, in terms of empirical-analytical unified science, the separation of the subject and object of science is also to be maintained in the social sciences, then this demand could only signify that society must be split up into those who are controlled and those who control. This practical consequence of this ambiguous demand today finds its methodological recognition and explication, it would appear, in a functionalist systems theory of society which thereby places itself at the service of 'technocracy'. If this systems-related functionalist interpretation and evaluation of all socially relevant processes is then also applied, as Luhmann appears to suggest,[24] to the cognitive and communicative achievements of science (including systems theory itself), then the whole technological relevance of science for practice finds itself in a paradoxical situation that indicates the possibility and necessity for a different kind of relevance for practice on the part of the 'critical social sciences'. These will neither abandon their practical technical relevance in an unreflected manner, in the sense of the value-free, theoretical, empirical-analytical sciences, nor will they, in the sense of functionalist systems theory, simultaneously reflect upon and absolutize the technological relevance of science. On the contrary, they must make precisely that practical relevance of science, which, together with its claim to truth, is presupposed in the postulate of the realization of an unlimited communication community, a theme and standard of their committed critique of society.

This, of course, also presupposes that the critical social sciences must hold in check their emancipatory engagement on a higher level of theoretical-philosophical self-reflection. It must be tested in attempts at both a normative and empirical reconstruction of the historical situation. The critical social sciences, with this philosophical self-reflection, attain once more te *stage of self-knowledge of knowledge* that was already postulated by Hegel as the goal of the 'phenomenology of mind'. The distinction between the critical social sciences and absolute idealism, however, lies in the fact that the attainment of this highest stage of philosophical reflection may today no longer be *confused*, as it was for Hegel, with a 'transcendence' of historical-social praxis in the concept's movement in reflection. At least, as the Young Hegelians replied to Hegel, the future, in principle, evades reflexive-theoretical interpretation; it can, as Kierkegaard and Marx both unanimously postulated, only be considered as a whole by means of practically engaged thought. Yet precisely that thought which guides and introduces concrete practice itself unavoidably runs the risk of dogmatism if left to itself. The 'anticipation of partiality'[25] required by Marx cannot simply be equated with the 'will to reason' (Fichte) that is implicit in reason itself, or engagement in the sense of emancipation for the maturity of mankind in general (Habermas).[26] Rather, over and above this, it must at all times enter into an engagement that can no longer be covered by knowledge.[27] It must do this in order to mediate *critical theory* with the *transformation of the world*. Yet in order to transcend the contradiction between the risk of dogmatism that emancipatory praxis must take upon itself and the will to emancipation in the sense of the maturity of reason, the party commitment of practical reason – demanded by Marx – must once more be capable of being reduced by theoretical reflection to the status of a hypothetical suggestion and of being placed in question.[28] This is precisely what occurs in the 'theoretical discourse' of practically engaged philosophy: it represents, in terms of its critical claim, the permanent attempt to anticipate the standpoint of the ideal unlimited communication community within the community of participants in argumentation, and to confront it with the idiosyncrasies of the present.

'Methodological solipsism' as the transcendental presupposition of the idea of 'unified science'

I shall not be able in what follows to introduce *in extenso* this outlined programme for a theory of science which commences from the *a priori* of the (both presupposed and yet still to be realized) communication community. I will limit myself to the explication and defence of this first step over the rubicon of the theory of science, namely, the recognition of human society as a subject-object of science. This first step is manifested methodologically (as has already been indicated) in the distinction between, and dialectical mediation of, 'understanding' and 'explanation'. In order now, after so much speculative programmatics, to restore contact with the analytical logic of science, I wish to make clear my own methodological theses through a critical confrontation with the unified science methodology of neopositivism. In so doing, our concern is first of all with the *confrontation of the a priori of the communication community with the hidden transcendental presuppositions of neopositivist 'logic of science'*. Within this context, my thesis states that the objectivistic conception of unified science can be traced back to a presupposition which, remarkably, neopositivism as an approach based on the analysis of language, shares with the traditional philosophy of consciousness of the modern period: *the presupposition of methodological solipsism*. Like Descartes, Locke, Russell and even Husserl, neopositivism ultimately also commences from the presupposition that, in principle, 'one alone' could recognize something *as* something and practise science in such a manner. In so far

147

as neopositivism, like the traditional metaphysics of the subject, fails to take into account the fact that knowledge based upon observation at the level of the subject-object relationship always already presupposes knowledge as understanding of meaning at the level of the subject-cosubject relationship, it cannot conceive of the 'understanding' practised in the human sciences from its appropriate dimension, namely, the cognitive interest in intersubjective understanding. Rather, it is compelled to treat understanding as 'empathy' towards behavioural data that can possibly lead to causal hypotheses.[29] In other words, it pushes understanding from the very outset into the transcendental horizon of objectively utilizable knowledge and examines its *explanatory* value, just as if agreement by *understanding* between people could ever be replaced by *one* amongst them making all the others the object of descriptions of behaviour and explanation. The paradoxical situation that our thesis must take into account lies, however, in the fact that the neopositivist 'logic of science' as a language-analytical *method* – as the syntactical and semantic reconstruction of scientific language – thus far does itself deal quite well with intersubjective understanding, e.g. with the *explication* of meaning. If, nevertheless, in unified science's *methodology* the hermeneutic interest in understanding is not paralleled with the language-analytical interest in meta-scientific understanding but rather, from the outset – and expressly within the context of a programme of logical reduction – is subordinated to the interest in objective explanation, then this seems to indicate a contradiction between the programme of the language-analytical *method* and the programme of scientific *methodology*.[30] In what follows I shall claim the existence of such a contradiction and try to present it. Over and above this, however, it must be asked *why* the contradiction between the presuppositions of the language-analytical *method* and the presuppositions of objectivistic *methodology* could remain unnoticed in neopositivism until the present.

In my opinion, the answer to this question lies in the fact that the even more fundamental contradiction between the language-analytical approach and the *methodological solipsism* of modern epistemology belongs amongst the unclarified transcendental presuppositions of the neopositivist 'logic of science'. Of course, transcendental presuppositions are not recognized by logical empiricism and hence they are also not reflected upon. If, none the less, one wishes to reveal them and subject them to critical discussion, then one must return to Ludwig Wittgenstein as the key figure in the analytical philosophy of language. In my opinion, Wittgenstein had introduced *methodological solipsism* as a transcendental pre-supposition in the analytical philosophy of language, and, also with the aid of the analytical philosophy of language approach, he ulti-mately superseded it. I wish in what follows to substantiate and clarify these theses.

If one wishes to raise the *question of the ultimate presuppositions of the neopositivist 'logic of science'*, then certainly several answers are to be expected which amplify and correct one another. The first reply might run as follows: the sole *a priori* presupposition that is involved in the logical empiricist position refers to the *validity of formal logic*. All scientific knowledge must, with its assistance, be derived from the observation of given facts. This reply might most faithfully express the original self-understanding of the supporters of logical empiricism. After some reflection, however, it becomes clear that some further *a priori* presuppositions are contained within logical empiricism. Thus it is not simply a fact that these are facts. Rather, it is an *a priori* presuppostion that facts exist which are independent of human thought and which can be recognized as facts by observation in an intersubjectively valid form. Thus it proves to be the case that we have specified two of Leibniz's metaphysical principles as the ultimate presuppositions of logical empiricism: that there exists logical truths of reason (*vérités de raison*) and experiencable factual truths (*vérités de fait*).[31] And there is presented here yet another *a priori* presupposition that logical empiricism, at least originally, has in common with Leibniz. In order to bring logic together with observational facts, i.e. in neopositivist terms, in order, with the aid of logic, to be able to extract scientific knowledge in an unambiguous manner from observational data, an *ideal scientific language* – along the lines of mathematical logic – is presupposed; or in Leibniz's terms, a *lingua philosophica sive calculus raciocinator* that will bring to an end the eternal philosophers' disputes over words is presupposed.[32] Actually, there exists in this idea (of a universal calculus language of science) the typical motive of a neo-Leibnizian metaphysics that logical empiricism took over from Bertrand Russell and the young Wittgenstein. Furthermore, it can, in my opinion, be asserted that logical empiricism had at its disposal a theoretical basis for its promised 'transcendence of metaphysics by the logical analysis of language'[33] just so long as it held on to the secret metaphysics of neo-Leibnizianism. For, at the moment at which it abandoned the presupposition of the *single* calculus language of science in favour of the 'principle of tolerance or conventionality' of constructive semantics,[34] it also lost the theoretical basis for a critique of metaphysics.[35]

Yet what does this discussion of the metaphysical presupposition of logical empiricism have to do with 'methodological solipsism'? Is not the transcendental value of intersubjective understanding recognized precisely by the Leibnizian demand for an intersubjectively valid scientific language? And is not the methodological solipsism of the return to my own data of consciousness, that is implicit in traditional empiricism, overcome through Carnap's return to the *language* of the data of consciousness and overcome completely through exchanging this language for the intersubjectively verifiable *'thing-language'* of *physicalism?*[36] None the less, my thesis is that it is precisely the postulate of the objectivistic unified language of physicalism that presupposes *methodological solipsism* as it arises in the young Wittgenstein's *Tractatus.*[37]

Before I go on to discuss the *Tractatus,* I wish to discuss a prior consideration. A formalized calculus language of science does not serve intersubjective understanding in that is seeks to make the latter superfluous as the transcendental presupposition of knowledge. The aim of the construction of formalized scientific languages lies precisely in the fact that it seeks to replace the hermeneutic problematic of the reciprocal understanding of subjective intended meanings by the establishment of a semantic system that *a priori* only releases intersubjective meaning (namely, possible 'facts' as the content of 'propositions') as intentional. Thus, in principle, formalized scientific languages cannot be used for reaching agreement in the full sense of this word. If one excludes all meta-problematics and presupposes the – none the less – successful interpretation of calculus language, then at best *propositions* concerning possible *facts* (not *assertions* of *facts!*) and logical consequences can be expressed in it but not 'speech-acts'.[38] Above all, it cannot express such *speech-acts* as certain personal identifiers such as 'I', 'you', 'we', 'they', etc. that, as a result, express the situation of intersubjective communication. Speech-acts – such as assertions, questions, requests, protestations, etc. – that testify to the linguistic 'communicative competence'[39] of human beings, in so far as they activate the propositional content of statements in discourse, can find no place in formal language since they do not belong to the objective syntactic-semantic dimension but to the subjective, pragmatic dimension of language as a sign system.[40] This pragmatic dimension of communicative utterances or speech-acts must, in a physicalist scientific language, itself be made the object of semantic reference, and that means the object of a behaviouristic science.[41]

Yet at this point one could counter with the argument that in the case of formalized scientific language a *metaproblematic of interpretation* cannot, in principle, be excluded and in this context it produces the necessity for intersubjective agreement as the transcendental presupposition of all conventions that enter into the construction of scientific languages. In short, in the light of this, one could indeed postulate a *transcendental pragmatics* of the communication community of science – just as Peirce in fact postulated.[42] This counter-argument seems to me to be fully justified and I shall return to it again later. In the meantime, however, it must be shown how far the radicalization of the idea of the unified language of an objective natural science in the sense of a *transcendental onto-semantics*[43] prevents consideration of a *transcendental pragmatics* of the communication community.

The *transcendental radicalization of the idea of the unified language* of science mentioned earlier is present in the young Wittgenstein's *Tractatus*. In my opinion, the *Tractatus*'s central theme is that the logical form of the ideal language which represents the world is not constructable arbitrarily but lies hidden as the precondition for the possibility of all construction[44] in everyday language.[45] Since the logical form of language is the transcendental precondition for all linguistic representation of the world, and hence for all discussion about the world, there can be no metaphysical discussion, according to Wittgenstein, about the relationship between language and the world. Such a metaphysical discussion would amount to the confusion of 'internal relations' that belong to the transcendental form of language and the world, with 'external relations' between things and states of affairs that occur in the world. In the light of this conception, the 'theory of types' and the 'hierarchy of meta-languages' are superfluous whereas the reflection on language – practised by Wittgenstein himself in the *Tractatus* – can no longer be actually conceived of within a transcendental pragmatics of communication.[46] The 'transcendental' logical form of language that is identical with the logical form of the describable world can only 'appear'.

On the basis of these presuppositions, however, what happens to the *subject of science* that, certainly for Kant – as 'consciousness as such' – was the agent of the transcendental unity of possible knowledge of the object? The reply is as follows: in so far as the concern is here with empirical human beings then there is no subject but rather merely objects of scientific language (of natural science). However, in so far as the concern is with Kant's *transcendental* subject, then its function rises or sinks in the transcendental function of language as the limit of the world.

Wittgenstein expresses it as follows (*Tractatus,* 5.631): 'There is no such thing as the subject that thinks or entertains ideas'. This statement may be viewed as the starting-point for the rigorous *behaviourist programme* within the realm of the neopositivist conception of physicalism's unified language. However, Wittgenstein himself did not forget the transcendental (subjective) presuppositions of this unified scientific thing-language. He condenses this in the following statement which, on the face of it, seems to contradict the previously cited statement concerning the subject of knowledge (5.641): 'Thus there really is a sense in which philosophy can talk about the self in a non-psychological way. What brings the self into philosophy is the fact that "the world is my world"'. According to Wittgenstein, the apparent contradiction between this statement (on the philosophical concept of the self) and the previous one which disputes the existence of a thinking subject, is solved by the transcendental reflection that the self, which is expressed in the statement 'the world is my world', does not exist *in* the world but marks the limit *of* the world which can be described in the language of science (5.632): 'The subject does not belong to the world: rather, it is the limit of the world.' And (5.62): 'The world is *my* world: this is manifest in the fact that the limits of *language* . . . mean the limits of *my* world.'

Hence, according to Wittgenstein, the *transcendental unity of the self* lies in the *transcendental unity of language,* which, for its part, is the precondition for the possibility and validity of (natural) science – just as for Kant it is the 'transcendental unity of consciousness of the object'. Of course, Kant's 'transcendental unity of consciousness of the object' should be identical with the 'transcendental unity of self-consciousness'. In Wittgenstein's transcendental unity of language, i.e. in terms of a reflection-free representational logic (or 'isomorphic' logic) this identity cannot be conceived of.[47] With this formal-logical reduction of Kant's 'transcendental logic' Wittgenstein at the same time abandons the *transcendental pragmatic dimension of intersubjective understanding.* For at the same time as the transcendental separation of the self as 'self-consciousness' disappears, the possibility of conceiving of the transcendental dependency of the objective-consciousness and self-consciousness upon a dialogical understanding also disappears. For Wittgenstein, thinking of the world in the 'logical space' of language is not a 'conversation of the soul with itself' (Plato) and therefore *a fortiori* is not a function of transcendental communication. If the transcendental ego or subject in the sense of formal logic is identical with the world-limiting form of language, in such a way that for each ego the same ideal form of description of the world is *a priori* valid, then it requires no intersubjective communication (in the sense of a pre-understanding) of the world. In short, a *transcendental pragmatics or hermeneutics* of the world as the practically significant 'life-world' or situational world is neither necesssary nor possible. Indeed, in the transcendental dimension, there exist only 'solitary'[48] natural scientists. Each of them functions completely self-sufficiently as the transcendental subject of the description of the world in the objective thing-fact-language that, by means of a guarantee – one might even say, a mystical, transcendental or metaphysical guarantee[49] – is the language of all other subjects.

Wittgenstein expresses this as follows (5.62):

> For what the solipsist *means* is quite correct; only it cannot be *said,* but makes itself manifest. The world is *my* world: this is manifest in the fact that the limits of *language* (of that language which I alone understand) means the limits of *my* world.
> (5.621) The world and life are one.
> (5.63) I am my world.

The latter statement is, of course, ambiguous; it may be understood in Heidegger's or Merleau-Ponty's terms and would then, in fact, refer to a dimension of transcendental philosophy that itself still expressed the reflexive self-relationship of 'being-in-the-world' in terms of a transcendental hermeneutics.[50] More significant in terms of Wittgenstein's onto-semantics and his transcendental difference between the describable object-world and the inexpressible dimension of subject-monads – co-ordinated by a 'pre-established harmony' – is the following passage (5.64):

> Here it can be seen that solipsism, when its implications are followed out strictly, coincides with pure realism. The self of solipsism shrinks to a point without extension, and there remains the reality co-ordinated with it.

In my opinion, Wittgenstein's statement formulates precisely the (modern) *significance of methodological solipsism in the analytical philosophy of language* inasmuch as it is presuppposed by logical empiricism. It does not deny the *existence* of other subjects but rather the transcendental pragmatic or transcendental hermeneutic *presupposition* of communication with other subjects for my world and self-understanding. In accordance with the presupposition of *methodological solipsism* found in the *Tractatus*, it must, in principle, be possible for a scientist to reduce all other scientists – not to mention the remaining existent human beings – to objects of his 'description' and 'explanation' of their behaviour. My thesis is indeed that precisely this position becomes the ultimate, no longer reflected upon presupposition of the neopositivist notion of an objectified unified science (in the 'thing-language' of description and explanation according to laws). And this hidden presupposition, too, remains effective in the *conventionalist principle* of constructive semantics that *logical expiricism* established to replace the abandoned metaphysics of *logical atomism* (Russell or Wittgenstein). This statement requires further elucidation.

As is well known, logical empiricism took to heart the encouragements of the *Tractatus* in that it sought to keep the promise to provide a 'transcendence of (meaningless) metaphysics by the logical analysis of language' through a constructive syntax and semantics of scientific language. Yet, in fact, it was apparent that two of the previously advanced postulates could not be fulfilled; namely: 1   the idea of a single syntactic-semantic system as the universal language 'of' science; 2   the idea of elementary observational statements as the representation 'of' observed facts that could be viewed as independent of theoretical contexts (protocol statements). It was shown that, on the one hand, the construction of languages (their semantic structure) applied in science already differentiated itself with reference to its interpretability by particular observational languages, i.e. with reference to particular facts whilst, on the other, the description of observational data as facts already implied an 'anticipation' of theoretical systems. In this context, and from my transcendental-philosophical perspective, there was yet another *a priori presupposition of the neopositivist 'logic of science'* (besides logic, facts and formalized language); namely, the presupposition of 'conventions'. *Conventions* were required in order to construct the 'semantical frameworks' with reference to their interpretability as scientific languages. *Conventions* were likewise required in order to attain observational statements that, as 'basic statements', could function as the confirmation or falsification of hypotheses or theories. But what are 'conventions'?

One could maintain that the fact that conventions are presupposed for the construction of semantic systems which, for their part, primarily make scientifically meaningful statements possible, is an indication of the fact that – in contrast with the early Wittgenstein's transcendental conception of semantics – a *transcendental pragmatics* of intersubjective communication forms the ultimate presupposition of the logic of science. Certainly, with this conjecture we are pushed on once more towards the process of action. For logical empiricism would be prevented precisely by the motif of the onto-semantic system introduced by Wittgenstein, that from the outset makes meaningful and intersubjective valid discussion possible, from erecting a philosophical problematic of rational communication as a metaproblematic of constructive semantics.[51] Furthermore, reflection upon the transcendental hermeneutic structure of such a metaproblematic would endanger the programme of an objectivistic unified science. One would be compelled to presuppose the scientist at least not only as the object of 'description' and 'explanation' in the 'thing-language' but also as the *co-subject* of linguistic understanding – on the basis of the understanding of intended meanings. And from this point one would not have to travel very far to the insight that 'understanding' in the *empirical-hermeneutic* human or social sciences does not simply form a psychological auxiliary function for 'explanations' according to laws but forms a continuum with the meta-scientific problem of explicative understanding of constructive language analysis. In my opinion, Carnap's admission that all constructive 'explication' of concepts (that is certainly not to be confused with 'explanation'), in the light of its 'conditions of adequacy', is related back to the everyday or educated linguistic 'explicanda',[52] in fact amounts to an implicit recognition of the continuum between *empirical-hermeneutic* and *constructive-semantic* methods on this side of the methodology of unified science.

One must, of course, concede that the methodological recognition of such a meta-scientific and meta-semantic problematic of understanding implies a difficult exacting demand for the formalistic – i.e. 'indirect'[53] – method of linguistic-reconstruction. It would indeed imply revoking the Leibnizian hope of the replacement of difficult everyday linguistic understanding mediated by a completely artificial language.[54] A more decisive barrier to the recognition of the transcendental problematic of understanding might indeed be the presupposition of *methodological solipsism* which, as we have shown, lies at the basis not only of empiricist and rationalist philosophy of consciousness in the modern period but of the programme of constructive semantics itself. If one reads the works of logical empiricism, one gains the unmistakable impression that under 'convention' is to be understood an absolutely *irrational* factor that must precede all rational discourse or transcend it. 'Convention' seems to be identical with 'arbitrary decision' – similar to the sense in which, according to Hobbes, the sovereign master interpreted the laws by means of the authority of his will; or, to go back even further to the history of nominalism, when, for the Franciscan theologians, the 'fiat' of God's will preceded all reason.[55] In a similar sense, Carnap seems to understand that 'praxis' which answers external ('onto-logical' or, rather, 'onto-semantic') questions in terms of the 'conventional' assertion of a 'semantic framework', i.e. the questions to which semantic-dependent science cannot give the answers.[56]

Yet in fact it cannot be denied that 'conventions' must precede all rational intellectual and cognitive operations in the sense of neo-positivism. (Conventions cannot be deduced from ultimate principles in a calculus[57] and just as little can they be immediately produced by empirical observations.) But the fundamental philosophical question that arises out of our previous deliberations is precisely this: is the concept of human rationality exhaustively defined by the logic of science's concept of scientific rationality so that, over and above these limits, only the irrationality of arbitrary decisions exists?[58]

In my opinion, this question can only be answered positively, i.e. in favour of the scientistically limited concept of rationality, if – at least in principle – 'one alone and only once' could follow a rule. In this case, in fact, 'conventions', to a certain extent as 'agreements' of the scientist with himself, must be irrational personal decisions. Yet from whence are these 'conventions' to obtain their *meaning* and *validity*? Here the question seems to be raised – in a vague form – through which the later Wittgenstein prepared to overcome the *methodological solipsism* of the analytical philosophy of language, which he himself had newly founded, and thereby at the same time to overcome the *methodological solipsism* of the philosophical tradition (since Ockham or, perhaps, since Augustine).

Society as the subject-object of critical social science, or the transcendental language-game in 'given' language-games

In Wittgenstein's later work the central problem seems to me to be precisely that which was raised but remained unreflected upon in the neopositivist 'logic of science' by the transition from the metaphysics of 'logical atomism' to the 'conventionality principle' of constructive semantics: the problem of the transcendental-pragmatic foundation of the conventions for establishing or interpreting rules.

On the other hand, the later Wittgenstein first of all makes manifest the fundamental philosophical meaning of the analytical philosophy of language's transition from the metaphysics of logical atomism to the principle of conventionality. It is not an onto-semantic system of ideal language (in which the 'determinacy of the meaning' of statements is *a priori* established by the 'logical space' of the representation of possible facts) that is belatedly utilized by human beings but rather it is the *use* of signs by human beings that determines their meaning. This leads – especially in the *Remarks on the Foundations of Mathematics* (Oxford, 1964) – to the hitherto most radical presentation of *conventionalism* known in the history of philosophy. For not only is the *meaning* of signs made dependent upon the *rules* for their usage; even the *meaning* of *rules* for their usage depends at any moment – so it seems – upon the *conventions* concerning their usage.[59] (There not only exist no Platonic entities that, as logical atoms, would establish the meaning of signs independently of human sign usage. Even the rules governing usage introduced by human beings may not be conceived as components of a system that can be hypostatized independently of their use. Even rule-Platonism is, according to the later Wittgenstein, a superstition.) If one interprets *these* reflections under the traditional presupposition of *methodo-*

157

logical solipsism, then, in my opinion, one must view Wittgenstein's *conventionalism* as an extreme expression of that irrational, arbitrary decisionism whose nominalist tradition I have already sought to interpret.[60]

Yet, on the other hand, however, one finds a motif in Wittgenstein's later work that, in my opinion, may be interpreted as the *counterpoint to the irrationalist version of conventionalism* – though from the outset I would concede that, in so doing, one must somehow counterpose Wittgenstein with Wittgenstein. In my opinion, the counterpoint to arbitrary conventionalism lies in the *conception of the 'language-game'*. More precisely, it lies in the application of this conception in the thesis that 'one alone and only once' cannot follow a rule. If this were indeed possible, i.e. if methodological solipsism were correct, then the question of the criteria of meaning or the validity of speech-acts which, for their part, must make us aware of the meaning of knowledge and actions, would be quite unable to be answered. (We would have reached a position that in Plato's *Theaitetos* is ascribed to those – the Heracliteans – who do not recognize anything fixed that could serve as an object or standard of knowledge.) For in his later work, Wittgenstein had not only suspended all objective-metaphysical criteria of validity but also, so it appears, all Kantian subjective preconditions for the possibility of objectivity. None the less, in my opinion this latter 'appearance' is transcended by the *refutation of methodological solipsism.* The fact that 'one alone and only once' cannot follow a rule, that rather actions, interpretations of the world and linguistic usage must be 'interwoven' in the language-game as constituent elements of a *social life-form,* in my opinion signifies the new pivotal point of philosophy that the later Wittgenstein *nolens volens*[61] made available. It is precisely because, according to Wittgenstein, no objective or subjective metaphysical guarantee exists for the meaning of signs or even for the validity of rules that the 'language-game', as the horizon of all criteria of meaning and validity, must possess a *transcendental value.* To anticipate, one might say: We human beings, as creatures of language, so to speak – in contrast to animals – are condemned to 'agreeing' amongst ourselves about the criteria of meaning and validity of our actions and knowledge.[62]

The possibility of such an agreement as to the criteria (paradigms, standards) of correct decisions in all conceivable situations in life, however, presupposes, in my opinion, that linguistic agreement itself is *a priori* bound to *rules* in each possible language-game *that cannot be first established by 'conventions', but rather that make 'conventions' possible at all*: for instance, the norm of respecting rules in the social context, and this implies – amongst other things – the norm of fair and truthful (veracious) discussion. In my opinion, *such meta-rules* of all conventionally established rules do not belong to specific language-games or forms of life but to the transcendental language-game of the unlimited communication community.[63]

Yet is this still Wittgenstein's argument? I do not wish to attempt to answer this question here[64] but rather to attempt to show in a – perhaps dialectical – construction which misunderstandings or erroneous interpretations of the idea of the language-game are to be avoided if it is to fulfil the transcendental function of a foundation for the theory of science – as I conceive of it – and especially a foundation for the social sciences. First of all, there exist two difficulties that are *polar opposites*.

1 The first difficulty emerges if one understands Wittgenstein's discussion of 'given' language-games or forms of life, which the philosopher can only 'describe' but not change, in terms of *methodological behaviourism,* thereby making language-games into the objects of empirical-analytical science in the sense of the 'logic of science'. In this case, of course, the transcendental value of the language-game is immediately lost and it results in exactly the same paradox as the reduction of the pragmatic sign dimension to an object of empirical-analytical science which is common in logical empiricism. As data that are to be merely observed and described, the language-game would, like all observational data in empirical-analytical science, already presuppose a language-game in whose context they could be identified and described as objective data. Were this latter language-game to be described, then it would once more presuppose an *ungiven* language-game, and so on *ad infinitum*. In short, the language-game as the precondition for the possibility and validity of establishing and interpreting rules – e.g. the rules for describing the world – could just as little be discussed at any time as could the pragmatic meta-dimension of conventions – as in Carnap – that lies at the basis of the construction and interpretation of artificial languages with the aid of everyday language.

2 However, one would also reach this aporia – already thought out to its ultimately paradoxical consequences in the *Tractatus* – if,

in terms of Kant's traditional transcendental philosophy, one were to understand the language-game merely as *the subjective precondition for the possibility of the description* of the world. One could then in no way speak of 'given language-games' but, at most, on the basis of *a single* – world-limiting – language-game, identify and describe such objects as having nothing to do with language. In this case, however, to speak of the 'interwoven' nature of linguistic usage with actions and external expressions in the sense of given 'forms of life' would no longer have any meaning. In short, the language-game would now lose its character as a phenomenon imprinted by the world just as, on the basis of a behaviouristic interpretation, it loses its transcendental value.

The conclusion that is reached from this dialectical confrontation of two interpretative fictions lies, in my opinion, in the insight that the conception of the language-game cannot in any way be conceived of in an uncontradictory manner on the basis of the traditional, Cartesian-Kantian separation of subject and object. It would appear that the subject-object distinction can, at most, clarify – in the sense of a methodological auxiliary conception – the distinction between empirical and transcendental aspects of the language-game concept. At the same time, this implies that the notion of the language-game cannot be conceived of in terms of the 'logic of science'. For, with regard to the subject-object relationship, the latter distinguished itself from Descartes' metaphysical dualism or from the *Critique of Pure Reasons*'s transcendental scientism only by virtue of the fact that it no longer *reflects* upon *its own* transcendental presuppositions and hence completely elevates the subject-object-separation that is successful in classical physics into being the self-evident presupposition of all theories of science and respectable philosophies. But to put it more precisely, wherein lies the *incompatibility of the language-game concept with scientism's subject-object-separation*?

On this occasion, one should remember, in my opinion, that the philosophy of the historical spirit (Hegel) – basically first established after Kant – and – partly dependent upon Hegel and partly in competition – the foundation of the historical-hermeneutic human sciences (by Schleiermacher and the members of the 'Historical school' up to Dilthey, Max Weber and Collingwood) has more or less negated scientism's subject-object separation. Leaving aside all the significant differences in their theory of science, for all these approaches society is – to speak dialectically – a 'subject-object' with which one can identify through self-understanding and not merely treat as an object of description or explanation according to rules derived from outside. This notion of society as a subject-object is also valid, in my opinion, for Marx's 'historical materialism' provided one does not dogmatize it into a scientistic objectivism but rather places it back in the originally outlined context of the emancipation of subjective and intersubjective praxis and views it as a critique of ideology corrective to bourgeois human sciences. On the basis of what has just been said, we must ask the question: How does the conception of a language-game relate to the traditional dialectical-hermeneutic foundation of the human or social sciences?

As far as I know, the first person to ask this specific question and to produce the connection between the later Wittgenstein's language-game concept and the fundamental problem of the social sciences was Peter Winch in his book, *The Idea of A Social Science and Its Relation to Philosophy.*[65] In 1964 whilst working on a similar project,[66] I myself came across this book in the middle of writing my own. I found, first of all, that Winch had asked the decisive question that enabled him (a) to develop the behaviouristic interpretation of Wittgenstein *ad absurdum* and, at the same time, enable him (b) taking Wittgenstein as his point of departure, to ground afresh the fundamental distinction between 'understanding' as the method of the human sciences and 'explanation' as the method of the natural sciences.

The question that Winch, along with Wittgenstein, asked may be formulated in our context, as follows: How, then, does one know that a person actually – for his part – follows the rules with whose aid one describes his behaviour; that our concern is not merely with rules which we have applied to his behaviour from outside? In this context, Winch is inclined to suggest 'that any series of actions which a man may perform can be brought within the scope of some formula or other if we are prepared to make it sufficiently complicated'.[67] This question seems to me in fact to make manifest in a modern and not a psychological form the indispensable interest of the social sciences in the 'understanding' of the 'meaning' of actions. The reply to this question could indeed be seen to be unnecessary if the social researcher were to be satisfied with providing descriptions of behaviour in the service of technologically applicable knowledge.[68] Yet even in this case, which neopositivists seem always to have in front of them, the social scientist could hardly avoid 'understanding' on heuristic grounds. Otherwise he could never know whether the described behaviour actually dealt with the behaviour of people, e.g. with language.[69] This latter point of view refers to the answer that Winch (in the spirit of hermeneutic interpretation of Wittgenstein's work) ultimately provides to the question that he asked: I can only show that a person follows a rule, e.g. speaks or acts meaningfully, if his behaviour is capable of being made intelligible from the context of a language-game as publicly checkable rule-following. Yet I can show this only on the basis of participation in this language-game.[70]

It seems to me even today that in this solution, which I could only outline very roughly, there still lies the decisive step over the rubicon of the objectivistic 'logic of science' – a step behind which one should no longer fall back. In the notion of *participation in a common language-game* – that, of course, requires further elucidation – there is opened up precisely that *transcendence of the subject-object separation* which can only be meaningfully required for the interpretative human or social sciences and which in the nineteenth century – because of the psychologistic theory of understanding as 'empathy' or 'empathetic reconstruction' – could not be sufficiently established. In my opinion, it is quite another matter with regard to the consequences which Winch believes he must draw from his approach that is based on Wittgensteinian premises. They seem to me to reproduce, on the one hand, the idealistic, on the other, the relativisitic poverty of German philosophy of the *Geisteswissenschaften* at the turn of the century in the extreme elevation of an abstract and unhistorical mode of thought.[71] I believe that this result is determined by a deep ambiguity of some of these consequences and even by a deep ambiguity in Wittensteinian presuppositions.

With a certain justification, Winch sees the logical distinction between natural scientifically (i.e. with the aid of causal or statistical laws) explicable connections between events and interpretable connections between actions and concepts in a language-game as lying in the fact that the former represent 'external', whilst the latter represent 'internal' relations. That is, the former can only be 'explained' as necessary on the basis of hypothetically imputed, empirical natural laws, whereas the latter can only be 'understood' as necessary on the basis of the reconstruction of intended meanings (of actions or concepts). From this Winch draws the following methodologically extreme conclusion, that the social sciences can (or may) only make their object intelligible – the behaviour or institutions within human societies or cultures – in such concepts as can be understood by the members of the relevant society; *in principle,* in the concepts of their language-game and that means on the basis of the paradigm of their 'form of life'. In turn, Winch concludes from this quasi-postulate that a critical questioning and evaluation of a particular social form of life and interpretation of the world – in the sense of Durkheim's, Pareto's or Labriola's (and that means Marx's!) critique of ideology – is, in principle, inadmissible.[72] There are, of course, different language-games or forms of life and these are, at the same time, the ultimate transcendental horizons and standards for possible norms and their infringement. Outside these horizons there exist no *criteria* for what is true or false;[73] or good and evil. Accordingly, Winch comes to the conclusion that, 'To take an *uncommitted view* [my emphasis] of such competing conceptions [i.e. the recognizability of things in 'different competing forms of life'] is peculiarly the task of philosophy; it is not its business to award prizes to science, religion or anything else. It is not its business to advocate any *Weltanschauung* . . . In Wittgenstein's words, "Philosophy leaves everything as it is".'[74]

It seems to me that in his later writings Winch has attempted to correct or to qualify his relativistic – and, as is still to be shown, paradoxical – basic position. Thus, for example, Winch shows in the important and interesting article 'Nature and Convention',[75] that it would be meaningless to call the norm of truthful (veracious) discourse a 'social convention', upon which a society could be agreed or even not agreed (or the convention that in one form of life it might be the foundation of communication whereas in another it would not be accepted). Rather, the norm of truthful discourse is, as Winch shows, a precondition for the possibility of any functioning language-game and must therefore not merely be accepted in principle in every society but, to a certain degree, must be fulfilled in order for communication to be possible at all: 'the supposition that telling lies could be the norm and telling the truth a deviation from it is self-contradictory. And again, if *per absurdum* the incidence of "true" and "false" statements were statistically random, there could be no distinction between truth and falsity at all, therefore no communication.'[76] In a similar manner, Winch shows that, in principle, it is not possible to explain intersubjective agreement

163

between people in some society in terms of the reciprocal manipulation of individuals as in Hobbes's state of nature or the Sophist's
idea of rhetoric: 'For one can only use words to manipulate the
reactions of other men in so far as those others at least think they
understand what one is saying. So the concept of understanding is
presupposed by the possibility of such manipulation of reactions
and cannot be elucidated in terms of it.'[77] Finally, Winch generalizes
the point of his example in the sense that 'integrity' is an indispensable
presupposition for the functioning of social institutions (for role
behaviour) in the same sense as 'fair play' is indispensable for the
possibility of games. And he summarizes the fact of his reflection
upon 'the relationship of the general idea of these virtues and their
particular social manifestations' in the following aphorism from
Vico: 'There must in the nature of human things be a mental
language to all nations, which uniformly grasps the substance of
things feasible in human social life, and expresses it with as many
diverse modifications as these same things may have diverse aspects.'[78]

Viewed from my perspective, Winch himself here points to the
preconditions for the possibility of all communications and social
interaction that are no longer relativizable to individual language-
games but rather lie in the nature *of* the (transcendental) language-
game. I would put it as follows. He points to the both hermeneutically
and ethically (and natural law-like) relevant norms of the ideal
language-game that we must presuppose – even though imperfectly
realized or marred by socially-specific malformations – in any
language-game and that means in any human form of life. But this
'transcendental hermeneutic' approach obviously did not prevent
Winch from adhering to certain basic presuppositions of his earlier
language-game relativism. Thus in his study 'Understanding a
Primitive Society',[79] he draws from the Wittgensteinian assumption
of a 'paradigm' specific to the language-game the provocative inference that a critique of belief in witches and the particular magical
practices in Azande cultures that are described by Evans-Pritchard[80]
is, in principle, impossible on the basis of the standards of our culture
which is permeated by science.

In this context, it seems to me to be understandable and justified
that both philosophers and practising social scientists have expressed
sharp criticism of Winch's conclusions.[81] Unfortunately, in so
doing, most of them have also roundly rejected Wittgenstein's and
Winch's basic assumption and have therefore fallen back upon the

position of the objectivistic 'logic of science' (of a neopositivist or Popperian variety). In contrast, I believe it is necessary to critically reconstruct the basic approach associated with the language-game that is interwoven in a social form of life by confronting Wittgenstein with Wittgenstein or Winch with Winch.

We commence with a paradox. If – as Wittgenstein, in fact, suggested – the innumerable diverse language-games or forms of life as 'given' (pre-) facts are also to be the ultimate quasi-transcendental rule-horizons for the understanding of meaning, then one cannot understand how these different rule-horizons themselves can be understood and hence 'given' as language-games. *One* language-game at least is excluded and presupposed as a transcendental language-game when one speaks of given language-games as quasi-transcendental facts (in the sense of a language-game relativism). On the other hand, the *diverse* language-games may not only be 'given' as *observable* phenomena for the transcendental philosophical language-game. Rather, the latter must, in principle, be capable of interpretative participation in all 'given' language-games if such a thing as understanding alien forms of life is to be possible.[82] Here, with compelling necessity, there is already the question of a *transcendental unity of the diverse rule-horizons* that cannot be *given* but which, none the less, create *a priori* a communication connection between the quasi-empirically given language-games. How, in fact, could someone – a philosopher or a social scientist – be in a position to undertake a comparison of 'given' language-games? Yet the philosopher or social scientist must be capable by means of a specific language-game of transcending comparative participation in the given language-games. In this respect, Winch's mention of an 'uncommitted view' that the philosopher should maintain is already paradoxical.[83] For it is clear from Winch's and Wittgenstein's presuppositions that the philosopher too can understand and evaluate only in terms of the specific presuppositions of a language-game. According to Winch, he must interpret and evaluate since otherwise he cannot judge as to correct or incorrect rule-following. In short, the philosopher and also the interpretative social scientist must, in some manner, participate in all language-games or forms of life 'given' to him and not merely hover above them and observe them. At the same time, however, he must be in a position to maintain a critical distance from all language-games or forms of life in order that he can compare them as 'given' in the world and not, as it were, sink down into one of them. In my opinion, the task outlined here is only soluble if the philosopher or critical social scientist can relate himself to a language-game that, on the one hand, is presupposed in all given language-games and, on the other, however, can be considered as a (still) unrealized ideal. Thus far, however, we have still not taken into account the concrete historical relationships between the language-games.

The postulate of a transcendental language-game is clearly distinguished from a solution to the problem of inter-cultural understanding *solely* on the basis of the factual similarity of human circumstances of life – demonstrable by empirical-anthropological comparison – e.g. on the basis of institutions related to birth, death and sexuality. At the end of his article on 'Understanding a Primitive Society', Winch seems to have in mind such a solution to the problem of relativism. In so doing, he has recourse, as he did earlier in 'Nature and Convention', to Vico's foundation of the 'New Science' of the institutions of the 'mondo civile' and, in particular, to the following passage (*The New Science*, §§ 332-3):

> Now since the world of nations has been made by man, let us see in what institutions men agree and always have agreed. For these institutions will be able to give us the universal and eternal principles (such as every science must have) on which all nations were founded and still preserve themselves.
> We observe that all nations, barbarous as well as civilized, though separately founded because remote from each other in time and space, keep these three human customs: all have some religion, all contract solemn marriages, all bury their dead . . .

Now two interpretations of this passage are possible in my opinion. Either, the *principles* of understanding should be derived fom the comparative generality of the indicated circumstances of life as social facts. In this case, it would not be clear why here – in contrast, for instance, to the behaviour of animals – one should speak of intelligible *institutions*. Or, the principles of cross-cultural understanding lie in the fact that birth, death and sexuality are always *understood linguistically*, and *in the context of a language-game* are the reference point of institutions in all *human* societies. In this case – which Winch seems to favour when he speaks of birth, death and sexuality as 'limiting notions' or 'limiting concepts' – it is the comparative general circumstances of life as the common 'paradigms' of all human *language*-games that are to make *understanding* possible. In my opinion, however, this already pre-supposes a *linguistic competence* in the sense of 'grammatical competence' (Chomsky) and, over and above that, in the sense of 'communicative competence' (Habermas)[84] that all human beings have in common. In short, the genuine precondition for the possibility and validity of understanding is here the *transcendental language-game* that, of course, has its *real* basis and its genetic starting-point in the basic fact of the life of the human species. Wittgenstein once said: 'If a lion could speak, then we could not understand it.' This seems to me to be not very plausible since it is precisely linguistic competence and not, for instance, the conditions of life (birth, death, sexuality) – conceived of as independent of linguistic competence – that separates us from lions.

If it is the case that the requirement of a transcendental language-game *in* all language-games is *in principle* already established by means of this still very abstract 'dialectic', then this requirement may be made more concrete if we turn our attention to the specific form of participation in two language-games that lie in the skilful ('hermeneutic') understanding of an alien form of life. This under-standing could not commence at all as the confrontation of two completely opposing, closed, incommensurable systems of rules, yet for all that it is usually historically brought about by the shock and fascination of confrontation with strange peoples – also by confrontation with one's own tradition when it has become alien or artificially alienated. Thus, 'hermeneutic understanding' commences – in contrast to what Dilthey termed 'pragmatic understanding' that does not overstep the context of a 'general sphere' of life[85] – with a 'confrontation' between two horizons that, at the same time, already presupposes a *transcendental unity of interpreta-tion*[86] as the precondition for its possibility. Since only this makes possible the synthesis of understanding and not, for instance, the diverse, actually established rules of language-games, then at this point the ambiguity of Winch's thesis may be clarified; namely, that human behaviour can or may be made intelligible only through such concepts as, *in principle,* can be understood by the actors them-selves. The ambiguity here concerns the words 'in principle'. If it is interpreted in terms of the *already established* rules of a 'given' language-game, then it leads to the paradoxes of relativism already outlined: there emerges the demand to understand any language-game (any form of life) *only within its own terms*. Yet this must be impossible for the not already initiated ('drilled': Wittgenstein) members of a foreign form of life. If, on the contrary, the demand for the intelligibility of social scientific concepts is established *in principle* for the subject-object of science with reference to the *possibility* of an already presupposed understanding between language-games (of the social scientist and his objects) – in other words, if it refers to the *synthetic unity of the transcendental language-game* – then, in my opinion, Winch's thesis represents a fundamental hermeneutic principle. It represents a principle that, as will be shown, is not cancelled out by the questioning of human forms of life and language-games by the critique of ideology. It now commences from the presupposition – not explicitly reflected upon by Wittgenstein – that, in principle, any 'language-game' as a *language-*game (and this means, any *human* form of life) is capable of being transcended and expanded by *self-reflection* through philosophy or critical social science.

The *dialectical* relationship between the unity *and* diversity of the transcendental language-game and the quasi-empirically given language-games or forms of life, becomes more clear if Winch's distinction between *internal* and *external* relations is included in the discussion. On the face of it, this distinction is very well suited to clarifying the radical distinction between *interpretable* relationships between (intentional) actions and concepts (in which the actors themselves can, in principle, make explicit the meaning of their actions) and – causal or statistical – *explicable* relationships between natural events. In so doing, it should be borne in mind that Winch's distinction is obviously taken from the early Wittgenstein's *Tractatus* where it characterizes, on the one hand, a *transcendental difference* in terms of the Cartesian-Kantian *subject-object separation* and, on the other, a logical difference in terms of the distinction between *analytic* and *synthetic*. Yet from the outset, it is questionable whether such a distinction can be applied without considerable modification to the later Wittgenstein's intended relationship of 'interwovenness' between actions and linguistc usage. But even if, from the outset, one assumes a sphere for reciprocal interpretation of elements interwoven with one another in 'forms of life' and one only maintains that no contradiction may exist between them, difficulties emerge. It is certainly correct to say that human actions and words (concepts) *should* interpret each other without contradiction. This *demand* lies, in my opinion, in the transcendental presupposition of an *ideal* language-game. Consequently, can *this* relationship be assumed without further ado in 'given' language-games or forms of life?

At this point, in my opinion, the reproach of methodological *idealism,* that has been made against Winch's language-analytical foundation of the social sciences, is justified to some extent.[87] In fact Winch seems to assume *ideal* intelligibility (in accordance with *internal relations*) – anticipatable only as the norm of the transcendental language-game – precisely where it cannot *a priori* be introduced: in the case of the – in his view – untranscendable diversity of actual language-games or forms of life. The ideological confusion of the ideal with what was socially present at the time, that characterized the *methodological idealism* of the human sciences in the nineteenth century, proves to be identical here with a *relativism* for which history can hold no regulative principle for its possible transcendence. In this context, I would speak of an 'idealistic fallacy' that forms the counterpoint to the 'naturalistic fallacy' of the scientistic reduction of interpretable to explainable relationships. At the same time, I would propose to interpret the 'interwovenness' of linguistic usage, activity, expression of life and interpretation of the world in Wittgenstein's 'language-games' or 'forms of life' in terms of a *dialectical unity* that does not exclude *contradiction* between its *elements.* In my opinion, it is only given this proviso that talk of 'internal relations' is transferable from logico-mathematical systems to 'given' social circumstances of life.

This would imply, on the one hand, that one always has to take human actions and words seriously *hermeneutically* in terms of their potential intelligibility and even truth or normative and ethical correctness in the context of an ideal language-game with *internal relations* between words and actions (and knowledge). *This* demand (Gadamer's 'anticipation of perfection'),[88] results from the transcendental assumption of ideal unity of understanding that each person, who himself speaks or who listens to another, has always already made. (And since, in my opinion, a 'private language' is unthinkable, so also are the solitary thoughts and actions of each individual always already related to the ideal language-game in the ideal communication community.) On the other hand, however, one must at the same time take into account the fact that, in given language-games or forms of life, there exists a more or less great discrepancy, even contradictions between actions and concepts. If one seeks to make these discrepancies or contradictions intelligible then, in my opinion, one also has to deal throughout with 'external relations' – that is, for example, with 'explainable' causal relationships – between unconscious ideas and constrained modes of behaviour or between interests that are immanent to practice (i.e. meaningful motives that are not conceptually explicated) and official linguistic regulations *qua* 'institutional fictions'.[89] Of course, these *external relations* cannot be *explained* solely on the basis of causal hypotheses but must also, at the same time, be *understood* as such latent *internal relations* as could be taken up into the language-game of a given form of life because of certain rules of taboo. In my opinion, it is precisely this combination of quasi-causal explanation and deep-hermeneutic understanding (especially of unconscious teleological behaviour) that extends beyond actual linguistic usage and actual self-understanding of social forms of life, which characterizes the *methodological* procedures of the *critique of ideology*. Hence, this does not damage the basic transcendental-hermeneutic claim that their motivational assumptions must *in principle* be capable of being understood by the members of the form of life that is criticized. This is testified by the fact that critique of ideology, as public critique, also provokes *in principle* those criticized to a deeper self-understanding. Indeed, from the outset, it lays claim to the synthetic unity of the transcendental language-game and thereby assumes that this unity can, in principle, be realized for any language-game by reflexive self-transcendence of the actual rules including the 'paradigm'.

Indeed, I believe that one has to take into account ideological relationships even more the further actions and concepts are distanced from the functional sphere of work – even in primitive cultures that already anticipated experimental science's control for error. This should not be intended to imply that in the so-called higher or 'superstructural' realms of culture, in the realms of 'formative' and 'salvational knowledge'[90] as they were termed by Max Scheler, no language-game free of contradiction can *eo ipso* be presupposed.

None the less, it should be remembered here – along with Peirce,[91] Dewey[92] and Marx – that, in these spheres, we are concerned most seriously and in greatest detail with limitations upon rational communication and social 'association' (Marx) by the authoritarian repressions and tabooing of words and actions; in short, with the ideological fixations of the self-alienation of socialized human beings. However, where such overt distortions indeed confront the ideal function of the language-game, then, in my opinion, we have to suppose alien horizons of rules that, as the final standards or paradigms of world-understanding, have equal rights with those of such a culture that has placed itself under the hermeneutic ideal of an unrestricted understanding. This already also implies that we are in no way concerned with measuring all myths, religions and, if possible, all metaphysical outlines of world-views by the standards of a modern, Western science in the sense of 'science' and 'techno-logy'.[93] Only in as much as primitive practices themselves as pseudo-technologies – that both recognize empirical evidence and immunize themselves against unwished-for results – subject themselves *nolens volens* to the standard of experimental science and technology are they to be judged according to this standard. In fact, this seems to me to be the case with the Azande's sorcery tests and with all comparable magical practices[94] – but not, on the other hand, with Indian yoga practices, for example, in which at least a rational core, in the sense of a type of knowledge and faculty that is irreducible from the standpoint of objectivistic science and tech-nology, may be inherent within it.[95] Similarly, there seems to me to be a distinction between 'mysticism' – perhaps understood in the sense of the adherents of scientism – i.e. ritual-magical practices of restriction or tabooing of rational communication and major intel-lectual mysticism such as Shankara's or Meister Eckhart's, which did not in fact possess the function of ritual fixation and isolation of cultural forms of life but rather introduced an intellectual emanci-patory movement.[96]

Naturally, these reflections are not primarily concerned with the correctness of my appraisal of these examples but rather with an illustration of the concept of concrete social and intellectual history, in which the closed rule-horizons of language-games as forms of life do not exist at all – in contrast to primitive cultures, at least, where their existence can perhaps be confirmed. In this universal history of humanity, that has, of course, essentially been made possible by Western culture, I believe that concern not only in the scientific-technical sphere but also in all dimensions of culture is concentrated on the progressive realization of the always transcendentally presupposed ideal language-game in the given forms of life and in opposition to irrational limits to communication in these forms of life. This *goal of a hermeneutic enlightenment* that does not *leave everything as it is* cannot, of course, be achieved without the inclusion of the *critique of ideology*[97] which must also be entrusted with the task of engaging in a critique of whole forms of life and their official language-games. This task requires, in my view, sailing between the Scylla of a relativistic hermeneutics, which sacrifices its own conditions for its possibility to the pluralism of language-game monads, and the Charybdis of a dogmatic-objectivistic critique that no longer admits of any real discourse. Indeed I believe – and in so doing I return to the thesis announced in the introductory title – that this goal of philosophy and the critical social sciences can be achieved in the long run only along with the *practical realization* of the unlimited communication community in the language-games of social systems of self-assertion.[98]

Notes

1 On this thesis of so-called critical rationalism, see H. Albert, *Traktat über kritische Vernunft*, Tübingen, 1969. For an attempted metacritique of 'Critical Rationalism', see K.-O. Apel, 'The Problem of Philosophical Fundamental Grounding in the Light of a Transcendental Pragmatic of Language', *Man and World*, 18, 1975, pp. 239–75.

2 The rejection of a transcendental foundation rests on this limitation for K. Popper (cf. *Conjectures and Refutations*, London, 1965, pp. 190 ff.), and S Körner (cf. 'The Impossibility of Transcendental Deductions', in *The Monist*, 51, 1967; and 'Zur Kantischen Begründung der Mathematik und der Naturwissenschaften', in *Kantstudien*, 56, 1966).

3 This is demonstrated in the 'reconstruction' – based on H. Dingler's work – of the Kantian foundation as 'protophysics' by P. Lorenzen (*Methodisches Denken*, Frankfurt, 1968, pp. 120 ff.), that is in fact both confirmed and relativized by C. F. von Weizsäcker in terms of a 'methodological a priorism' (cf. 'Das Verhältnis der Quantenmechanik zur Philosophie Kants', III, 3, in his *Weltbild der Physik*, Stuttgart, 1958). A cognitive-anthropological foundation of the complementarity of the *a priori* of 'life' and 'reflexion' could, in my opinion, solve this apparent difficulty by a reconstructed transcendental philosophy: the protophysicalist validity of Euclidean geometry and classical physics as the methodical *a priori* of experimental action may be traced back to the *a priori* of a centric life-engagement (the mediation of knowledge through praxis), the possibility of an objectification and relativization of the methodical *a priori* may be traced back to the eccentric *a priori* of

reflection. (Cf. provisionally, K.-O. Apel, 'Das Leibapriori der Erkenntnis', *Archiv für Philosophie*, 12, 1963, pp. 152–72).
4 On this point, see K.-O. Apel, 'C. S. Peirce and the Question of the Truth-Conception of Modern Empirical Science', *Proceedings of the Peirce Society,* 1979, forthcoming.
5 See ch. 3 in this volume.
6 Cf. L. Wittgenstein, *Philosophical Investigations*, p. 100^e.
7 A decision in the light of an alternative itself still presupposes the *transcendental language-game* for those who perform the decision as *meaningful* action. For 'one person alone and only once' cannot follow a rule (Wittgenstein); and even self-decision is, as meaningful action, also basically a public following of rules. Cf. my argument against Popper in 'Sprache als Medium und Thema der Reflexion', in *Transformation der Philosophie*, vol. 2, Frankfurt, 1973, pp. 311–29.
8 According to Husserl, 'methodological solipsism' should be the starting-point for every sincere thinker.
9 See ch.3 in this volume.
10 See ch. 4 in this volume.
11 For a corresponding mediation between Hegel and Marx, cf. K.-O. Apel, 'Reflexion und materielle Praxis: zur erkenntnisanthropo-logischen Begründung der Dialektik zwischen Hegel und Marx', *Hegelstudien*, Beiheft 1, 1964, pp. 151–66 (reprinted in *Transformation der Philosophie*, vol. 2, pp. 9–27).
12 For the sense-critical approach as a whole cf. K.-O. Apel, *Der Denkweg von C. S. Peirce*, Frankfurt, 1976, and 'C. S. Peirce and the Question of the Truth-Conception of Modern Empirical Science'.
13 Cf. especially the Preface to *The Phenomenology of Mind*. Also, M. Heidegger, 'Hegel's Begriff der Erfahrung', in *Holzwege*, Frankfurt, 1950, pp. 105–92 and H.-G. Gadamer, *Truth and Method*, London, 1975, pp. 310 ff.
14 Cf. Popper, 'What is Dialectic?', in *Conjectures and Refutations*, 3rd ed., pp. 312 ff.
15 This need not be equated, in my opinion, with 'historicism' in Popper's sense but rather with a *critical historicism* in the sense of both the normative and empirical reconstruction of the history of the 'open society' that Popper himself implicitly attempts as a philosopher of history and society.
16 Moreover, Weber's emphasis on *value-free* science presupposes his own *affirmative evaluation* of the possibility of historical progress in (value-free) science and his *non-value-free interpretation* of history as a 'rationalization' process. Hence this *non-value-free* interpretation of social history is – as in the case of Popper's philosophy of the 'Open Society' – not just a hypothesis based on an arbitrary decision, but a normative precondition for the possibility of an account of the value-freedom of science – which then, of course, has to be restricted to technologically relevant natural science and quasi-nomological social science. On this problem, see K.-O. Apel, 'Types of Social Sciences in the Light of Human Interests of Knowledge', *Social Research*, 44, no.

3, 1977, pp. 425–70, and 'Types of Rationality Today: The Continuum of Reason between Science and Ethics', *Proceedings of the International Conference on 'Rationality Today'* (Ottawa, October, 1977), ed. T. Geraets, Ottawa, 1978.

17 I am thinking here especially of the works of Niklas Luhmann which not only relate the functions of social systems but also system formation itself to the so-called cognitive-anthropological meta-problem of the 'reduction in the complexity of the world'. Cf. especially, 'Soziologie als Theorie sozialer Systeme', *Kölner Zeitschrift für Soziologie und Sozialpsychologie,* 19, 1967; and N. Luhmann, *Zweckbegriff und Systemrationalität,* Tübingen, 1968. Cf. also n. 39 below.

18 Cf. for example, Hans Albert, 'Wertfreiheit als methodisches Prinzip', in E. Topitsch (ed.), *Logik der Sozialwissenschaften,* Cologne/Berlin, 1965, pp. 181–212. Further, D. Junker, 'Über die Legitimität von Werturteilen in den Sozialwissenschaften und der Geschichtswissenschaft', *Historische Zeitschrift,* 211, no. 1, 1970, pp. 1–33.

19 For a discussion of this topic see my 'Sprechaktheorie und transzendentale Sprachpragmatik zur Frage ethischer Normen', in K.-O. Apel (ed.), *Sprachpragmatik und Philosophie,* Frankfurt, 1976.

20 Cf. J. Habermas, 'Wahrheitstheorien', in *Wirklichkeit und Reflexion,* Pfullingen, 1973, pp. 211–65; and ch. 7 in this volume.

21 Cf. Apel, *Der Denkweg von Charles S. Peirce.* Further, G. Wartenberg, *Logischer Sozialismus,* Frankfurt, 1971.

22 Cf. the approach of P. Lorenzen, *Normative Logic and Ethics,* Mannheim/Zürich, 1969; and his 'Szientismus versus Dialektik', in R. Bubner (ed.), *Hermeneutik und Dialektik,* Tübingen, 1970, pp. 57–72.

23 This assertion of an *a priori* interlocking of interests of 'science' and technology, conditioned by the cognitive-anthropological structure of the experiment, has nothing to do with a vulgar pragmatic (instrumentalist) reduction of the truth of science. Cf. my essay, 'Types of Social Science'.

24 Cf. n. 17 above, n. 89 below.

25 On this point, K. Marx, *German Ideology,* Moscow, 1965. Cf. also K.-O. Apel, 'Reflexion und materielle Praxis', *Hegelstudien,* Beiheft 1, 1964, pp. 151–65. See also D. Böhler, *Metakritik der Marxschen Ideologiekritik,* Frankfurt, 1971, pp. 42 ff., 108 ff., 232 ff.

26 Cf. K.-O. Apel, 'Wissenschaft als Emanzipation', *Zeitschrift für Allgemeine* Wissenschaftstheorie, 1, 1970, pp. 173–95 (reprinted in *Transformation der Philosophie,* vol. 2, pp. 128–54).

27 Cf. Goethe's aperçu: 'The actor is always reckless.'

28 Cf. Bohler, *Metakritik der Marxschen Ideologiekritik,* pp. 47 f., 95 ff., 113 ff., 237 ff.

29 Cf. my critical assessment of this theory of understanding that was established by Otto Neurath and has been developed by Carl Hempel, Theodor Abel and Wolfgang Stegmüller and others in 'Communication and the Foundations of the Humanities', *Acta Sociologia,* 15, no. 1, 1972, pp. 7–26. See further, K.-O. Apel, *Die*

'*Erklären-Verstehen*' *Kontroverse in transzendentalpragmatischer Sicht,* Frankfurt, 1979.

30 Cf. K.-O. Apel, *Analytic Philosophy of Language and the '*Geisteswissenschaften*',* Dordrecht, 1967.

31 The fact that, according to Leibniz, this distinction is only relatively valid for a finite reason, while for the infinite reason of God 'contingent truths' are *a priori* demonstrable as 'necessary truths' – this rationalistic speculation naturally does not enter into the metaphysics of logical empiricism. One could say that, in this manner, the neo-Leibnizian metaphysic of logical empiricism, mediated via Bertrand Russell, is distinguished from Baroque rationalism.

32 Cf. L. Couturat (ed.), *Opuscules et fragments inédit de Leibniz,* Paris, 1903, pp. 153 ff.

33 Cf. R. Carnap, 'Überwindung der Metaphysik durch logische Analyse der Sprache', *Erkenntnis,* vol. 2, 1931, pp. 219–41.

34 Primarily in R. Carnap, *The Logical Syntax of Language,* London, 1937, foreword (pp. xiii ff.) and p. 51. Cf. also R. Carnap, *Introduction to Semantics,* Cambridge, Mass., 1942, p. 247.

35 Cf. K.-O. Apel, 'Heidegger's Radikalisierung der Hermeneutik und die Frage nach dem Sinnkriterium der Sprache', in O. Loretz and W. Strolz (eds), *Die Hermeneutische Frage in der Theologie,* Freiburg/Vienna, 1968, pp. 86–155 (reprinted in *Transformation der Philosophie,* vol. 1, pp. 276–334).

36 Cf. R. Carnap, 'Replies and Expositions', in P. A. Schilpp (ed.), *The Philosophy of Rudolf Carnap,* La Salle, Ill./London, 1963, p. 945.

37 With reference to the philosophical tradition, which only reveals attempts at overcoming *methodological solipsism* in very few places (e.g. in Herder, Hegel, Humboldt, Peirce, G. H. Mead, Heidegger), one could advance the following thesis: Both a philosophy that starts out – introspectively – from the contents of consciousness, and on this basis poses questions as to the existence of a real external world and possibly of 'other selves' and, on the other hand, a philosophy in which language is conceived as the unreflexive reflection of reality, must both remain within *methodological solipsism.* Only a philosophy that does not conceive of consciousness as a *receptaculum* but as the language-mediated interpretation of the real *as* something and, on the other hand, does not conceive of the cognitive function of language as representation but as the hermeneutic synthesis of predication, can integrate the *a priori of intersubjective understanding.*

38 Cf. J. L. Austin, *How to do Things with Words,* also John R. Searle, *Speech Acts.*

39 Cf. J. Habermas, 'Vorbereitende Bemerkungen zu einer Theorie der kommunikative Kompetenz', in J. Habermas and N. Luhmann, *Theorie der Gesellschaft oder Sozialtechnologie,* Frankfurt, 1971.

40 Cf. Charles Morris, 'Foundations of the Theory of Signs', in *International Encyclopaedia of Unified Science,* vol. 1, no. 2, Chicago, 1938.

41 Cf. Carnap, *Introduction to Semantics,* §§ 5, 38 and 39.

42 See p. 139 above.
43 The term 'onto-semantics' was first introduced by G. Jánoska, *Die Sprachlichen Grundlagen der Philosophie,* Graz, 1962. Cf. also E. K. Specht, *Sprache und Sein: Untersuchungen zur sprachanalytischen Grundlegung der Ontologie,* Berlin, 1967.
44 Cf. *Tractatus,* 5.555. 'Is it really possible that in logic I should have to deal with forms that I can invent. What I have to deal with must be that which makes it possible for me to invent them?'
45 Cf. ibid., 5.5563, 'In fact, all the propositions of our everyday language, just as they stand, are in perfect logical order'. And 4.002, 'Everyday language is a part of the human organism and is no less complicated than it. It is not humanly possible to gather immediately from it what the logic of language is. Language disguises thought.'
46 There emerges here the problem of an illegitimate philosophical 'ladder'-language in which, for example, the polemical 'introductions' and other philosophical utterances of the neopositivist supporters of constructive semantics are in fact written. This is a problem that is raised at the end of the *Tractatus.*
47 If I am not mistaken the unsolved problem of the relationship between formal logic and dialectics is to be found here.
48 'Solitary' in the sense of a metaphysical metaphor that Heidegger and the later Wittgenstein exposed as meaningless by recourse to the language-game with the word 'solitude' which is *a priori* inconceivable without the other language-games.
49 I do not believe that a distinction exists between these conceptions in Wittgenstein's *transcendental onto-semantics.*
50 In contrast, Wittgenstein specifically maintains that 'nothing *in the visual field* allows you to infer that it is seen by an eye', because the section – as in Descartes and Kant – runs between the body that belongs to the world of objects and the subject as the limit of the world. For a critique of this position, cf. K.-O. Apel, 'Wittgenstein und Heidegger', *Philosophische Jahrbuch,* 75, 1967, pp. 56–94 (reprinted in *Transformation der Philosophie,* vol, 1, pp. 225–75).
51 Cf. on this problem, Y. Bar-Hillel, 'A Prerequisite for Rational Philosophical Discussion', in Bar-Hillel, *Aspects of Language,* pp. 258–62.
52 Cf. R. Carnap, 'Meaning and Synonym in Natural Languages', in R. Carnap, *Meaning and Necessity,* Chicago, 1956, supplement.
53 Cf. Y. Bar-Hillel, 'Argumentation in Pragmatic Languages', in Bar-Hillel, *Aspects of Language,* pp. 206–21.
54 A way out of this dilemma is promised by the 'direct' – i.e. located in the transcendental-pragmatic dimension of everyday linguistic communication – method of linguistic reconstruction by the Erlangen school. Cf. W. Kamlah and P. Lorenzen, *Logische Propädeutik,* Mannheim, 1967. Further, K. Lorenz, *Elemente der Sprachkritik,* Frankfurt, 1970, vol. 2, 'Die Möglichkeit einer wissenschaftlichen Sprache'.
55 In this context, cf. K.-H. Ilting, 'Hobbes und die praktische

Philosophie der Neuzeit', *Philosophische Jahrbuch,* 72, 1964, pp. 84–102.

56 R. Carnap, 'Empiricism, Semantic, and Ontology', in L. Linsky (ed.), *Semantics and the Philosophy of Language,* Urbana, Ill., 1952, pp. 208–30.

57 Cf. pp. 136 f. above and the reference to the problem of ultimate justification.

58 Cf. my essay 'Types of Rationality Today'.

59 Cf. W. Stegmüller, 'Ludwig Wittgenstein: Philosophy II', in *Main Currents in Contemporary German, British and American Philosophy,* pp. 423 f.

60 There is much in the *Remarks on the Foundations of Mathematics* that *seems* in fact to speak in favour of such an interpretation.

61 It should not be disputed, at this point, that Wittgenstein's own intention was primarily to 'show the fly the way out of the fly glass' and that means to finally cure the disease of linguistic usage called 'philosophy' by means of philosophy itself – which is indeed, paradoxical. In this respect, Walter Schulz is correct (W. Schulz, *Wittgenstein: die Negation der Philosophie,* Pfüllingen, 1967). But I do not think this interpretation is a fruitful one.

62 This, I suggest, is the point of departure for a transcendental-pragmatic *consensus* theory of meaning and truth. For a Peircean approach to this same conception see my 'C. S. Peirce and the Question of the Truth-Conception of Modern Empirical Science'.

63 For an elaboration of these rules see Habermas's and my own contribution in K.-O. Apel (ed.), *Sprachpragmatik und Philosophie,* Frankfurt, 1976.

64 Cf. however Apel, 'Wittgenstein und Heidegger', as well as ch. 1 in this volume.

65 London, 1958.

66 K.-O. Apel, *Analytic Philosophy of Language and the 'Geisteswissenschaften'.*

67 Winch, *The Idea of a Social Science,* p. 29.

68 The form of description which Winch has in mind and which can be readily found seems to me in fact to be identical with the 'systematization' of knowledge in the sense of the natural-scientific interest in an 'explanation' according to laws only on the presuppositions of classical neopositivism. From the standpoint of Kant, Peirce, Toulmin, Ryle and the Popperians – in my view, justifiably – a sharp distinction should be made between a merely technologically utilizable generalization of symptoms (technique of prognosis) and a 'theory-laden' explanation. None the less, in the latter case, the question as to whether natural objects, for their part, follow the law as a rule is obviously meaningless. Thus, Winch has in fact adequately explicated the distinction between the questions of the 'explanatory' natural sciences and those of the 'interpretative' human or social sciences.

69 Cf. N. Chomsky's critical 'Review of B. F. Skinner's *Verbal Behavior',*

Language, vol. 35, 1959, pp. 26–58.

70 Cf. Winch, *The Idea of a Social Science,* p. 89: 'any more reflective understanding must necessarily presuppose, if it is to count as genuine understanding at all, the participant's unreflective understanding. And this in itself makes it misleading to compare it with the natural scientist's understanding of his scientific data.'

71 Cf. my critique in *Analytic Philosophy of Language and the 'Geisteswissenschaften'.*

72 Cf. Winch, *The Idea of a Social Science,* ch. 4.

73 The same problem – how the theoretical criteria of falsification are themselves capable of being falsified – stands at the centre of the controversy between Thomas Kuhn and Karl Popper in I. Lakatos and A. Musgrave (eds), *Criticism and the Growth of Knowledge,* Cambridge, 1970. And the final result of paradigm-relativism has been presented in the meantime in the form of Feyerabend's slogan: 'Anything goes'.

74 Cf. Winch, *The Idea of a Social Science,* p. 103.

75 In *Proceedings of the Aristotelian Society,* 1959–60, pp. 231–52.

76 Ibid., p. 243.

77 Ibid., p. 249.

78 Ibid., p. 251. Cf. on this my interpretation of the same passage in K.-O. Apel, *Die Idee der Sprache in der Tradition des Humanismus von Dante bis Vico,* pp. 377 f.

79 In *American Philosophical Quarterly,* 1, 1964, pp. 307–24.

80 Cf. E. Evans-Pritchard, *Witchcraft, Oracles and Magic among the Azande,* Oxford, 1937.

81 Cf. for example, the discussion in I. Lakatos and A. Musgrave (eds), *Problems in the Philosophy of Science,* Amsterdam, 1968, pp. 377–432.

82 This paradox is obviously identical with the paradox of the subject-object relationship referred to above as the presupposition of the hermeneutic sciences.

83 It calls to mind Karl Mannheim's paradoxical presupposition of a 'free-floating intelligentsia' that is intended to transform an engaged *critique of ideology* into a neutral *sociology of knowledge.* The 'suspicion of ideology' is thus both universalized and robbed of its critical function. For a critique of the sociology of knowledge, cf. K. Lenk (ed.), *Ideologie,* Neuwied, 1961.

84 Cf. n. 39 above.

85 Cf. Wilhelm Dilthey, *Gesammelte Schriften,* vol. 7, 5th ed., Stuttgart, 1968, pp. 146 f.

86 Cf. also my semiotical postulate of a *unity of sign interpretation* in chs 3 and 4 in this volume.

87 Cf. E. Gellner, 'The New Idealism: Cause and Meaning in the Social Sciences', in Lakatos and Musgrave (eds), *Problems in the Philosophy of Science,* pp. 377–406.

88 Cf. Gadamer, *Truth and Method.*

89 Cf. A. Gehlen, *Urmensch und Spätkultur,* Bonn, 1956.

90 Cf. Max Scheler, *Die Wissensformen und die Gesellschaft,*
    Bern/Munich, 3rd ed., 1960.
91 Cf. especially the article 'The Fixation of Belief', in C. S. Peirce,
    Collected Papers, Cambridge, Mass., 1934, vol. 5, §§ 358 ff. Cf. also on
    this my *Der Denkweg von Charles S. Peirce.*
92 Cf. especially J. Dewey, *Reconstruction in Philosophy,* New York,
    1920.
93 This seems to me to be Winch's strongest argument against critics of the
    Azande. Cf. 'Understanding a Primitive Society', *American
    Philosophical Quarterly,* 1, 1964, and also 'Reply to I. C. Jarvie', in R.
    Borger and F. Cioffi (eds), *Explanation in the Behavioural Sciences,*
    Cambridge, 1970, pp. 249 ff.
94 I would distinguish the concept of 'magic' in this sense from that of
    'myth'. Both are certainly 'interwoven' with one another in primitive
    cultures, but myth can contain a 'preview' (Ernst Bloch) of the truth,
    whereas, in my opinion, magical practices can be defined as the
    perversion of the notion of technique.
95 In my opinion, this may be made plausible on the basis of a cognitive-
    anthropological interpretation of depth psychology and 'autogenic
    training'.
96 In my opinion, the critical social sciences should just as fully distance
    themselves from a dogmatic scientism that allows one to see in
    mythical, metaphysical and the ontological traditions including their
    secularization in the humanities, only nonsense ('empty formulae')
    that has an ideological function (Ernst Topitsch, Hans Albert), as from
    a hermeneutic relativism that has abandoned history as the dimension
    of emancipatory progress (cf. 'Scientistics, hermeneutics and the
    critique of ideology', in this volume).
97 See ch. 2 in this volume, also Apel, 'Types of Social Science' esp. last
    section.
98 Cf. Habermas and Luhmann, *Theorie der Gesellschaft oder
    Sozialtechnologie.*

CHAPTER 6

Noam Chomsky's theory of language and contemporary philosophy: a case study in the philosophy of science

The problem and programmatic theses

There is no need for me to discuss the specific content and significance of Chomsky's theory of language for contemporary linguistics. In view of my subject, I would hardly possess the necessary competence for such an undertaking. If, however, in the course of this study I am forced to adopt a standpoint on these issues, then this is due to the practical inseparability of the methodological problem of the linguistic revolution which Chomsky and his pupils have undertaken, from the question – which I wish to discuss – concerning the relationship between this theoretical position and contemporary philosophy.

The relationship between linguistics and philosophy has, in fact, never been so close as it is today. Chomsky himself would, perhaps, be more precise and add: not since the rationalist and romantic philosophy of language and 'philosophical grammar' were superseded by comparative Indo-European studies and so-called modern empirical descriptive linguistics.[1] Be that as it may, the fact is that between the linguistics of the Chomskyan school and modern philosophy, i.e. primarily 'analytical' philosophy, there exists a kind of symbiosis that is not always peaceful – a far-reaching amalgamation of language games which also involves areas of mathematics and automata theory. On the one hand, therefore, it is immediately evident that Chomsky's theory of generative transformational grammar is inconceivable without the background of modern analytical philosophy and its logico-mathematical aids. On the other hand, it is precisely this close contact that had made it possible for his theory of language to have revolutionary effects, as an epistemologically and perhaps even meta-logically relevant theory of mind, upon analytical philosophy itself.

Katz, in particular, has attempted to give a comprehensive summary of these effects from the perspective of MIT linguistics. Since the early 1960s he has attempted – initially with Fodor – to extend Chomsky's syntactic theory by a *universal semantics* and to ground logic linguistically on this basis.[2] Finally, in his *Philosophy of Language* (1966) he presented a critical reconstruction of the entire development of analytical philosophy in this century and claimed to have overcome the one-sidedness of Carnap's 'constructive semantics' on the one hand, and 'ordinary language philosophy' on the other, in the form of a synthesis based on a theory of language.

Chomsky's interpretation of his own work in the realm of the philosophy and history of science is more cautious in its philosophical claims.[3] One is especially struck by his reticence concerning *semantics* and by his awareness of the problem of what must still be achieved both here and in a theory of 'performance'. Nevertheless, I believe that what is philosophically revolutionary about his approach and his line of reasoning when compared with the normal presuppositions made by analytic philosophy, emerges from Chomsky's writings more distinctly than from Katz's explicit philosophy of language.

In the following attempt at a critical appreciation and, to some extent, location of the philosophically relevant orientation of Chomsky and his school, I should like to draw upon two relevant areas. Unlike Katz,[4] who only sees Chomsky's theory in relation to analytic philosophy, I should like to refer to a wider area of reference that is not exclusively Anglo-American, namely, the distinction in terms of ideal types between three currently competing forms of the philosophy of science: (a) logical empiricism, (b) critical rationalism and (c) the hermeneutic-dialectical philosophy of the human and social sciences. The attempt to locate or evaluate Chomsky's ideas with this system of reference leads to one difficulty – as we shall demonstrate – which is closely connected with the relationship to the second and third alternatives. In my view, this difficulty lies in the object itself, namely, in the essence of language as something that is both natural and artificial, as the medium of transition from the realm of nature to the realm of freedom, but one which still has affinities with instinct. But the difficulty might also arise because

Chomsky's theory of language is one-sided or, rather, incomplete. I believe that its one-sidedness or incompleteness is to be seen above all in the absence of an adequate *semantics* and in the absence of a *pragmatically* expanded theory of linguistic *competence*, which actually makes possible the *theory of performance* that Chomsky postulates.

In order to demonstrate this and also to indicate the possibility of a solution to Chomsky's difficulties in the domain of the theory of science, I shall draw upon Morris's[5] and Peirce's *three-dimensional semiotics* in the last part of my paper, namely, the differentiated system of *syntactic, semantic,* and *pragmatic* sign dimensions or the science of signs. But I shall refer to this framework in a free manner, i.e. not in the sense of its adaptation by Morris to behaviourism or logical empiricism but rather in the sense of a transcendental pragmatic or transcendental hermeneutic semiotics,[6] which was developed from Peirce, Royce and Mead. In addition, I shall take up recent papers on the foundation of a 'systematic pragmatics' in which Chomsky's conception of 'competence' is extended or complemented in the form of a theory of 'communicative competence'.[7] I hope this will enable me to suggest how Chomsky's approach might be extended. In this connection it might be possible to answer the question as to which type of philosophical theory of science can most readily do justice to Chomsky's linguistic theory. In my view, it will then become clear that this type of linguistics must 'explain', on the one hand, the quasi-natural phenomenon of an instinctual linguistic competence as an anthropological fact on the basis of both the quasi-natural law of grammatical rule-generation and the limiting conditions governing the selection of specific grammars. On the other hand, it must 'understand' the free, creative and – in terms of a normative consciousness – self-explanatory application of grammatical rules in 'speech' and 'understanding' on the basis of the grammatical and communicative competence of the subject and object of linguistics. Moreover, it must reconstruct this application in a normatively correct manner. It is precisely this intermediate position of modern linguistic theory-formation, namely between nomothetic, explanatory natural science on the one hand, and interpretative social science on the other, which makes it the paradigmatic topic of a case study in the philosophy of science.

Chomskyan linguistics and its relationship to the philosophy of science

First of all, I should like to present the three major positions in contemporary philosophy of science in a simplified form as ideal types:

1   The first is (classical) *neopositivism* or *logical empiricism*. By this I understand the extension of classical empiricism in the sense that formal logic in its symbolic mathematical form is recognized as an independent factor of theory-formation alongside empirical data. But this means that, with its help, i.e. with the aid of a formalized calculus language, all the theory-formation of science, especially concept formation, is to be reduced to observational data. When the later Carnap found himself forced to distinguish between the 'language of theory' and the 'language of observation', and when he realized that the so-called 'theoretical concepts' (which are to be found in Newton's theory of gravity or Quantum theory) represent a function of the whole theory and consequently cannot be immediately reduced to empirical data with the aid of logic,[8] he had – in my view – already transcended the framework of logical empiricism and was progressing towards the second type, namely *critical rationalism*. The crucial feature of this step is very well expressed in the following characterization by Stegmüller (to quote an unimpeachable witness):[9]

> According to the notion of the older empiricists, a theorist in the empirical sciences may introduce only such concepts as are definable by means of the conceptual apparatus available to the observer, and the theorist has no more to do than sum up the data of observation and generalize them in the form of statements of universal laws. But now a new picture emerges of the tasks of the theorist, one that goes far beyond the mere generalization of observed regularities. He must construct a new system of concepts, some of which are only partially reducible to what is observable and the others not reducible at all. He must also devise a system of laws that contain these newly created concepts; and finally he must give an interpretation of his system that is required to provide only a partial empirical meaning, yet at the same time must suffice to enable the theoretical system to be used for predicting observable processes.

2   In the light of *critical rationalism,* I believe that this characterization must be radicalized. It is quite impossible for the theorist to
presuppose anything like fixed intersubjectively available data from
which, with the aid of logic – e.g. inductively – he could derive
theories. Rather, he must display spontaneous creativity and approach
the phenomenon with idealizing concepts or theories. Only in the
light of these concepts or theories can he demonstrate the scientific
relevance of the data. Critical rationalism recognizes the characteristic
feature of the classical theory-formation of modern mathematical
physics in the establishment of 'theory-laden' explanatory hypotheses,
that are not to be confused with merely descriptive 'generalization
of symptoms'[10] but rather they dare to assume a reality behind the
so-called 'observational data'. In short, critical rationalism sees the
foundation of science not primarily in the empirical data and logic,
but rather in *creative* theory-formation, in the context of which logic
and data first become relevant – relevant, that is, in terms of a
theory-formation in physics or linguistics. The standpoint adopted
here – as represented by Popper and his school – is compatible not
only with a recourse to Kant's Copernican turn, but also with the
recognition of the 'heuristic', 'explanatory' and 'science-critical'
function of a rationalist metaphysics in the pre-Kantian style.[11] This
metaphysics will, so to speak, be incorporated into the strategic,
methodological horizon of science as an indispensable background
– a science whose theory-formations, however, must always be
empirically testable, and (however indirectly) falsifiable.

3   *Critical rationalism,* however, as a logic of science shares with
logical empiricism – and, one could add, with the scientistically
orientated philosophy of the modern age before Hegel – one essential
presupposition, namely the presupposition of *a strict separation
between the subject and object* of knowledge, which is indeed essential
for all natural science.[12] This means that both types of logic of
science do not regard it necessary, in principle, to take into account
the fact that in the social sciences *qua* human sciences the object of
knowledge itself is, in principle, a virtual subject of science. Or, to
put it more precisely, the object is a co-subject of the scientist that
interests him, not merely as an entity whose behaviour is to be
observed, described and 'explained', but also – and even primarily –
as a partner in communication. Therefore, social science entails the
'understanding' of intended meaning. (In fact, the termination of
communication with nature, i.e. the willingness to forgo the 'under-

standing' of intended meanings, was the precondition for modern natural science.[13]) But the question that has aroused the interest of at least some German philosophers since Hegel and especially since Dilthey is whether a fundamentally new problematic for the philosophy of science arises if man or society is the subject matter. If this question receives an affirmative reply and society is dealt with as a *subject-object* of science that must first of all be 'understood', then I wish to refer to such a standpoint as the *hermeneutic-dialectical* position within the philosophy of science.

In order to draw upon this basic position as a system of reference for modern linguistics, I should like to reconstruct two of its basic postulates in a more modern form. The following account of the *hermeneutic-dialectical* position was itself only made possible by the quasi-linguistic ('language-analytical') method of the philosophy of this century. It does not fully take the historical-critical function of a hermeneutic-dialectical philosophy of science into account, but rather it concentrates on the formal limiting case of the analysis of rules. But for precisely this reason, it becomes relevant for linguistics in terms of the philosophy of science.

I   If one takes the later Wittgenstein or Winch's interpretation of Wittgenstein[14] as a starting-point, one can assert that the decisive question which the social scientist, as opposed to the natural scientist, must raise and answer is whether the rules that the scientist must correlate with the behaviour of the human objects of science even to 'describe' the so-called 'data', are followed by these objects as behavioural subjects. What, for instance, are the criteria which I require in order to *know* that a person whose behaviour I am 'observing' is reading, listening to the radio, playing chess, operating the light switch, etc.? How can the linguist *know* that a so-called 'native speaker' is actually *speaking*, and that in so doing he is following certain rules? The answer to such questions can only be derived from a language-game communication with the object, no matter how reflectively detatched and indirect this might be. This implies a method of 'interpretation' (*Verstehen*). Consequently, the concepts that are to be applied in the social sciences must, *in principle,*[15] be capable of being used by the objects *qua* possible subjects of science for their own self-understanding. I believe that this is a basic starting-point for a modern justification of hermeneutics or the 'subject-object-dialectic'.

II   The second basic demand of this position as a 'transcendental-

utic' one can be formulated in the following manner. For a
ental justification of the sciences in general it is necessary
recourse to the critical discourse of an unlimited, ideal
communication community. It is only with reference to the consensus
of such a community that the idea of scientific truth can be defined.[16]
In other words, the subject-related *pragmatic dimension of language*
cannot be reduced to an (observable) object of empirical science as
it is in 'scientism'. Rather, in accordance with the transcendental
pragmatism of Peirce and Royce, it must be discussed within the
framework of the 'interpreting community' of scholars. As a modern
equivalent to Kant's 'transcendental unity of consciousness as such',
one must demand the *transcendental unity of interpretation* in the
unlimited communication community of scholars. But in the case of
the social sciences, this postulated ideal communication community
cannot include merely the scientists for it is evident that the correctness of hermeneutic hypotheses cannot be corroborated or falsified
by pure 'observation'. The scientist must abandon his standpoint as
an observer, at least partially, in favour of a *participation* which is a
result of heuristic reflection in the language-game that is to be
understood. Since this participation is ultimately made possible by
the fact that the subject-object of the social sciences is, in principle,
capable of following rules that have been reflected upon (to a
certain extent, capable of 'meta-communication'), the ideal communication community as the precondition for the possibility of
reaching scientific consensus, must ultimately incorporate society as
the subject-object of science in the case of the social sciences. At
this point, the semiotic transformation of transcendental philosophy
merges with the non-psychologistic approach of hermeneutics in the
form of a *transcendental hermeneutics*.

Against the background of this system of reference, we shall now
attempt to examine the relationship between Chomskyan linguistics
and the philosophy of science. It is relatively easy to decide between
logical empiricism and critical rationalism. Chomsky's writings which
take up problems within the philosophy of science – from his critique
of Skinner's behaviourism (1959), via *Current Issues in Linguistic
Theory* (1964) to *Cartesian Linguistics* (1966) and *Language and
Mind* (1968) – represent a concerted plea for strong theory-formation
along the lines of critical rationalism and against all those 'discovery
procedures' of so-called 'modern linguistics',[17] which are considered
to be inductive and related to observation in the sense of logical

empiricism. Chomsky's basic distinction between linguistic 'competence', as the real topic of linguistics, and 'performance', which is found in a corpus of linguistic utterances, is also a methodological decision in favour of a (*generative*) theory-formation – derived from the mathematical theory of recursive functions – which transcends, in principle, all observational data and can only be tested in a very *indirect* manner on the basis of experience.[18] In a discussion of Carnap and Bar-Hillel,[19] Chomsky – like Katz[20] later – had already described the value of logical syntax and semantic for linguistics as being extremely slight. In contrast to logical empiricism, which seeks to prevent ambiguity and contradiction in each particular instance of theory-formation through the mathematical formalization of scientific language, and thereby provide paradigms for an ideal language as measuring standards for linguistics, Chomsky claims that his mathematization of grammar is derived directly from linguistic theory-formation itself – just as Newton's mathematization of physics was derived from his theory of gravity. The 'formation' and 'transformational' rules of his mathematized grammar do not in fact rest upon mere convention – unlike the corresponding rules in Carnap's constructed language. Rather, they correspond to the speculative, theoretical approach of generative grammar. This theory claims that, given the formation rules (and the lexicon) it must be possible to generate first the 'deep structure' with the aid of transformation rules and then the 'surface structure' of all the sentences in a language. Here Chomsky, like the later Popper, turns to the theory-formation of the seventeenth century as the paradigmatic foundation of modern science. Finally, with his provocative revival of the rationalist philosophy of the Baroque period (e.g. Descartes' notion of the *res cogitans,* the doctrine of innate ideas, and – in this context – Leibniz's Platonic belief in an *a priori* order of 'simple ideas' as combinable features of a 'universal semantics'),[21] Chomsky seems to go much further towards the rehabilitation of metaphysics than, for instance, the Popperian school does. One should, of course, not overestimate the systematic role of this tradition-conscious attitude. When Chomsky draws upon traditional rationalism he assumes, as if it were *self-evident*, that such doctrines concerning the *a priori* preconditions for cognition are not themselves true *a priori*. They must be incorporated as a substantive content into the *empirically* testable hypotheses of modern linguistics which – as a theory of language capability or language acquisition – is integrated into psychology. Chomsky, therefore, transforms the epistemological position of *a priorism* or rationalism into the empirical-psychological hypothesis of the innate device or scheme of language acquisition.[22] In so doing, he would ultimately like to do the same with Descartes' *res cogitans* that Newton achieved with Descartes' *res extensa.* As he makes clear in *Language and Mind,* he would like to realize a possibility which was overlooked in the seventeenth and eighteenth centuries and establish a theory of mind that is both analogous and complementary to Newtonian physics.[23] One might say, somewhat provocatively, that Chomsky would like to become the Newton of the *res cogitans.*

This programme, however, which revives *scientifically* traditional *philosophical* rationalism gives rise to quite remarkable philosophical problems. Is it his actual aim to make all the *a priori* preconditions for cognition in the sense of traditional epistemology the object of the *empirically* testable formation of hypotheses in the individual science, for example, by making Leibniz's belief in an *a priori* order of combinable ideas the object of an empirical hypothesis concerning the inventory of features of a universal linguistic semantics?[24] Or is his aim to make the belief in the spontaneous creativity of the human mind – a belief which stretches from Descartes via Kant and German idealism to Wilhelm von Humboldt – the object of a linguistic or psychological hypothesis concerning an instinctive mechanism that is both restrictive and generative? In *Language and Mind* this seems to be Chomsky's actual intention. This suggests a view of metaphysics that tests itself empirically through the formation of hypotheses in individual sciences. Such a conception was outlined in the nineteenth century, for example, by Peirce, whom Chomsky also seeks to follow in his abductive logic of conjecture or the instinct-guided formation of hypotheses.[25]

But this problem becomes very paradoxical when one recalls that – partially at least – Chomsky seems to translate the programme of Kantian transcendental philosophy into that of an empirically test-able epistemology.[26]

This linguistic-psychological theory of the human language faculty would then constitute an empirical science that also had as its object the preconditions for its own possibility and validity. This would certainly correspond to Bierwisch's postulate of a linguistic justi-fication of logic which, in turn, falls back upon Katz's claim to be able to resolve in linguistic terms the question of the distinction between analytical and synthetic judgments (through developing Kant's ideas in a positive manner).[27] But how can one conceive of an empirically testable theory that does not need to make presuppositions for this purpose – at least, no presuppositions in the logical sense – which cannot be empirically questioned?[28]

In a discussion with Stuart Hampshire,[29] Chomsky indicated how he envisaged the solution of such problems. Since scholars are in a position to conceive of a language that is not bound to the structure of the formal universals which Chomsky postulates, he concludes 'that there are faculties beyond the language faculty'. He believes, however, that these mental faculties should be looked upon and studied in a manner analogous to that used for the language faculty which he postulates. He believes that these faculties would also prove to be empirically limited. But with this reply which is consistent with the theoretical approach that we have described, Chomsky merely heightens the paradox of the transcendental aspect, for he assumes that *we* would also discover these *empirical-universal* limitations and consequently demonstrate that they can be transcended. The problem that arises here can hardly be resolved by the assertion that we are able to 'tell what a frog's limitations are, and some more complicated organism than us might be able to tell what our limitations are'. For it is *we* who, in the course of Chomsky's method, both discover and transcend our own empirical-universal limitations. Within this problematic it seems that there are only two philosophically relevant and possible solutions. One either denies the transcendental philosophical relevance of Chomsky's possible discoveries, but this would imply, most implausibly, that the basis of the human language faculty has nothing to do with that of the (logical) faculties of argumentation and cognition. Or one adopts a dialectical view of the transcendental preconditions for human thought and cognition. This view would hold that the 'innate forms of experience' are also the transcendental preconditions for the possibility of experience as long as they are merely postulated philosophically and cannot be made the object of an empirically testable set of hypotheses. But if this latter alternative is successful the creative spirit would have transcended itself historically to some extent and distanced itself from the merely empirically relevant fact; similarly, in biological evolution, the development of spontaneous creativity – which is improbable according to the law of entropy – leaves the extreme specializations of organic life behind.

189

It is not surprising that these fundamental philosophical questions arise from the basic problems of Chomskyan linguistics. If the scientist is to discuss the human language faculty adequately – and, as Chomsky has recognized, this cannot be achieved by an empiricist theory of habit formation – he is confronted, in terms of the philosophy of science, with a fundamentally different type of task from that which confronted Newton when he established his physics. The scientist does not then have the subjective (transcendental) presuppositions of his own knowledge behind him but rather he has to place them before him, to some extent, as the object of scientific knowledge. Even at this point it is problematical whether such an ambitious linguistic theory as Chomsky's can completely identify itself with the type of theory that is completely compatible with an explanation on the basis of laws similar to those in the natural sciences. Surely it must at least partially be a theory that normatively *reconstructs* human competence based on rules? In so far as it were a *normative* reconstruction, generative linguistics would not be understood by analogy with an empirically testable theory (e.g. Newtonian physics) but rather by analogy with *constructive* (*operational*) logic and mathematics whose crucial instance lies in the dialogue of those who argue competently.[30] But since, on the other hand, it must also be regarded – to a much higher degree than logic and mathematics – as a *re*-construction of an actual and, in the light of the empirical variety of language systems, differentiated competence based on rules, it would have to be understood on the basis of an analogy with the *hermeneutic* sciences. These sciences must always *construct possible* meaningful relationships and also *re-construct* linguistic documents that are *empirically* given. Such a reconstructive science must ultimately reconstruct its own rule-based competence in the rule-based competence of the 'ideal speaker-hearer' (Chomsky) and to this extent, unlike a theory based on observations, it could not uphold the separation of subject and object which is prescribed by the empiricist and rationalist logic of science. I do not think that this would prevent it from making the anthropological natural preconditions for the unconscious construction of a grammar the object of an *explanatory* theory. But if this reconstruction of human grammatical competence which claims to reveal the theoretical preconditions – e.g. the initial restrictions of possible unconscious constructions – penetrates through to the 'surface level', it must permit a hermeneutically-mediated corroboration since it is a reconstruction of normative competence. To some extent, this would imply the 'transcendence' of the second ideal type of the philosophy of science by the third.

But after this speculative preview, let us turn to more concrete problems of linguistic *methodology* in order to clarify further through them the place of generative transformational grammar within the philosophy of science. Once again it seems that it is impossible to doubt that Chomsky with his paradigmatic arguments has helped to overcome the partially dogmatic bias of the American social sciences in particular, and also structuralist linguistics, in favour of an *empiricist* theory. Even here his arguments, when taken as a whole, seem to support *critical rationalism*.

Chomsky's critique of Skinner's *Verbal Behavior*[31] provides a crucial model for questioning social scientific *behaviourism* in general. It demonstrated that a basic anthropological (or social) phenomenon, such as grammatical competence – i.e. the ability of every person to produce or understand sentences that are, in principle, unlimited in number – cannot even be noticed, let alone explained, if the social scientist merely applies such weak theoretical terms as 'stimulus', 'response' and 'stimulus reinforcement' to the so-called data.[32] In this context, Chomsky is especially critical of the scarcely controllable metaphysical extension of basic behaviouristic concepts in Skinner's work. If they are precisely defined and applied in accordance with this definition, the connection between observable stimuli and linguistic responses can be merely a statistical one, and as a result, grammar and grammatical rules could only be interpreted statistically in terms of the frequency of occurrence.

But in Chomsky's view, even American structuralism of the Bloomfield school (including his own teacher Zellig Harris) attempted to describe the rules of linguistic usage in this manner by means of taxonomic and distributional methods of analysis that were applied to a fixed corpus of linguistic utterances. In other words, they regarded these rules as 'habits' that were acquired inductively (i.e. on the basis of association) and that had to be described by the linguist himself by means of inductive methods which were made explicit taxonomically and statistically. As he repeatedly emphasizes, Chomsky recognizes in this attempt to establish an empiricist form of linguistics an example of a theory that is intended to be inductive and empiricist and which is the best developed model to date and consequently the easiest to check.[33] Since Chomsky considers that

191

this attempt – as a kind of methodological crucial experiment – has failed, he believes that the inadequacy of empiricist methodology in general has been demonstrated.[34]

The force of Chomsky's arguments is underlined by the fact that Carnap's pupil Bar-Hillel[35] and the linguist Helmuth Schnelle[36] both support Chomsky in his assessment of taxonomic linguistics, although they both still believe themselves to be adherents of logical empiricism.[37] Such an extension of the concept of 'logical empiricism' becomes historically intelligible in the light of the later Carnap's acceptance of the primacy of 'theoretical concepts'. But I do not believe that it helps to clarify questions of principle in the philosophy of science from a historical standpoint. One point in any case does not seem questionable. This is that the acknowledgment of the principle that so-called empirical data can only be recognized as scientifically relevant in the light of theories[38] implies for the philo- sophy of science the transition from *logical empiricism* to *critical rationalism* in the sense which we have outlined above.[39] Similarly, the transition from a corpus-based heuristics to one guided by a theory which tests its hypotheses that extend far beyond any finite corpus of data by the *method of examples and counter-examples,* illustrates fairly closely the transition from inductivism to falsifi- cationism in Popper's sense.[40]

But what connection exists between Chomsky's methodological self-understanding and the third ideal type in the modern philosophy of science which sees in man's scientific discussion of man a funda- mentally new problem with regard to the relationship between the subject and object of cognition? We have already mentioned the fact that it is quite difficult to make the quasi-transcendental- philosophical or epistemological and perhaps meta-logical claims of a theory of the creative mind compatible with the conception of an empirically testable, explanatory theory that is modelled on the natural sciences. But this difficulty could perhaps be overcome by restricting the philosophical claims.[41] The situation is different, however, with regard to the central claim of Chomskyan linguistics to deal with the partial conditions of linguistic behaviour (i.e. the production and understanding of linguistic utterances) that are to be found in *linguistic competence.* One might suppose that the social scientific character of linguistics must become evident here in that the question of *rule following* by the human subject-objects of linguistics becomes acute. With the question of the empirical testing

of the hypotheses of transformational grammar, the condition th
Winch postulates for all social sciences – namely the possible partic
pation of the subject and object of science in a common 'language-
game' – ought to become relevant in some form.

I believe that this is actually the case. But one must be aware of
the complex unique status of linguistics *between* the explanatory
and the interpretative sciences before one approaches Chomsky's
methodology with false expectations. Linguistics *qua* science of
man's linguistic competence – linguistic competence in general and
linguistic competence with reference to specific languages – is not
concerned with the *ad hoc* 'understanding' of individual utterances;
for example, textual interpretation in the sense of literary studies.
Nor is it concerned with the understanding of the strategies of
individual speakers as they were dealt with in the tradition of the
artes sermonicales by rhetoric. Rather, linguistics is concerned with
the 'description' and, since Chomsky, with the 'explanation' of
fundamental *partial conditions* of such 'understanding', namely the
conditions governing the rules of the grammar that is internalized
during the process of socialization, and these rules are followed to a
large extent unconsciously both in the interpretation and production
of utterances. According to Chomsky, linguistics is also concerned
with the partial conditions of internalization itself as language
acquisition. What must be *explained* in this connection by means of
the hypothesis of innate dispositions (e.g. the possibility that the
child constructs a relevant grammar on the basis of the hypothetical
initial restriction and the possibility of the successive selection of the
optional construction by means of an evaluating function) is itself
presupposed as an anthropological *conditio sine qua non* for the
unconscious following of grammatical rules. The assumption that
rules are followed unconsciously then 'explains' the creative production and understanding of well-formed sentences. One can speak
of *explanation* here in so far as *theoretically grounded predictions*
about the structure of all grammatically well-formed sentences are
possible. Nevertheless, a problem arises for the philosophy of science
in the inevitable assumption that human beings as *speakers* and
listeners who understand what they hear *select* and *follow* the hypothetically established rules. This problem cannot simply be resolved
in accordance with the standard *logic of science*.

No matter how unconsciously people follow the *rules* of grammar,
they are certainly not followed in the same manner in which falling

193

stones or celestial bodies obey the *laws* of gravity. Even in cases where they are not *de facto* followed or are wrongly applied, they must be *understood* as *normatively valid* rules. These are cases in which a corroboration through the so-called 'observation' of predicted data cannot occur. Why can the linguist have grounds for maintaining his grammatical theory even in such cases? What conception of human 'linguistic competence' enables him to do this?

Basically, it is meaningless to speak of *rule-following* in the case of stones or celestial bodies since there can be no question here of either a *failure* to follow the rules (i.e. a *violation* of the rules) or of an *incorrect* following of the rules. In cases where the behaviour does not correspond to the assumed rules of behaviour or natural laws, one would consider the *rules themselves to be false.* Or, one might draw upon further rules in order to explain the deviant behaviour which must form a consistent law-like connection with the rules that were initially presupposed. But the linguist only proceeds in this manner if, *as a result of his communication with a competent native speaker,* he has reason to believe that his hypothesis does not correspond to the rule which the speaker follows as a norm. In other cases, however – once again, as a result of communication with a competent native speaker – he will conclude that the speaker did not follow or followed *incorrectly* the legitimately assumed rule or is *unable* to follow it. At this point, however, he has two alternatives[42] for further justifying his findings: he can fall back on natural laws to *explain* a linguistic *slip* or – on account of the linguistic competence that he shares with the speaker – he is able to detect an *intentional deviation* from the rule which is still *intelligible* precisely because of the assumed rule.

The latter possibility provides a further perspective in the comparison of the problems facing the natural and linguistic sciences. It is not only rule-following as quasi-objective behaviour that must be fundamentally distinguished from behaviour that is determined by laws (or statistically). Even the various ways in which we apply the theoretical knowledge of natural laws – in themselves instances of intelligible rule-following – are very different from the intuitive or linguistically reflected upon application of our knowledge of the grammatical rules. In the former case, the practical application consists of the technical utilization of our knowledge of invariable laws that we cannot violate (in accordance with the motto: *natura nonnisi parendo vincitur*). In the case of linguistic competence, however, the practical application lies in what Chomsky himself refers to as the 'rule-governed' and 'rule-changing creativity' of our linguistic behaviour. We can indeed treat the grammatical rules as something that we discuss, that we carefully follow, but that we also change and can even consciously violate. This happens, for instance, in the ironic, poetic, metaphoric and in the philosophical-speculative use of language.

In passing, the objection might be raised here that we cannot alter the rules that Chomsky postulates as 'universals'. I believe one could counter this with the following. In so far as we are only dealing with the so-called 'substantive' universals (e.g. Roman Jakobson's phonological 'distinctive features' and the analogously conceived universal repertoire of 'semantic features') it is still necessary to presuppose an area of 'unconscious selection' from this repertoire for the acquisition of a given language, and consequently an area of pragmatically and communicatively determined historical rule-changing remains. But in so far as we are concerned with so-called 'formal' universals (e.g. the 'transformational cycle' of phonology in particular) we are indeed dealing with 'laws' in the sense of an *explanatory* theory of the *conditiones sine qua non* of the human language faculty. Even in this case, however, it might be appropriate to speak of 'quasi-laws'. For if it is true that the 'formal universals' of human language are not *cognitively necessary* (as Chomsky argued against Putnam)[43] and if, as Chomsky assumes,[44] it is possible on account of the knowledge of 'formal universals' to construct languages that are not bound to them and that are, consequently, impossible or very difficult for children to learn, then we could even do something with the natural laws of the human language faculty that we cannot do with genuine natural laws. Since they are 'rules' (quasi-norms) which can be altered or not followed we could place them, to some extent, *before us*. We cannot cognitively place natural laws as rules before us in this manner. For the moment we derive technical applications from their recognition we must presuppose that they are unchangeable.

Here, too, the functional distinction between grammatical *rules* and *natural laws* is revealed. Neither natural bodies nor human beings can follow or fail to follow natural laws. In other words, both the relationship of natural bodies to natural laws and our technological relationship to inviolable natural laws must be clearly distinguished from our relation to rules that are either followable or not. Con-

195

sequently, it is completely incorrect to attempt to reduce Chomsky's reference to the tacit knowledge of grammatical rules to absurdity – as Goodman does[45] – by comparing rule-based competence with the capacity of a stone to fall precisely towards the centre of the earth. In this connection, Harman's comparison between grammatical competence and the ability to ride a bicycle is also misleading.[46] In the case of gravitation the distinction is obvious. But even in the case of riding a bicycle as a form of physical skill the connection with mechanics which Harman suggests can certainly not be compared with grammatical competence. The behaviour of a cyclist can still be subsumed under the laws of mechanics even if he falls off his bicycle, whereas a speaker who is unsuccessful in formulating a sentence or who intentionally constructs an irregular sentence does *not* follow the rules of grammar. The following distinction which bears directly on Chomsky's problem of 'tacit knowledge' is also connected with this. We know that every competent native speaker can make explicit his ability to follow rules correctly, to a certain extent, in statements about correct or incorrect usage. In the case of the cyclist, making the laws of mechanics explicit has nothing directly to do with making his ability explicit. His ability is only perhaps made explicit in the trainer's reflections upon the art of riding a bicycle. But this art consists of the *technically* (purposive-rationally) *skilful* exploitation of mechanical laws, and not of correctly following quasi-institutional rules and norms. In view of the indisputable capacity of every competent native speaker to discuss his rule-following competence in the form of meta-linguistic statements, we can appreciate why Chomsky regards Harman's comparison as irrelevant and also refuses to be restricted in his terminology to Ryle's *disjunction* between 'knowing how' and 'knowing that'.[47]

In short, the *rules of grammar,* even if they are selected quasi-automatically by everyone by virtue of an innate instinctive device from a class of possible systems of rules, are nevertheless internalized as a component of social *norms,* i.e. in the sense of a *normative consciousness.* Incidentally, when Chomsky emphasizes that language acquisition can take place neither on the basis of the 'conditioning' of conditioned reflexes in Skinner's sense, nor on the basis of a 'training' in Wittgenstein's sense,[48] this observation contains two relevant points for the philosophy of science. On the one hand, it is directed against the fortuitousness of an empiricistically conceived learning process and emphasizes instead the rational systematic character of the innate preconditions for language acquisition. On the other hand, it is directed against the naturalistic character of the notion of conditioning and understands language acquisition more in Plato's and Leibniz's sense, namely, as a maieutically stimulated process of 're-generation' (*Wiedererzeugung*)[49] (and, in a certain sense, of re-calling) of ideas *qua* norms.

Chomsky confirms the methodological indispensability of a normative consciousness by the introduction of the concepts 'grammaticality' and 'acceptability'.[50] It is, of course, only the notion of the 'acceptability' of 'utterances'[51] that describes a social norm of linguistic usage ('performance'), and numerous pragmatic conditions which stretch beyond grammatical competence have to be taken into account here. Nevertheless, the 'grammaticality' of 'sentences' is a necessary partial condition for their 'acceptability', which itself must be capable of being reflected upon by a 'competent speaker' in the sense of a – to some extent, abstract – *social norm,* if it is to be followed at all as a rule. For Wittgenstein's statement that 'one person alone and only once' cannot follow a rule seems to be incontestable. One can speak meaningfully of rule-following only in connection with a public language-game within which rule-following can, *in principle,* be checked by every participant by virtue of publicly available criteria. If, therefore, one wishes to call the 'unconsciously' followed rules of grammar (unconscious in the sense of 'tacit knowledge') – and perhaps even the universal 'rules' for constructing a grammar which Chomsky claims that every child follows – 'rules', then it must be possible to conceive of them 'from above', i.e. from the rules that are followed (or not followed) within the framework of the language-game. Only to this extent can the rules of grammar that Chomsky presupposes as tacit knowledge be corroborated at all by the 'competent speaker'.

But it seems to follow from these considerations that Chomskyan linguistics correspond more closely to the third type of philosophy of science than to the second. In the light of what has already been said, linguistics cannot represent a *merely* explanatory theory which applies theoretical concepts, constructs and law-like hypotheses from outside, as it were, to its object and tests the correctness of its theoretical standpoint by means of carefully selected observations. Rather, the so-called object must be able to *participate* in some form in the corroboration or falsification of hypotheses concerning rules.

Chomsky partially confirms this assumption, but only partially.

In my view, it is definitely confirmed by the often cited thesis that the *intuition of the competent speaker* is an ultimate, irreducible crucial instance in the empirical testing of the 'descriptive adequacy' of a linguistic theory.[52] As a fundamental insight, I believe that this thesis represents the non-natural scientific aspect of linguistics and cannot therefore be invalidated in the foreseeable future by more advanced methods of observation and measurement.[53] But nor can it be interpreted in such a manner that what a speaker is able to say about his language could simply represent his knowledge of the language in the sense of competence and could, to this extent, be crucial.[54] (This assumption is not valid in any social or human science. Even the interpretation of an author in literary studies cannot be *replaced* by interviews with the author about his so-called intentions.) The *hermeneutic* communication with the human being as the subject-object of *science* must be *methodologically* mediated in so far as it must seek ways and means of revealing the text's meaning or the meaning of his behaviour (or the behavioural rules followed) to a certain extent along the lines of the human subject's approximate ideal self-understanding.[55]

For this undoubtedly difficult operation,[56] methods can certainly be employed which explain in a quasi-naturalistic manner in order to 'unmask' a false – e.g. ideological – self-understanding. But the term 'unmask' itself expresses the notion that, in principle, communication must be established with the subject-object. As we emphasized above, in the social sciences no concept may be used to explain behaviour which cannot *in principle* be transformed or 'transcended' by the objects *qua* human beings in a heightened self-understanding.

Yet, it is precisely at this point that the ambiguity of Chomsky's theory of language for the philosophy of science is revealed. This is evident if one considers its claim to 'explanatory adequacy' upon which Chomsky's distinctive pathos rests. On the one hand, he emphasizes the fact that the crucial instance for his theory is the ideal speaker-hearer with respect to his grammatical competence. Here one *might* see confirmation for my postulate concerning the third type of philosophy of science. On the other hand, he repeatedly expresses his conviction that the abstract rule device, with whose aid not only the generation of sentences in terms of a given grammar but also the selection or construction of the grammar itself is to be 'explained', cannot basically be made explicit by introspection.[57] To this extent, Chomsky's theory does not represent a deep-hermeneutic 'quasi-explanation' in the sense of psychoanalysis,[58] but rather a reconstructive theory whose correctness can perhaps be tested, like that of mathematics, by means of maieutically elicited 'anamnesis' in Plato's sense.[59]

Chomsky himself believes that we are dealing here with a mathematically constructed *model* that contains the individual possible grammars merely as 'theoretical constructs'. These constructs are to lead to 'an explanation for the intuition of the native speaker' which far exceeds any possible consciousness of the latter 'on the basis of an empirical hypothesis concerning the innate predisposition of the child to develop a certain kind of theory to deal with the evidence presented to him'.[60] If one examines more closely the mathematical structure of Chomsky's projected theory[61] then one might form the impression that transformational grammar is not primarily intended to explain human linguistic behaviour, but rather to develop linguistic computer programmes as part of the theory of finite automata and, therefore, part of algebra.[62] In this case, the *experimentum crucis* for transformational grammar as a linguistic theory would lie in the possibility of a successful simulation of linguistic behaviour by computers. Its success, however, could ultimately only be demonstrated by incorporating computers into successful communication with competent speakers. The prospects for such an undertaking – in view of the 'theorems of undecidability'[63] which, in the last analysis, are surely an expression of the non-formalizable self-reflexivity of human thought in the form of language[64] – cannot be discussed here.

But even if we ignore the question whether it is possible for automata to simulate human linguistic competence, the fact that such automata are considered as models for generative linguistic theory does not speak as decisively as some people think for the *explanatory* character – in the sense of the 'logic of science' – of generative theory. For the *construction* and programming of abstract automata, like the construction of formalized calculus language, must be looked upon as the indirect procedure for a reconstruction of human rule-based competences. In other words, the relevant point for the philosophy of science in mathematical linguistics as part of the theory of finite automata does not so much lie in the mechanical explanation of predictable facts as in the normatively correct objectification of possible paradigms for constructing and following grammatical rules. This is revealed by the proposed semantic-pragmatic interpretation of the peculiar dual-level structure of Chomsky's theory. This can be understood, on the one hand, as a universal theory of human linguistic competence that contains all the possible grammars as 'theoretical constructs'. To this extent, we are confronted with an *explanatory* theory which derives the laws of specific grammars that are valid under specific limiting conditions from a universal law. The universal linguistic theory can, however, also be understood as a 'meta-theory' of the specific grammars where, according to Chomsky, the latter in turn can be understood as possible individual instances of human linguistic competence that are realizable by the child in the language-learning process. If one adopts the latter perspective then the 'evaluation measure', which is part of the universal theory, emerges as the *objectifying reconstruction* of the child's ability – on the basis of the linguistic data offered him (which must also be evaluated since they are often corrupt or irrelevant) – to select by means of successive construction and self-correction the *normatively adequate* grammar from the set of possible grammars. This means that the meta-theory has a *normative* function in the process of theory-formation which the child must perform unconsciously, just as *methodology* is accorded such a function in the formation of scientific theories. Such an 'evaluation measure' is normally – i.e. in the case of natural science – not a part of empirical-analytical theory, but rather it is the task of the *normative logic of research* as the *meta-theory of creative theory-formation*. One can appreciate, however, that the situation can be different in linguistics if one recalls that Chomsky considers human linguistic competence to be the unconscious initial stage of the competence to form linguistic theories.[65] Their empirical-analytical 'explanation' must also possess the character of a *normative reconstruction* of the capacity for theory-formation that is identical in both subject and object.

This reconstruction must, of course, adhere to empirically demonstrable 'restrictions' on the formation and transformational rules of grammar, both those which are possible in general and those of a specific language. It would seem that, at this point, the *empirical-analytic* character of Chomsky's theory is established as a falsifiable explanatory hypothesis in the sense of critical rationalism. Yet even the empirical corroboration of this substantive core of the explanatory theory – the proof of the 'formal' and 'substantive universals' as anthropological characteristics of linguistic competence in Chomsky's sense – is methodologically bound to the communication between

subject and object that is presupposed for each hermeneutic reconstruction. Indeed, Chomsky's linguistic theory appears to fulfil a
dual task. On the one hand, it permits a prognosis of the structure
that all correctly formed sentences actually possess and which is
derived from law-like hypotheses and antecedent conditions. To
this extent it is an *explanatory* theory. But this explanation and
prediction of the structure of all well-formed sentences coincides
with a *reconstructive illuminating function* concerning the potential
normative correctness of sentences. Strictly speaking, only the latter
function can be corroborated on the basis of the so-called *introspection* of the competent native speaker. For the sake of this
corroboration, however, generative linguistics must transcend the
separation of the subject and object of science that is required by
the standard 'logic of science'.[66] Since such a transcendence is
identical with the incorporation of *self-reflection* into the
methodological procedure of science, it is possible that, given this
presupposition, one might be able to understand why generative
linguistics, unlike physics, for example, can transform the preconditions for its own possibility and validity – at least partially – into
its object, even in so far as it can only reveal the *syntactic* universals
of human linguistic competence.

Syntactics, semantics, pragmatics: the perspectives created in the philosophy of language by a possible or necessary extension of Chomsky's theoretical approach

I believe that the above mentioned preconditions for the possibility
and validity of linguistics can be made clearer if one takes into
account not only the *syntactic* but also the *semantic* and *pragmatic*
preconditions for the *use of language* and even for *linguistic competence*. As we shall attempt to demonstrate, this amounts to a
complementing or extension of Chomsky's notion of *competence* in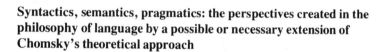
the form of 'communicative competence'. At this stage in the
development of generative linguistics the same problem recurs –
mutatis mutandis – that is already familiar to the historian of philosophy in the development of Carnap's theory from 'logical syntax'
via 'logical semantics' to the postulate of a *constructive pragmatics,*
and, on the other hand, in the development of analytical philosophy
as a whole. This development goes beyond the logical construction

of language to the pragmatically orientated *ordinary language philo-sophy*.[67] Contrary to Katz's opinion,[68] the hitherto projected semantic integration of generative transformational grammar does not seem to be capable of providing the linguistic synthesis of the existing philosophical positions of this century, but rather it requires its pragmatically mediated extension. For instance, if we consider the mediation of tradition as the linguistic mediation of meaning, we must include as a constitutive part of semantics not only a *universal component* but also an aspect that is determined by the *pragmatics* of communication. This is an aspect in which, to some extent, the historical world experience of nations is reflected.

It is highly probable that this demand leads to a reciprocal extension or correction of *syntagmatic* semantics (i.e. based on combinations of features) which has hitherto been monopolized by the Chomsky school, and actual structuralist semantics (e.g. word-field theory)[69] which is based upon *paradigmatic* oppositions of meanings. Within the framework of a paradigmatically orientated semantics, one would have to deal with that side of what Wilhelm von Humboldt calls the 'inner form of language' which cannot be traced to the universal capacity of human beings to construct specific grammars and to generate 'speech anew each time' with the aid of a specific grammar. Rather, this aspect can be traced back to the presupposed historically formed 'structural functions'[70] with whose aid individual languages have elaborated both grammatically and lexically specific meaning contents and have thereby created the precondition for specific collective 'world-views'.[71] In this manner, the concept of the language system would regain the social aspect intended by Saussure, which it has lost in Chomsky's psychological reduction of the concept of linguistic competence. Of course, this should not lead one to abandon the association which Chomsky has established between linguistics, on the one hand, and both a theory of human language capacity and of language use on the other. As 'energeia' language certainly cannot be reduced to a repertoire of words and phrases. In other words, the intended meanings that are objectified semantically in language cannot be understood – as was recently postulated in a critique of Chomsky[72] – on the basis of the primacy of words.

In order to make clear, at least in principle, the necessity for the *pragmatic* extension or even correction of Chomsky's approach I shall begin with a fictitious interpretation of Chomsky's notion of competence, which deviates from the one that I have hitherto followed, but is still undoubtedly in accordance with Chomsky's Cartesian presuppositions. This interpretation was explicated by Jürgen Habermas as a 'monological model of the transmission of information'[73] and would indeed reduce Chomsky's theory of language to a (natural scientific) theory in the sense of critical rationalism. In my view, however, it would also reveal Chomsky's conception of competence to be not only in need of extension but also to be downright inadequate.

Habermas argues that linguistic competence in Chomsky's sense represents a 'monological capacity', i.e. in Wittgenstein's terms, a capacity to apply private rules.[74] Concrete linguistic competence would not then be *constituted* in part by the *internalization* of the accepted norms of language usage in the process of socialization but would merely be *stimulated* by this process. As a capacity for applying rules it would rest *solely* upon the internal device that is analogous to instinct, which Chomsky hypothetically presupposes in his theory of language acquisition.[75] This interpretation of Chomsky's intentions is supported not only – as we have indicated – by the affinities with the Cartesian tradition of *methodological solipsism*. It is also supported by the fact that Chomsky seems to consider the *pragmatic* presuppositions for speech only as *psychological restrictions* on competence in the sense of extra-linguistic limiting conditions (such as memory limitations, shifts of attention and interest, etc.).[76] It is further supported by the fact that both Chomsky and Katz presuppose an *a priori* structure of meaning as an anthropological repertoire, analogous to the universal structure of sound, on the basis of which – to a certain extent – each isolated speaker can construct, in principle, independently of agreement as to the meaning of words, all the possible semantic contents by virtue of an *ars combinatoria* (Leibniz) that is also innate.[77] The *monological* model of linguistic competence corresponds to the model of an *explanatory* theory in the sense of logical empiricism or even of critical rationalism in so far as the pragmatic dimension of the communicative use of language would not function as a transcendental precondition for the possibility of linguistic competence, but rather merely as the empirical 'limiting condition' of an 'explanation' for the limitations of ideal linguistic competence. In other words, the level of *intersubjective agreement on the use of language* (which, in the case of human beings, cannot, in my view, only be counted as the result but also as the transcendental precondition for both communication and learning to communicate, and ultimately for the scientific study of communication) would apparently vanish in favour of the total empirical objectification of the linguistic and extra-linguistic conditions for communication.[78]

The price to be paid for such a (scientistic-rationalistic) simplification and clarification in terms of the philosophy of science is, however, that the theory of language as a whole reverts to the level of the young Wittgenstein's or Russell's 'logical atomism'. Instead of making possible a synthesis of the achievements of constructive semantics and the philosophy of language that developed from the later Wittgenstein, as Katz had promised, such a theory would basically reproduce the philosophical paradox of the *Tractatus logico-philosophicus*. To what extent is this statement justified?

As Habermas emphasizes,[79] a theory which regarded linguistic competence as a 'monological capacity' would logically have to conceive of communication itself *monologically,* since the linguistic competence of the individual participants in communication is supposed to contain *a priori* all the linguistic preconditions for communication. In terms of a technical model for transmitting information, the 'inter-subjectivity of the validity of identical meanings' must be reduced to the fact that 'sender and receiver, each as an entity in itself, have been previously equipped with the same programme'.[80] The process of communication itself, as the a priori of reaching agreement, would not be necessary presupposition for the constitution of meaning. It would be merely a phonetic process of transmitting information from sender to receiver, who would 'encode' or 'decode' their private thoughts with the aid of their own linguistic competence in the form of the language system that was *a priori* common to both. This is, in fact, precisely how one must conceive of human communication on the basis of the *Tractatus logico-philosophicus*, according to which, of course, 'realism' should coincide with 'solipsism', since every language user is confronted *a priori* – i.e. on account of the *logical form* of language – with the same world.[81] In his essay 'Form and Content', Moritz Schlick drew the conclusions for communication theory. He concluded that the interpretation of a language system by a sender or receiver of information was strictly private and in no way altered the pre-supposed formal structure of language.[82] But what is paradoxical about this conception?

Firstly, it can be recognized in the fact that – given the presuppositions that I have indicated – *meta-communication,* communication about linguistic usage or even about the structure of language, is neither necessary nor possible. Consistent as he was, the young Wittgenstein therefore finally dismissed as 'nonsensical' the reflective meta-communication that he had conducted with the readers of the *Tractatus.* Yet I believe that the possibility and necessity of meta-communication, i.e. reaching agreement about linguistic usage, that is consistently denied here, represents the *differentia specifica* of human linguistic usage when compared with so-called 'animal languages' on the one hand and the formalized programming language of information theory on the other. We know that programming languages presuppose a transcendental pragmatics in the form of human agreements. For 'animal languages', like that of the bees, it is reasonable to assume a kind of programming of the individual participants in communication in the form of an innate *signal code.* In both cases it is neither necessary nor meaningful to presuppose a kind of accompanying meta-linguistic and meta-communicative consciousness,[83] which alone is compatible with understanding communication as symbolically mediated interaction between partners. To this extent, we are confronted here with 'monological' models of communication in Habermas's sense. They can indeed be 'explained' by law-like hypotheses and limiting conditions (i.e. on the basis of the presupposed signal programme and the specific storage and transmission conditions that exist in or between the senders and receivers of signals).[84]

The decisive question is whether we must interpret Chomsky's theory of language in this manner. Is the child's learning of language to be comprehended as the construction of a grammar on the basis of an innate set of rules and repertoire of features – a process that is merely *stimulated* by the environment? Is linguistic communication between ideal speaker and the ideal hearer to be considered therefore as private encoding and decoding on the basis of a repertoire of rules that is *a priori* common to both? In Chomsky's view, would the communication process itself then be simply a process of transmitting information that has nothing to do with the *constituting* of language systems – and especially with the constitution of the semantic component?

Habermas seems to presuppose this 'monological' model for Chomsky's theory, and for this reason he seeks to extend Chomsky's notion of linguistic competence through that of 'communicative competence'.[85] I believe, however, that in this case such an *extension* would not be possible. This is because a 'monologically' conceived 'grammatical competence' (in the sense of private rule-following) and a 'communicative competence' which was not mediated through a 'grammatical competence' that was specific to one language would be incompatible. In other words, even the *grammatical competence* to form correct sentences must be conceived of as a publicly controllable competence to apply rules if communicative competence is to be realizable in 'verbal utterances'. I believe that even from Chomsky's standpoint it is not necessary (although it might be an obvious conclusion) to interpret linguistic competence as a 'monological' capacity in the sense criticized by the later Wittgenstein. For in Chomsky's view, what individual organisms are provided with is not the competence to apply *grammatical rules,* but merely the *innate disposition to acquire competence* under the (language-game) conditions of the socialization process. Let us attempt to make this clearer.

Here, I have basically adopted the later Wittgenstein's view that, in principle, 'one person alone' cannot follow a rule and I have opposed the view that linguistic competence is a 'monological' capacity to apply private rules. Instead I have assumed that the *intuitive normative consciousness* which belongs to human linguistic competence cannot be understood on the basis of the individual's innate predispositions which Chomsky assumes exist, but solely on the basis of the internalization of accepted linguistic norms in the process of socialization. In other words, even if the acquisition of linguistic competence can only be 'explained' with the aid of the hypothesis concerning an innate instinctual mechanism, the meaning of linguistic competence itself can only be 'understood' if one presupposes that a *communicative* competence is acquired together with *grammatical* competence (in Chomsky's sense). Stated more precisely, a *linguistically moulded communicative competence* must be acquired. For, on the one hand, there can be no grammatical (syntactic and semantic) competence without pragmatic, communicative competence. But on the other hand, without grammatical competence in Chomsky's sense there can be no pragmatic communicative competence in the sense of linguistic behaviour. The communicative behaviour of the small child, which already contains the basic foundations for social role-playing, apparently develops during the phase in which the innate language disposition is not yet sufficiently mature and consequently communicative behaviour cannot yet be 'moulded' in terms of the child's mother tongue. But this 'moulding' of communicative behaviour in a specific language must apparently take place in order that grammatical competence in Chomsky's sense can be acquired simultaneously with communicative competence. Without grammatical competence, however, which basically must make possible a potential grammaticalization in a specific language and must therefore permit the explication of discourse constitutive 'speech acts', this communicative competence would not be a linguistic or human competence.[86]

These reflections on the need for grammatical and communicative competence to mutually presuppose one another are not intended to question the necessity for an extension of Chomsky's notion of linguistic competence in the form of a communicative competence. My first task was to elucidate the preconditions for the possibility of such an extension. The aim of this proposed extension can be demonstrated much more precisely and in a much more concrete manner with the aid of more systematic study of linguistic pragmatics. From a philosophical standpoint, the writings of Austin[87] and Searle[88] deserve special mention. In his presentation of 'speech acts', Searle has not merely redefined the distinction between 'sentences' (in the sense of a 'language system') and 'utterances' as actual 'speech acts' by drawing upon Austin and explaining utterances through the *performative* use of language. On the other hand, he has also shown that the distinction as between 'sentences' and 'speech acts' cannot simply lead to the latter being abandoned to psychology. For, every speech act that is not only constituted implicitly by the pragmatic context of the utterances but can also be constituted explicitly by the performative use of language must correspond to a possible sentence in the language system. Part of the notion of a 'speech act' is that it can explicate itself linguistically through *performative expressions* (such as 'I hereby promise', 'I hereby request', 'I hereby assert', etc.) and specify its role in discourse (which it helps to establish). In short, 'speech acts' not only form a topic in the study of *parole* in Saussure's sense but also a topic in the study of *langue*.[89] Nevertheless, Searle's thesis that 'an adequate study of speech acts is a study of *langue*' is somewhat imprecise, since *langue* consists of 'sentences' which can, at best, include *potential* speech acts – an account of the explicit form – but not *actual* 'speech acts'. The imprecision that would characterize a total reduction of *linguistic pragmatics* to *system-orientated linguistics* (which Searle does not practise) would inevitably lead to a failure to notice that human 'communicative competence' *transcends individual languages.*[90] It can, of course, only be acquired together with competence in *one* language and is organized *a priori* in such a manner that it can be verbalized in terms of a given language. None the less, communicative competence is apparently the transcendental precondition for the possibility and validity of 'translation', 'hermeneutic understanding' and 'linguistic reconstruction'. It cannot, therefore, be reduced to a linguistic competence that is restricted in its realization to single languages. In my view, communicative competence represents an element of reflective distance and creative sovereignty in the relationship of human beings to each specific language. As a result, it reveals an element of truth in the ancient ($\vartheta\acute{\epsilon}\sigma\epsilon\iota$) theory of the invention of language. In passing, we should note that this theory has quite rightly been questioned by Wilhelm von Humboldt and Chomsky and replaced by the $\phi\acute{v}\sigma\epsilon\iota$ theory in the form of an anthropological instinctual *a priori* of language.

Despite Katz, Anglo-American linguistics has continued to derive inspiration from ordinary language philosophy and this has apparently led recently to the incorporation not only of semantic but also pragmatic presuppositions into the deep structure postulated by transformational grammar.[91] I believe that a decisive breakthrough in the direction of a systematic pragmatics of language can be found in Dieter Wunderlich's writings,[92] whose philosophical significance has been recognized and demonstrated by Habermas in particular.[93] On the one hand, Wunderlich draws upon the work of those rebels within the Chomsky school (such as James D. McCawley[94] and John R. Ross[95]) who have incorporated not only semantic but even pragmatic presuppositions of linguistic competence into the deep structure of transformational grammar. But unlike these linguists, Wunderlich apparently does not wish to complement the syntactic-semantic theory as such. Instead he seeks to reflect upon the pragmatic presuppositions of linguistic competence as the expression of a 'meta-competence' at the level of a 'pragmatic meta-language'. Taking Searle as his starting-point, Habermas rightly criticizes this conception in so far as pragmatics cannot presuppose that the general structures of the speech situation 'exist independently of speech like empirical objects'.[96] Indeed, it is actually people themselves who create 'the conditions for possible communication' with the aid of utterances in the form of speech acts and who thereby establish the speech situation as the level of intersubjectivity. If, however, in so doing they also reveal a *meta-linguistic* and *meta-communicative competence,* then this represents the precondition for the possibility of linguistic and communication science. But as *systematic pragmatics,* this science in particular should not mistakenly consider itself to be an empirical objectivation of actual language behaviour (in the sense of empirical-analytical psychology). Rather, it should regard itself as that transcendentally reflexive explication of the ideal speech situation which we always counterfactually anticipate as the level of intersubjectivity, and in which all interpretative or reconstructive sciences have their normative basis.[97]

Wunderlich, in fact, is not concerned with psycholinguistics in the normal sense of the term. He is concerned with a theory of the 'idealized speech situation'. The point that he is making with regard to the necessary complementing or correction of Chomsky's approach is, apparently, that the pragmatic theory he proposes is 'not a theory of linguistic performance' such as that which both Chomsky and all the syntactically-orientated or syntactically and semantically orientated logicians and linguists have always required in the form of a psychological extension. He writes: 'Actual utterances which, for psychological reasons, or on account of the finite character of memory, etc., can deviate in some way from grammatical utterances, and even misunderstandings that are produced by unintentional ambiguities or by the incorrect combination of meanings are not of interest at this point.'[98] Wunderlich defines the positive relationship between this postulated 'pragmatics' and Chomsky's theory in the following manner: 'The sentences (or, at best, texts) of idealized speakers in the existing syntactic-semantic theory are replaced by the *utterances* of speakers in idealized speech situations.' 'As a result,' Wunderlich concludes,[99] 'the notion of linguistic competence also acquires a wider meaning. It signifies the capacity of speakers or hearers to articulate themselves intelligibly in speech situations (conceived in an idealized manner) or the capacity to understand what is articulated.'

As linguistic arguments for the thesis that 'a theory of linguistic competence must necessarily include a pragmatics of the speech situation', Wunderlich enumerates various types of linguistic phenomena. Here he uses a method adopted by Wittgenstein and ordinary language philosophy that was systematized by the Chomskyan school. Grammatically deviant sentences are detected and the reasons for this deviation are sought in a linguistic 'deep structure'. It becomes apparent that the reasons for deviation in the case of the types of phenomena selected by Wunderlich cannot be found in a *syntactic-semantic deep structure* in Chomsky's sense. Rather, they can be located in a pragmatic deep structure of the speech situation.

This is true, for instance, of 'deictic expressions'.[100] The structure of grammatically deviant sentences such as 'I am apparently/evidently hungry', 'I fear that it is raining here (now)', 'I assume that I am just having dinner now' cannot be understood if one merely considers the deictic expressions *I, here, (just), now,* in terms of Chomskyan grammar to be *noun phrases* or *adverbials. I* must be interpreted as the self-reflexive indication of the speaker in a speech situation, the *here* and *now* must be interpreted as situationally bound indicators of place and time, before one can understand that the structure of these sentences is irregular.[101] In other words, the 'grammaticality' or 'non-grammaticality' of 'sentences' is revealed here to be dependent *a priori* upon *pragmatic universals* which structure the human speech situation in general. Wunderlich's other examples are the *vocative case, honorific forms, the imperative* (e.g. the sentence 'Love your neighbour as himself/myself' would be incorrect), *questions, direct and indirect speech* (e.g. a transformation of the sentence 'Thomas told his friend in great detail that he was writing a new novel' into direct speech would be a deviant sentence).

Habermas has adopted Wunderlich's linguistic approach and has systematized and radicalized it, in the light of Searle's theory of speech acts, into a 'universal pragmatics' or a theory of communicative competence.[102] Following Wunderlich's suggestion, Habermas does not wish to use the term 'communicative competence' as it had already been introduced in socio- and psycholinguistic literature[103] in the sense of an empirical-theoretical concept for the mastery of given linguistic codes. Instead, he wishes to use it in the sense of a basic universal pragmatic concept for the mastery of 'dialogue-constitutive universals'. In the light of this radicalization, which – I believe – is similar in many respects to my conception of a 'transcendental pragmatics', within the framework of a semiotic transformation of transcendental philosophy,[104] I should like to return to the question

210

posed initially, namely, that of the place of Chomsky's theory of language within the philosophy of science.

Even in presenting Chomsky's theory, I maintained that the difficulty in classifying the generative theory of language in terms of the philosophy of science is based on the fact that here the attempt is made, on the one hand, to provide an empirical-analytical *explanation* for linguistic competence and its acquisition by recourse to unvariable conditions of human nature and, on the other, to achieve a *reconstruction* of linguistic competence as a basically self-reflexive capacity to follow, or fail to follow, rules or norms ('rule-governed creativity' and 'rule-changing creativity'). I believe that the detour via the pragmatic extension of the notion of linguistic competence was instructive in that it threw more light on to the second quasi-hermeneutic aspect of generative linguistics. It was shown that 'grammatical competence' can, at best, be distinguished from 'communicative competence' (i.e. the capacity for intersubjective communication which also makes communication with oneself possible), but the two cannot be *separated* since each capacity mutually presupposes the other. 'Grammatical competence' too must participate in that *meta-linguistic competence* that can only be constituted at the level of the dialogue. Consequently, even language learning cannot be regarded *merely* as a stimulated process of construction. It must also be comprehended as an intersubjective process of communication whose outcome is mastery of the dialogue-constitutive universals.

The preconditions for this communicative process are presumably both innate dispositions to acquire rules in Chomsky's sense and, on the other hand, the prelinguistic ability of the child to communicate and interact. This ability is preserved as the extra-verbal communicative competence of the adult that is, however, related to language.[105]

It is through this interweaving of *grammatical* and *communicative* competence that the simultaneity of 'rule-governed creativity' and 'rule-changing creativity' in Chomsky's sense becomes at all intelligible. Only as an unconscious, quasi-organic spontaneity is this creativity in applying or changing rules made a topic of generative grammar *qua explanatory* theory. As a capacity in the sense of the meta-linguistic normative consciousness, it is to a certain extent merely a deficient mode of the meta-communicative competence which enables us, if necessary, to establish situations of discourse even by transcending a given competence in one language – either

211

through translation or through the utilization or creation of linguistic 'interference'.[106] But in this meta-communicative competence that belongs to communicative competence one can apparently also detect a fundamental precondition for the possibility of *linguistics*. Only through the mediation of the communicative-meta-communicative competence of both the subject and object of science can linguistics ascertain the grammatical competence of native speakers as a 'mental reality' in Chomsky's terms. To this extent, generative linguistics is apparently an interpretative social or human science which, instead of the scientistic separation of the subject and object of science, presupposes a dialectical identification of both sides.

Notes

1 See N. Chomsky, *Language and Mind*, ch. I.
2 Cf. J. J. Katz and J. J. Fodor, 'The Structure of a Semantic Theory', *Language*, 39, 1963, pp. 170–210; and also the relevant articles in Fodor and Katz (eds), *The Structure of Language: Readings in the Philosophy of Language*. Cf. Y. Bar-Hillel's critique in *Language*, 43, 1967, pp. 526–50 (reprinted in Bar-Hillel, *Aspects of Language*). Similarly in M. Bierwisch, 'Strukturalismus: Geschichte, Probleme und Methoden', *Kursbuch*, 5, 1966, pp 144 ff. linguistics is considered to be the 'grounding discipline of logic'.
3 Cf. N. Chomsky, *Current Issues in Linguistic Theory; Cartesian Linguistics; Language and Mind;* 'Linguistics and Philosophy', in Sidney Hook (ed.), *Language and Philosophy,* New York, 1969, pp. 51–93.
4 Cf. J. J. Katz, *The Philosophy of Language,* New York, 1966.
5 Cf. C. Morris, 'Foundations of the Theory of Signs', in *International Encyclopaedia of Unified Science,* vol. 1, no. 2, Chicago, 1938.
6 See chs. 3, 4 and 5 in this volume.
7 Cf. D. Wunderlich, 'McCawleys Tiefenstrukturen', Third Linguistic Colloquium in Stettenfels, 1–4, October 1968; D. Wunderlich, 'Pragmatik, Sprechsituation, Deixis', in *Zeitschrift für Literaturwissenschaft und Linguistik (LiLi),* vol. 1, nos. 1–2, 1971, pp. 153–90; and D. Wunderlich, 'Die Rolle der Pragmatik in der Linguistik', *Der Deutschunterricht,* 22, no. 4, 1970 pp. 5–41. Cf. also J. Habermas, 'Einführende Bemerkungen zu einer Theorie der kommunikativen Kompetenz', mimeographed working paper, 1970; and J. Habermas, 'Vorbereitende Bemerk ungen zu einer Theorie der kommunikativen Kompetenz', in J. Habermas and N. Luhmann, *Theorie der Gesellschaft oder Sozialtechnologie,* pp. 101–41.
8 Cf. R. Carnap, 'The Methodological Character of Theoretical Concepts', in H. Feigl and M. Scriven (eds), *Minnesota Studies in the Philosophy of Science,* vol. 1, Minneapolis, 1956, pp. 38–76.

9 W. Stegmüller, *Main Currents in Contemporary German, British and American Philosophy,* Dordrecht, 1969, pp. 349–50.

10 Cf. S. Toulmin, *Foresight and Understanding: an Enquiry into the Aims of Science.*

11 Cf. L. Schäfer ('Über die Diskrepanz zwischen Methodologie und Metaphysic bei Popper', *Studium Generale,* 23, 1970, pp. 856–77) on Popper.

12 If, in micro-physics, statements about the location or impulse of an elementary particle cannot be formulated without reference to the observer, then (1) this is not a mediation between the subject and object of knowledge in the sense of a self-identifying 'understanding' and (2) the separation of the subject and object of knowledge can be re-established at the level of statistical statements about the behaviour of a set of particles.

13 Cf. K.-O. Apel, 'Das "Verstehen": eine Problemgeschichte als Begriffsgeschichte', *Archiv für Begriffsgeschichte,* 1, 1955, pp. 144 ff.

14 P. Winch, *The Idea of a Social Science.* Cf. K.-O. Apel, 'Die Entfaltung der sprachanalytischen Philosophie und das Problem der "Geisteswissenschaften"', *Philosophisches Jahrbuch,* 72, 1965, pp. 239–89 (English trans. *Analytical Philosophy of Language and the 'Geisteswissenschaften',* Dordrecht, 1967); and ch. 5 in this volume.

15 It is not necessary for the concepts of the social science to be *actually* understood by random members of the society described. Nor is it necessary for them to be understandable on the basis of the *existing rules* of the language-game of an objectified society. It is, however, necessary – precisely for a description or quasi-explanation of human social behaviour that distances itself from and transcends its object through a critique of ideology – for even the objects of this description or explanation to have, in principle, the opportunity to transcend their own linguistic self-understanding through critical self-reflection and become members of the communication community to which the social scientists themselves belong. Cf. my critique of Winch in 'Die Entfaltung der sprachanalytischen Philosophie und das Problem der "Geisteswissenschaften"', and ch. 5 in this volume.

16 Cf. K.-O. Apel, Introduction to C. S. Peirce, *Schriften I,* Frankfurt, 1967, pp. 13–154 (reprinted in K.-O. Apel, *Der Denkweg von Charles S. Peirce,* pp. 11–151). Introduction to C. S. Peirce, *Schriften II,* Frankfurt, 1970, pp. 11–214, and chs. 3 and 4 in this volume.

17 Chomsky regards the work of his teacher Zellig Harris (especially *Methods in Structural Linguistics,* Chicago, 1951) as a paradigm of the empiricist corpus-orientated attempts by the Bloomfield school to resolve the problem of discovery procedures. Before the publication of *Syntactic Structures* in 1957 Chomsky himself tried to define this approach more precisely and arrived at the conclusion that there is a fundamental difference between sentences that can be generated by a grammar and a sample of utterances. In his later writings he develops from this the distinction between competence and performance. Cf. J. Lyons, *Chomsky,* pp. 34, 38 ff.

18 The following defence of the 'rationalist' hypothesis of 'innate ideas' against the empiricist Nelson Goodman is typical: 'In linguistics, as in any other field, it is only in such indirect ways . . . that one can hope to find evidence bearing on non-trivial hypotheses. Direct experimental tests of the sort that Goodman mentions are rarely possible', Chomsky, *Language and Mind,* p. 72.

19 N. Chomsky ('Logical Syntax and Semantics: their Linguistic Relevance', *Language,* 31, 1955, pp. 36–45) on Bar-Hillel (1954).

20 Cf. Katz, *The Philosophy of Language*, pp. 24 ff.

21 Cf. Chomsky, *Language and Mind,* ch. 1.

22 Nevertheless, Chomsky rejects the term 'resourceful empiricism' that was suggested by Gilbert Harman, since it is neutral with regard to the following alternative: 'The issue that concerns one is whether there are "ideas and principles of various kinds that determine the form of the acquired knowledge in what may be a rather restricted and highly organised way", or, alternatively, whether "the structure of the acquisition device is limited to certain elementary peripheral processing mechanisms . . . and certain analytical data-processing mechanisms or inductive principles".' Chomsky, 'Linguistics and Philosophy', p. 90 with reference to Chomsky, *Aspects of the Theory of Syntax,* pp. 47 f. Even with this kind of argument, which heuristically incorporates the speculative spirit of a priorism into the framework of an empirically testable theory-formation, I believe that Chomsky complies with the methodological principles of *critical rationalism.*

23 Chomsky, *Language and Mind,* ch. 1.

24 As Bierwisch, 'Strukturalismus, Geschichte, Probleme und Methoden', pp. 96 ff, demonstrates, the hypothesis concerning the universal inventory of semantic features can be developed in analogy to Roman Jakobson's hypothesis concerning the universal basic inventory of phonological features. We would then be faced with an empirical anthropological explanation of the *a priori* preconditions for the possibility of *meaning constitution* (cf. Husserl!) that is possible for humanity as a whole. This is a theory that is very similar to the biological-ethological hypotheses concerning the human instinct *a priori*, which were developed by Jakob von Uexküll and Konrad Lorenz. Cf. Chomsky, *Language and Mind,* pp. 81 ff.

25 Cf. Chomsky, *Language and Mind,* pp. 78 ff., and 'Linguistics and Philosophy', p. 64.

26 Chomsky, *Language and Mind,* pp. 81 ff. Chomsky refers here to Peirce and Lorenz who actually claimed to revive the Kantian position. Cf. on Peirce's fusion of the normative claim of a transcendental logic of research with the conception of an empirical (abductive-inductive) metaphysics of the evolution of instinct, the second part of my Peirce monograph, *Der Denkweg von Charles S. Peirce.*

27 Cf. Bierwisch, 'Strukturalismus: Geschichte, Probleme und Methoden', pp. 144 ff.

28 This question also arises in a more general form from the philosophy of *critical rationalism* which tries to extrapolate the falsification principle

of empirical science with respect to philosophy and hence to its own presuppositions. Thus Hans Albert (*Transzendentale Träumereien, K.-O. Apels Sprachspiele und seine hemeneutischer Gott*) does not recognize that critical rationalism can only distinguish its own position from plain scepticism if, or in as far as, it excepts its own principles and their presuppositions from the principle of fallibilism.

29 See Noam Chómsky and Stuart Hampshire discuss the study of language (BBC Third Programme, 8 June 1968). Reprinted in Mark Lester (ed.), *Readings in Applied Transformational Grammar*, pp. 100–13.

30 I am thinking primarily of Paul Lorenzen's 'constructive' or 'operational' foundation of logic and mathematics.

31 Cf. N. Chomsky, 'Review of B. F. Skinner's *Verbal Behavior*', *Language*, 35, 1959, pp. 26–58.

32 Cf. Chomsky ('Linguistics and Philosophy', p. 61): 'One cannot hope to study learning or perception in any useful way by adhering to methodological structures that limit the conceptual apparatus so narrowly as to disallow the concept "what is perceived" and the concept "what is learned".'

33 Ibid., p. 93, n. 14 (directed against Harman).

34 Cf. n. 17 above.

35 Cf. Bar-Hillel, *Aspects of Language*, pp. 160, 164, 178, 180.

36 Cf. H. Schnelle, 'Theorie und Empirie in der Sprachwissenschaft', *Bibliotheca Phonetica*, no. 9, 1970, pp. 51–65.

37 Cf. Bar-Hillel, *Aspects of Language, passim*; Schnelle, op. cit., p. 51.

38 Schnelle, op. cit., pp. 58 ff. correctly asserts that this was the significance in terms of the philosophy of science of the foundation of phonology by the Prague school.

39 Cf. also Chomsky's recourse to Popper in Chomsky, *Current Issues in Linguistic Theory*, pp. 98 f.

40 Cf. Schnelle, op. cit., pp. 63 ff. Does he regard Popper to be a logical empiricist despite the latter's self-understanding?

41 This would, of course, mean that Bierwisch's claims for the linguistic *justification* of logic would have to be abandoned. For logic certainly cannot be *justified* by means of an explanatory, empirically testable theory that necessarily presupposes logic. Chomsky's arguments against Putnam's thesis that language universals – e.g. the 'phrase-structure' of the 'base' as the simplest algorith 'for virtually any computing system' – are not at all surprising, but rather are *cognitively necessary*, reveal that Chomsky is primarily concerned with developing an *empirically relevant* hypothesis concerning the origins of the human language faculty and consequently concerning the structure of all languages. Cf. Chomsky, 'Linguistics and Philosophy', pp. 78 ff. and also pp. 62 and 85.

42 I am ignoring here the possibility of a dialectical mediation between the 'explanation' and the 'deep-hermeneutic understanding' of meaningful slips, such as is typical for psychoanalytical methods. Cf. Apel, 'Die Entfaltung der sprachanalytischen Philosophie und das Problem der "Geisteswissenschaften"', and ch. 2 in this volume.

43 Cf. Chomsky, 'Linguistics and Philosophy'.

44 Cf. Chomsky, *Language and Mind*; cf. p. 186 above.

45 Cf. N. Goodman, 'The Epistemological Argument', in 'Symposium on Innate Ideas', *Synthese,* 17, no. 1, 1967, p. 26.

46 Cf. G. Harman, 'Some recent Issues in Linguistics', *Journal of Philosophy,* 64, no. 2, 1967, p. 81.

47 Chomsky, 'Linguistics and Philosophy', p. 87.

48 Cf. Chomsky, *Aspects of the Theory of Syntax,* p. 51.

49 Ibid., pp. 24 and 51.

50 Ibid., p. 11.

51 On the distinction between 'sentences' and 'utterances', see Bar-Hillel, *Aspects of Language,* pp. 364 ff.

52 Cf. Chomsky, *Current Issues in Linguistic Theory,* p. 26; and Chomsky, *Aspects of the Theory of Syntax,* pp. 18 ff., esp. pp. 20 and 26 f. Here Chomsky even ascribes to the 'child learning a language' the 'intuitive knowledge' of linguistic universals.

53 In his reply to Henry Hiz, Chomsky seems initially inclined to admit such a possibility but then continues: 'Obviously, any such procedure would first have to be tested against the introspective evidence. If one were to propose a test for, say, grammaticalness, that fails to make the distinctions noted earlier in the proper way, one would have little faith in the procedure as a test for grammaticalness.' Chomsky, 'Linguistics and Philosophy', pp. 81 f.

54 Ibid., pp. 82 f.

55 Cf. Chomsky, *Aspects of the Theory of Syntax,* pp. 22 ff., esp. p. 24. As a result of this discussion, however, it is not clear how the question raised by Henry Hiz, namely by what method one arrives at the real linguistic knowledge of a speaker or hearer, is claimed to be irrelevant for Chomsky's elevation of competence to the object of linguistics. Cf. Chomsky, 'Linguistics and Philosophy', pp. 81 f.

56 As Chomsky frequently emphasizes it is certainly true that the procuring of reliable data on the basis of the intuition of the competent speaker creates relatively minor difficulties in linguistics, when compared with the difficulties of theory-formation. It is, of course, a completely different matter in those social sciences in which the adequate understanding of singular utterances is at stake.

57 Cf. Chomsky, *Language and Mind,* p. 83. Further, the following detailed statement in Chomsky (Discussion with Stuart Hampshire on the study of language, pp. 110 f.): 'I would want to use "knowledge" in the sense in which Leibniz uses it: as referring to unconscious knowledge, principles which form the sinews and connections of thought but which may not be conscious principles, which we know must be functioning although we may not be able to introspect into them. The classical rationalist's view is that there are many principles which determine the organisation of knowledge which we may not be conscious of. You can think of these principles as propositional in form, but in any event they're not expressible. You can't get a person to tell you what these principles are. Incidentally, I think that the

rationalists didn't go at all far enough: in fact the one fundamental mistake that I think is made by the Leibnizian theory of mind is its assumption that one could dredge out these principles, that if you really worked hard at it and introspected, you could bring to consciousness the contents of the mind. I don't see any reason to believe that sinews and connections of thought, in Leibniz's sense, are even in principle available to introspection. They may interrelate in some complicated way with certain principles that are available to introspection, but there's no more reason to suppose these principles to be available to introspection than there is to suppose that the principles that determine visual perception should be accessible to introspection – the principles, as in the case of Descartes' example, that make us see a certain irregular figure as a distorted triangle.' In this comparison of grammatical principles with those of spatial conception, however, the fact that competence in one language is acquired by means of 'internalizing' social norms is not taken into account. Cf. pp. 199 ff. below.

58 Cf. on this point T. Nagel, 'Linguistics and Epistemology', in S. Hook (ed.), *Language and Philosophy*, pp. 175 f. On the notion of deep-hermeneutic quasi-explanation cf. also J. Habermas, *Erkenntnis und Interesse*, pp. 262 ff.; Apel, 'Die Entfaltung der sprachanalytischen Philosophie und das Problem der "Geisteswissenschaften";' K.-O. Apel, 'Heideggers Radikalisierung der Hermeneutik und die Frage nach dem Sinnkriterium der Sprache', in *Die hermeneutische Frage in der Theologie*, and ch. 2 in this volume.

59 Cf. Chomsky, *Aspects of the Theory of Syntax*, p. 24.

60 Cf. ibid., p. 26.

61 Cf. ibid., pp. 31 f., where he establishes the following requirements:
   (i) an enumeration . . . of possible sentences . . .
   (ii) an enumeration . . . of possible structural descriptions
   (iii) an enumeration . . . of possible generative grammars
   (iv) a function which assigns to each sentence its structural description by means of a given grammar
   (v) an 'evaluation measure' which selects a given grammar from potential alternatives.

62 Cf. N. Chomsky, 'On the notion "rule of grammar",' in Roman Jakobson (ed.), *Structure of Language and its Mathematical Aspects*; see also J. Klüver, 'Wissenschaftstheoretische Bemerkungen zur Transformationsgrammatik Chomskys', working paper, Philosophy Institute of the University of Saarbrücken, 1971; but also a contrary view in Chomsky, *Current Issues in Linguistic Theory*, p. 25.

63 Cf. W. Stegmüller. *Unvollständigkeit und Unentscheidbarkeit – Die metatheoretischen Resultate von Gödel, Church, Kleine, Rosser und ihre erkenntnistheoretische Bedeutung.*

64 Cf. G. Frey, *Sprache: Ausdruck de Bewusstseins.*

65 Cf. Chomsky, 'Linguistics and Philosophy', p. 63.

66 Following Nicolas Ruwet (*Introduction à la grammaire générative*, pp. 18, 50–51, and 390–1), Klaus Heger, 'Zur Standortbestimmung der

Sprachwissenschaft', *Zeitschrift für Romanische Philologie,* 87, 1971, pp. 9 ff., has compared Saussure's distinction between *langue* and *parole* with Chomsky's distinction between *competence* and *performance.* If I have understood him correctly, he supports Ruwet's critique of an interpretation – attributed by Ruwet to Saussure – that transfers the *aspect créateur,* which is included in Chomsky's notion of 'competence', to *parole* and understands *langue* in a static-taxonomic manner. Nevertheless, he sees the decisive advantage of the notion of *langue* over that of 'competence' in the fact that the former is exclusively restricted to the *object language,* whilst the latter seems to imply the requirement that *metalinguistic statements* (judgments) by the competent native speaker be taken into account as verifying or falsifying instances for a description of competence. In his critique of this requirement, that is explicitly set up by Ruwet, Heger refers to Eugenio Coseriu ('Sincronia, diácronia, y tipologia', in *Actas del XI Congresco Internacional de Linguistica y Filologia Románicas,* Madrid, 1968, pp. 274 f.) who criticizes *generative grammar* on the grounds that the concept of grammaticality 'ought to be justified by the language itself and not by the judgments of the speaker'.

In terms of the philosophy of science, I think that there is a basic difficulty here. On the one hand, it cannot be disputed that it is possible and desirable to *distinguish* between object language and meta-language, and to look upon the object language as the goal or topic of linguistic description. In this respect, meta-linguistic *statements* (which, of course, as verbal *utterances* can also be manifestations of the object language described) cannot ultimately be crucial for the 'justification' of the description's validity. In my opinion this distinction can be conceded, and even required, by the notion of competence. For the *competence* of the native speaker does not consist of what he knows about his language, but rather it consists of his *command of a language,* which can at best be characterized as 'implicit' knowledge about the language (if one assumes with Chomsky that, in this case, Ryle's dualism of 'knowing how' and 'knowing that' can, in principle, be overcome). On the other hand, I cannot see how a linguistic description – of either *competence* or *langue* (if the latter is to be interpreted as 'dynamic' in the sense of 'rule-governed creativity') – can be tested empirically at all if no meta-linguistic utterances are permitted as verifying or falsifying instances, that must, to some extent, be assessed critically.

If this were not permitted, not only positive or negative judgments as to *acceptability* (especially for generated sentences that were unusual and whose confirmation, therefore, would be particularly relevant) on the part of the non-linguists, but also all the corresponding – silent – affirmations or negations by the linguist himself on account of his intuition would be precluded. Instead of reflective communication between the subject of the object-language and the subject of the meta-language, merely a description of the object-language with the aid of the meta-language would be possible, as if the states of affairs to be described linguistically could be observed or recalled like *physiological data* not only in other people but also in the case competent native speaker himself. As it is, however, linguisti behavioural *rules* – both those followed by others *and* those we ourselves follow – are not given. They are only revealed in reflection, where the competent native speaker attempts to *reach agreement* with himself about the valid rules of a language-game, and he seeks to convert his 'knowing how' into a 'knowing that'. In my opinion, this means that the linguist, no matter whether he relies upon 'informants' or upon so-called 'introspection' (an extremely unfortunate term that suggests 'observing oneself' as opposed to 'observing others') cannot avoid taking up *communicative* contact with the 'accompanying metalinguistic consciousness' (Heger) of the subject of linguistic competence and in order through this mediation to make *langue* or *competence* itself the object of research. Of coure, he can bring the scientific knowledge of *langue* itself (or *competence* itself) to bear against superficial meta-linguistic statements by competent native speakers in the form of empirical criticism, but even this criticism is basically dependent upon potential meta-linguistic corroboration by competent native speakers.

In the light of the philosophy of science, it is not surprising that the methodological recognition of these facts encounters resistance. In the analytical theory of science, the demand for a strict separation (not merely a distinction) between the object language and the meta-language of science was initially associated quite naturally with the programme of a behaviouristic reduction of all the social sciences. Anyone who, like Chomsky, considers this programme has failed neither can nor need insist upon the strict separation of object language and meta-language. In my opinion, he must tackle the more difficult problem of the distinction between object language and meta-language within the framework of – and with the aid of – man's meta-linguistic self-reflection upon his rule-based competences. I think that this problem is characteristic of what one can (and, in my view, must) call the *subject-object dialectic* in the social sciences' methodological relationship to their object. It is remarkable that, unlike Chomsky, even Fodor and Katz adhere to the quasi-behaviouristic presuppositions of the scientistic, reductionist philosophy of science. In the light of this theory, they even tried to convince the representatives of ordinary language philosophy that their 'intuitive' linguistic knowledge was based on empirical observations and generalizations, similar to those of physiology. In my opinion, the long dispute between Fodor and Katz, on the one hand, and Cavell, Hanson, Vendler and Searle on the other (cf. the documentation in Colin Lyas (ed.), *Philosophy and Linguistics*), produces results that support the line of argument I have advanced here.

67 Cf. E. Tugendhat, 'Tarskis semantische Definition der Wahrheit und ihre Stellung innerhalb der Geschichte des Wahrheitsproblems im logischen Positivismus', *Philosophische Rundschau*, 8, 1960, pp.

131–59; K.-O. Apel, 'Sprache und Wahrheit in der gegenwärtigen Situation der Philosophie', *Philosophische Rundschau*, 7, 1959, pp. 161–84; and ch. 4 in this volume.

68 Cf. Katz. *The Philosophy of Language.*

69 Chomsky (*Aspects of the Theory of Syntax*, p. 164) himself postulates an extension in this direction: 'further structure being necessary in the lexicon to account for field properties'. Cf. also Bar-Hillel, *Aspects of Language,* pp. 186 f. Earlier (p. 158) Bar-Hillel draws attention to a very interesting comparison between the dependency of theoretical concepts on a theory and the possible functional relatedness of semantic units to linguistic world-views.

70 Cf. Coseriu, 'Sincronia, diacronia y tipologia'.

71 Cf. the writings of Leo Weisgerber.

72 Cf. H.-M. Gauger, 'Die Semantik in der Sprachtheorie der transformationellen Grammatik', *Linguistische Berichte*, 1, 1969, pp. 1–18.

73 Cf. Habermas, 'Kritische Bemerkungen zum elementaristischen Programm einer allgemeinen Semantik'.

74 In my opinion, however, the term 'monological' as Habermas uses it, namely as a counterpart to 'dialogical' or 'communicative', is ambiguous. In the sense in which I use it below, the 'monological' application of rules means something which, according to Wittgenstein, cannot exist, but which, however, has been widely assumed in the philosophical tradition – alongside the prejudice concerning *methodological solipsism.* That is, it means that 'one person alone' can follow a rule, e.g. logical, mathematical, or grammatical rules. There are many indications that at least the Cartesian Chomsky has not overcome this prejudice. On the other hand, however, I believe, for instance, that the point of the dialogical justification of logic by Paul Lorenzen is only intelligible if we presuppose that the application of a rule itself basically presupposes the monitoring of a language-game. A *monological logic,* therefore, would merely be a matter for abstract calculi and automata, i.e. the objectivations and simulations of human operations in the service of the 'indirect' elucidation of dialogical-pragmatic argumentations. I think that Habermas sometimes uses the term 'monological' in this sense, which means in a radical, critical sense. More frequently, however, he assumes that the monological capacity and the monological application of rules is something which exists and which always *presupposes* a language-game in Wittgenstein's sense. It is distinguished, however, from the dialogical-communicative application of rules, e.g. the application of logical and grammatical rules as opposed to the application of such rules that presuppose *communicative competence* for their application as, for instance, adopting roles in the speech situation. In my view, these are two separate problems which have yet to be seen in the proper relationship to one another.

75 Chomsky's most recent statements on his model of language learning do not permit a definite answer to the question raised here, even if a

weakening of the distinct a priorism can be detected. Chomsky ('Linguistics and Philosophy', p. 83) writes: 'In the case of language-acquisition, furthermore, it must be emphasized that the model I am suggesting can at best only be regarded as a first approximation to a theory of learning, since it is an instantaneous model and does not try to capture the interplay between tentative hypotheses that the child may construct, new data interpreted in terms of these hypotheses, new hypotheses based on these interpretations, and so on, until some relatively fixed system of competence is established.'

76 Cf. Chomsky, *Aspects of the Theory of Syntax,* p. 3 and *passim.*
77 Cf. ibid., pp. 15 f. (198) 160; Chomsky, 'Linguistics and Philosophy', p. 54; but cf. also ibid., p. 55 where, in contrast to the earlier hypothesis that the surface structure cannot contribute anything to the semantic interpretation, such a possibility is envisaged as a result of the studies on 'referential opacity'.
78 Total objectification through description and explanation, i.e. the failure to take into account transcendental reflection upon the preconditions for the possibility of scientific objectification – and also of intersubjective communication – is, of course, self-evident for the two scientistic types of modern philosophy of science (i.e. those committed to the conception of an objectivistic unified science). With reference to what follows, however, one can ask whether, given the scientistic presupposition, 'communicative competence' that is postulated alongside grammatical competence in the pragmatic dimension can be discovered at all, let alone explicate it as the set of 'dialogue-constitutive universals' (Habermas). It could be that just as the phenomenon of 'grammatical competence', (re)-discovered by Chomsky, disappears in the behaviourist approach, so for a scientistic approach the phenomenon of communicative competence also disappears.
79 Habermas, 'Kritische Bemerkungen zum elementaristischen Programm einer allgemeinen Semantik', p. 63.
80 Ibid., pp. 63 f.
81 Wittgenstein, *Tractatus logico-philosophicus,* §§ 5.64 f. and 5.62 ff. See also ch. 5 in this volume.
82 Cf. M. Schlick, *Gesammelte Aufsätze,* pp. 151–250; cf. K.-O. Apel, 'Sprache und Ordnung', in *Das Problem der Ordnung,* pp. 215 ff.
83 Cf. K. Heger, 'Zur Standortbestimmung der Sprachwissenschaft', *Zeitschrift für Romanische Philologie,* 87, 1971, pp. 1–31; and Heger, *Monem, Wort und Satz.*
84 In this sense, however, *we* can only speak meaningfully of 'animal languages' and the 'application of rules' by animals since *we* tacitly presuppose the transcendental pragmatic dimension of the monitoring of language-games, which is part of our application of both language and rules, in the case of the – privatively reductive – interpretation of animal behaviour. Without these transcendental hermeneutic presuppositions the data of research into animal behaviour ('ethology') – unlike the 'data' of physics – cannot be constituted for us.

221

85 Cf. Habermas, 'Einführende Bemerkungen zu einer Theorie der kommunikativen Kompetenz'.
86 This does not exclude the fact that 'communicative competence' also includes the active and passive command of *paralinguistic* and *extralinguistic* means of communication (e.g. intonation, mime, gesture). Cf. U. Maas and D. Wunderlich, *Pragmatik und sprachliches Handeln,* Frankfurt, 1972.
87 Cf. J. L. Austin, 'Performative Utterances', in *Philosophical Papers,* pp. 220–39; and Austin, *How to do Things with Words.*
88 Cf. J. R. Searle, *Speech Acts.*
89 Cf. ibid., pp. 17 f.; and also Habermas, 'Vorbereitende Bemerkungen zu, einer Theorie der kommunikativen Kompetenz', pp. 103 f.
90 See, on what follows, my dispute with Searle in 'Sprechakttheorie und transzendentale Sprachpragmatik zur Frage ethischer Normen', in K.-O. Apel (ed.), *Sprachpragmatik und Philosophie,* Frankfurt, 1976.
91 Cf. Wunderlich, 'McCawleys Tiefenstrukturen'.
92 Cf. ibid.; Wunderlich, 'Pragmatik, Sprechsituation, Deixis', and Wunderlich, 'Die Rolle der Pragmatik in der Linguistik'.
93 Cf. Habermas, 'Einführende Bemerkungen zu einer Theorie der kommunikativen Kompetenz', and Habermas, 'Vorbereitende Bemerkungen zu einer Theorie der kommunikativen Kompetenz'.
94 J. D. McCawley, 'Where do Noun Phrases Come From?'
95 'On the Cyclic Nature of English Pronominalization'.
96 Habermas, 'Vorbereitende Bemerkungen, zu einer Theorie de kommunikativen Kompetenz', pp. 109 f.
97 Cf. Habermas, 'Vorbereitende Bemerkungen zu einer Theorie der kommunikativen Kompetenz', p. 110; chs. 4 and 5 in this volume, and Apel, 'Sprechakttheorie und transzendentale Sprachpragmatik zur Frage ethischer Normen'.
98 Wunderlich, 'Pragmatik, Sprechsituation, Deixis', p. 20.
99 Ibid., pp. 19 f.
100 As 'indexical expressions' or 'token-bound sentences' these were already familiar to us in their reference to the pragmatic situation through the work of C. S. Peirce. Cf. Y. Bar-Hillel, 'Logical Syntax and Semantics', *Language,* 30, 1954, pp. 30–7; Bar-Hillel, 'Indexical Expressions', *Mind,* 63, 1954, pp. 359–79; and Apel, Introduction to C. S. Peirce, *Schriften II.*
101 One can, of course, conceive of an ironical context in which these sentences would be acceptable in empirical-pragmatic terms. But even then the understanding – itself systematic-pragmatic in character – of their *ungrammaticality* would be presupposed. The situation becomes more difficult if the problematic use of deictic expressions is regarded not as an ironical but rather as a philosophically necessary use of language, as, for example, in the sentence: 'I (alone) know that I am in pain (now).' It is well known that the later Wittgenstein (*Philosophical Investigations,* 1958) took great trouble to unmask such sentences as nonsensical or, more precisely, as symptomatic for the creation of philosophical problems through the misuse of language. Wittgenstein

referred in this connection to the deep structure of everyday language. In his view, the sentence 'You know that I am (now) in pain' would be justified in terms of deep pragmatics since the language-game with the word 'know' must be understood analogously to the language-game with the word 'assume'. A *systematic deep-pragmatics* would presumably corroborate Wittgenstein's keen insight into the deviations of philosophy from the ordinary use of language. But the decisive question for Wittgenstein and ordinary language philosophy would still not have been answered; namely, whether in this case the philosophers' linguistic usage is simply nonsensical or whether, as *rule-changing creativity* – similar to properly appreciated metaphors – it reveals insights that cannot be attained without deviation in applying the rule. I believe that at this point a perspective is opened up on to the problem of the distinction and connection between *systematic pragmatics* and *hermeneutics* – a problem that, at present, is still hardly understood. A philosophical *critique of meaning* (e.g. under the motto of the suspected meaninglessness of all metaphysics) has hitherto been undertaken in the name of 'logical syntax' or 'logical semantics' (early Wittgenstein, Carnap) and in the name of deep pragmatics (Peirce, later Wittgenstein). It will surely be found, however, that such a critique must be performed at the level of hermeneutics, which is more concrete and transcends the abstraction of pragmatics from the *historical* situation of human discourse. At the level of hermeneutics, even systematically deviating language does not immediately represent a criterion for meaninglessness. Cf. provisionally, Apel, 'Heideggers Radikalisierung der Hermeneutik und die Frage nach dem Sinnkriterium der Sprache'.

102 Cf. Habermas, 'Einfuhrende Bemerkungen zu einer Theorie der kommunikativen Komptenz'; Habermas, 'Vorbereitende Bemerkungen zu einer Theorie der kommunikativen Kompetenz'; and Habermas, 'Was heisst Universalpragmatik?' in K.-O. Apel (ed.), *Sprachpragmatik und Philosophie*, pp. 174–272.

103 Cf. D. Hymes, 'Models of the Interpretation of Language and Social Setting', *Journal of Social Issues*, 23, 1967, pp. 8–28; Hymes, 'On communicative competence', in J. J. Gumperz and D. Hymes (eds), *Directions in Sociolinguistics*. Also, Lyons, *Chomsky*, p. 28; and E. Oksaar, 'Sprachliche Interferenzen und kommunikative Kompetenz', in *Indo-Celtica: Gedächtnisschrift Alf Sommerfelt*, Munich, forthcoming.

104 See chs. 3, 4 and 5 in this volume, and Apel, 'Sprechakttheorie und transzendentale Sprachpragmatik zur Frage ethischer Normen'. In this essay I am unable to deal with the problems raised by Habermas concerning the analogy with and distinction between a *theoretical idealization* at the level of ('monological') 'grammatical competence' on the one hand, 'communicative competence' on the other, and the related problem of the relationship between philosophy and empirical linguistics at the level of *universal pragmatics*. I believe, however, that the present study has established the following: Since we cannot gain

reflective distance from 'communicative competence' and transcend it as an anthropological fact by means of a *communicative competence* as is the case with 'grammatical competence', a *universal pragmatic* theory cannot be understood as a theory that can merely be tested empirically. Rather, it must be grounded in a directly transcendental-philosophical manner in reflective contemplation of a normative ideal – that is also ethically relevant – of the 'ideal speech situation' in the 'ideal communication community', a situation which we always anticipate counterfactually. In my opinion, this by no means excludes a heuristic mediation of 'universal pragmatics' through the methods of linguistics or psycho- and sociolinguistics.

105 I would disagree with Wunderlich ('Die Rolle der Pragmatik in der Linguistik', pp. 30 f.) and support Habermas's view that the postulate of a non-distorted and basically unlimited verbalization of extra-linguistic communicative competence is the presupposition of all critiques of ideology *qua* transcendence of alienation, and to this extent it cannot be interpreted as a mere extrapolation of the bourgeois form of life. The demand for a 'naturalization of man' that is also a 'humanization of nature' is not opposed to this but rather it constantly presupposes anew the overcoming of what is merely 'natural' for it to be fulfilled.

106 Cf. Oksaar, 'Sprachliche Interferenzen und kommunikative Kompetenz'.

CHAPTER 7

The *a priori* of the communication community and the foundations of ethics: the problem of a rational foundation of ethics in the scientific age

Contents

2.3.   The heuristic question of the ethical presuppositions of (value-neutral) science as the decisive strategy of argument.

2.3.1. The attack on the presupposition of the ethical necessity of science and the radicalization of the heuristic question as the question of the ethical presuppositions of any rational argument.

2.3.2. The strategic meaning of the question of ethics as the presupposition of logic.

2.3.3. The logical (syntactic-semantic) aporetic of 'fundamental grounding' and the possibility of a transcendental-pragmatic reflection upon the irreducibility of the *a priori* of argument.

2.3.4. The recognition of a basic ethical norm as the necessary presupposition of argument.

2.3.5. The content of the basic ethical norm and its strategic implications: the self-assertion of the real communication community and the realization of the ideal communication community.

1   The paradoxical problem

1.1   Anyone who reflects upon the relationship between science and ethics in modern global industrial societies is, I believe, confronted with a paradoxical situation. On the one hand, the need for a universal ethics, i.e. one that is binding for human society as a whole, was never so urgent as now – a time which is characterized by a globally uniform civilization produced by the technological consequences of science. On the other hand, the philosophical task of rationally grounding a general ethics never seems to have been so difficult as it is in the scientific age. This is because in our time the notion of intersubjective validity is also prejudged by science, namely by the scientistic notion of normatively neutral or value-free 'objectivity'.

Let us first consider one side of this paradoxical situation: the present need for a universal ethics (I would say: the need for a macro-ethics of humanity on the finite earth).[1] Today the technological consequences of science have secured for human actions and inactions such a range and scope that it is no longer possible to be content with moral norms which regulate human life in small groups and to abandon the relationships between groups to the struggle for existence in Darwin's sense. If the assumption of the ethologists is correct that even cannibalism amongst early human beings must be interpreted as a consequence of the invention of the mallet or *celt*, i.e. as the result of the disturbance – that was essential for *homo faber* – of the equilibrium between the available organs of aggression and the inhibiting instincts that are analogous to human morals, then this imbalance has been made far more acute by the development of modern weapons systems. Today, however, there is the additional problem that the group-specific morals which are mostly rooted in archaic institutions and traditions are no longer able to compensate for the loss of equilibrium that is basic to *homo faber*. For there is probably no example more typical of the 'uncontemporaneity' of human cultural spheres than the imbalance between the expansion of scientific and technical possibilities and the tendency of group-specific morals to remain static.

If, in terms of the possible effect of human actions, one distinguishes between a micro-domain (family, marriage, neighbourhood), a meso-domain (levels of national politics) and a macro-domain (the fact of mankind),[2] then it can be shown that the moral norms which currently operate in all nations are still principally concentrated in the intimate domain (especially in the regulation of sexual relations). Even in the meso-domain of national politics, they are largely reduced to the archaic impulses of group egoism and group identification, whilst the actual political decisions count as problems of a morally neutral *raison d'état*. But in so far as the macro-domain of vital human interests is affected, concern about them is left, for the time being, to a still relatively small number of initiates. But now this situation in the conservative moral sector is confronted with a completely different situation in the sphere of the consequences of human actions, especially the risk rising out of them. As a result of the planetary expansion and the internationally interlocked technical-scientific civilization, the consequences of human actions – e.g. within industrial production – can largely be localized in the macro-domain of humanity's common interests.

The ethically relevant aspect of this phenomenon becomes most clear if one considers the risk involved in action, for instance the threat to human life. Even if, until recently, it was possible to interpret war as an instrument of biological selection and also as an instrument of the spatial expansion of the human race by pushing the weaker party into unsettled regions, this view has been made completely obsolete by the invention of the atom bomb. The risk of destruction through war is no longer restricted to the micro- or meso-domain. It threatens the existence of mankind as a whole. But the effects and side-effects of industrial technology in general present a similar problem. In recent years, this has been made clear to us most forcibly through the awareness of progressive environmental pollution. Amongst other things, this ecological problem of the side-effects of a technical civilization has raised the question as to whether the economic and technological theory of growth which prevails in competing industrial nations should not be radically revised if the human ecosphere is to be saved.

These few examples should be sufficient to demonstrate that the results of science present a moral challenge for mankind. Scientific-technical civilization has confronted all nations, races and cultures, regardless of their group-specific, culturally relative moral traditions, with a common ethical problem. For the first time in the history of the human species, human beings are faced with the task of accepting collective responsibility for the consequences of their actions on a world-wide scale. One might expect that this obligatory collective responsibility corresponds to the intersubjective validity of norms or at least to the basic principle of an ethics of responsibility. So much for the first aspect of the problem that is suggested by the topic 'ethics in a scientific age'.

The second aspect of the problem which, as I have indicated, makes it paradoxical is suggested to the professional philosopher when he contemplates the theoretical – or rather, meta-theoretical – problem of the relationship between science and ethics. This problem is characterized by the conviction that is widely held, especially by undaunted and honest theoreticians, that the possibility for the intersubjective validity of arguments is already covered by the possibility of scientific objectivity in the domain of the logico-mathematical formal sciences and in the domain of the empirical-analytical substantive sciences. But since norms or value judgments can be derived from facts neither through the formalism of logico-mathematical inferences nor through inductive inferences, the idea of scientific objectivity seems to banish moral norms' or value judgments' claim to validity to the domain of an unbinding subjectivity. It seems as if the validity claims made by ethics either explicitly or implicitly within ideological contexts must be reduced to irrational, emotional reactions or equally irrational arbitrary decisions.

Accordingly, it is not the ethical norms but only the value-free descriptions of the operative moral norms and the causal or statistical explanations of the emergence of moral norms or value systems by the so-called empirical social sciences, that can be rationally grounded.

But these sciences, which also include in this context history and cultural anthropology as well as sociology and psychology, seem to provide an additional empirical argument for the subjectivity and irrationality – that has already been postulated by the logic of science – of moral norms and values. One frequently hears that they have reached the objectively valid factual judgment that the norms which human beings either recognize or follow in practice are, to a large degree, relative to the particular culture or epoch, i.e. they are subjective.

It seems only consistent, therefore, if ultimately professional philosophy, which regards itself as scientific, has abandoned the business of ethics in the sense of a direct justification of ethical norms, or of an ultimate principle for ethical norms. In this connection, there developed from traditional ethics or practical philosophy an analytical 'meta-ethics' which generally considers itself to be a value-free, scientific-theoretical description of the linguistic usage or of the logical rules of the so-called 'moral discourse'. Each type of philosophy which does not concur with this transformation, i.e. a philosophy that attempts to replace the 'neutrality thesis'[3] of analytical meta-ethics by a justification of moral norms, appears to derive norms from facts and thereby to violate Hume's principle of the strict distinction between what *is* and what *ought* to be.[4] Consequently, every normative ethics seems to have been made obsolete by logic. Its foundations, like those of 'natural law', are shown to be dogmatic or ideological by 'scientific' philosophy, and its validity claim is stigmatized either as a regrettable illusion or as authoritarian repression and a threat to human freedom (in the latter case, it is, however, interesting to note the quasi-moral engagement of 'scientific' philosophy which is meant to function as a critique of ideology in the name of liberalism. We shall return to this point). This must suffice for the present on the second aspect of the paradoxical problem with which we are confronted by the question concerning the relationship between science and ethics. A universal, i.e. intersubjectively valid ethics of collective responsibility thus seems both necessary and impossible.

This paradoxical feature of the present problem can be elevated

229

to a contradiction in the sense of Hegelian dialectics; i.e. it can be characterized as a real antagonism between two contemporary philosophical currents and, to this extent, as a driving force behind a dialectics that can offer a heuristically useful illustration and explication of our problem. What are the tendencies in the philosophy of our times which represent this antagonism in a real and not merely academic sense?

1.2   From the standpoint indicated, I believe it is impossible to doubt that Marxism in all its versions represents the positive but also the more or less dogmatic side of this antagonism. Marxism has classically expounded the view (and developed its consequences) that mankind faces the task of overcoming its natural 'prehistory', but this means overcoming the era of particular group or class interests which, reified into quasi-natural historical forces, impair the transparency and effective self-control of human activity and make it impossible for human beings to assume responsibility for history in collective action. In the era anticipated by Marxism in which history is made by truly socialized human beings, a praxis which is collectively planned and for which people are collectively responsible is to replace the illusory freedom of the conflicting actions of individuals and groups.

But in view of the theoretical difficulties already indicated, how can Marxism provide the ethical foundations and consequently the preconditions for the possibility of a collective praxis and responsibility for such a praxis? As a dialectical philosophy (in the Hegelian sense), Marxism does not accept Hume's distinction between what is and what ought to be as an insurmountable separation of scientifically knowable facts and subjectively established norms. In its orthodox version, at least, it adheres more or less avowedly to the classical Aristotelian-Thomist postulate of a teleological ontology, according to which what exists, if understood correctly, is identical with what is good. Stated more precisely: Marxism, following Hegel, interprets the historically real as what is rational and the rational as what is real. It interprets this in the sense of a historical-dialectical transformation of classical ontology. But it transcends Hegel's position in that it seeks to interpret the unity of historical facticity and its determinate negation, which is to constitute the historical-dialectical unity of rational reality, not only speculatively *ex post* but rather it believes that it can make this unity – including the future that has still to be recreated through 'critique' and 'revolutionary practice' –

the object of an objective, materialistic scientific analysis. (This claim is raised at least by 'orthodox' Marxism, despite Marx's appraisal of 'subjective practice' – which was discovered by German idealism – in the 'Theses on Feuerbach'.)[5]

As the critically engaged 'subjective practice' of revolutionaries is integrated in this manner into the dialectical concept of the objectively knowable reality (of history), the impression is created that an ethical foundation of the totally committed subjective praxis becomes superfluous for Marxism.[6] The dialectical analysis and synthesis of the necessary course of history seems from the outset to sublate Hume's distinction between what is and what ought to be into the totality of reality that is interpreted as rational.

It is obvious, however, that precisely this 'dialectical' concept of reality as the objectively necessary course of history contradicts both the modern idea of scientistic objectivity and the modern idea of a free, moral decision of conscience.

In fact, along with Whitehead,[7] one can object to Hume and the analytic philosophy which follows him that – in both causal analysis and the distinction between facts and norms – they fail to come to terms with the concrete reality of a temporal world process by separating (through abstract concept formation) the past as what has become fact 'for us', and therefore objectively given, from the future as that which is undecided 'for us' and therefore reserved for the subjective domain.[8]

But this objection on the part of 'speculative reflection' to the modern analytical idea of objective reality also demonstrates that the dissection of the 'concrete' process of reality – like the distinction between the three subjective 'time ecstasies'[9] – has its necessary origin in the situation of the acting human being; or, more precisely, in the situation of the human being who must project the knowledge he has gained from experience onto the uncertain and undecided future, and thereby presupposes principles of action which he cannot derive from experience. The speculative-dialectical concept of 'concrete' reality as a temporal reality in process, which is common to Hegel, Marx and the later Whitehead, is unable to 'transcend' this practically and ethically relevant distinction between that which exists now and that which ought to be. Its legitimacy with regard to Hume's abstract analytical distinction lies in the fact that reflection upon the totality of reality in process (which we must also help to constitute) compels us, however, to conceive of, i.e. to postulate, the real transcendence of this distinction as the transcendence of a dialectical contradiction. Consequently, the acting human being himself is charged with the transcendence of the distinction; i.e. there exists no super-science which might guarantee the unity of theory and practice through objective analysis. Rather, an ethics is required which provides a mediation between theory and practice by means of a normative principle in the historical situation.

The objections just raised to the possibility of a transcendence – itself still objectively scientific – of the practically relevant distinction between *is* and *ought*, facts and norms, must also be raised against the related notion of a total mediation between *objectivity* and *subjectivity* through a dialectical super-science. Of course, here too the demand for a *mediation* as such is justified as the result of a radical epistemological reflection upon the situation of the human sciences. Where *interpretation* takes place in the sense of 'hermeneutics', i.e. where a science's concept formation develops, in principle, from a language-game that includes both the subject and object of science,[10] the dialectical mediation between subjectivity and objectivity has always occurred. In this sense, a dialectical-critical sociology's demand that scientific practice itself be considered a part of the social reality of the 'subject-object' (Ernst Bloch) that is to be analysed, is legitimate as long as the 'total mediation' in Hegel's sense is not envisaged, or – even worse – Hegel's speculative attempt at a total mediation is confused with the possibility of an empirical, objective science of history as a whole (allegedly founded by Marx). But it is precisely this demand for both a dialectical and scientific solution to the subject-object opposition in epistemology that is suggested by Marxist orthodoxy and neo-orthodoxy. The question why someone subjectively takes up the cause of the proletariat, for example, is answered by reference to the objective results of scientific socialism whilst the understanding and acceptance of these results is made dependent upon taking up the cause of the proletariat. Here, the total mediation of subjectivity and objectivity postulated by Hegel as a speculative *ex post* reflection is presented as the result of a scientific, objective analysis.

Instead of the open hermeneutic circle involving tentative, practical, ethical engagement and the hypothetical reconstruction of the historical process,[11] which must indeed be derived from the mediation between objectivity and subjectivity that is always initiated in *understanding*, a closed, logical circle of presuppositions is produced.

This makes it impossible for an outsider – i.e. for someone who is not already a believer – to enter into a critical discussion with orthodox Marxism.[12]

Given these presuppositions, the Marxist notion of a mediation between theory and practice and science and ethics must seem a dogmatic rejection of both the spirit of science and free ethical responsibility. As a historical-dialectical transformation of teleological ontology, Marxism seems to transcend the dogmatism of traditional metaphysics by a prophecy that includes future praxis. As *scientific* socialism, it replaces the qualified prognoses of empirical-analytical (natural) science with the unqualified prognoses of 'historicism' that Popper has criticized.[13] On the other hand, as scientific *socialism* it replaces the ethical justification of social engagement with reference to the historically necessary and thereby corrupts – again, in Popper's view – ethical responsibility in the present situation by a 'moral futurism'.[14] Nor can it be denied that this critique of orthodox theory is largely corroborated by the analysis of orthodox practice. In the domain in which Marxist orthodoxy is in control, the extremely reasonable requirement that human society collectively takes over responsibility for historical practice apparently leads to that class of party officials taking over which, since Lenin's time, has monopolized insight into the necessity of the historical process and has consequently supervised the mediation of theory and practice. The ethical responsibility of individuals is not extended into the political domain. Rather, it is drastically restricted even in the domain of ideological decisions which modern liberalism wrested from the authority of church and state.

Against this background, one can understand why modern philosophy in the Western tradition of liberal democracy has taken on the (ideological) function of an antithesis with regard to the Marxist conceptions of a dialectical mediation between theory and practice and between science and ethics. This function becomes evident if, in the light of our heuristics of the basic paradox of the problem, we examine the difference between so-called 'analytical philosophy' and 'existentialism', which is usually regarded in the West as the most profound contradiction within modern philosophy. From our perspective, however, it immediately becomes clear that analytical philosophy and existentialism by no means contradict each other in their ideological function, but rather they complement one another. They corroborate each other through a kind of division of labour by mutually assigning to one another the domain of objective scientific knowledge, on the one hand, and the domain of subjective ethical decisions on the other.[15]

Even a philosopher like Soren Kierkegaard believed that 'objectivity' in the sense of the universal, intersubjective validity of knowledge is a privilege of value-free science. This conviction was, in fact, the presupposition underlying his thesis that what is ethically binding is only revealed to the 'subjectively interested' thought of individuals in what he ultimately called the 'extreme situations' of ultimate decisions of faith. The difference between Kierkegaard's attitude and that of modern scientism lies solely in the fact that for him subjectively interested thinking was 'fundamental thinking', whilst he regarded the objectivity of science as existentially irrelevant and therefore not fundamental.

But even this existentialist accentuation of the relationship between the complementary domains can also be found in the form of an implicit suggestion in a work by one of the intellectual fathers of modern neopositivism, namely, in Ludwig Wittgenstein's *Tractatus logico-philosophicus*. After he has initially restricted the possibility of meaningful statements to the domain of natural science, Wittgenstein writes at the end of the *Tractatus* (6.42): 'Hence also there can be no ethical propositions. Propositions cannot express anything higher'.

And in a letter to Ludwig von Ficker in 1919, Wittgenstein characterizes the whole of the *Tractatus* in the following way:[16]

> the meaning of this book is an ethical one. I once wanted to include in the preface the statement that my book consists of two parts: of what is presented here, and of all that which I have *not* written down. And it is this second part that is important. For through my book, the ethical is circumscribed as it were from within; and I am convinced that it can *only* be *strictly* circumscribed in this manner. In short, I believe that by remaining silent I have defined what *many* people today *babble about.*

The connection between mysticism and existential subjectivism or 'transcendental solipsism' in Wittgenstein's comments on the ethical realm corresponds to a characteristic problem of modern existentialism, from Kierkegaard's method of 'indirect communication' to Karl Jaspers's 'illumination of existence' (*Existenzerhellung*). The difficulty here is always how theoretical philosophy with its claim to intersubjective validity can discuss what, by definition, is subjective and singular. A specific aspect of this problem also occurs in analytical metaphysics. There the question arises as to how an objectively descriptive meta-ethics, that considers itself to be a value-neutral science, can obtain the criteria for determining the morally relevant use of language, since such criteria can by no means be derived from the objectively describable grammatical structures of language.[17]

But before we reflect in more detail upon these aporetic features of the official complementarity of existentialism and scientism, let us examine the ideological function of this system in mediating theory and practice in the Western world.

1.3 The complementarity between the value-free objectivism of science, on the one hand, and the existential subjectivism of religious acts of faith and ethical decisions, on the other, proves to be the modern philosophical-ideological expression of the liberal separation of the public and private spheres of life which has developed in the context of the separation of church and state. For in the name of this separation, and that means with the aid of secularized state power, Western liberalism first of all made religious belief less binding and then, correspondingly, increasingly restricted the binding character of moral norms to the sphere of private decisions of conscience. Today this process is still continuing. One instance is the removal of moral arguments and principles from the foundations upon which the law rests. In general, one can assert that in all sectors of public life in Western industrial societies, *moral* justifications of praxis are being replaced by pragmatic arguments that can be provided by 'experts' on the basis of objectifiable, scientific-technological rules.

In this manner, part of human praxis can, indeed, be 'objectified' in accordance with the value-free standards of science. The instrumental, technical part and the strategic part of praxis can be grounded by objective if-then rules that can be regarded as logical transformations of scientific law-like knowledge.

The first detailed historical, sociological analysis of this aspect of the mediation of theory and practice was carried out by Max Weber with his notion of the 'rationalization' of the public sphere of Western industrial societies, and also the 'rationalization' of trade, production and bureaucratic government organization.[18] Nowadays this analysis and objectification is being continued and generalized – partially with the aid of cybernetics – by means of a functionalist systems theory of society. In philosophical terms, this scientifically and technologically objectifiable aspect of the mediation between theory and practice was first emphasized and virtually raised to the paradigm of practical reason by John Dewey. Today, this pragmatism and instrumentalism has become an essential part of both analytical philosophy and the public wisdom in the broader sense. One can indeed claim that pragmatism is the operating philosophy of public life in Western industrial societies.[19] It is therefore very significant that a philosophy like Popper's, which is so representative of the West, has hitherto only formulated the instrumentalistically objectifiable part of the rational mediation of theory and practice that it propagates. Hitherto, the Popperian school has seen the paradigm for the rational mediation of theory and practice solely in 'piecemeal social engineering', or in the corresponding and necessary analysis of the conditions for the realizability of, and the anticipated consequences of, political projects. On the other hand, the foundations and criteria for an engaged philosophy of the (evolution of the) 'open society' that is implicitly drawn upon – foundations and criteria that are derived from hermeneutics, the critique of ideology and ethics – could hitherto only be articulated in the limiting concept of 'critical conventionalism'.[20] It would seem that in this restriction of the idea of methodological rationalism to what can be objectified in a value-free manner plus convention, a limitation of the currently conceivable idea of undogmatic reason is expressed.

Yet the rules of instrumental and strategic rationalization of the technical sector of praxis that are capable of value-free objectification appear to presuppose *decisions* about the goals of human praxis. They do not provide a rationalization of the selection of the goals themselves. Stated more precisely: they also make a very important contribution towards the rationalization of goals in that, by revealing the technical possibilities for their realization and the probable effects and side-effects, they limit the possibilities for the rational establishment of goals.[21] Nevertheless, they are incapable of providing positive criteria for the desirability of the goals themselves. The fact that an ethical problem still exists, over and above the 'intelligent mediation of ends and means' propagated by Dewey, is especially evident in those situations, which are not uncommon today, where it is necessary to establish rationally grounded resistance to scientific, technical suggestions of practicability that are generally also supported by economic interests.[22] Here the ethical problem of rationality establishing goals can apparently no longer be excluded pragmatically. But it is at precisely this point that the limitation of the scientific-technological concept of a value-free, objectivating rationality is revealed.

Unlike the instrumentalist Dewey, who questioned the practical necessity of ultimate goals as such,[23] Max Weber, who was closely associated with neo-Kantianism, recognized precisely in politics the limitations of pragmatic rationalization when it is confronted with what his pupil Karl Jaspers later called the 'extreme situations' of responsible decision-making. But even Weber himself at this point could only follow the logic of the system of complementarity that we have outlined, and he had to relegate the ethical problem of the evaluation of goals to the domain of ultimately irrational, subjective decisions. In contrast to the neo-Kantians, who still adhered to the idea of a formal value-rational argument, Weber saw the truth of ancient polytheism reaffirmed in the sphere of ultimate value pre-ference. Each individual must choose his god here in a situation of responsible decision-making.[24]

It hardly needs to be mentioned that both the so-called existentialist situationalist ethics (e.g. of the young Sartre) and political decisionism (e.g. of Carl Schmitt) follow the same logic. It is the *logic of the alternative between objective-science and subjective value-decision* which even today largely determines the ideological structure of the mediation of theory and practice in the West. In its liberal-democratic version, the public part of life-practice should ideally be regulated by value-free rationality, which is formulated in 'analytical philosophy' in the broadest sense. What cannot be resolved in terms of this rationality – the problem of ultimate preferences for values and goals – devolves automatically upon the private sphere of subjective decisions of conscience that is formulated in 'existentialism' in the broadest sense. The so-called analytical 'meta-ethics', which was developed by pupils of G. E. Moore and Wittgenstein in the English-speaking world, has merely confirmed this situation through its 'neutrality-thesis'. Taking up a statement by the later Wittgenstein, we can say that analytical meta-ethics 'leaves everything as it is'.

1.4   But given these presuppositions, what about the above-mentioned necessity for assuming responsibility for the results and side-effects of human practice in the age of global industrial tech-nology? This much seems to be clear: the value-free scientific-technological mediation of theory and practice cannot assume this responsibility. It can, at best, provide the necessary 'information' for exercising this responsibility. It must, however, presuppose the existence of ethical standards for responsibility. But who can assume responsibility and on the basis of what principles? If one recalls the philosophical foundation of the Western system of complementarity, then ultimately only isolated decisions of conscience by individuals can claim to be morally binding. How can these individual decisions of conscience be made to coincide in accordance with normative rules so that they can assume the collective responsibility for societal practice?

One may recall here the public formation of the will through convention ('agreement') which, in the domain of liberal democracy, gives rise to the grounding of both positive law and the conception of politics. It seems as if, through conventions, the subjective decisions of conscience and – mediated through these – even the subjective needs of individuals are drawn together in a specific situation in the form of a willed decision for which everyone assumes responsibility – even if this comes about through compromise solutions such as votes. Moreover, the 'decisions' reached in this manner themselves create the basis for all intersubjectively binding norms, in so far as they can lay claim to validity in the public sphere. This seems to be the answer that can be derived from the philosophical presuppositions of the Western system of complementarity; and this answer seems to render superfluous the philosophical grounding of a universally valid ethics.[25]

As in the analytical theory of science, even in the sphere of practical reason conventionalism seems to define those subjective-intersubjective bases for decision which can and must augment the objective criteria of rationalization – logic and empirical information – in order to constitute intersubjective validity pragmatically, both in the sphere of theoretical knowledge and in the sphere of practical norms. To a certain extent, the actual conventions seem capable of establishing the normatively relevant synthesis between the domain of private (existential) decisions and the domain of objective validity.

We should certainly not underestimate the practical significance of the pure mechanism of *convention* (*qua* agreement) as a criterion of democratic freedom. Nevertheless, I believe that our problem is masked rather than clarified by recourse to the possibility of 'conventions'. For the ethically relevant question which is raised by the reference to conventions is whether it is possible to state and justify a basic ethical norm that makes it a duty for all individuals to strive, in principle, for a binding agreement with other people in all practical questions and furthermore to subsequently adhere to this agreement. Or, if this is not possible, is it possible at least to act in the spirit of an anticipated agreement? This requirement is by no means grounded, and certainly not fulfilled, by mere reference to the existence of convention. For if actual conventions develop under the pre-suppositions of the Western system of complementarity (of value-neutral objectivity and private morality that is not intersubjectively binding), then they can only be interpreted in terms of Hobbes's contract theory as purposive-rational manifestations of good sense on the part of individuals. As such, they certainly do not presuppose any intersubjectively valid basic moral norm. But as measures of strategic good sense, I believe that they are incapable of grounding the morally binding character of conventions. (In this sense, for instance, 'positive law' as such without the tacit presupposition of an ethics is not normatively binding but, at best, effective. It is, however, most indicative that a legal system which loses its moral credibility in society normally also forfeits its effectiveness in the long run.)

I believe that this argument is directed against all those versions of a liberal contract theory of law and morality that seek to ground the intersubjective validity of norms in terms of a *methodological individualism* or *solipsism*,²⁶ i.e. solely on the basis of the empirical unification or mediation of individual interests or arbitrary decisions. If there exists no ethical principle that is both normatively binding and intersubjective, then ethical responsibility is basically unable to transcend the private sphere. This not merely implies, however, that in *formal* terms the conventions which are fundamental to every democracy (treaties, constitutions, laws, etc.) do not possess any morally binding force. Furthermore, it implies that *substantively* the moral decisions of individuals (in everyday life and in existential crisis situations), which are not explicitly regulated by agreement, are not obliged to take into account the demand for a collective responsibility of mankind. (In practice, the moral decisions of individuals in our modern mass society that have been released from archaic and religious communal bonds do, indeed, rarely transcend the horizon of solidarity established by the intimate group.)

If, however, the so-called 'free' decisions of conscience by individuals are isolated from each other *a priori* – as the notion of a purely subjective private morality suggests – and if they do not, in practical terms, obey any norm of solidarity, then they will have little prospect of success in the world of public, social practice from which the macro-effects today emanate. Given these presuppositions, does not the idea of human freedom (which liberalism associates with the privatization of both morals and ideology) become an illusion, as Marxism, in fact, asserts? (In practice, this insoluble problem seems to coincide with an already existing problem faced by the Lutheran-Kantian ethics of inwardness (*Innerlichkeit*), which only thinks it necessary to ascertain the integrity of goodwill or pure sentiment, and believes it has to abandon success in the political world to the value-neutral play of forces.) Given these presuppositions, it is not surprising if the 'lonely crowd' in Western industrial societies eventually avails itself less and less of the possibility which is postulated in the ideological system. Nor is it surprising if it now acts in an 'other-directed' rather than an 'inner-directed' manner; or, to use a different sociological vocabulary, if it lets itself be 'manipulated', right into the so-called existential domain of private life, along the lines of consumer behaviour.

It should be clear that if this sociological analysis were correct, then the whole system of complementarity in Western ideology would collapse. For in this case the private sphere of alleged existential decisions of conscience is dissolved since it is increasingly determined by the complementary sphere of so-called 'objective constraints', which by definition cannot assume any moral responsibility (this would be the realization of Schelsky's vision of 'technocracy').[27] Yet even if this stage is not reached it is difficult to see how the Western type of scientific-technical civilization, given the presuppositions of the ideological system of complementarity, is supposed to assume the above-postulated moral responsibility for the effects of industrial technology.

It hardly needs to be mentioned that the so-called 'New Left' movement, which met with a world-wide response from the younger generation, took reflections similar to those presented here as its starting-point. I would agree with their critique of the Western system in so far as the chances for a macro-ethics in modern industrial societies are extremely slight, given the presuppositions of the ideological system of complementarity. At the same time, however, I wish to emphasize that, under the Eastern 'system of integration', i.e. under the dogmatic presupposition that an élite of party philosophers guarantees the unity of scientific knowledge and morality on the basis of a dialectical 'superscience', it is also impossible to speak of an ethics of collective responsibility. I believe that the difference between the insoluble ideological contradiction of the West and that of the East can be traced back to the following fact. In the former case, moral decisions of conscience by all individuals are postulated, yet an intersubjective validity of ethical norms, and consequently a moral solidarity, cannot be grounded. In the latter case, the collectivity of society's moral responsibility is postulated, but it cannot be mediated, either theoretically or in political, practical terms, by individuals' decisions of conscience. Such decisions are basically superfluous and – the practical consequence is similar to that of the Western system of complementarity – they are relegated to the private sphere.

This concludes my comments on the dialectical problem of the relationship between science and ethics in modern industrial society. In what follows, I should like to reflect upon the possibility of resolving the difficulties that I have presented.

2   Reflections on resolving the paradox

2.1   As I have indicated, analytical philosophy adheres to certain basic presuppositions which make a grounding of normative ethics seem virtually impossible. Let us attempt to present the most important of these presuppositions:

1   *Norms* cannot be derived from *facts* (or: *prescriptive* statements and, consequently, 'value judgments' cannot be derived from *descriptive* statements). For the sake of brevity we shall refer to this principle as Hume's principle or Hume's distinction.

2   *Science*, in so far as it provides us with substantive knowledge, deals with *facts*. Consequently, a *scientific* grounding of *normative ethics* is impossible.

3   It is only science that provides us with *objective* knowledge. *Objectivity* is identical with *intersubjective validity*. For this reason, an intersubjectively valid grounding of normative ethics is absolutely impossible.

If one wishes to demonstrate that a rational grounding of *normative* ethics is possible, then after what has already been said it seems to be necessary to place in question at least one of these premises. Two strategies for argument seem promising here.

1 One can try to question the *relevance* of Hume's distinction (and consequently the first premise) for our problem. Even if it is not logically possible to derive norms from facts, it is still highly questionable whether all the sciences with an empirical content are, for this reason, pure factual sciences, and in the present context this means morally value-free factual sciences. It could be that only the natural sciences and neither the empirical human sciences nor philosophical 'meta-ethics' are able to constitute their phenomenal object without some moral evaluation.

2 The second strategy for argument does not bother to question the value-neutrality of science, including philosophical meta-ethics. It does not, therefore, doubt the relevance of Hume's distinction for the present topic; but rather it presupposes such a distinction. This strategy raises the question as to whether the objectivity of value-neutral science itself can be understood philosophically if one does not presuppose the intersubjective validity of moral norms. This line of argument would directly place in question the validity of the third premise.

In what follows, I shall attempt to demonstrate that both lines of argument are legitimate and can complement one another. The first approach, however, even if it attains its goal, cannot prove that it is possible to ground ethics rationally. Rather, it can be demonstrated that its consequences only become relevant for our subject matter if it is presupposed that the second approach can prove that it is possible to ground ethics rationally.

2.2 As I have indicated above, the first line of argument could assert that, viewed phenomenologically, the objects of the human sciences cannot be *constituted* without some moral evaluation. Modern experimental and theoretical natural science was, of course, only able to constitute its object as the 'existence of things inasmuch as they form a law-like connection' (Kant) by basically sacrificing communicative understanding and a corresponding evaluation in terms of whether behaviour conforms to, or violates, norms. This initial sacrificing of *understanding* and *evaluation* that is constitutive for the phenomenon corresponds here to the previous cognitive interest in making available, if possible, processes based upon the law of causality as means that serve *human objectives*. For, as

Francis Bacon recognized, only if one dispenses with the teleological evaluation of the natural processes themselves is a science made possible whose results can be tested experimentally and, to this extent, can basically be technically utilized.

Consequently, an epistemological subject-object relationship is created here in which the world as the sum of value-free facts is given, and – in contrast to Aristotle's teleological ontology – the concept of being no longer implies the concept of 'good' or 'ought'. It is true that for Galileo, for instance, the object is by no means constituted without idealizations. But these do not represent goals or behavioural norms for natural bodies – which they might deal with less adequately in the sub-lunar sphere than in the stellar sphere. Rather, they simply represent methodological norms for the natural scientist, whose mind – initially in the sense of an *adaequatio ad intellectum divinum*[28] – prescribes the (formal) law for nature. Understanding goals and behavioural norms falls back to some extent in this case upon the methodological self-understanding of natural science. Despite all the suggestions made by a reductionist scientism, however, the human sciences have found it impossible to seriously follow the natural sciences in their *initial renunciation of an evaluative understanding that is constitutive for phenomena.*

Stated more precisely, in a subsequent remodelling of phenomena the so-called 'empirical-analytical' social sciences were able to simulate the value-free constitution of the object that one finds in the natural sciences inasmuch as it was possible to abstract from the intersubjective communicative relationship and thereby also achieve an experimental and technological manipulation of the human 'objects'. To this extent, the reciprocal presupposition of a value-free concept of experience and a possible technological utilization of experience – a presupposition that was already constitutive for the experimental natural sciences – was confirmed in the social sciences. Yet even this scientific, technological interpretation of the human sciences presupposes a heuristic application of the evaluative understanding of behaviour that conforms to or deviates from norms, if the motives underlying behaviour – that are, however, treated like quasi-causes – are to be made accessible. But when the human sciences are not concerned with making available (for possible technological utilization) the facts of quasi-law-like behaviour, but rather are attempting to reconstruct human actions, achievements and institutions interpretatively: in short, when they are dealing with the self-understanding of human life-practice, then the evaluative characteristics can no longer be meaningfully eliminated from the primary constitution of the object.

Even here, positivist 'historicism' attempted to make a value-free objectivity binding in terms of methodology. It attempted, for example, to reduce both the selection of historical topics – that are fascinating on account of their significance – and the evaluation of human actions (or at least of their purposive rationality) – which makes understanding possible – to merely heuristic preconditions for the actual scientific operations of establishing facts and providing a causal explanation. It is indeed possible, for the political historian at least, to have the interpretation of human tradition in the sense of a merely 'empirical, historical hermeneutics' serve the reconstruction of pure facts and to consciously reduce the constitution of the significance of historical events methodologically to relationships between effects that are immanent to history and that can themselves be objectified in a value-free manner.[29] But this methodological neutralization can never remove the so-called 'pre-scientific' perspective of evaluation. Even if the historian attempts to ground judgments on meaning in an objective manner that remains immanent to history itself, his selective conception and narrative representation of history as a whole – and especially his 'appreciative' understanding of individual persons and epochs – are fundamentally influenced by the evaluative perspective which derives from the fact that the historian is part of history in a practical sense. Since this also affects the constitution of the object (which cannot be separated from its linguistic presentation), it cannot be treated as a merely pre-scientific aspect in the same manner as an external (e.g. economic) evaluative interest that determines the selection of an object of natural scientific research. As a possible instance of law-like explanation, such an object at no stage represents a subject of progressive, individual appraisal. But, in my opinion, this negative statement is far less fundamental than the positive statement that the political historian's methodological neutralization of the value judgment cannot be intended to definitively eliminate the evaluation of the object as in the natural sciences of the modern age. Rather, it must possess a completely different significance: that of qualitatively placing in question the quasi-natural evaluation which human beings associate with the traditionally mediated understanding of their history by means of the objectivation of a spatio-temporal causal connection, an objectivation that is, as far as possible, value-free. This means that a new, critically mediated evaluation is made possible.

Consequently, the activity of the political historian can, in fact, be incorporated into the hermeneutic circle of value-'prejudice' (*Wert-'Vorurteil!'*) and purified 'value judgment' (*Werturteil*), which has hitherto basically characterized the function of the interpretative human sciences in the sense of a normatively non-neutral hermeneutics – e.g. in the sense of a critical and appraising history of literature and philosophy. A confirmation of this assessment of the reconstructive human sciences – one that is striking since it is, as yet, involuntary – has been provided recently by the Popperian school which was originally committed to methodological monism and therefore to the conception of value-free empirical, analytical social sciences. In its steady course of development from the normative logic of science to an interpretative reconstruction of the 'internal history of science' – in which the school's normative concept of rationality and the immanent rationality of the exemplary achievement of the classic writers on the history of science mutually correct one another in terms of the 'hermeneutic circle' – the Popperian school itself provides the paradigm of a *Geisteswissenschaft* that neither explains on the basis of laws, nor is value-free, but is, in the best sense, a 'normative-hermeneutic' human science.[30]

Another example of the difficulty involved in the serious attempt to reduce the reality of human behaviour to observational data that can be described in a value-free manner is provided by the above-mentioned meta-ethics which is committed to the 'neutrality thesis'. In perspicacious studies, Hans Lenk has been able to demonstrate that 'all three goals' of analytical meta-ethics – 'the preservation of the neutrality of meta-ethics, the consistent application of the descriptive analysis of everyday language and the unambiguous meta-ethical identification of what is specifically moral . . . are incompatible in pairs and are even less compatible all together'. In the present context, it is particularly important that the mere 'description' of linguistic material ('sentences') cannot lead to an unambiguous identification of the normative. For this to take place, an interpretation of the 'utterances' in their pragmatic context is necessary. Yet in order to provide such an interpretation, meta-ethics cannot simply be neutral (non-normative).

Meta-ethics certainly cannot prescribe *actions,* but they do prescribe what is to count as 'moral' or even as a 'morally good' action. Meta-ethics are, so to speak, normative at a higher level. But the normative-ethical statements are dependent upon the normative part of the particular meta-ethic. For the meanings of expressions like 'good' or 'ought' which occur in such statements are determined by meta-ethical 'rules'.[31]

Contrary to the Popperian school, which Lenk seems to follow in interpreting his findings, I do not think that the fact that the un-ambiguous identification of what is moral is not possible with the aid of a normatively neutral meta-ethics can simply be reduced to the fact that even 'meta-ethics' possesses the character of a scientific *theory* and as such must introduce rules that are already normative (idealizing definitions of the object).[32] For, unlike the normative rules of natural-scientific theories, those of meta-ethics – as Lenk himself realizes – must be mediated through an *understanding* of their object: human utterances in the pragmatic context. (They must basically be capable of being used by human objects in the reconstruction of their self-understanding.) I believe, therefore, that the methodological difficulty of 'analytical' meta-ethics with the neutrality thesis, like the previously mentioned continuum of the normative logic of science and the history of science, ultimately arises from the fact that we are not confronted here with a *theory* whose object is already constituted as a phenomenon in the value-free subject-object relationship. Rather, we are dealing with a *meta-theory* in the reflection-mediated approach of *hermeneutic reconstruction.* The latter's primary 'constitution of the object' must be determined in part by a communicatively realizable engagement that is not only *methodologically normative* but also *morally normative.*

In my view, the difficulties of analytical meta-ethics, and even the methodological difficulties of 'ordinary language philosophy' in general can be traced back to the failure of the later Wittgenstein to reflect upon his own communicative and reflexive relationship with the 'language-games' or 'life-forms' which he 'described'. Consequently, they represented for him *both* the quasi-transcendental horizons of all meaningful speech and action *and* the hard facts, present in the world, that – with the exception of metaphysical language-games – cannot be critically placed in question. I believe that ordinary language philosophy has never sufficiently reflected upon the resulting contradiction between a quasi-transcendental and a quasi-behavioural analysis[33] – with the exception of Peter Winch who, however, does not realize that the transcendental-hermeneutic interpretation of Wittgenstein which he puts forward must be grounded in the presupposition of a normative, ideal 'transcendental language-game'. Otherwise it will revert to a quasi-empiricist behaviourism that also incorporates ethical relativism.[34] If one sought to locate the notion of 'hermeneutics' within this language-analytical version, then one might indeed be inclined to interpret the maxim of the 'irreducibility of everyday language' as a rejection of every attempt at a normative reconstruction of human practice.[35]

In terms of a normatively non-neutral hermeneutics, however, I should like to establish the following. Anyone who seeks to understand human actions (including 'speech acts'), must heuristically at least – even if this occurs with the methodological reservation that a subsequent estrangement and neutralization can take place – engage himself communicatively in the sense of accepting joint responsibility for the intentions underlying actions. That is to say, *understanding* presupposes the regulative principle of *hypothetical justification*. (This is corroborated by each 'good reason essay' of purposive-rational understanding even if the methodological intention only extends as far as the evaluation of the selection of means and not to the selection of ends.) As far as the interpretative social sciences (including philosophy) are concerned, it will not suffice, therefore, to argue with Popper against logical empiricism that the relevant data can only be constituted as data in the light of (methodologically and normatively non-neutral) 'theories'. In Popper's view, this also applies to the data of natural science that is established independently on any evaluation. Furthermore, it must be pointed out that *even* the so-called 'data' in the case of the human sciences are characterized by subjective norm-following. But this means that *primarily* – even given the reservation that there can be subsequent estrangement and neutralization – they must be constituted by an approach which is not value-free by being both communicative and self-reflective, and this means a hermeneutic approach. And it may be added that what we call reconstructive human science finally cannot withdraw to subsequent neutralization. This is shown in the case of a relevant history of science which can figure as the paradigm of a *normative-hermeneutic* approach.

If we attempt to draw from these remarks the consequences for our problem of the grounding of ethics, then one might assume that, through the phenomenological constitution of the object in the *normative-hermeneutic* human sciences, Hume's distinction between pure facts and pure norms may not have been shown to be false, but certainly epistemologically irrelevant. Consequently, it appears that we have found the way back from value-neutral meta-ethics to ethics. Given the presuppositions that we have outlined, one does not reach the point at which, contrary to Hume's verdict, one attempts to derive norms from purely factual judgments. Rather, one corrects and enriches one's ever-present normative engagement in interpretative communication with morally suggestive actions, achievements of life-styles of other people and alien cultures. In fact, it was the conviction of humanism – especially influential in the sphere of education – from the Italian Renaissance (if not from the Hellenic Stoics) via Humboldt to Dilthey, that through the under-standing of all that is human – i.e. in terms of the hermeneutic circle, through the extension of the 'humanitas' that is presupposed in 'understanding' – an aesthetically and morally relevant, normative process of education is made possible.

I do not wish to underestimate, let alone refute, this humanistic conception of the not yet, or no longer, morally neutral human sciences, a conception that has recently been revitalized, in terms of the binding authority of the classical tradition by Hans-Georg Gadamer. Nevertheless, I cannot concede to it a decisive function in the attempt to 'ground ethics in the scientific age'. The reasons for this are as follows:

1   The 'hermeneutic circle' of 'understanding' *and* 'evaluation' which, in the context of a hermeneutic-phenomenological conception of ethics in accordance with Hume's distinction, must function, to some extent, as the vehicle of normative rationality, cannot itself take over the function of a 'grounding' of ethics. Certainly, it may guarantee a moral education in the sense of moral sensitization and thus be indispensable as a means against 'value-blindness' (in Max Scheler's and Nicolai Hartmann's terminology). This kind of moral education is, however, not only inadequate but also ambivalent even in moral terms. An important demonstration of this fact has been provided by the development of the humanistic *Geisteswissen-*

schaften in Germany (from Herder to Dilthey and beyond Dilthey). Ultimately, the *exclusively hermeneutic* education, in the sense of a historical, cultural-anthropological *relativism* that can no longer be overcome *normatively,* led to a paralysis of moral judgment and moral, political engagement within the German intellectual élite.[36] The enticing step towards terrible simplification with the aid of ultimate values that were established with pseudo-biological arguments seems to have suggested itself particularly to over-sensitized 'humanists' who were either decadent or felt themselves to be decadent. Possibly it offered an existentially effective 'reduction' of moral 'world complexity', to express it in Niklas Luhmann's terminology. From this example it is clear that hermeneutics must always *presuppose* a normative grounding of its ethically evaluatory understanding.

2   Even if one could presuppose the normative, ethical grounding of hermeneutics, the hermeneutic method *alone* would not be sufficient for its hermeneutic application. This becomes evident if the *material* conditions of the socio-cultural life-forms that must be understood are considered as *empirical* premises of the possible *justification* of systems of morality. By virtue of its methodology, hermeneutic understanding must always 'transpose' itself to alien or past life-situations and understand human behaviour within its particular historical situational context. Moreover, one of the ethically relevant basic postulates of hermeneutics is that there must be a serious attempt to reconstruct methodically the situational context *qua* subjective state that is to be elucidated. Nevertheless, such reconstructive understanding (*Nachverstehen*) of life-situations cannot in itself provide the sufficient preconditions for the ethical evaluation of actions and institutions as answers to given conditions. The fundamental insight into the lack of transparency in a human being's understanding of the world and of the self, which is tantamount to the methodological postulate of reflexively transcendent understanding, forces hermeneutics itself to leave behind Schleiermacher's and Dilthey's postulate of identical reconstructive understanding and to attempt to understand human beings (and also cultures or societies) 'better than they understand themselves'. Yet if such an attempt is to be successful in the long run and not to resign itself – as Gadamer does – to the awareness of understanding that is always merely 'different', then the attempt must be made to reconstruct, in addition to the ethical foundation of hermeneutics, the

material living conditions of human society. Such a reconstruction must certainly be hermeneutically mediated, but it must also be historical and objective. It is only such a social-historical reconstruction of the situational conditions that are not contained in the subjective consciousness of one's situation which can, in the long run, overcome the moral confusion of 'understanding everything' in favour of an ethically relevant reconstruction of history. For example, the expulsion or killing of old people who are no longer able to work by certain Eskimo tribes, not only becomes *intelligible* but can even prove to be compatible with human purposes if one considers the living conditions of a primitive archaic culture.[37] On the other hand, in the age of the already-mentioned 'macro-influence' of hostilities, in the form of a threat to the existence of humanity, the spirit of readiness to fight for one's country can no longer lay claim to that high moral value which it was previously accorded in virtually all systems of morality – as is confirmed by world literature from the time of the heroic sagas onwards – from the epoch of the hordes of primitive hunters to the nationalistic, imperialist era of the world expansion of Western civilization. Such an assessment was only correct inasmuch as the expansive self-assertion of humanity as a whole and even the advancement of culture could be promoted for a long time through the 'unsociable sociability' (Kant) of belligerent group-egoism. Nor is recourse by traditional and especially religious systems of morality to the instinctive feelings of goodwill and magnanimity and to the human 'catalyst qualities' that provoke them, sufficient any longer in an age when human actions have 'macro-effects'. Rather, it seems to be necessary to mobilize moral imagination in the sense of a *prima facie,* abstract 'love of strangers' (*Fernstenliebe*).[38]

In terms of what concerns us here, these examples illustrate the 'non-contemporaneity' between the very conservative moral traditions of groups and cultures, and the progressive change in human living conditions achieved by the unified scientific-technical civilization. This is not a phenomenon which could be dealt with by a purely hermeneutic discussion of moral traditions. It is only revealed to an objectifying reconstruction of history that can proceed methodically beyond the interpretation of systems of morality that have actually been handed down to us. Here we encounter the ethically relevant aspect of an argument developed in the philosophy of science that has recently been advanced, especially by a Marxist-inspired science of society and philosophy of history, against a universalization of the hermeneutic perspective or method. Pure hermeneutics fails to notice that social reality, whose life is lived out in technical and politico-economic practice, is neither sufficiently nor adequately expressed in the 'objectified mind' of tradition that is, in the broadest sense, linguistic. Especially in view of a normative, ethical engagement, the hermeneutically interpretable 'objectified mind' can and must be rendered problematic through a critique of ideology by consciously confronting the non-verbally manifested aspects of social history and their real living conditions with the hermeneutic mediation of tradition. Such aspects must be used as a corrective to this hermeneutic mediation of tradition.

Accordingly, 'hermeneutics' claim to universality', in so far as it draws upon the *method* (or *methodology*) of what are traditionally called 'the humanities' (*Geisteswissenschaften*), must be decisively rejected.[39] However, this does not impinge upon 'hermeneutics' claim to universality' in the *quasi-transcendental* aspect that has been developed by Heidegger and Gadamer. Here I am referring to the thesis that the life-world has always been interpreted linguistically and that the *a priori* of communicating in everyday language within the context of the life-world is, in a precisely definable sense, the irreducible precondition for the possibility and intersubjective validity of all conceivable philosophical or scientific theory-formation and even of the 'reconstruction' – an 'indirect' reconstruction from Carnap's standpoint,[40] a direct one from Lorenzen's – of language itself.[41] Even the results of the historical-objective reconstruction of the material living conditions of society, and consequently the results derived from the critique of ideology, must be realized through *communication*. This implies that they must basically be capable of being transformed into the reflective consciousness of all human beings. (This regulative principle is even valid with regard to those who can no longer reply and should, for example, persuade the interpreter of a text to envisage counter-factually the potential answers of the authors criticized.) In my opinion, this transcendental-hermeneutic thesis, if it is understood correctly, is still valid today. Naturally, this presupposes that the transcendental primacy of everyday language or communication is not reduced ontologically – or even in terms of a history of being – to an 'event' or even reduced quasi-behaviouristically to empirical language-game facts.[42] Communication in everyday language is only *irreducible* in so far as the *normative ideal* of communication can be realized in everyday language – and only there – and must, therefore, always be anticipated.[43] It is precisely for this reason that one cannot question communication in everyday language as a whole, because one must potentially place it in question in each particular individual case in the interest of the ideal of communication that must still be realized.

There are, however, grounds for believing that a normatively relevant advance in communication in the sense of hermeneutics cannot be conceptualized without at the same time conceiving of an ethically relevant advance in the societal formation of humanity as a community of interpretation and interaction. As we have already indicated, if a *normative hermeneutics* – in the sense of *understanding better* in the long run, and not merely in the sense of 'understanding in a constantly different manner' that is guaranteed by Gadamer's ontology of the 'event' and 'game' of truth – is to be possible, then it must presuppose a normative ethics. Yet this makes it clear that a hermeneutic phenomenology which, in terms of the 'hermeneutic circle', eludes Hume's distinction between facts and norms cannot function as a foundation for ethics. If one could take as given ethical principles of interpersonal communication (in the broadest sense) and, consequently, ethical principles of a 'normative hermeneutics' of the mediation of tradition, then hermeneutics could incorporate the engaged critique of ideology and would have to become the methodological vehicle for the *substantive development* of ethics. Then the ethically engaged human sciences could come to terms with the diversity of actual norms and values in a critical appraisal and – complementary to society's scientific technological 'information'[44] – could develop its *own* relationship to praxis in the 'formation' of an ethically committed society.

It need hardly be pointed out here that even 'criticism' in the Popperians' sense of Theodor Geiger's and Ernst Topitsch's critique of ideology, presupposes a normative ethics.[45] Even the engagement of neopositivist critics of the critical social sciences, and perhaps of ethics itself, reveals all too clearly that more is at stake than value-free empirical data and formal logic. Most recently, Habermas[46] has pointed out that, of course, the 'critical theory' of Frankfurt neo-Marxism, like Marxism in general, presupposes a – not yet explicitly developed – ethics that should be explicated in the interests of an undogmatic self-understanding. Habermas has, therefore, begun to develop a positive justification of ethics in critical co-operation with the Erlangen school. We shall return to this approach later.

The reflections presented here, which were intended to place in question the scientistic principle of value-freedom, thus lead to an ambivalent result. On the one hand, they are liable to reinforce our suspicion that the modern disjunction between the value-free objectivity of the sciences and subjective private morality is untenable and is still refuted even today by the existence of the human sciences. On the other hand, it was revealed that ethics must apparently already have been grounded before one can establish the human sciences as the organon of ethics. This first finding in itself leads to the second, already outlined line of argument that does not question the relevance of Hume's distinction but rather the scientistic thesis of the reducibility of all inter-subjective validity of arguments to the objective validity of value-free statements. Moreover, this second strategy is supported by a further reflection which seems to directly demonstrate the relevance of Hume's distinction for our task and, in connection with this, it even seems to demonstrate the primacy of meta-ethics in terms of the methodological outcome of the neutrality thesis. Although, given Hume's distinction, one cannot make intelligible the primary, phenomenological *constitution of data* in the life-world and the hermeneutic human sciences, I believe that it cannot be disputed that in *justifying* the *validity* of propositions in the human sciences – and even in ethics (including normative, prescriptive ethics) – one must methodologically presuppose the subject-object relationship, which is free from evaluation, and one must consequently also presuppose Hume's distinction. If one seeks to avoid dogmatism as a starting-point, then the 'theoretical discourse' of philosophy (that began with the Greeks' $\phi\acute{v}\sigma\epsilon\iota$-$\vartheta\acute{\epsilon}\sigma\epsilon\iota$ controversy and was given its transcendental philosophical form – which adopts a critical stance toward scientific knowledge – in Kant's formulation of the *quaestio iuris*) must, to some extent, be able to detach itself from the 'universe of human discourse', just as in the philosophical (metaphysical) presupposition of theoretical natural science,[47] the latter detaches itself from the universe of things or given objects. I consider this *analogy of theoretical detachment* to be the presupposition for the 'validity' of propositions being potentially 'bracketed off' and therefore placed in question in a similar manner to Husserl's 'Urdoxa' of the 'existence' of things. Moreover, the validity of moral norms (i.e. the validity of the

253

imperative claims of *practical propositions*) must, in principle, be bracketed off and placed in question to the same extent as the truth-value of theoretical propositions about facts. However, in this attempt to place normative validity in question, it is precisely the *actual existence* of the normative *claim* to validity that cannot be bracketed off. Rather the problematized validity of norms must be methodologically reduced tentatively (temporarily) to the fact of the claim to validity, in order to justify the validity which is claimed. It seems to me that ultimately the legitimacy of the meta-ethical *neutrality thesis* is established here. The significance of the latter does not, therefore, lie in analytical philosophy's dismissal of normative ethics but rather in the radicalization of the philosophical claim to ground normative ethics undogmatically.[48]

I believe that the above-mentioned detachment of the 'theoretical discourse' of philosophy from the 'universe of human discourse' also contains the reason for philosophers' obstinate demands for a (meta-ethical) term which, analogously to the truth predicate of theoretical propositions, can be used for justifying practical propositions on what *ought* to be.[49] It is precisely the acknowledgment of the distinction between facts and norms – an acknowledgement mediated by *reflection* – that compels metaphysics to treat both the ought-claims and the justification of the undoubtedly different claims to truth of theoretical propositions as problems of reflective – and, consequently, *theoretical* – 'insight'. The only alternative to such an *analogy of justification* – which, in my opinion, should not be confused with the intellectualist reduction of goodwill to correct knowledge – is represented by the reduction of the ethical problem of justification to that of an actual 'acknowledgment' of norms through an arbitrary human act. On the other hand, I believe that the theoretical, philosophical *unity* of the problem of theoretical and practical justification, and consequently the requirement that philosophical ethics develop methodologically (and tentatively) from the meta-ethical neutrality thesis – seen in cognitive-anthropological terms – is grounded in the 'excentric positionality' of the human being.[50] If it is to be radical, human thought must make use of this possibility – itself constitutive for human thought – of detachment from the world and the self. To this extent, the methodological approach of Augustinian-Cartesian doubt and Husserl's neo-Cartesian approach are binding for ethics *qua* meta-ethics.

Nevertheless, radical world-detachment as *thought*, and this means as *argument,* is immediately caught up in the 'transcendental language-game' that is presupposed in 'theoretical discourse'. At this point, the 'methodological solipsism' of the Cartesian mode of thought is immediately refuted by the *sense critical* insights into the pre-suppositions for both theoretical and practical discourse. As far as theoretical detachment from the world is concerned, this means that the 'bracketing off' of the 'general thesis' about the existence of the world leads to the critical insight that, as a result, both the existence of an ego arguing within the framework of a language-game and the possibility of 'real doubt' in the existence of certain things is invalidated. For the claim that something is 'merely in my imagination' or 'merely a dream', etc., obviously presupposes the 'transcendental-language-game' with the 'paradigm' of the existence of a real world.[51] The tentative placing in question of the real world itself can obviously only be intended to gain an *undogmatic reflective insight into the transcendental preconditions for the possibility and validity of the 'theoretical discourse' of philosophy* itself through radical detachment.[52] But I believe that similar consequences must arise for the radical questioning of moral norms that draws upon theoretical detachment from the world through the meta-ethical neutrality thesis. Certain moral norms or imperative requirements cannot be placed in question with regard to a possible justification or non-justification so long as the validity of moral requirements in general is placed in question. Even here a transcendental critique of meaning is able to demonstrate that the *presupposition of the validity of moral norms in general is a 'paradigmatic' precondition for the possibility of the language-game associated with the justification of norms.* Should it not, then, be possible to derive from this para-digmatic presupposition of the 'theoretical discourse' on the validity of norms a 'basic moral norm' or a 'principle of ethics'?

We have now reached a point of view which prompts us to attack the third premise of analytical philosophy, namely the scientistic thesis that it is impossible for moral norms to be proved to be intersubjectively valid. In fact, such an attack seems promising even on the presupposition – and, indeed, precisely on this presupposition – that one accepts Hume's distinction and the associated neutrality thesis of modern meta-ethics as the methodological starting-point of the discussion. Contrary to the ideological suggestion of the 'Western system of complementarity' it appears by no means impos-sible to find the way back to normative ethics from the meta-ethical position. But this can only be achieved if one does not confuse the method of philosophical meta-ethics in a scientistic manner with that of the 'empirical, analytical' sciences. Rather, it is essential to recognize the characteristic demand of philosophical meta-ethics for normative neutrality as the methodological starting-point of *transcendental reflection*. Once we have adopted the methodological standpoint of '*transcendental reflection*', we can take a step further and investigate the preconditions for the possibility and validity of value-free, empirical-analytical science itself. In so doing, we shall take into account the fact that the 'intellectual actions' which Kant posited can and must be concretized in terms of the 'transcendental language-game', as interpersonally-directed communicative actions within the framework of a communication community of scholars. Given this presupposition, would it be possible to state the pre-conditions for the possibility and validity of the value-free objectivity of the empirical-analytical statements of science without having previously posited the intersubjective validity of moral norms? Our second line of argument will develop from a reply to this question.

2.3   Our second and, in my view, decisive approach develops heuristically from the *thesis* that even the '*objectivity' of value-free science still presupposes the intersubjective validity of moral norms*. By exploring the consequences of this thesis, we shall first undermine the prejudice concerning the irrational subjectivity of all moral norms and judgments and then attempt to determine the basic principle of ethics in the scientific age. Methodologically, I should like to develop this approach by attempting to defend it as a strategy for argument against possible objections and misunderstandings.

2.3.1   The *first*, immediate *objection* to the proposed line of argument could assert that if it is possible to demonstrate that certain ethical norms are the preconditions for science, then this would enable us, at best, to ground 'hypothetical imperatives' in Kant's sense, but not a 'categorical imperative' as an essential basic moral norm. For, in this case, the decisive question would be: is science something that *ought* to be? One could then argue that, in order to answer this question, an ethics is necessary which, for its part, must have recourse to subjective, irrational decisions. One could make the following reply to such an objection. Proof that the intersubjective validity of moral norms is a precondition for the possibility and validity of science can at least demonstrate that, contrary to widespread belief, the idea of scientific 'objectivity' in itself cannot constitute a fundamental argument against the possibility of an intersubjectively valid ethics. The approach would therefore be sufficient to refute the ethically relevant version of 'scientism', which makes the possibility or impossibility of ethics dependent upon whether its form of validity can be 'reduced' to that of value-free objectivity. For it would at any rate be possible to demonstrate that – contrary to the hitherto accepted presupposition of the Western system of complementarity – the normatively neutral objectivity of the empirical sciences can only appear possible if one simultaneously assumes a *complementary intersubjective validity of ethical norms*. At this point, an interesting parallel is established between *ethics* and *hermeneutics*, for even the latter can best defend its own methodological legitimacy against scientism not by claiming an *explanatory* function for *understanding* but rather by demonstrating that objectively descriptive and – causally or statistically – explanatory science always presupposes methodological agreement about meaning and thereby about its truth claims in the dimension of (transcendental) intersubjectivity.[53] The refutation of scientism in the manner indicated would not, of course, prove the possibility of a categorical imperative, but it would reveal the logical necessity of the intersubjective validity of ethics in the *scientific age*. It will become evident, however, that the basic ethical norms that are presupposed by science are not simply 'hypothetical imperatives' in the restricted sense which we have mentioned, but rather that, ultimately, they even provide an answer to the question as to whether science *ought to exist*. In order to demonstrate this, we must radicalize our *thesis*, such that the *rational argumentation* that is presupposed not only in every science but also in every discussion of a problem, in itself presupposes the validity of universal, ethical norms. This thesis, however, must first be defended against a possible misunderstanding.

2.3.2 My thesis does not imply that even the principle of rationality, that is manifested in following the logical rules of consistent thinking, represents *eo ipso* a foundation for ethics. I am completely of the opinion (together with Peirce, Popper and Lorenzen) that logic, and especially the logic of science, must be regarded as a *normative science*. An interesting consequence is that the modern, reconstructive history of the exact sciences provides us with a model, not of a value-free (empirical-analytical) science, but rather of a *normative, hermeneutic* science that can always presuppose a principle of normative evaluation in logicity.[54] This principle, however, does not represent in itself the discovery of an ethical principle.

The validity of this statement is revealed, for instance, by the attempt to overcome the limits of a value-neutral meta-ethics simply by establishing a parallel to the normative logic of science. This attempt merely leads to a programme in which existing systems of morals are to be tested for their logical consistency and empirical efficiency in the same manner as scientific theories. But it can be readily recognized that, unlike scientific theories, it is only possible to speak of the empirical efficiency of systems of morals if one posits, over and above logical consistency, an ethical standard of efficiency.[55]

On the other hand, however, it should not be denied – and certainly not in our context – that the somewhat vague expression 'ethics of logic'[56] contains something that is true. It is for instance incorrect, in a sense that I hope to clarify, to assert with reference to Kant that even the Devil could be a logician. It cannot, of course, be disputed that the logically correct use of intellect can be employed simply as a means to an end by an evil will.[57] To this extent, logic as a theory of the normatively correct use of the intellect is a morally value-free technology (which, just like all other technologies, is accommodated into the system of complementarity of value-free objectivity and the subjective positing of values). Consequently, one cannot assert that logic logically *implies* an ethic. One can, nevertheless, assert that logic – and, *at the same time,* all the sciences and technologies – *presupposes* an ethic as the precondition for its possibility. This can be demonstrated by the following argument.

The logical validity of arguments cannot be tested without, in principle, positing a community of scholars who are capable of both intersubjective communication and reaching a consensus. Even the *de facto* solitary scholar can only explicate and test his line of argument in so far as he is able to internalize the dialogue of a potential community of argumentation in the critical 'discourse of the soul with itself' (Plato). This proves that the *validity* of solitary thought is basically dependent upon the justification of verbal arguments in the actual community of argumentation.

'One person alone' cannot follow a rule and create validity for his thought within the framework of a 'private language'. This is, in principle, public. This is how I would interpret the famous thesis of the later Wittgenstein in our context.[58] Together with the real community of argumentation, however, the logical justification for our thought also presupposes the following of a basic moral norm. Lies, for instance, would obviously make the dialogue of people engaged in argument impossible. But the same is also true of the refusal to understand arguments critically or to explicate and justify them. In short, in the community of argumentation it is presupposed that all the members mutually recognize each other as participants with equal rights in the discussion.

Since all linguistic utterances and, moreover, all meaningful human actions and physical expressions (in so far as they can be verbalized)[59] involve 'claims' (in German '*Ansprüche*') and hence can be regarded as potential arguments, the basic norm of mutual recognition by the participants in the discussion potentially implies that of the 'recognition' of all human beings as 'persons' in Hegel's sense. In other words, all beings who are capable of linguistic communication must be recognized as persons since in all their actions and utterances they are potential participants in a discussion, and the unlimited justification of thought cannot dispense with any participant, nor with any of his potential contributions to a discussion. In my view, this demand for the mutual *recognition of persons as the subjects of logical argument,* and not merely the logically correct use of intellect, justifies the use of the phrase 'ethics of logic'.

This point can be clarified further if one distinguishes in terms of 'speech-act' theory[60] between the *performative* and the *propositional* aspect of human speech. Then it becomes evident that in the dialogue of those engaged in argument not only are value-neutral statements made about states of affairs, but also that these statements are connected, at least implicitly, with *communicative actions* – with actions that make moral claims on all members of the communication community. Each statement of fact, therefore, as one which must be logically justified, presupposes in its pragmatic deep structure a *performative* complementation such as: 'I hereby assert, against all potential opponents, that . . .' or 'I hereby call upon everyone to test the following statement.' Consequently, the performative complementation of the statements necessary in order to carry out the test is as follows: 'I hereby dispute that A is the case' or 'I confirm that A is the case.' Following our heuristic approach, it is at this level of intersubjective communication about the meaning and validity of statements and not before, at the level of substantive intellectual operations, that an ethics is presupposed.

If the question as to whether someone is following a rule in his intellectual operations can only be meaningfully raised and answered within the framework of a language-game, then the logic that has to *justify* the rules for the monological use of intellect *must* enter at the level of the dialogue. *Arguments* cannot then be understood, as they are in modern (syntactic-semantic) logical calculus, in abstraction from the pragmatic dimension,[61] but rather they must always be understood simultaneously as meaning and validity *claims* that can only be explicated and decided upon in an interpersonal dialogue. In my opinion, it was along these lines that Paul Lorenzen, by recourse to the pre-Aristotelian origins of logic, was able to ground the meaning and validity of predicate logic at the level of the dialogue. From here he could, whilst remaining internally consistent, turn to the transition from normative logic to the grounding of ethics.[62] In contrast to the Popperian approach, the 'ethics of logic' is not simply sought here in a constructive parallel between meta-ethics and the meta-scientific 'logic of research'. Instead, I believe it is sought in the reconstructive recourse to the *transcendental-pragmatic* pre-conditions for the possibility of logic and thus of science – namely in the *a priori* of the communication community.[63]

In my opinion, the consequences of this distinction for the philosophy of science can be located in the fact that the value-neutral, empirical-analytical sciences do not presuppose an ethics simply because they presuppose intellectual operations in the sense of a normative logic. They do so because these monological operations of science presuppose a dialogical agreement on meaning and a dialogical justification of validity in a communication community. In short, the *normative logic of science* (scientistics) presupposes *normative hermeneutics* and, at the same time, *normative ethics*,[64] because 'one person alone' cannot practise science and reduce his fellow human beings to mere objects of 'description' and 'explanation' with the aid of a private logic. I believe that what ultimately makes possible the transition from (normative) logic to (normative) ethics is the overcoming of 'methodological solipsism' that is initiated in Lorenzen's work, as it was in Peirce's and the later Wittgenstein's.

Moreover, in my opinion, the overcoming of methodological solipsism illustrates that the ethics presupposed by logic can also answer the question as to if and why logic and even science itself *should exist*. It becomes evident that the ethics of argumentation which is presupposed in logic is not only a precondition for the possibility of the logically and empirically scientific justification of opinions, but can prove to be a claim made by all the members of the community of argument on all the others and therefore represents a moral duty. An ethics that was not charged with the justification of opinions in this manner could not – *qua* ethics of argumentation – be the precondition for the possibility of logic. The ethics *presupposed* by logic as the precondition for its possibility *implies,* therefore, the obligation to apply logic and science. But does this line of argument not create a logical circle? The ethics of argumentation, which makes logic and science a duty, is *only* automatically presupposed *if* we desire logical argumentation at all. Indeed, the decisive – independent – argument for the 'final grounding' of logic together with the ethics that it presupposes is still lacking. We shall return to this point. Here, let it suffice to say that the entire complex of science, logic and the ethics of argumentation must apparently either be accepted as a whole or – if this is meaningful and possible – negated as a whole.

At this point, too, we should draw attention to the *complementarity thesis* of the philosophy of science. Empirical-analytical (*descriptive* and *explanatory*) science presupposes *hermeneutic communication* in the communication community of those human beings who practise science. Yet hermeneutic communication also implies the utilization of all the available factual information and this means – under contemporary conditions – empirical-analytical sciences. But in so far as hermeneutic communication is also communication about needs and goals, it presupposes an ethics and is, at the same time, required by the ethics that is presupposed – together with the information from empirical-analytical science.

But what about the possibility of a *meaningful negation* of this interrelated complex of science, logic, hermeneutics and ethics? Here one might object, with reference to Kant, that even the Devil, given an instrumentalist reservation – such as the improvement of his art of persuasion or the mastery of the 'know-how' of scientific technology – could participate in Lorenzen's dialogue game for grounding logic and thus take part in the community of argumentation without abandoning his evil will. To state it in Kant's terms: he can behave 'dutifully' without acting 'out of a sense of duty'. This appears to indicate that even recourse to the ethical preconditions for the possibility of logic is at best able to reveal 'hypothetical imperatives' and is therefore incapable, in Kant's sense, of revealing a principle of ethics.

One could immediately reply that Kant's distinction is not relevant for our undertaking if it can be demonstrated that the basic norm of 'dutiful' behaviour that we can establish cannot, in practical terms, be distinguished from that of behaviour 'out of a sense of duty'. Given this presupposition, it is not Kant's argument – that even devils who can use their intellect *can,* in principle, behave 'dutifully' – which is relevant, but rather the argument that even devils *must* behave dutifully if they wish to partake of the truth. Peirce pointed out that truth, in the sense of the consensus postulate of the logic of science, cannot be attained by finite individuals and that, for this reason, membership of the argumentative community of scholars incorporates a basic transcendence of the egoism of finite beings – a kind of self-surrender in terms of a 'logical socialism'.[65] This means that the Devil, inasmuch as he desired to be a member of the community of argumentation would for ever more have to behave towards its members (i.e. all rational beings) as if he had overcome egoism and, consequently, himself. The instrumentalist reservation that we assumed in his case loses its significance here since it cannot basically be verified. This appears to indicate that the moral norm which is presupposed by the will to truth and, therefore, by membership of the unlimited community of argumentation cannot be a 'hypothetical imperative' *in the sense in which Kant intended.* The corresponding hypothetical imperative is at least not motivated by a 'pathological interest' in an empirical goal but rather, to some extent, by the practical interest of theoretical reason itself. The fact that the search for truth must also anticipate the morality of an ideal communication community when it presupposes intersubjective consensus will most probably reveal a modern analogue to the classical doctrine of 'transcendentals'. What classical metaphysics posited as existing *sub specie aeternitatis* – The identity of *unum, bonum* and *verum* – must still be posited by the modern philosophy of a historically precarious mediation between theory and practice as a *necessary postulate* in terms of a *critique of meaning* and, with regard to its realization, as the 'principle of hope'.

2.3.3 But it appears that our thesis – that logic presupposes ethics – gives rise to a more serious objection to the possibility of a *rational grounding* of ethics. One might argue that every 'grounding' already presupposes the *validity of logic.* Yet if the latter, for its part, presupposes the validity of ethics then neither a grounding of ethics nor logic would appear to be possible, since every such attempt must lead to a circular argument or a *regressus ad infinitum*. This long familiar difficulty has been emphasized recently by both Popper and Albert in particular as a basic insight of critical rationalism concerning the impossibility of a 'final grounding' of philosophy.[66]

It is easy to appreciate that this argument would indeed condemn our attempt at a 'grounding of ethics' to failure if one had to interpret *fundamental grounding* in philosophy as deduction within the frmeowrk of an axiomatic system. But is not the very reference to the fact that one *cannot* ground logic in this sense, since *it is always presupposed for every attempt* to ground something, the typical starting-point of a 'philosophical grounding' in the sense of a *transcendental reflection* upon the *preconditions for the possibility and validity of argumentation*. If, in the context of a philosophical discussion about basic matters, we establish that something cannot in principle be grounded since it is the precondition for the possibility of all grounding, then we have not simply established an insoluble contradiction in the deductive procedure. We have also gained an *insight* in terms of *transcendental reflection*.

I believe that the virtual failure to notice the character and heuristic value of *transcendental reflection* as a specifically *philosophical* method in the contemporary discussion of a 'final grounding' is connected with the fact that the abstraction from the *pragmatic* dimension of argument, which is characteristic of analytical philosophy, leads one to conceive of the problem of 'final grounding' solely as a problem of *logical* (*syntactic-semantic*) presuppositions for *statements* or *propositions*. It is actually trivial to state that given this presupposition – practised in logic since Aristotle's distinction between 'dialectics' and 'apodeictics' – nothing final can be envisaged and all recourse to 'evidence' must appear to be an arbitrary breaking-off of argument – a 'recourse to dogma'.[67] If one abstracts from the pragmatic sign-dimension, then there is no human *subject* of argumentation. As a result, there is no possibility of *reflection* upon the preconditions for the possibility of argumentation that *we always* presuppose. Rather, there is, of course, the infinite hierarchy of *meta*-languages, *meta*-theories, etc. in which the *reflective competence* of the human being as the *subject of argumentation* both makes itself apparent and conceals itself. It makes itself *apparent* in that the meta-mathematical studies of Gödel, Church, Rosser, and Kleene have demonstrated that the possibility of *formalizing* thought is basically limited, and consequently the *non-contradiction* of logico-mathematical systems in the sense of a *final grounding* cannot be proved.[68] In this finding, however, *reflective competence* is *concealed* inasmuch as it does not come face to face with itself. In terms of formalizable languages, *statements,* or more precisely, *propositions,* cannot, without being contradictory, be self-referring – a fact with which we have been familiar since Bertrand Russell's 'theory of types'.[69] In terms of *formalized languages, semantics* systems must, therefore, as Tarski demonstrated, be split into the 'object language' and the 'meta-language' in order to eliminate contradictions *a priori.* For a 'theory of proofs', this does indeed give rise to the 'second horn' of Fries's 'trilemma' that is invoked by Popper and Albert; the attempt at a final grounding becomes involved in an *infinite regress.*

Yet we are fully aware that our *reflective competence* – or more precisely, the self-reflection of the human subject of intellectual operations, which is ignored *a priori* at the level of syntactic-semantic systems – is concealed behind the aporia of infinite regress and makes possible, for example, something like Gödel's *proof* of in-decidability. In other words, it is precisely when one establishes that the subjective preconditions for the possibility of argumentation are *not objectifiable* in a syntactic-semantic *model* of argumentation that the *self-reflective* knowledge of the transcendental-pragmatic subject of argumentation is expressed. Charles Morris, the founder of three-dimensional semiotics, *know*, for instance, that the *semantic* function of signs presupposes an 'interpretant' that is defined in the *pragmatic* dimension of sign usage. Moreover, he knows that the 'interpretant', as the rule by virtue of which it can be said of a sign that it 'denotes' certain types of objects of situations, cannot itself be an object of this set. Nevertheless, Morris does not utilize this *transcendental* pragmatic reflective knowledge, and attempts to ground pragmatic semiotics as a behaviouristic discipline.[70] Yet can this 'pragmatic dimension', which is part of argumentation or sign-mediated cognition itself, simply be ignored? Can one act as if the semiotic relationship that is involved in all argumentation and cognition were merely a *two-place* relationship? I believe that this is precisely what the modern 'logic of science' does when it relegates the 'pragmatic dimension' of argumentation, together with *reflection,* to empirical psychology. Naturally, the reflection to which we are referring can no more be discussed in empirical psychology than it

The communication community and the foundation of ethics

can in the meta-mathematical theory of proofs. For even if one overlooks behaviourism, an empirical psychology can only discuss the phenomenon of reflection as an infinite regress of the introspective objectivation of the act, and not as reflection upon reflection as the transcendental precondition for the possibility of all cognition, which also means the possibility of all argumentation.

The fact that there is a genuine problem here and that, in particular, one cannot resolve the Kantian problem by merely realizing the (synthetic) *a priori* character of *semantic systems*[71] (and, in terms of the latter, the implicit *a priori* character of theories)[72] and leaving out of consideration the transcendental subject of the semiotic relationship, seems to have been hardly noticed for decades (if one ignores Neo-Hegelianism which, however, lacked an adequate contact with the problem of the foundations of modern logic).[73] Recently, however, it has gradually been recognized, even in the modern 'logic of language', that semantically interpreted logical calculi can only act as models of an 'indirect' elucidation and control of our *pragmatic argumentation* in (pragmatic) everyday language. Moreover, it has also been recognized that an 'abstractive fallacy' would result if one sought to interpret truth as the predicate of *propositions* in a *semantic system* and not as the predicate of *statements* that are asserted by arguing human subjects in *speech acts*.[74] Should one wish to infer from this that even the transcendental-philosophical problem of 'final grounding' cannot be judged on the basis of abstractly presented systems of propositions? If this question received an affirmative reply, then it would in my view imply that one must consider a 'transcendental pragmatics of language' to be possible in which the subject of argumentation is able to reflect upon the preconditions for the possibility and validity of argumentation that are always presupposed in the speech-situation (and in the mental situation as the internalized speech-situation). I believe that the fact that the possibility of antinomies has been demonstrated in so-called 'closed' *semantic systems,* has neither proved the so-called 'inconsistency of natural languages',[75] nor has it proved that the transcendental-pragmatic self-reflection of speech *must* lead to contradictions. Rather, I am more inclined to assume that the *indirect self-referentiality* of argumentation, which is contained in the transcendental-pragmatic discussion of (the preconditions for the possibility of) *argumentation as such,* only becomes self-contradictory if it denies or fails to credit itself with its own truth, as

265

is the case in radical scepticism or in a discussion of the *fundamental inconsistency of discussion in everyday language about the truth of discourse.*[76]

It is interesting to note that the Popperian school, immediately after having proclaimed the impossibility of philosophical *fundamental grounding* in the sense of Fries's trilemma, and having replaced this demand by that of the *critical test* that is potentially universal, encounters a new kind of problem of justification which the Popperians had apparently not foreseen. They are faced, in fact, with the question of the preconditions for the possibility and validity of the critical test.[77] Bartley was the first to recognize that logic 'cannot be part of the totality that is brought under test' because 'the practice of critical argument and logic are bound together'. He believes, therefore, that logic is 'an absolute presupposition of argument'.[78] Hans Lenk counters Hans Albert's objection that he 'cannot see how the situation here with regard to logic is supposed to be *completely* different from the usual one' by defining Bartley's thesis more sharply, such that 'at least *some* logical rules are basically removed from rational revision'.[79] Lenk attempts to establish as complete a list as possible of these rules by reflecting – as I would interpret him – upon what aspects of logic one cannot reject without having recourse to them – in the sense of a *petitio tollendi* – in the critique itself. He concludes that it is the rules of the 'logic of consequences' themselves which Popper himself established in harmony with Paul Lorenzen's operative grounding of logic, that constitute 'the components of logic which cannot be abolished by means of rational criticism'.[80]

In my opinion, what is fundamental to this line of argument is that – contrary to Albert's attempt to incorporate logic, so to speak, in the empirical *intentio recta* into the universe of what can be critically tested – something irreducible in terms of transcendental pragmatics was established through the operation of *reflection upon the preconditions for the possibility* of critical testing, an operation which differs characteristically from empirical testing.[81] Accordingly, if one interprets Kant's question as the heuristic approach to an indirect philosophical final grounding, then in my opinion it follows that the actual business of *philosophical foundation* must consist of reconstructing the necessary preconditions for human argumentation as completely as possible. In this connection, Kant's reference to the organic or teleological, systematic 'nature of reason'[82] indicates that the transcendental reconstruction of the preconditions for the possibility and validity of cognition is very similar to *functional analysis*. Like the latter, it must presuppose, to some extent teleologically, a certain 'achievement of the system' – in Kant's case, this is the 'transcendental synthesis of apperception' – as the 'highest point' of the 'transcendental deduction' of the functional preconditions.

Similarly, I should like to reconstruct the ethical preconditions for the possibility and validity of human argumentation and, consequently, of logic. This attempt differs, however, from Kant's classical transcendental philosophy in that it does not see the 'highest point' – which transcendental reflection takes as its starting-point – in the 'unity of consciousness of the object and self-consciousness' that is posited in a 'methodologically solipsistic' manner, but rather in the 'intersubjective unity of interpretation' *qua* understanding of meaning and *qua* consensus of truth.[83] This unity of interpretation must, in principle, be attainable in the unlimited community of those engaged in argumentation by virtue of the experience derived from experiment and interaction, if argumentation is to have any *meaning* at all. To this extent, my attempt is conceived as a *transformation of transcendental philosophy that is critical of meaning*, one which develops from the *a priori* fact of argumentation as an irreducible, quasi-Cartesian starting-point.

The significance of this programme can initially be elucidated by means of a confrontation with Popper's theory of 'critical rationalism'. It seems that the *tertium comparationis* can easily be found since Popper has established an ideal within the so-called 'criticist frame' of rational discussion that is very similar to our posited *a priori* of the unlimited communication community. This is especially true since it obviously contains ethical (and political) implications that were, as we know, developed by Popper in his philosophy of the 'open society'.[84] The difference between the theories lies, first, in the fact that Popper thinks he must draw the following conclusion from his renunciation of 'final grounding': from the standpoint of a potential grounding of validity, the principle of the 'criticist frame' cannot, for example, be conceded any basic advantage over that of 'irrationalism'. Instead of a fundamental grounding, 'an act of faith', an 'irrational moral decision' must in Popper's view settle the issue between the two opposing principles.[85] Popper believes that in a discussion of philosophical fundamentals, it is at best arguments of pragmatic expediency which can be advanced in favour of the principle of critical rationality. Yet these cannot be used to 'determine' our decision: 'it is always we who decide'.[86]

I believe that one must concede with Popper (and, in this connection, with scepticism) that the decision of the will in favour of the 'criticist frame' cannot be 'determined'. But this is not because it cannot be rationally grounded. Nor does it make the decision an 'irrational' act of faith. Even if the principle of the 'criticist frame' itself could be deduced from principles, this would not 'determine' our decision of will (not even in the light of Popper's presuppositions). To this extent, the *practical realization of reason* through (good) will always requires a commitment that cannot be proven and that one can, consequently, term 'irrational'. But this restriction of 'rationalism' – which one has to concede – does not mean the renunciation of a *rational grounding* of primary engagement on behalf of reason, as Popper and Albert seem to believe. The renunciations of a rational grounding for the choice of the criticist frame – and consequently, in accordance with our thesis, the choice of a basic moral norm – is only plausible if, like Popper, one equates the possibility of *philosophical grounding* with the possibility of *deduction* and does not draw upon *transcendental reflection* or *contemplation* (in the sense that I have outlined). If one does this, however, then it becomes evident that participants in a discussion of philosophical fundamentals – and this means all those who look to (philosophical) thought for an answer to their questions – have already *implicitly* acknowledged the operative rules of the criticist frame.[87] They are, none the less, constantly required to *endorse* this acknowledgment *through an act of will*. To this extent, the *realization of reason* in the world is left to their free engagement, a decision that must be renewed constantly and that no one else can either take over or force upon them. Nevertheless, the choice of the criticist frame as a philosophical position in a philosophical discussion is not an *irrational* act of faith. Rather, it is the only possible decision that is *semantically* and *pragmatically consistent* in terms of the ongoing language-game. It is the only one that is consonant with the preconditions for the possibility and validity of discussion – preconditions that have to be established through *transcendental contemplation*. Anyone who does not make this choice but instead chooses obscurantism, for instance, terminates the discussion itself and his decision is, therefore, irrelevant *for the discussion*.

I think that this line of argument is basically sufficient to refute Popper's thesis that the choice of a basic principle of critical discussion is an 'irrational' one, and for this reason, a 'moral' one. The choice is not 'moral' because it is 'irrational', but rather because it endorses through an act of will itself the *principle of discussion,* which must be established through reflection. I should like to go further, however, in order to counter the objection that the decision to enter into (rational) discussion – the decision to philosophize – could still represent an *irrational,* moral decision in Popper's sense.[88] If this were true, it ought to be possible in terms of a discussion – i.e. an intended communication about good and bad reasons – to put oneself in the position of a person who has *yet* to enter this very discussion. It seems to me that this is precisely what Popper pre-supposes in his line of argument. In my view, he thus reveals in a very interesting manner that – like virtually all the classical figures in philosophy since Descartes (or since Augustine?) – he makes 'methodological solipsism' his basic presupposition. That is, he believes that one can think and take meaningful decisions before one has acknowledged, even *implicitly,* the rules of argumentation as those of a critical communication community; or – and this amounts to the same thing – that one can philosophize about critical communication from a standpoint outside it.

In opposition to this, I believe that – within the framework of a transcendental-philosophical radicalization of the later Wittgenstein's work – one must point out that everyone, even if he merely *acts* in a *meaningful* manner – e.g. takes a decision in the face of an alternative and claims to understand himself – already implicitly presupposes the logical and moral preconditions for critical communication. (We have yet to establish what those conditions are.) This becomes evident, for instance, from the fact that – as Wittgenstein demon-strates – no language-game is possible on the basis of permanent lying and therefore no meaningful action is possible. Anyone who takes the obscurantist decision in Popper's sense can nevertheless only *understand* it by presupposing what he himself negates. He still takes it within the *transcendental language-game of the transcendental communication community.* If he takes the decision in a radical and fundamental sense, then in so doing he leaves the transcendental communication community and thereby relinquishes the possibility of both self-understanding and self-identification.[89] (If one wished to express this in speculative, theological terms, then one might say that the Devil can only become independent of God through the act of self-destruction.)

2.3.4   At this point, we can resume the discussion of the first objection which asserted that our approach can, at best, ground 'hypothetical imperatives'. This objection is even now still valid inasmuch as the validity of basic moral norms (which we must ground) is dependent upon the will to argumentation. At the same time, however, we can point out that this rational will can and must be presupposed in every philosophical discussion of fundamentals – otherwise the discussion itself has no *meaning*.

In terms of argumentation, we – as philosophers – cannot go back on our will to argumentation. To this extent, the will to argumentation is not *determined empirically* but rather it is the precondition for the possibility of every discussion of hypothetically posited, empirical preconditions. In so far as we admit that our discussion of fundamentals must be meaningful *unconditionally* – i.e. regardless of empirical conditions – we can, accordingly, call the basic moral norm which is implied in the will to argumentation *unconditional* or *categorical*.

It seems to me that this argument concerning a transcendental critique of meaning is also a match for the following modification of the first objection: One might consider that our recourse to the fact that the participants in a discussion of philosophical fundamentals have always already implicitly accepted the basic moral norms of a critical communication community is unable to ground any moral norm since no *norm* can be derived from a *fact*, namely the *fact* of having accepted.

I do indeed believe that this argument is valid against the attempt to ground the moral binding force of norms on the fact of 'free acknowledgment'. The free acknowledgment of norms by human subjects is only a *necessary* but not a *sufficient* condition for the moral validity of norms. Even immoral norms can be acknowledged as binding, either erroneously or in the belief that it will be other people (weaker people!) who suffer. Examples of this are the supposed duty to sacrifice human beings to the gods, or the legal norm that all social considerations be subjected to the free play of economic competition – or even the biological selection of the strong.[90] Naturally, all contracts – in order to be binding – presuppose the free acknowledgment of genuine moral norms on the part of the contracted parties, but the moral validity of the presupposed norms cannot itself be grounded on the fact of acknowledgment – i.e. using the model of a concluded contract. As I indicated above, I think that this is the fallacy of an ethical 'liberalism'.[91] Does this line of argument, however, also apply to our recourse to those moral norms which must be acknowledged together with the will to engage in argument?

The transcendental critique of meaning can argue against this last *objection,* which rests upon Hume's distinction, that accepting the rules of a critical communication community is not an empirical fact. Rather, it is one of the preconditions for the possibility and validity of the empirical-scientific establishment of facts. Moreover, the problematized acknowledgment of a basic moral norm, as has been demonstrated, is one of the preconditions for the possibility of all argumentation and, in so far as methodological solipsism can be considered to be refuted, it is one of the preconditions for the possibility of all valid self-understanding. In my opinion, this means that accepting the basic moral norm itself takes on the modal character of *ought* – on condition, however, that the questions of the philosophical discussion of fundamentals – and, indeed, questions in general – *ought* to be raised meaningfully. This presupposition is – as we have already established – not the precondition for a hypothetical imperative, for it cannot be *meaningfully* negated unless the discussion itself is to be suspended. In other words, in so far as it must be necessarily presupposed, the acceptance of the basic moral norm of the critical communication community does not possess the character of a Humean 'fact', but rather the character of the Kantian 'fact of reason'.

This interpretation is obviously linked with the claim to critically reconstruct Kant's justification of the 'categorical imperative' through the 'fact of (practical) reason'.[92] In my opinion, it cannot be doubted that in the form in which it exists historically Kant's reference to the 'fact of reason' as the foundation for a 'categorical imperative' is open to criticism of the Humean kind or to the charge of representing the 'naturalistic fallacy'. As Ilting in particular has convincingly demonstrated,[93] Kant's claim to have justified the validity of a 'categorical imperative' rests – in the *Groundwork of the Metaphysic of Morals,* at least – upon the fact that, in an analogous manner to the 'transcendental deduction' of thematical 'principles' in the *Critique of Pure Reason*, he believes that he has demonstrated the 'objective reality' of the basic ethical principle as a synthetic *a priori* practical judgment. Here Kant transforms – tacitly and contrary to his critical intention – the question of the *moral validity* of the 'categorical imperative' *qua* basic principles of ethics into the question of the 'facticity' of the corresponding 'constraint' upon conscience. Eventually, he answers this question by means of the – ultimately Christian-Platonic – metaphysics of constraint upon the empirical will, which is affected by the sensual, through the 'prime will' of the 'intelligible ego' who established the law for himself. Even in the *Critique of Practical Reason,* where the claim to provide a 'transcendental deduction' of the 'categorical imperative' has been abandoned and the latter has been reduced to a 'fact' that cannot be grounded any further, the metaphysical notion of the 'reality' of this fact is preserved. For the distinction between the 'categorical imperative' and the 'principles' of theoretical reason is, in Kant's opinion, that the latter are the precondition for the possibility of the 'appearance' of objects for a (sensually stimulable) consciousness, whilst the self-determination of the will through the moral law is the 'reason for the existence of its objects' through the causality of a rational being.

Given the critical preconditions for discussion in our time, one cannot regard this metaphysical 'grounding' or 'explanation' as an answer to the problem of the justification of validity. This opinion would be shared by all those who have taken part in the meta-ethical discussion that has developed since G. E. Moore's work. Nevertheless, to metaphysically reduce the basic moral 'norm' to a moral 'law' *qua* 'fact of reason' is not so confusing as to mistake the norm for an empirical fact in Hume's sense.[94] The metaphysical – and also the mythically or speculatively theological – mode of presenting a problem or its 'resolution' can also be considered as the preservation of the problem-substance and the 'pre-illusion' of the true resolution of the problem, which is directly opposed to empirical 'reductions' and attempts to ease the problem. The 'analogical' language of metaphysics is to some extent legitimate as long as a more adequate formulation of the problem is not available. This especially applies to Kant's metaphysics, which is itself the expression of an undogmatic attempt to undertake a critique of knowledge. Moreover, the author is occasionally aware of the 'analogical' character of his mode of expression.[95]

In this manner I believe that we can interpret Kant's reference to the 'fact of reason' *qua* uncontestable *fact* of moral self-determination (through a self-imposed law of self-transcendence) as a result of transcendental self-contemplation, that can be reconstructed in the sense in which we have indicated, namely, as an implication of the *a priori* of argumentation. To this extent, in my opinion, Kant's theory, even in its metaphysical wording, asserts its greater legitimacy, not only against a 'naturalistic fallacy' in the sense of an empirical reduction, but also against all decisionistic justifications of the validity of norms (and even the grounding of this validity as the 'free acknowledgment' of finite human beings is a decisionistic justification!). The peculiar dialectic – and involuntary self-irony – of the modern disjunction and complementarity of facts and decisions is constituted by the very fact that, for reflexive (meta-ethical) judgment, 'decisions' are still only 'facts' in that they have not been proved to be *inevitable pre-decisions of argumentative reason* through transcendental contemplation and critique of meaning, so that they take on the character of an '*a priori* perfect'.[96] In terms of this '*a priori* perfect', I believe that Kant's doctrine of the 'fact of reason' can be reconstructed – especially if one considers that, according to Kant, practical reason proves 'its reality and that of its concepts through the deed'.[97] In fact, Fichte was the first to attempt a 'self-reconstruction of reason' in retracing the 'actions of the ego' which ground both the validity of ethics and that of the 'theory of science'.[98] Fichte describes his method as follows:[99]

> Our procedure is nearly always that we a) perform something, undoubtedly guided by a rational law that is directly active within us. – What we actually are in this case, in our own supreme point, and in which we are absorbed, is still facticity. – We then b) investigate and reveal the law that has just directed us in this first performance; that is, we appreciate indirectly by virtue of the principle and reason for its 'being-so' [*Sosein*] what we have previously appreciated indirectly; that is, we penetrate it in the genesis of its determinacy. In this manner we shall proceed from the actual members to the genetic ones. This genetic aspect can, however, be actual in another respect, and then we are consequently obliged to proceed again to the genetic with reference to this facticity, until we reach the absolute genesis, the genesis of the theory of science.

Fichte, therefore, seeks to gradually dissolve the 'fact of reason' in its mere facticity through both immediate and subsequent reconstruction. By reason appropriating or reconstructing itself, both the dogmatic recourse to a merely existent metaphysical fact and the arbitrariness of an ungrounded decisionistic postulate are to be avoided. Yet even Fichte himself – as his later philosophy in particular shows – was unable to free himself from the presupposition of one metaphysics (of the 'absolute ego' of God as a prime fact). Nevertheless, he was the first to move forward towards a 'reconstructionist' transcendental philosophy, which, in a sense, was later developed further by Hugo Dingler and Paul Lorenzen. But I believe that this modern 'reconstructivism' is in danger of seeking to elude Fichte's metaphysical residual dogmatism by easing the problem of the starting-point of the reconstruction not in the direction of a metaphysical fact but rather in the direction of decisionism. Thereby, it would in my opinion abandon the point of (*transcendental*) *reconstructivism* that is dependent upon *reflection* in favour of a *constructivism that is dependent upon decisions.*

Consequently, Lorenzen, like Popper, believes that he must concede that the principles on whose basis alone moral norms can be justified can themselves not be justified, but rather must be accepted through an 'act of faith' in terms of a belief in reason.[100] Lorenzen claims that the reason for the inevitability of the act of faith is that 'the term "justification" makes sense only after one has accepted such principles'.[101] Even Oswald Schwemmer believes that he must accept these typical conditions of modern *logical semantics* (e.g. of Carnap's type), although he previously demonstrated, by drawing upon Fichte, that the moral principle itself can be made 'understandable' on the basis of participation in the reciprocal practice of communication. For Schwemmer, the reason for the reference to a decision or act of faith that cannot be meaningfully justified any further is that one must always *participate* in the reciprocal practice of communication in order to appreciate the validity of the moral principle through the joint reconstruction of practical reason.[102]

Yet anyone who raises the question of the justification of the moral principle – a question that is, in my view, very meaningful – is already *participating* in the discussion, and one can make him 'understand' – entirely along the lines of a reconstruction of reason as practised by Lorenzen and Schwemmer – what he has 'always' accepted as a basic principle, and also that he should accept this principle as the *precondition for the possibility and validity of argumentation* through conscious affirmation. Anyone who does not appreciate or accept this is automatically excluded from the discussion. But anyone who does not take part in the discussion cannot raise the question of the justification of basic ethical principles at all and it is, as a result, meaningless to speak of the meaninglessness of his question and to recommend that he take an honest decision of faith.[103] The fact that it is, nevertheless, meaningful in life-practice to *call upon* people to attain moral autonomy and to posit their own ego – this means, assuming that 'methodological solipsism' has been overcome, that they are called upon to participate in the communicative praxis of the reconstruction of practical reason – can be seen from the following: on the one hand, anyone who speaks or who simply acts meaningfully is already participating in a potential discussion; on the other hand, everyone – even the philosopher – must *consciously affirm* his participation in the transcendental language-game of the transcendental communication community at every moment of his life. But this 'conscious affirmation', which Lorenzen must actually have in mind, is not an irrational act of faith or an irrational decision that replaced transcendental justification.[104]

In my opinion, it is precisely Schwemmer's attempt to reconstruct Lorenzen's theory as the realization of Kant's and Fichte's actual intentions which demonstrates that one need not call the demand for a *justification* of the basic moral norm or the principle of ethics 'meaningless' as long as one has not discarded the methodological possibility of a *transcendental reflection or contemplation* – and, consequently, of a *reconstruction* that depends upon *reflection* – in favour of the procedure that is suggested by neopositivism; namely, that every philosophical argument is made dependent upon presuppositions that have been made binding in an explicit manner through definitions or entire 'semantic systems'. Given the presupposition of the latter, one cannot even meaningfully raise – let alone resolve – the problem of the non-arbitrary start in philosophy, a problem which Lorenzen brought back to our attention. The representatives of the *linguistic-construction* of a logical semantics that is dependent upon *decisions* no longer regard a 'transcendental reflection' upon the *implicit* pre-decisions of reason as a legitimate move in the philosophical language-game. As a result, they are faced with the problem of everyday language – which has not been reconstructed philosophically – as the final meta-language or paralanguage of philosophical discourse.

I believe that this typical situation of the 'indirect' reconstruction of language along Carnap's lines can only be avoided if, for the purpose of *normative reconstruction*, one consciously enters from the outset the 'hermeneutic circle' (or 'hermeneutic spiral') of *normative and actual reconstruction* which also means: the 'hermeneutic circle' of the traditional *cultivated language* of philosophy, *everyday language* and the reconstructed cultural language of philosophy.[105] Yet I believe that this means that the Erlangen school's fight against the *transcendental-hermeneutic* principle of the 'non-reducibility of language'[106] rests upon a self-misunderstanding, since the school seeks to question or eliminate precisely what makes its own approach possible.[107] For anyone who strives for a *non-arbitrary reconstruction* of (practical and theoretical) reason – and not for the construction of paradigmatic fragments of axiomatic reason that is dependent upon *decisions* – has, in my opinion, every reason to begin with the transcendental contemplation of the 'fact of reason' which, affiliated with a language community, can 'have always' been presupposed in the sense of an '*a priori* perfect'. This *a priori* can be reconstructed, but not overlooked.

2.3.5 It is now time, however, to answer a final question which is probably the most important one in terms of our present topic. What is actually achieved by transcendental reflection upon the moral norms of the communication community that are also presupposed in the *a priori* of argumentation? On the basis of these presuppositions, can an ethics be developed that will serve as the foundation for a collective[108] assumption of moral responsibility in the scientific age?

At this point, it becomes evident once again that it is not sufficient to reconstruct those moral norms which are presupposed in the sense of 'hypothetical imperatives' for the fact of science – although proof of the existence of such norms is necessary in order to break the paralysing spell of scientism. The following critical reflections upon Peirce's conception of the ethics of science may show that the ethics of science is not sufficient to ground an ethics for humanity in the scientific age. Peirce recognized – rightly in my opinion – the specific moral commitment that is implicitly presupposed by every member of the community of natural scientists in a certain abstraction from the finite (individual) life interests.[109] According to Peirce, the natural scientist must be in a position to identify himself (as an interchangeable member) with an unlimited community of experiment. Moreover, the natural scientist knows that this community will not attain its goal – the establishment of definitive truth – within his lifetime. In the attitude of self-surrender of individuality that is implied here, Peirce[110] seems to have recognized something like the paradigm of moral sentiment in general. Accordingly, he looked forward to the rationalization of the universe, even in the sense of an ethic of 'evolutionary love', as a consequence of the extrapolation of the ethics of science. The attempt to reconstruct this extrapolation and to formulate an ethical imperative along the lines of Peirce's 'self-surrender' reveals, however, that here a *single* life interest would be made absolute – a need that can only be justified in the 'community of those engaged in argument'.

This reflection demonstrates that the community of those engaged in argument is not identical with the community of scholars, although it is presupposed by the latter. The *a priori* of argumentation contains the *claim* to *justify* not only all the 'assertions' of science, but also all human *claims* (including the implicit claims of human beings upon one another that are embedded in actions and institutions).[111] Anyone who takes part in an argument implicitly acknowledges all the *potential claims* of all the members of the communication community that *can* be jutified by rational arguments (otherwise the claim of argumentation would restrict itself in subject matter). He also commits himself to eventually justifying all his claims upon other people through arguments. Furthermore, I believe that the members of the communication community (and this implies all thinking beings) are also committed to considering all the potential claims of all the potential members – and this means all human 'needs' inasmuch as they could be affected by norms and consequently make *claims* on their fellow human beings. As potential 'claims' that can be communicated interpersonally, all human 'needs' are ethically *relevant*. They must be *acknowledged* if they can be justified interpersonally through arguments. This necessary readiness to justify personal *needs qua interpersonal claims* represents an analogy to the 'self-surrender' demand by Peirce in that the 'subjectivity' of the egoistic assertion of one's interests must be sacrificed in favour of the 'transsubjectivity' of the argumentative representation of interests.[112] Yet this readiness also represents the demand that one should not unnecessarily sacrifice a finite, individual human interest. The meaning of moral argument could almost be expressed in the by no means novel principle that all human *needs* – as potential *claims* – i.e. which can be reconciled with the needs of all the others by argumentation, must be made the concern of the communication community.[113]

I believe that this outlines the basic principles of an ethics of communication, a principle which also represents the hitherto non-existent foundation for an ethics of the democratic formation of the will through *agreement* ('convention'). The basic norm that I have outlined acquires its binding character not merely through the *factual acknowledgment* of those who reach an agreement (the 'contract model'). Rather, it commits all people who have acquired 'communicative competence' through the process of socialization to strive for an agreement for the purposes of the collective formation of the will in every matter that affects the *interests* (the potential *claims*) of others. Moreover, it is only this basic norm – and not, for instance, the *fact* that a given agreement has been reached – that guarantees to individual norm conforming agreements their binding moral character. The *subjective, individual decisions of conscience* that were demanded by the Christian tradition which was secularized during the period of liberalism and existentialism are now mediated *a priori* with the *demand for intersubjective validity*; namely, by each individual acknowledging from the outset that public argument is the explication of all possible criteria of validity and, consequently, of all criteria for a rational formation of the will. 'Methodological solipsism' is therefore also overcome within the ethical domain.

Understanding the principle that we have outlined, however, implies recognition that little is achieved by the establishment of the principle if the long-term tasks that were set up with the principle cannot be fulfilled. These entail, first, developing the *method of moral discussion* (i.e. of practical 'consultation' in general),[114] and, second, effectively institutionalizing this method under finite, political and legal conditions. In my opinion, however, this indicates a certain limitation of the principle that we have discussed up till now.

The foundation of an ethics of communication that has been developed up till now is based on idealized presuppositions. Basic-ally, it does not take into account the fact that it is not only intellectual difficulties which must be considered when the moral discussion is institutionalized, but rather the fact that this institutionalization must be realized in a concrete historical situation which has always been determined by the *conflict of interests*. It does not, for example, take into account the fact that even those who have achieved complete insight into the moral principle cannot as a result immediately become members of an unlimited community of communicating people who share equal rights. On the contrary, they remain bound to their *real* social position and situation. Through this real bond they are condemned to assume a *specific moral responsibility* that cannot be satisfactorily defined by means of the formal principle of 'transsubjectivity' in the sense of the community of argumentation. As 'experts', for example, in the sense of a certain knowledge or skill, they possess an authority that must be brought to bear even if it is not acknowledged by fellow human beings – for example, the inhabitants of the earth who are threatened by 'biocide'. As members of an oppressed class or race, they possess *a priori* a *moral privilege vis-à-vis* the *socially privileged,* a right to bring about equality even prior to acknowledging the rules that only have to be accepted once real equality exists. As politicians, moreover, they are committed to considering carefully all the chances of realizing morally desirable goals, and also all their effects and side-effects. In short, the moral principle as we have developed it so far does not take into account the moral situation of all those who have to take decisions of conscience at short notice outside institutionalized communication. Such people have to take into consideration not only moral maxims of conscience, but also – contrary to Kant's assumption[115] – possible or probable effects. Max Weber threw light on this situation with his thesis that an 'ethics of political responsibility' must come into conflict with every consistent 'ethics of conviction'.[116] It is, for instance, often impossible for the politician – and not only for him – in view of the consequences for which he must bear the responsibility, to adhere to the fundamental commandment of every ethics of communication (as it was of Kantian ethics) which forbids lying. The same applies to the prohibition on treating a human being merely as a means and not as an end in himself. At this point, the basic problem of modern existentialist situation ethics evidently recurs and the question arises as to whether one should abandon the field to irrationalism or whether one can at least derive *regulative principles* from our approach even for a situational ethics of solitary decisions.

Without underestimating the force of the tragic in human extreme situations, I wish nevertheless to give a positive reply to the last question and attempt to outline the consequences of the *a priori* of the communication community for the long-term *strategic* orientation of moral action.

279

In the first place, one could follow Sartre and formalize Kant's categorical imperative or Lorenzen's principle of transsubjectivity such that it can also be applied to the limiting case of the absolutely unique situational decision. According to Sartre, even in a situation from which communication and comparisons are excluded and which apparently compels the individual to violate all the moral norms, the individual can act as a representative of humanity as far as his intention is concerned. By choosing himself, he may choose humanity. In this case, every other person who is able to put himself in this person's position should, in principle, subsequently endorse his action and thereby be able to establish that the moral norms of the communication community have been fulfilled. (With this demand, Sartre himself overcomes the phase of the irrational, arbitrary existentialism of 'The Flies' in order to demonstrate that 'existentialism is humanism'.)[117] Yet precisely this radical formalization clearly reveals the substantive vacuum for which Kant's categorical imperative has been criticized. Consequently, the question arises whether – contrary to Kant's opinion – it is not possible to derive a *substantive goal* as the regulative principle of all moral actions from the 'fact of reason' inasmuch as the latter is understood as the *a priori of the communication community.*[118] To this end, let us reflect more precisely upon the unique character of the *a priori* of the communication community, as the sense-critical precondition for the possibility and validity of all argumentation, in contrast to the *a priori* of traditional transcendental philosophy.

The first point to emerge is the fact that we are not concerned with a purely *idealistic* presupposition in the sense of an *a priori* of consciousness. Nor, however, are we concerned with a purely materialistic presupposition – such that Kant's ideal and normative 'consciousness as such' is to be replaced by the 'being' of empirical society.[119] I believe that the point of our *a priori* is that it marks the *principle of a dialectics* (on this side) *of idealism and materialism.* For anyone who engages in argument automatically presupposes two things: first, a *real communication community* whose member he has himself become through a process of socialization, and second, an *ideal communication community* that would basically be capable of adequately understanding the meaning of his arguments and judging their truth in a definitive manner. What is remarkable and dialectical about this situation, however, is that, to some extent, the ideal community is presupposed and even counterfactually anticipated *in* the real one, namely, as a real possibility of the real society, although the person who engages in argument is aware that (in most cases) the real community, including himself, is far removed from being similar to the ideal community.[120] But, by virtue of its transcendental structure, argumentation is left no choice other than to face this both desperate and hopeful situation.

We have established, therefore, that our transcendental pre-supposition contains a 'contradiction'; not a genuine or obvious contradiction of formal logic, but rather a *dialectical contradiction*. The possibility that we are faced with a genuine, formal-logical contradiction is excluded from the outset since our problematic presupposition is evidently meaningful and, as we shall demonstrate, has by no means arbitrary logical consequences. *Prima facie,* it seems more plausible to assume that it is merely an apparent (formal-logical) contradiction that can be resolved at any time with logical means, namely by distinguishing between aspects of it. One could, for instance, attempt to separate the presupposition of the real communication community from that of the ideal community and interpret the former as the common-sense presupposition of the rhetorical pragmatician who takes up premises ('prejudices') that are accepted here and now.[121] One could then interpret the latter, however, as a regulative principle or as a mere fiction on the part of the solitary thinker who is not concerned with a real audience. Actually, in the time-honoured dispute of philosophers and rhetors about the primacy of *sapientia* such dissection and weakening of the dialectics of the *a priori* of the communication community, which we have presented here, probably played a central role.[122]

It is, however, evident from what has been said that a philosopher who has recognized the illusion of 'methodological solipsism' and appreciated that solitary thought is a deficient mode of communication, cannot accept this separation of the two presuppositions. In solitary thought he must automatically presuppose dependence upon the real discussion yet, as a result, he must presuppose that both he and the people with whom he is engaged in communication belong to the *real* communication community which has developed socially and historically, and he must *also* presuppose that he and those communicating with him possess competence in the sense of the *ideal* communication community. This is obviously a 'contradiction' not in the metaphorical sense of formal logic but rather in the literal sense of the hitherto undecided dialectics of history. This is a contradiction which – as Hegel says – we must endure. Within the framework of a 'dialectical relationship between Hegel and Marx',[123] one can anticipate a resolution of this contradiction only in the historical realization of the ideal communication community *in* the real communication community. In fact, one must morally postulate the historical resolution of this contradiction.

I believe that two *fundamental regulative principles* for the long-term moral strategy of action for every human being can be derived from this (implicit) demand on the part of all philosophical argumentation. First, in all actions and omissions, it should be a matter of ensuring the *survival* of the human species *qua real* communication community. Second, it should be a matter of realizing the *ideal* communication community in the real one. The first goal is the necessary condition for the second; and the second goal provides the first with its meaning – the meaning that is already anticipated with every argument.

The strategy which is governed by the regulative principle of securing the survival of the species must provide an answer today for the fact, originally mentioned, that in the age of scientific technology all human activities have *macro-effects* that are capable of threatening the survival of the species. To this end, this strategy must itself utilize scientific instruments that, in my opinion, should basically be found in the functionalist systems theory of modern sociology and political science. This means that human society as a whole can, may and must be analysed under the aspect of the strategy for survival as a *system of self-assertion* (also in terms of Luhmann's 'reduction of complexity').[124] Even truth can, may and must be interpreted functionalistically (in a normative analytical manner) under this aspect – for scientific truth is undoubtedly also a means in the human species' strategy for survival. But this functionalist interpretation certainly does not amount to a 'reduction' in Nietzsche's or Luhmann's sense for, according to our presuppositions, the entire strategy of survival only acquires its meaning through the strategy – required by argumentation – of the social realization of the ideal communication community in which truth can be attained. In other words, the *strategy for survival* acquires its meaning through a long-term *strategy for emancipation*.

At this point, it seems to me that our approach is in a position to concede an ethically grounded function to the strategy of a non-orthodox, non-dogmatically deterministic Marxism; in other words, to a humanitarian, emancipatory and, to some extent, hypothetical, experimental Marxism or – more correctly – neo-Marxism. For it is evident that the task of realizing the ideal communication community also implies the transcendence of a class society, or – formulated in terms of communication theory – the elimination of all socially determined asymmetries of interpersonal dialogue.[125]

'Taking up the cause of the proletariat' can possibly, therefore, be justified in ethical terms if one adopts our philosophical *a priori.* It can, in fact, be justified ethically when 'the' proletariat in the sense in which Karl Marx characterized it in 1843 – and this means in the sense of the 'categorical imperative' established at that time – actually exists.[126] It is obvious that Marxist 'neo-orthodoxy' has little use for such a philosophical 'final grounding'. It is satisfied with the – ostensibly more concrete – grounding of commitment to the cause through the objectively assumed class standpoint of the 'proletariat' which cannot be questioned further. It is, of course, obvious to any-one who attempts to concretize his political commitment in terms of this assumption that this is the paradigmatic case of a breaking off of justification through dogmatic assertion (in Popper's and Albert's sense). Suppose, in fact, that the *neo*-Marxist thesis were incorrect in assuming that the revolutionary proletariat has disintegrated in modern industrial states, even then one would at least have to concede that there are, so to speak, several proletariats. Stated in very simple terms, there is, for instance, the Third World proletariat to which Marx's term 'pauperization' applies but hardly the term 'agent of the forces of production'. There is also the proletariat of Western industrial society to which Marx's term 'alienation' can undoubtedly still be applied, even in the economic sense, but hardly the term 'pauperization'. But even worse is the following: Even if one could still ascribe a revolutionary potential to *both* these pro-leteriats one could by no means ascribe to them the same material interests. Such an illusion would make a mockery of every 'materialist analysis'. One cannot even ascribe the same interests to the two 'victorious proletariats', or – expressed in more simple language – the Russian and Chinese proletariats. Moreover, I believe that this is not only because of economic reasons but also because of the struggle for power and prestige in foreign policy, the 'struggle for recognition unto death' which, in Hegel's view, precedes the 'master-slave' dialectic and consequently the class struggle, and will most probably outlive the latter.

From these illustrations alone, I think that the following becomes evident. Anyone who really thinks in a concrete and radical manner must be prepared to justify his or her social commitment in a particular situation through philosophical ethics. The latter is, of course, unable to deduce the concrete situational commitment, yet it can provide a critical standpoint against which the commitment itself – its success or failure – can be measured. This necessity will not 'die off' with the 'bourgeoisie', but only when philosophy is also 'transcended' by its 'realization'.

Even the strategy of emancipation will have to use scientific instruments in the scientific age. Here one will always primarily think of the historical, hermeneutic communication sciences. (In the age of empirical-analytical 'science' and 'technology', they are by no means dispensable or scientifically reducible. Rather, in proportion to scientific-technological advance, they are constantly confronted with complementary tasks. These involve the establishment of an adequate understanding of meaning and a normatively adequate agreement upon goals between scientific, technological experts, on the one hand, and between them and society as a whole, on the other. In this connection, one need only consider the new hermeneutic disciplines of the history of science and technology and the interdisciplinary 'science of science'.)[127] These disciplines, which are so controversial today, derive their *regulative principle* through the postulate of the *realization of the ideal communication community* in the methodological *and* in the ethical-normative sense of a non-subjectively arbitrary grounding of value judgments. Consequently, they serve an empirical and normative reconstruction of the historical situation[128] and, therefore, they serve the 'formation' of public opinion.

However, the traditional, humanist *Geisteswissenschaften* will not suffice as the scientific instruments of the strategy of emancipation. Their boundary lies where the actual obstacles to understanding, and consequently to communication, are encountered in the *real* communication community; obstacles in the sense of the lack of transparency or ideological masking of material interests that impede the realization of the ideal communication community. Here the ethically grounded strategy of emancipation must first create its specific scientific instruments so that, via the detour of a quasi-naturalistic 'explanation' of the reified structures, it can provoke the reflexive self-understanding of human beings to the emanci-

patory penetration of its own barriers. I believe that this task falls to
the critical, emancipatory social sciences – to psychoanalysis and
the critique of ideology[129] – which must draw upon all the empirical-
analytical and normative-analytical social sciences, including
economics.

In connection with this outlined strategy of emancipation there
arises, however, an extremely delicate moral problem. This is the
following question: In what situations and by virtue of what criteria
may one participant in a communicative exchange claim for himself
an emancipated consciousness and consider himself, therefore, to
be authorized to act as a social therapist? But this question is
ultimately identical with the more general problem of the responsible *assessment* of the situation and the *decision* taken in a particular
situation, a decision which – even given the presupposition of our
regulative principles – cannot be taken away from anyone. 'Taking
up a cause' in a concrete, historical situation will always involve a
precarious commitment that can be covered neither by philosophical
nor by scientific knowledge.[130] At this point – and not earlier when
the cause of emancipation is taken up, which, as we attempted to
demonstrate, can be philosophically justified – everyone must take
upon himself a non-groundable – or not completely groundable –
'moral' decision of faith. There exists, however, even in this situation
of the solitary[131] decision apparently no better ethical regulative
than to realize the possible critique of the ideal communication
community in one's own reflexive self-understanding. I believe that
this is the principle of potential moral self-transcendence.

Notes

1 The first part of the present study was my contribution to the panel
discussion on 'Modern Science and Macroethics on a Finite Earth' of the
international colloquium on 'The Meaning and Function of Science in
Contemporary Society', Pennsylvania State University, 6–18
September 1971.
2 Cf. H. Groenewold, 'Science and Macro-ethics on a Finite Earth' (a
contribution to the above-mentioned panel discussion).
3 Cf. Hans Albert, 'Ethik und Metaethik', *Archiv für Philosophie*, 2,
1961, pp. 28–63 (reprinted in H. Albert and E. Topitsch (eds),
Werturteilsstreit, Darmstadt, 1971, pp. 472–517). Also Hans Lenk, 'Der
"Ordinary Language Approach" und die Neutralitätsthese der
Metaethik', in H.-G. Gadamer (ed.), *Das Problem der Sprache*,
Munich, 1967, pp. 183–206 and his 'Kann die sprachanalytische

Moralphilosophie neutral sein?', *Archiv für Rechts-und Sozialphilosophie*, 53, pp. 367–82 (reprinted in *Werturteilsstreit*, pp. 533–51).

4 It is important to note that Kant's ethic of the categorical imperative does not escape such criticism. After being declared inadequate by Hegel on account of its formalism it has been revealed since G. E. Moore as a metaphysical version of the 'naturalistic fallacy' on account of the justification of the 'reality' of moral laws through the 'fact of reason' – not to mention its justification by means of the 'intelligible ego' *qua* 'thing in itself' in the *Groundwork of the Metaphysic of Morals*. Cf. most recently K. H. Ilting, 'Der naturalistische Fehlschluss bei Kant', in M. Riedel (ed.), *Die Rehabilitierung der praktischen Philosophie*, vol. 1, Freiburg, 1972.

5 For evidence of the initial stages of this objectivistic-scientistic-dogmatic reduction of the problem of the mediation of theory and practice even in Marx himself see Dietrich Böhler, *Metakritik der Marxschen Ideologiekritik*, Frankfurt, 1971.

6 Cf. typical of this view is Hans Jörg Sandkühler's introduction to his selection of texts on neo-Kantian socialists, *Marxismus und Ethik*, Frankfurt, 1970.

7 Cf. Alfred N. Whitehead, *Process and Reality*, 1929.

8 Cf. for this analysis of time K.-O. Apel, *Der Denkweg von Charles S. Peirce*, Frankfurt, 1975, pp. 342 ff.

9 In the sense of Martin Heidegger's *Being and Time*, Oxford, 1962.

10 Cf. Peter Winch, *The Idea of a Social Science*, K.-O. Apel, *Analytic Philosophy of Language and the 'Geisteswissenschaften'*, Dordrecht, 1967, and the preceding essays in this volume.

11 Cf. K.-O. Apel, 'Reflexion und materielle Praxis: Zur erkenntnis-anthropologischen Begrundung der Dialektik zwischen Hegel und Marx', *Transformation der Philosophie*, Frankfurt, 1973.

12 Cf., recently, Helmut Seiffert, *Marxismus und bürgerliche Wissenschaft*, Munich, 1971.

13 Cf. K. R. Popper, *The Poverty of Historicism*, 2nd ed., London, 1960.

14 Ibid., p. 54.

15 Cf. also 6.41, 6.421–6.43. One should compare these with the statements on transcendental solipsism, 5.62–5.641.

16 Quoted from G. H. von Wright's 'historical introduction' to the *Prototractatus*, London, 1971, p. 15.

17 Cf. the writings of Albert and Lenk cited above (n. 3).

18 Cf. G. Abramowski, *Das Geschichtsbild M. Webers*, Stuttgart, 1966.

19 Cf. my introduction to C. S. Peirce, *Schriften I*, pp. 13 ff. (reprinted in *Der Denkweg von Charles S. Peirce*, pp. 11–151). However, Peirce himself, the father of 'pragmatism', is not a 'pragmatist' in the sense intended here.

20 Cf. pp. 256 ff below. Like Popper, Dewey was able to present for discussion the ethical implications of his radical democratic conception of a mediation of all individual needs in the organized communication community only in a scientistic, technological reduction.

21 Cf. Hans Albert (*Traktat über Kritische Vernunft,* Tübingen, 1968, pp. 76 ff.) on the so-called 'bridging-principles' that mediate between 'is' and 'ought', facts and norms. Albert sees a possibility for rational critique of moral norms that transcends these bridging principles in an 'ethical pluralism' which is conceived of as a parallel to the 'pluralism of theories' in science. Cf. pp. 256 f. below.

22 Even the individual who finds himself compelled to decide between entire social systems and to place them totally in question is certainly able – contrary to Dewey's opinion (with which Albert, ibid. p. 77, seems to agree) – to raise the question of the ultimate goals of human life.

23 Cf. Sidney Hook, 'The Desirable and Emotion in Dewey's Ethics', in John Dewey, *Philosophy of Science and Freedom,* New York, 1950. Cf. on the other hand, C. S. Peirce: 'the only moral evil is not to have an ultimate aim' (*Collected Papers,* 5.133) and 'In order to understand pragmatism, therefore, well enough to submit it to intelligent criticism, it is incumbent upon us to inquire what an ultimate aim, capable of being pursued in an indefinitely prolonged course of action, can be' (*Collected Papers,* 5.135).

24 Cf. Max Weber, 'Science as a Vocation', in H. Gerth and C. W. Mills (eds), *From Max Weber,* London, 1948, p. 151; cf. also Max Weber, 'Politics as a Vocation', ibid., pp. 77–128.

25 It is indeed not an easy task nowadays to explain to a critical, non-philosophical audience where the *significance* of a philosophical grounding of an intersubjectively valid ethics might lie.

26 By 'methodological individualism' or 'methodological solipsism' I mean the belief, which has still hardly been overcome, that even if a human being, viewed empirically, is a social being, the possibility and validity of forming judgments and intentions can still be basically understood without the *transcendental-logical presupposition of a communication community,* i.e. to a certain extent, as a creative achievement of the individual consciousness. In theoretical philosophy, this results in the hopeless alternative and controversy between the 'introspective' and 'behaviourist' (subjectivistic and objectivistic) grounding of self-understanding and the understanding of others; in practical philosophy, it results in the alternative of 'decisionism' versus the 'naturalistic fallacy'.

27 Cf. H. Schelsky, *Auf der Suche nach Wirklichkeit,* Düsseldorf, 1965, pp. 456 ff.

28 Historically speaking, in its early stages during the modern age, natural science heuristically replaced the empathetic teleological understanding of nature in terms of a Christian Platonism by the methodologically correct reconstructed understanding (*Nachverstehen*) of the divine construction of the world. Cf. K.-O. Apel, 'Das "Verstehen", eine Problemgeschichte als Begriffsgeschichte', *Archiv für Begriffsgeschichte,* 1, 1955, pp. 143 ff.

29 Cf. most recently Karl-Georg Faber, *Theorie der Geschichtswissenschaft,* Munich, 1971, pp. 128 ff. and pp. 165 ff. Also

Detlef Junker, 'Über die Legitimität von Werturteilen in der Geschichtswissenschaft', *Historische Zeitschrift*, 211, no. 1, pp. 1–33.
30 Cf. Imre Lakatos, 'History of Science and its Rational Reconstructions', in R. C. Buck and R. S. Cohen (eds), *Boston Studies in the Philosophy of Science,* vol. 8, Dordrecht, 1971. Unfortunately, the Popperians have still not yet realized that they themselves are helping to provide a better model for the conception of the historical human than the – as yet still predominant – conception of the empirical social sciences. Cf. for a contrasting view, G. Radnitzky, *Contemporary Schools of Metascience,* 2nd ed., Göteborg, 1970; Chicago, 1973. For a more adequate account of this problem, see K.-O. Apel, *Die 'Erklären-Verstehen' – Kontroverse in transzendental pragmatischer Sicht,* Frankfurt, (forthcoming).
31 Cf. Hans Lenk, 'Kann die sprachanalytische Moralphilosophie neutral sein?', in *Werturteilsstreit.*
32 On this point, the Popperian school agrees with Paul Lorenzen and consequently the Popperians themselves must have overcome 'scientism' in Lorenzen's sense since – unlike 'analytical philosophy' – they believe that reason can and must 'be practical'.
33 This has been my thesis ever since my paper 'Sprache und Ordnung', *Akten des 6. Deutschen Kongresses für Philosophie,* Munich, 1960, pp. 200–25 (reprinted in K.-O. Apel, *Transformation der Philosophie,* vol. 1, pp. 167–96).
34 Cf. most recently, ch. 5 in this volume.
35 On this misunderstanding by the Erlangen school, cf. p. 274 below.
36 Of course, it must be admitted that the humanistic ethos in the hermeneutics of the late nineteenth century – when compared, for example, with Herder or Humboldt – was itself already paralysed by positivist objectivism, e.g. by the reduction of Hegel's 'absolute mind' to 'objective mind'. The practical consequences were that ultimately moral sensitization was neutralized in terms of a merely aesthetic sensitization, for instance, along the lines of a pseudo-moral substitution of what is genuine and powerful for what is good.
37 If one seriously considers this dependency of the validity of moral norms upon situational conditions then the ethical relativism that is presented as a finding of the empirical cultural sciences decisively loses its significance as a potential obstacle to the rational grounding of normative ethics.
38 Normally, the German expression would be '*Nächstenliebe*' (charity) but *literally* it corresponds to the English Biblical: 'Love thy neighbour [*Nächste*] as thyself'. Apel plays on this normal usage here to make his point that moral 'imagination' leads people to extend their love of their 'neighbour' to love of those who are far removed from us, i.e. strangers (trans. note).
39 This was the basic significance of my restriction of hermeneutics from the standpoint of the philosophy of science in ch. 2 in this volume. See also J. Habermas, 'Der Universalitätsanspruch der Hermeneutik', in

K.-O. Apel, *et al.*, *Hermeneutik und Ideologiekritik*, Frankfurt, 1971, pp. 120–59.

40 Cf. Y. Bar-Hillel, 'Argumentation in Pragmatic Languages', in Bar-Hillel, *Aspects of Language*, pp. 206–21.

41 In this sense, the thesis of the irreducibility of natural language was expounded in the introduction to my book, *Die Idee der Sprache in der Tradition des Humanismus*, Bonn, 1963. For an opposing view, cf. Kuno Lorenz and Jürgen Mittelstrass, 'Die Hintergehbarkeit der Sprache', *Kantstudien*, 58, 1967, pp. 187–208. On this hitherto completely unresolved controversy, cf. pp. 274 ff. below.

42 I believe that the advantage of the hermeneutic Heideggerian school (in the broadest sense) over the school of the later Wittgenstein can be seen in the fact that it can play off an historical conception against an abstract model conception. But the latent affinity between the two schools can be traced back to their inability to ground either a normative ideal or, as a result, a postulate of ethically relevant progress. Cf. S4 of my Introduction to *Transformation der Philosophie*, vol. 1.

43 Cf. ch. 4 in this volume also Habermas, 'Der Universalitätsanspruch der Hermeneutik', pp. 99 ff.

44 Cf. K. Steinbuch, *Die informierte Gesellschaft*, Stuttgart, 1966.

45 Karl Popper and Hans Albert would probably be willing to admit this. On Ernst Topitsch, cf. Peter Rohs, 'Wie wissenschaftlich ist die wissenschaftliche Naturrechtskritik?', *Philosophiche Rundschau*, 16, 1969, pp. 185–213.

46 Cf. Habermas's 'Introduction' to *Theory and Practice* (trans. J. Viertel), Boston/London, 1974, pp. 16 ff.

47 It can be noted here that I understand the modern theoretical and empirical natural sciences as the product of a synthesis between knowledge gained through labour (techniques of prediction) and Greek metaphysics (*theoria*) which detaches itself from the world.

48 The analogy of theoretical detachment dealt with from here may also be elucidated in terms of the distinction between unproblematized communicative interaction and argumentative discourse which must be unburdened by action in order to fulfil the function of an instance of the possible redemption of problematized validity claims. Cf. J. Habermas, 'Wahrheitstheorien', in *Wirklichkeit und Reflexion*, Pfüllingen, 1973, pp. 211–65.

49 Cf. recently Paul Lorenzen, 'Szientismus versus Dialektik', pp. 68 ff., and critical comments in K.-H. Ilting, 'Anerkennung: zur Rechtfertigung praktischer Sätze', in G. G. Grau (ed.), *Probleme der Ethik*, Freiburg/Munich, 1972, pp. 83–107.

50 Cf. Helmut Plessner, *Die Stufen des Organischen und der Mensch*, Berlin/Leipzig, 1928.

51 In my view, the results of Peirce's 'meaning-critical' realism, interpreted in a transcendental-philosophical manner (cf. my Introduction to *Der Denkweg von Charles S. Peirce*), and the results of

the later Wittgenstein's critique of meaning converge at this point.

52 If one shared Augustine's, Descartes' and Husserl's belief that the 'ego' can be preserved even if one presupposes that the world has been cancelled out, then this only demonstrates, in my opinion, the theological background of the discovery of mankind's 'excentric positionality'. This theological background itself, however, reveals the structure of the 'transcendental language-game' – here it is that of the tacitly presupposed communication between the human being who places the world in question and the trans-terrestrial god who posits the world. In view of the – at least, methodological – atheism of modern philosophy, the 'methodological solipsism' of its classics was bound to enter a crisis. 'One person alone' cannot 'follow a rule' (Wittgenstein), i.e. he cannot 'think'. It is necessary to tacitly presuppose either God or the 'transcendental language-game'.

53 See ch. 2 in this volume, and also 'The *a priori* of Communication and the Foundation of the Humanities', *Man and World*, 5, no. 1, 1972. I believe that this ethically relevant 'complementarity thesis' is essentially confirmed by Oswald Schwemmer's *Philosophie der Praxis,* Frankfurt, 1971, which, in Paul Lorenzen's sense, attempts to lay the 'foundation for a theory of moral argument'. Following Peirce and Royce, I have discussed the regulative principle of the unlimited 'communication' or 'interpretation community' that is both presupposed and still to be established. Schwemmer develops this as follows: 'The establishment of this communality is essential both for the creation of knowledge and understanding. For knowledge and understanding are differentiated from merely believing and interpreting by the fact that the established, general unity is replaced by a necessary universal unity, i.e. it is replaced by the *communality* of believing and interpreting. The creation of knowledge and understanding therefore constitute the two parts of a discussion whose aim is to create a reasonable will. They are the *theoretical* and *hermeneutic* parts of *practical discussion*' (op. cit., p. 125).

54 Cf. n. 30 above.

55 Despite this distinction, which he recognizes in parts, the Popperian Hans Albert (cf. 'Ethik und Metaethik') adheres to this strategy of establishing a parallel between meta-ethics and the logic of science. He apparently works on the assumption that one can, and must, determine the ethical standards for the efficiency of moral systems in the same manner as the rational standards for the efficiency of scientific systems. This replacement of transcendental reflection and the 'reconstruction' – that is dependent upon reflection – of the complementary cognitive interests of the logic of research and ethics through the construction – that is dependent on decisions – of a *singular* rationality, in my view, obliterates the fundamental distinction between meta-scientific methodology and ethics – a residual scientism that is characteristic of the normativist Popperians (in contrast to the unrestricted scientism of the logical empiricists). This residual scientism is particularly crass when Albert suggests in his *Traktat über kritische Vernunft* (pp. 78 f.)

that the final grounding of ethics, which is in principle impossible, be replaced in accordance with the critique of science, by the methodological proliferation of alternative ethics along the lines of a 'pluralism of theories'. It should not be denied that the critical comparison of ethical theories is instructive. We owe this insight, however, to the historical human sciences and comparative cultural anthropology (and consequently Hans Lenk seeks to draw upon their methods in his proposed 'meta-meta-ethics' which even detaches itself from the various 'metaethics' (cf. *Werturteilsstreit*, pp. 546 ff.)). Yet the critical effect, anticipated by Albert (and Lenk?), can apparently only come about if one can already presuppose a normatively non-neutral meta-ethics of argumentative standards for the confrontation of ethics. Failing such a standard, the method of 'proliferation', that has long been anticipated by 'historicism', has hitherto tended to lead to moral relativism and nihilism. But in practical (moral) terms, the latter is not as harmless as the corresponding pluralism or conventionalism in the logic of science. This is connected with the distinction between scientific and historical experiments or, more accurately, with the distinction between 'experiments' and 'interactions' – a distinction that has never been recognized by the Popperians. As human beings, we cannot set ourselves up beyond (or besides) morals in the same manner in which we can decline to accept certain theories, as Descartes himself was aware. Nevertheless, we must justify morals in philosophical and theoretical terms. That is the problem.

56 Cf. especially Kuno Lorenz, 'Die Ethik der Logik', in H.-G. Gadamer (ed.), *Das Problem der Sprache*, pp. 80–6.
57 In this sense, Kant emphasizes that 'the problem of organizing a state . . . can be solved even for a race of devils, if only they are intelligent', I. Kant, 'Perpetual Peace', in L. W. Beck (ed.), *Kant: On History*, Indianapolis/New York, 1963, p. 112.
58 Cf. O. R. Jones (ed.), *The Private Language Argument*, London, 1971. In my opinion, Wittgenstein's thesis – if understood correctly – has nothing to do with behaviourism. In fact, behaviourism, which replaces the *understanding* of action – that is dependent upon communication – with the *observation of behaviour*, presupposes *methodological solipsism* on the part of the knowing subject just as much as so-called *introspectionism* does. Both classical positions of positivism are avoided by an approach that comprehends the *understanding of the self and others* under the presupposition – which is, I believe, a *transcendental-hermeneutic* presupposition – of the language-game of *communication*. Yet in order to comprehend understanding of the self and others, one must comprehend the preconditions for the possibility and *validity* of the understanding of *meaning*, e.g. the conditions which govern the meaning of 'rule' and 'following a rule'. The presupposition of the language-game as the precondition of the criteria for testing, and consequently for the *validity* of the *meaning* of 'rule' and 'rule-following', is at issue when Wittgenstein says: 'Never can one person alone have followed a rule' (*Philosophical Investigations*, vol. 1, § 199).

This is not to assert that the individual by himself, i.e. on his own
initiative or independently, is incapable – in terms of his capacities or
abilities – of following a rule. Even if, as Chomsky and Lenneberg
suggest, each individual *qua* human being possesses the innate
disposition to acquire a language, the establishment (testing) of his
'competence' is dependent upon the existence of a *public language-
game*. One consequence is that one cannot speak of 'grammatical
competence' (Chomsky) without presupposing the 'communicative
competence' (Habermas) of interlocutions in the *pragmatic*
dimension of *speech*. Cf. ch. 6 in this volume.
59 Wittgenstein's insight into the 'interwovenness' of linguistic
utterances, actions and physical expressions can be interpreted in this
sense. Moreover, the thesis that all actions and gestures can, in
principle, be verbalized, is suggested by Austin's discovery of
'performative utterances' and their generalization and radicalization in
John Searle's 'speech act' theory. CF. J. Habermas, 'Vorbereitende
Bemerkungen zu einer Theorie der kommunikativen Kompetenz', in
J. Habermas and N. Luhmann, *Theorie der Gesellschaft oder
Sozialtechnologie.*
60 Cf. J. R. Searle, *Speech Acts,* and Habermas, op. cit.
61 Cf. recently also Y. Bar-Hillel, 'Argumentation in Pragmatic
Languages'.
62 Cf. Paul Lorenzen, *Normative Logic and Ethics,* Mannheim/Zurich,
1969; and also his 'Szientismus versus Dialektik', pp. 57–72.
63 This interpretation implies, however, that it is not the fact that all
science presupposes norms and, therefore, 'practical reason', but
rather it is the fact that the *monological* following of norms
presupposes the *dialogical* explication of the meaning of norms and the
testing of the validity of norms, which makes possible the transition
from the normative logic of science to ethics. A certain vagueness at
this point on Lorenzen's part is, in my opinion, *one* reason why
Habermas believes that he must regard his approach, which develops
out of the 'dialogue-constitutive universals' of the 'ideal speech-
situation', not as an extension and elucidation, but rather as an
alternative to the ultimately 'monological' strategy of the 'ethics of
logic'. (Cf. J. Habermas, 'Einige Bemerkungen zum Problem der
Begrundung von Werturteilen', in L. Landgrebe (ed.), *9. Deutscher
Kongress für Philosophie* (Düsseldorf, 1969), Meisenheim, 1972, pp.
89–99.) But when Habermas distinguishes the 'logical competence' (as
well as the 'grammatical competence') as the pre-verbal capacity for
monological operations (in Chomsky's and Piaget's sense) from
'communicative competence', and places his 'hope' in the latter and
not in the 'ethics of logic', he seems to overlook the following: The
'logical competence' of following rules (like 'grammatical
competence') is indeed not a 'communicative competence' and
consequently not a 'moral' competence. Both types of competence
can, in fact, be strictly distinguished, and undoubtedly, the decision as
to the ethical meaning of sentences is taken at the pragmatic level of

speech acts, whose deep structure contains the linguistic conditions for the possibility of *interpersonal communication* and *interaction* – including 'personal deixis' as the linguistic precondition for the possibility of intersubjective 'recognition'. Nor, however, is 'logical' (and 'grammatical') competence identical with the pre-linguistic (innate) dispositions which both Piaget and Chomsky have assumed in order to 'explain' competence and have, in so doing, made plausible. Rather, it can only be formed in the process of socialization *together with* 'communicative competence'. This means that 'logical' competence presupposes communicative, and consequently moral, competence as the 'complementary' precondition for its possibility. Within the context of this study, I have relied upon the fact that logic pragmatically *presupposes* – and not logically implies – ethics. I have done so since I believe that providing a cogent foundation for ethics is *not only* a matter of explicating the ethics of the ideal (e.g. symmetrical, transparent, undistorted, etc.) speech and interaction situation that is implied by the system of 'dialogue-constitutive universals' but rather that one must also demonstrate that 'argument' – and consequently 'monological thought' – is not possible and cannot be valid if one does not presuppose dialogical ethics. Upon this – and, in this sense, upon the 'ethics of logic' – depends, as we shall show, the possibility of a final grounding of ethics. The other question raised by Habermas, namely the relationship between 'deontic logic' ('modal calculus') and 'universal pragmatics' thereby remains, of course, untouched. Cf. however pp. 262 ff. below.

64 See n. 52 above on the 'complementarity thesis'.

65 Charles S. Peirce, *Collected Papers*, vol. 5, §§ 354 ff; cf. also vol. 2, § 654.

66 Cf. Albert, *Traktat über kritische Vernunft*, ch. 1. For an attempted meta-critique of Albert's 'critical rationalism' see my essay 'The Problem of Philosophical Fundamental Grounding in the Light of a Transcendental Pragmatic of Language', in *Man and World*, 18, 1975, pp. 239–75. For a reply to this, see H. Albert, *Transzendentale Träumereien*, Hamburg, 1975.

67 Cf. Albert, *Traktat*, p. 14.

68 Cf. Wolfgang Stegmüller, *Metaphysik, Skepsis, Wissenschaft*, Berlin/Heidelberg/New York, 1959, 2nd ed. Also Hans Lenk, 'Logikbegründung und rationaler Kritizismus', *Zeitschrift für philosophische Forschung*, vol. 24, 1970, pp. 183–205. On the connection between the problem of the foundations of logic and mathematics, on the one hand, and the problem of transcendental reflection, on the other, cf. especially Gerhard Frey, *Sprache-Ausdruck des Bewusstseins*, Stuttgart, 1965.

69 In anticipation of this insight, Hegel had already concentrated on the 'speculative statement'. Today it ought at least to be evident that a real confrontation between modern logic and the logic of the 'existing concept' (i.e. 'thought') that Hegel sought to establish will only be possible when the *syntactic-semantic* abstraction of modern mathematical logic has been fully recognized as such and when a

'transcendental pragmatics' of argumentation has been developed.

70 Cf. Charles W. Morris, 'Foundations of the Theory of Signs', *Encyclopaedia of Unified Science,* vol. 1, no. 2, Chicago, 1938. Cf. ch. 4 in this volume.
71 Cf. for example, Rudolf Carnap, 'Empiricism, Semantics and Ontology', in Leonard Linsky (ed.), *Semantics and the Philosophy of Language*, Urbana, Ill., 1952.
72 This is, for example, Wilhelm Essler's standpoint. Cf. Wilhelm K. Essler, *Wissenschaftstheorie II:* 'Theorie und Erfahrung', Freiburg/Munich, 1971, ch. 1.
73 None the less, Theodor Litt, basing himself on Hegel, has clearly worked out the distinction between the psychological or mathematical expression of reflection as 'infinite regress' and the 'self-elevation' of transcendental reflection to the stage of 'meaning universals' (from the stage of comparative universals of empirical-generalizing 'science' via the hermeneutic stage of interpreted meaning of human intentions to the philosophical stage of transcendental concept formation and the noological self-reflection of this concept formation). Cf. T. Litt, *Denken und Sein,* Stuttgart, 1948; his *Mensch und Welt,* 2nd ed., Heidelberg, 1961; his *Hegel: Versuch einer kritischen Erneuerung,* 2nd ed., Heidelberg, 1961.
74 Cf. Habermas, who develops this from a discussion of Austin, Strawson and Searle in 'Wahrheitstheorien' in H. Fahrenbach (ed.), *Wirklichkeit und Reflexion: Festschrift für Walter Schulz,* Pfüllingen, 1973, pp. 211–65. Cf. also Y. Bar-Hillel, *Aspects of Language,* esp. chs 16 ('Argumentation in Natural Languages'), 17 ('Argumentation in Pragmatic Languages') and 24 ('Do Natural Languages Contain Paradoxes?').
75 Cf. Bar-Hillel, *Aspects of Language,* ch. 24.
76 Nevertheless, Alfred Tarski formulates in *natural language* the conjecture that 'the very possibility of a consistent use of the expression "true sentence" which is in harmony with the laws of logic and the spirit of everyday language seems to be very questionable'. *Logic, Semantics, Mathematics,* Oxford, 1956, ch. 8, p. 164 (cited in Bar-Hillel, *Aspects of Language,* p. 277).
77 On this and what follows, cf. the excellent study by Lenk, 'Philosophische Logikbegründung und Rationaler Kritizismus'.
78 Cf. William Warren Bartley, *The Retreat to Commitment*, New York, 1962, pp. 171 ff.
79 Lenk, 'Philosophiche Logikbegründung', pp. 201 f.
80 Ibid., p. 203.
81 I believe that the methodological correspondence between the heuristic mental procedure actually adopted by Bartley and Lenk, on the one hand, and the transcendental approach in Kant's sense, on the other, is not really placed in question by Lenk's quasi-Wittgensteinian reference to the 'analytical' connection between the rules of the logic of consequences and the (idea of the) institution of criticism. Cf. ibid., pp. 204 f.

82 Cf. I. Kant, *Critique of Pure Reason*, trans. N. Kemp Smith, London, 1933, 2nd imp., pp. xxiii, xxxvii.
83 Cf. ch. 3 in this volume. Incidentally, in the ability to anticipate the 'highest point' of a semiotically transformed transcendental philosophy – in the identification of a thinking human being with an unlimited community of interpretation – I would recognize, like Peirce, the precondition for the possibility of the 'unity of consciousness of the object and self-consciousness' in Kant's sense.
84 Cf. Karl R. Popper, *The Open Society and its Enemies*, 2 vols, 5th ed., London, 1966.
85 Cf. ibid., vol. 2, pp. 228 ff.
86 Ibid., p. 233.
87 It is quite simply incorrect to assert that logically a 'comprehensive irrationalism is tenable', for it cannot be defended *a priori*. Moreover, the fact 'that one can always refuse to accept arguments' (ibid., p. 231) is irrelevant for those engaged in argument and, therefore, for every individual thinker. That Popper and many others consider it relevant is connected, in my opinion, with 'methodological solipsism' which, to some extent, permits the refusal to accept arguments to count as a private para-argument.
88 Cf. K.-O. Apel, 'Sprache und Reflexion', *Akten des 14. Internationalen Kongresses für Philosophie* (Vienna, 1968), vol. 2, Vienna, 1969, pp. 417–29. Also K.-O. Apel, 'Sprache als Thema und Medium der transzendentalen Reflexion', *Sprache und Erkenntnis*, Meisenheim, 1972 (reprinted in *Transformation der Philosophie*, vol. 2, pp. 311–29).
89 I believe that this can be empirically corroborated in terms of clinical psychopathology.
90 It is obvious that at this point I can only assert the immorality of the norms mentioned. It is, however, sufficient here to give examples which prove that the free acknowledgment of immoral norms is conceivable.
91 Cf. p. 238 f. above. With the actual *acknowledgment* of a contract one, naturally, undertakes an obligation – similarly, one does so through the illocutionary act of *promising*. Yet I believe that it is misleading to interpret this statement of an 'institutional fact', as Searle does (*Speech Acts*, pp. 185 ff.), as the 'derivation of an "ought" from an "is"'. For our *judgment* that an obligation arises for someone who has committed himself is not identical with the empirical statement that the person in question has committed himself. It does not follow merely from this statement *alone*, but rather from it *and* the normative presupposition that obligations must be fulfilled if they do not run counter to any more serious duties. For a thorough discussion of this problem, cf. my essay 'Sprechakttheorie und transzendentale Sprachpragmatik zur Frage ethischer Normen', in K.-O. Apel (ed.), *Sprachpragmatik und Philosophie*.
92 Cf. also on the point, Schwemmer, *Philosophie der Praxis*, pp. 193 ff.
93 Cf. Ilting, 'Der naturalistische Fehlschluss bei Kant'.
94 Cf. Kant himself, *Critique of Practical Reason*, A56, A81, A163, A187.

On this, cf. Dieter Henrich, 'Der Begriff der sittlichen Einheit und Kants Lehre von Faktum der Vernunft', in D. Henrich *et al.* (eds), *Die Gegenwart der Griechen im neueren Denken: Festschrift für H.-G. Gadamer*, Tübingen, 1960, pp. 77–115, and Schwemmer, *Philosophie der Praxis*, p. 198.

95 Cf. E.-K. Specht, 'Der Analogiebegriff bei Kant und Hegel', *Kantstudien*, Ergänzungsheft 66, Cologne, 1952.

96 I have always thought that one of the fascinating aspects of Heidegger's *Being and Time* is to be found in the 'have always' or 'in each case' of the reference to the *'a priori* perfect' of existential presuppositions. These, of course, are not anchored by Heidegger in the uncontestable validity of an *a priori* of argumentation. Rather, they tend to form a continuum with the hermeneutic meaning *a priori* of historical facticity that certainly cannot be ignored but can nevertheless be criticized and, therefore, be corrected; cf. p. 276 below.

97 Kant, *Critique of Practical Reason*, A2; cf. Ilting, op. cit., pp. 14 ff.

98 Cf. Schwemmer, *Philosophie der Praxis*, pp. 198 ff. and also Dieter Henrich, *Fichtes ursprüngliche Einsicht*, Frankfurt, 1967.

99 J. G. Fichte, *Werke* (ed. Fritz Medicus), vol. 4, Leipzig, 1910–11, p. 206.

100 Paul Lorenzen, *Normative Logic and Ethics*, p. 74. K.-H. Ilting rightly points out that Lorenzen thereby fulfils the conditions of his own definition of 'scientism' in 'Szientismus versus Dialektik', op. cit., pp. 58 ff. and p. 72, in one sense at least (cf. 'Anerkennung: zur Rechtfertigung praktischer Sätze', p. 1).

101 Cf. Lorenzen, *Normative Logics and Ethics*, p. 74.

102 Cf. Schwemmer, *Philosophie der Praxis*, pp. 194 ff.

103 Even Ilting does not see that fortunately the difficult basic situation to which he draws attention, namely, that one must justify the basic moral norm without being permitted to presuppose any norm at all, cannot occur. Anyone who is interested philosophically in grounding the basic norm is able to appreciate through transcendental reflection that he is already presupposing this norm.

104 I must, therefore, also reject as a misunderstanding Habermas's remark in n. 160 of his *Legitimation Crisis*, Boston/London, 1975, pp. xx ff., that my insistency upon a *conscious (voluntary) affirmation (re-confirmation)* of one's membership in the community of argumentation amounts to preserving a 'residual stance of decisionism'. I believe that this assessment rests on a confusion of the question of *replacing the fundamental grounding of norms by decision* – a position that, in fact, should be called 'decisionism' – with the question of *committing oneself to the realization of the norms of reason*. Whereas Popper (and most analytical philosophers, including even Paul Lorenzen) seem to fall victim to this confusion by giving in to decisionism – i.e. by overlooking the possibility of grounding norms by transcendental-pragmatic reflection – Habermas seems to fall into the opposite extreme of overlooking the indispensable function of goodwill for putting into force, so to speak, the norms of reason in

ourselves. I completely agree with Habermas's claim that 'the fundamental error of methodological solipsism lies in the assumption of the possibility not only of purely monological *thought*, but also of purely monological *action*' (ibid.; cf. my own account for the presupposition of the transcendental language-game through the very act of decision as intelligible action). Nevertheless, I must insist on the possibility, in principle, of our *voluntary denial* of – I would say – the *normative conditions of the possibility* of our very identity as human beings. Without conceiving of this possibility, and hence also of the necessity of an 'existential act' of 'voluntary re-confirmation' of what we indeed must have already implicitly acknowledged as the normative precondition for the possibility of arguing (and, furthermore, of acting meaningfully), I could not conceive of the human dignity that lies in our being an addressee of an ethical 'right'.

105 It seems to me that the Erlangen school is quite correct when it interprets the later Wittgenstein's critical withdrawal from cultivated philosophical language – whose connections with everyday language had become obscure – and his recourse to everyday language as the 'destructive' part of an undertaking that only attains its goal in the *normative reconstruction* of cultivated philosophical language itself. Cf. Kuno Lorenz, *Elemente der Sprachkritik: eine Alternative zum Dogmatismus und Skeptizismus in der analytischen Philosophie*, Frankfurt, 1970.

106 Cf. Lorenz and Mittelstrass, 'Die Hintergehbarkeit der Sprache', *Kantstudien*, pp. 187–208. Cf. p. 251 above.

107 I think that *de facto* both Kamlah's and Lorenzen's 'logical propadeutics' and Schwemmer's 'philosophy of praxis' completely confirm that the 'direct' reconstruction of language is bound up with the 'hermeneutic circle', provided one ignores the occasional assurance that it could also be carried out quite differently than it is – if the author had the time and could go back to the immediate acquisition of language in practical life situations. If, however, the methodological reconstruction of language in a situation of paradigmatic teaching or learning is not to amount to 'drill' (as Wittgenstein formulated it in a serious misunderstanding of language learning and the process of socialization) then even the dialogical explication of the meaning and validity of the logic of junctors and quantors must always have presupposed a certain *linguistic competence* on the part of those engaged in the dialogue (even if – as Habermas no doubt correctly assumes along with Chomsky – an innate *preverbal disposition* makes the development of both *logical* and *grammatical competence* possible). But if it is a matter of reconstructing the substantive 'predicators' of cultivated language – if, for instance, we are dealing with 'protoethics' – then in my view the hermeneutic circle of the factual and normative genesis of history that Lorenzen himself calls for in order to create for the *formal* normative principle – in the spirit of Hegel – the *content* of its potential application (*Normative Logic and Ethics*, pp. 84 ff; cf. Schwemmer, *Philosophie der Praxis*, pp. 207 ff.)

will already be bound up with the reconstruction of language. It is indeed an illusion to think that one can introduce in an exemplary manner the predicators that are necessary for the construction of a protoethical terminology without already working on a speculative, thematical project and without entering into discussion with the philosophical tradition. Even without drawing upon such 'sorcery', the Erlangen approach – as a *reconstruction* of language that is dependent upon reflection – can, in my opinion, lead to philosophically relevant suggestions that are, however, open to criticism. Above all, as we are attempting to demonstrate here, the *starting-point* can consist of the *reconstruction of the principle* that is *implicitly* presupposed in the 'transcendental language-game' and, as a result, in every language-game of culturated and everyday language.

108 This is not a plea for 'collectivism' but rather for solidarity on the part of responsible people, cf. n. 130 below.

109 Cf. n. 64 above.

110 And also Henry James Sr. who – since he belonged to the tradition of Böhme, Swedenborg and religious socialism – saw in private idiosyncrasy the sign of sin *qua* estrangement from God. Cf. Gerd Wartenberg, *Logischer Sozialismus: die Transformation der Kantischen Transzendentalphilosophie durch Charles S. Peirce*, Frankfurt, 1971.

111 By 'justification' I do not understand the *definitive justification*, which – according to Peirce and Popper – cannot exist for scientific statements (assertions). Nevertheless, I believe that the traditional demand for 'justification' is still meaningful; in any case, it cannot be replaced by the demand for 'criticism' as the Popperians suggest. One cannot fail to notice that in his *Traktat über kritische Vernunft*, for example, Albert attempts to *justify* critical rationalism's approach against all criticism. The participants in communication do indeed have a moral claim to be informed by the person who is addressing them about everything that *rebus sic stantibus* speaks for an *assertion* – or for a *motion* or *suggestion*.

112 In this sense, Lorenzen rightly characterizes the basic moral norm as the principle of 'transsubjectivity'; cf. *Normative Logic and Ethics*, p. 82.

113 Conversely, one cannot – I believe – justify the claims of human beings by tracing them back to 'true needs', e.g. through the 'normative genesis' of 'cultural needs' from 'natural needs'. For it is precisely natural, human needs – i.e. food, shelter, sexuality, etc. – that are obviously morally relevant and can be ethically justified only as cultural needs. This means that they can only be justified ethically as *claims* that can be satisfied in a given social situation (e.g. at a given stage in the development of the 'forces of production'). I believe, however, that the normative genesis of cultural from natural needs indeed has a function within the practical discourse in terms of a critique of ideology. The justification of needs, however, also entails the confrontation of subjectively 'real' needs with the 'reality principle' (Freud), and this

confrontation, in turn, requires a normative and empirical genesis of the social situation, e.g. of the development of the 'forces of production' and the 'relations of production' (Marx) and *also* of the political power situation within a given state.

114 This is surely the focal point of the Erlangen school's approach.

115 The examples which Kant gives of the application of the 'categorical imperative' – especially in the treatise 'Concerning an alleged right, namely lying out of love of humanity' – demonstrates in my opinion that he did not sufficiently reflect upon the dependence of the validity of material norms upon situations. Nor did he reflect sufficiently upon the related problem of moral responsibility for all effects and side-effects. In order to make the truth apparent here, one might indulge in an exaggeration of the history of philosophy and claim that, with his justification of the 'autonomy' of the law-giving 'good-will', Kant overcame the era of the heteronomous 'ethics of commandments'. At the same time, however, he grounded an 'ethics of conviction' that still – secretly – assumes that human beings' 'goodwill', which is the sole essential factor, is rewarded (by a god who, to some extent, retains the real responsibility for what happens in the world, including its history?). Now, however, the era of a true 'ethics of responsibility' seems to have begun. Ultimately, 'goodwill' is not crucial, but rather that what is good is realized. Human beings must take upon themselves the responsibility for this undertaking.

116 Cf. Weber, 'Politics as a Vocation'.

117 Jean-Paul Sartre, *L'Existentialisme est un humanisme*, Paris, 1946.

118 Indeed, Kant himself did this *de facto* in his notion of the 'world-bourgeois society'.

119 We should leave this crassest form of the 'naturalistic fallacy', which evidently serves to relativize the will to argue and justify philosophically as an epiphenomenon of 'bourgeois' social structure, to a certain form of Marxist neo-orthodoxy.

120 Cf. on this and the following, Apel, 'Scientism or Transcendental Hermeneutics?'; cf. Habermas, 'Der Universalitätsanspruch der Hermeneutik', pp. 99 ff. and also Habermas, 'Vorbereitende Bemerkungen zu einer Theorie de kommunikativen Kompetenz', pp. 140 f.

121 Cf. Chaim Perelman and L. Olbrechts-Tyteca, *Traité de l'argumentation: la nouvelle rhétorique*, 2nd ed., Brussels, 1970.

122 Cf. Chaim Perelman, 'The New Rhetoric', in *The Great Ideas Today* (*Encyclopaedia Britannica*, 1970, pp. 273–312); and also Apel, *Die Idee der Sprache in der Tradition des Humanismus*.

123 Cf. K.-O. Apel, 'Reflexion und materielle Praxis: zur erkenntnis anthropologischen Begründung der Dialektik zwischen Hegel und Marx', *Hegelstudien*, Beiheft 1 (Heidelberger Hegeltage, 1962), pp. 151–66 (reprinted in Apel, *Transformation der Philosophie*, vol. 2, pp. 9–27).

124 Cf. Habermas and Luhmann, *Theorie der Gesellschaft oder Sozialtechnologie*.

125 Cf. Habermas, 'Vorbereitende Bemerkungen'.
126 Cf. K. Marx, 'Critique of Hegel's Doctrine of the State', in K. Marx, *Early Writings*, trans. R. Livingstone and G. Benton, London, 1975, pp. 146 f.
127 Cf. Radnitzky, *Contemporary Schools of Metascience*, 2nd ed. Further, G. Radnitzky, 'Der Praxisbezung der Forschung', *Studium Generale*, 23, 1970, pp. 817–55; G. Radnitzky and G. Anderson, 'Wissenschaftspolitik und Organisationsformen der Forschung' (Introduction to A. Weinberg, *Probleme der Grossforschung*, Frankfurt, 1970); W. Diederich (ed.), *Theorien der Wissenschaftsgechichte*, Frankfurt, 1974; and *Die gesellschaftliche Orientierung des wissenschaftlichen Fortschritts*, Starnberger Studien I, Frankfurt, 1978.
128 Cf. Lorenzen, *Normative Logic and Ethics*, pp. 88 ff.; and Schwemmer, *Philosophie der Praxis*, pp. 207 ff.
129 Cf. K.-O. Apel *et al.*, *Hermeneutik und Ideologiekritik*, Frankfurt, 1971, and J. Habermas, Introduction to *Theory and Practice* trans. J. Viertel, Boston/London, 1974. Further, Apel, 'Types of Social Science'.
130 Cf. K.-O. Apel, 'Wissenschaft als Emanzipation?', *Zeitschrift für allgemeine Wissenschaftstheorie*, 1, 1970, pp. 73–95 (reprinted in Apel, *Transformation der Philosophie*, vol. 2, pp. 128–54. Further, K.-O. Apel, 'The Conflicts of Our Time and the Problem of Political Ethics', in F. R. Dallmayr (ed.), *From Contract to Community: Political Theory at the Crossroads*, New York, 1978, pp. 81–103.
131 Even if a politically relevant decision is at issue, the responsibility will have to be borne by 'individuals' who can perhaps identify themselves with groups but cannot leave the decision to the collectivity. Existentialism, rather than Marxist neo-orthodoxy, is correct here since the individual can always identify himself, as a person engaged in argumentation, with the ideal communication community. He should presuppose this transcendental identification and adhere to it even if he identifies himself – in a precarious political-existential engagement – with an actual social group.

BIBLIOGRAPHY
(With special reference to Chapter 6)

ALBERT, HANS (1975), *Transzendentale Träumereien, Karl-Otto Apels Sprachspiele und seine hermeneutischer Gott,* Hamburg, 1975.

APEL, KARL-OTTO (1955), 'Das "Verstehen": eine Problemgeschichte als Begriffsgeschichte', *Archiv für Begriffsgeschichte* (Bonn), 1, pp. 142–99.

APEL, K.-O. (1959), 'Sprache und Wahrheit in der gegenwärtigen Situation der Philosophie', *Philosophische Rundschau,* 7, pp. 161–84 (reprinted in K.-O. Apel, *Transformation der Philosophie,* vol. 1, Frankfurt, 1973, pp. 138–66).

APEL, K.-O. (1960), 'Sprache und Ordnung', in *Das Problem der Ordnung* (6th German Philosophical Congress, Munich, 1960), Meisenheim am Glan (reprinted in K.-O. Apel, *Transformation der Philosophie,* vol. 1, Frankfurt, 1973, pp. 167–96).

APEL, K.-O. (1963), *Die Idee der Sprache in der Tradition des Humanismus von Dante bis Vico, (Archiv für Begriffsgeschichte,* vol. 8, Bonn, 1963; 2nd ed., 1975).

APEL, K.-O. (1965), 'Die Entfaltung der sprachanalytischen Philosophie und das Problem der "Geisteswissenschaften",' *Philosophisches Jahrbuch,* 72, pp. 239–89 (English trans., *Analytic Philosophy of Language and the 'Geisteswissenschaften',* Dordrecht, 1967).

APEL, K.-O. (1967), Introduction to C. S. Peirce, *Schriften I,* Frankfurt, pp. 13–154 (reprinted in K.-O. Apel, *Der Denkweg von Charles S. Peirce,* Frankfurt, 1975, pp. 11–151).

APEL, K.-O. (1968), 'Heideggers Radikalisierung der Hermeneutik und die Frage nach dem Sinnkriterium der Sprache', in *Die hermeneutische Frage in der Theologie,* Freiburg, 1968, pp. 86–155 (reprinted in K.-O. Apel, *Transformation der Philosophie,* vol. 1, Frankfurt, 1973, pp. 276–334).

APEL, K.-O. (1968), 'Szientistik, Hermeneutik, Ideologiekritik: Entwurf einer Wissenschaftstheorie in erkenntnisanthropologischer Sicht', *Wiener Jahrbuch für Philosophie,* I, pp. 15–45 (English trans. in this volume, ch. 2).

APEL, K.-O. (1970), 'Szientismus oder transzendentale Hermeneutik? Zur Frage nach dem Subjekt der Zeicheninterpretation in der Semiotik des Pragmatismus', in *Hermeneutik und Dialektik, Festschrift* for Hans-Georg Gadamer, vol. 1, Tübingen, pp. 105–44 (English trans. in this volume, ch. 4).

APEL, K.-O. (1970), Introduction to C. S. Peirce, *Schriften II,* Frankfurt, pp. 11–214 (reprinted in K.-O. Apel, *Der Denkweg von Charles S. Peirce,* Frankfurt, 1975, pp. 153–355).

APEL, K.-O. (1972), 'From Kant to Peirce: The Semiotical Transformation of the Transcendental Logic', in L. W. Beck (ed.), *Transactions of the Third International Kant Congress* (Rochester, 1970), Dordrecht, 1972, pp. 90–104 (reprinted in this volume, ch. 3).

APEL, K.-O. (1972), 'Die Kommunikationsgemeinschaft als transzendentale Voraussetzung der Sozialwissenschaften', *Neue Hefte für Philosophie,* 1, nos 2–3, pp. 1–40 (English trans. in this volume, ch. 5).

APEL, K.-O. (1976), 'Sprechakttheorie und transzendentale Sprachpragmatik zur Frage ethischer Normen', in K.-O. Apel (ed.), *Sprachpragmatik und Philosophie,* Frankfurt, 1976, pp. 10–173.

AUSTIN, J. L. (1961), 'Performative Utterances', in *Philosophical Papers,* Oxford, pp. 220–39.

AUSTIN, J. L. (1962), *How to do Things with Words,* Oxford, 1962.

BAR-HILLEL, YEHOSHUA (1954), 'Logical Syntax and Semantics', *Languge,* 30, pp. 30–7 (reprinted in Bar-Hillel (1964), pp. 38–46).

BAR-HILLEL, Y. (1954), 'Indexical Expressions', *Mind,* 63, pp. 359–79 (reprinted in Bar-Hillel (1970)).

BAR-HILLEL, Y. (1960), 'A Prerequisite for Rational Philosophical Discussion', *Synthese,* 12, pp. 328–32 (reprinted in Bar-Hillel (1970), pp. 258–62).

BAR-HILLEL, Y. (1964), *Language and Information,* Reading, Mass.

BAR-HILLEL, Y. (1967), Review of J. A. Fodor and J. J. Katz (eds) (1964), *Language,* 43, pp. 526–50 (reprinted in Bar-Hillel (1970), pp. 150–201).

BAR-HILLEL, Y. (1969), 'Argumentation in Pragmatic Languages', in Bar-Hillel (1970), pp. 206–21.

BAR-HILLEL, Y. (1970), *Aspects of Language,* Jerusalem, 1970.

BIERWISCH, MANFRED (1966), 'Strukturalismus: Geschichte, Probleme und Methoden', *Kursbuch,* 5, pp. 77–152 (English trans. *Modern Linguistics: Its Development, Methods and Problems,* The Hague, 1971).

CARNAP, RUDOLF (1956), 'The Methodological Character of Theoretical Concepts', in H. Feigl and M. Scriven (eds), *Minnesota Studies in the Philosophy of Science,* vol. 1, Minneapolis, pp. 38–76.

CHOMSKY, NOAM (1955), 'Logical Syntax and Semantics: their Linguistic Relevance', *Language,* 31, pp. 36–45.

CHOMSKY, N. (1957), *Syntactic Structures,* The Hague.

CHOMSKY, N. (1959), 'Review of B. F. Skinner, *Verbal Behavior',* *Language,* 35, pp. 26–58 (reprinted in Fodor and Katz (eds), 1964).

CHOMSKY, N. (1961), 'On the notion "rule of grammar"', in Roman Jakobson (ed.), *Structure of Language and its Mathematical Aspects,* Providence, Rhode Island.

CHOMSKY, N. (1964), *Current Issues in Linguistic Theory*, The Hague.
CHOMSKY, N. (1965), *Aspects of the Theory of Syntax*, Cambridge, Mass.
CHOMSKY, N. (1966), *Topics in the Theory of Generative Grammar*, The Hague.
CHOMSKY, N. (1966), *Cartesian Linguistics*, New York and London.
CHOMSKY, N. (1968), *Language and Mind*, New York.
CHOMSKY, N. (1968), Noam Chomsky and Stuart Hampshire discuss the study of language (BBC Third Programme, 8 June 1968). Reprinted in Mark Lester (ed.), *Readings in Applied Transformational Grammar*, New York and London, 1970, pp. 100–13.
CHOMSKY, N. (1969), 'Linguistics and Philosophy', in Sidney Hood (ed.), *Language and Philosophy*, New York, pp. 51–93.
COSERIU, EUGENIO (1968), 'Sincronia, diacronia y tipologia', in *Actas del XI Congresco Internacional de Linguistica y Filologia Románicas*, Madrid, 1968, pp. 269–83.
COSERIU, E. (1970), 'Semantik, Innere Sprachform und Tiefenstruktur', *Folia Linguistica*, 4, pp. 53–63.
FODOR, J. A. AND KATZ, J. J. (eds) (1964), *The Structure of Language: Readings in the Philosophy of Language*, Englewood Cliffs, New Jersey.
FREY, GERHARD (1965), *Sprache: Ausdruck des Bewusstseins*, Stuttgart.
GAUGER, HANS-MARTIN (1969), 'Die Semantik in der Sprachtheorie der transformationellen Grammatik', *Linguistische Berichte*, 1, pp. 1–18.
GOODMAN, NELSON (1967), 'The Epistemological Argument', in 'Symposium on Innate Ideas', *Synthese*, 17, no. 1, 1967, pp. 12–28 (reprinted in *Boston Studies in the Philosophy of Science*, vol. III, 1967, pp. 91–107).
HABERMAS, JÜRGEN (1967), *Erkenntnis und Interesse*, Frankfurt (English trans. *Knowledge and Human Interests*, Boston, 1971/London, 1972).
HABERMAS, J. (1970), 'Kritische Bemerkungen zum elementaristischen Programm einer allgemeinen Semantik', Mimeographed working paper.
HABERMAS, J. (1970), 'Einführende Bemerkungen zu einer Theorie der kommunikativen Kompetenz', Mimeographed working paper.
HABERMAS, J. (1971), 'Vorbereitende Bemerkungen zu einer Theorie der kommunikativen Kompetenz', in Habermas and Luhmann (1971), pp. 101–41.
HABERMAS, J. (1976), 'Was heisst Universalpragmatik?' in K.-O. Apel (ed.), *Sprachpragmatik und Philosophie*, Frankfurt, 1976, pp. 174–272.
HABERMAS, J. AND LUHMANN, NIKLAS (1971), *Theorie der Gesellschaft oder Sozialtechnologie: Was leistet die Systemforschung?*, Frankfurt.
HARMAN, GILBERT (1967), 'Some Recent Issues in Linguistics', *Journal of Philosophy*, 64, no. 2, pp. 67–87.
HEGER, KLAUS (1971), 'Zur Standortbestimmung der Sprachwissenschaft', *Zeitschrift für Romanische Philologie*, 87, pp. 1–31.
HEGER, K. (1971), *Monem, Wort und Satz*, Tübingen.

Bibliography

HYMES, DELL (1967), 'Models of the Interpretation of Language and Social Setting', *Journal of Social Issues*, 23, pp. 8–28.
HYMES, D. (1970), 'On communicative competence', in J. J. Gumperz and D. Hymes (eds), *Direction in Sociolinguistics*, New York and London.
KATZ, JERROLD J. (1966), *The Philosophy of Language*, New York.
KATZ, J. J. AND FODOR, J. A. (1963), 'The Structure of a Semantic Theory', *Language*, 39, pp. 170–210 (reprinted in Fodor and Katz (eds), 1964).
KLÜVER, JÜRGEN (1971), 'Wissenschaftstheoretische Bemerkungen zur Transformationsgrammatik Chomskys', working paper, Philosophy Institute of the University of Saarbrücken.
LYAS, COLIN (ed.) (1971), *Philosophy and Linguistics*, London and Basingstoke.
LYONS, JOHN (1970), *Chomsky*, London.
McCAWLEY, JAMES D. (1968), 'Where Do Noun Phrases Come From?', in R. Jacobs and P. S. Rosenbaum (eds), *Readings in English Transformational Grammar*, Waltham, Mass., 1969.
NAGEL, THOMAS (1969), 'Linguistics and Epistemology', in Sidney Hook (ed.), *Language and Philosophy*, New York, 1969, pp. 171 ff.
OKSAAR, ELS (1971), 'Sprachliche Interferenzen und kommunikative Kompetenz', in *Indo-Celtica: Gedächtnisschrift für Alf Sommerfelt*, Munich (forthcoming).
ROSS, JOHN R. (1967), 'On the Cyclic Nature of English Pronominalization', in *To Honor Roman Jakobson*, The Hague and Paris, 1967.
RUWET, NICOLAS (1967), *Introduction à la grammaire générative*, Paris (English trans. *An Introduction to Generative Grammar*, Amsterdam, 1973).
SCHAFER, LOTHAR (1970), 'Über die Diskrepanz zwischen Methodologie und Metaphysik bei Popper', *Studium Generale*, 23, pp. 856–77.
SCHLICK, MORITZ (1938), *Gesammelte Aufsätze*, Vienna.
SCHNELLE, HELMUTH (1970), 'Theorie und Empirie in der Sprachwissenschaft', *Bibliotheca Phonetica*, no. 9, pp. 51–65.
SEARLE, JOHN R. (1969), *Speech Acts*, Cambridge, Mass.
STEGMÜLLER, W. (1969), *Hauptströmungen der Gegenwartsphilosophie*, Stuttgart, 4th ed. (trans. A. Blumberg, *Main Currents in Contemporary German, British and American Philosophy*, Dordrecht, 1969).
TOULMIN, STEPHEN (1961), *Foresight and Understanding: An Enquiry into the Aims of Science*, London.
TUGENDHAT, ERNST (1960), 'Tarskis semantische Definition der Wahrheit und ihre Stellung innerhalb der Geschichte des Wahrheitsproblems im logischen Postivismus', *Philosophische Rundschau*, 8, pp. 131–59.
WINCH, PETER (1958), *The Idea of a Social Science and its Relation to Philosophy*, London.

WITTGENSTEIN, LUDWIG (1921–2), *Tractatus logico-philosophicus,* Vienna and London.

WITTGENSTEIN, L. (1958), *Philosophische Untersuchungen/ Philosophical Investigations,* G. Anscombe, trans. Oxford.

WUNDERLICH, DIETER (1968), 'McCawleys Tiefenstrukturen', Third Linguistic Colloquium in Stettenfels, 1–4, 1968 (mimeographed).

WUNDERLICH, D. (1968), 'Pragmatik, Sprechsituation, Deixis', in *Zeitschrift für Literaturwissenschaft und Linguistik (LiLi),* I, nos 1–2 (1971), pp. 153–90.

WUNDERLICH, D. (1970), 'Die Rolle der Pragmatik in der Linguistik', *Der Deutschunterricht,* 22, no. 4, pp. 5–41.

WUNDERLICH, D. (1972), in Utz Maas and Dieter Wunderlich, *Pragmatik und sprachliches Handeln,* Frankfurt.

INDEX OF NAMES